THE MEASURE
OF HER POWERS

THE MEASURE
OF HER POWERS

AN M.F.K. FISHER READER

EDITED BY DOMINIQUE GIOIA

WITH AN INTRODUCTION BY RUTH REICHL

COUNTERPOINT
WASHINGTON, D.C.

Library of Congress Cataloging-in-Publication Data
Fisher, M. F. K. (Mary Frances Kennedy), 1908-
A measure of her powers: an M. F. K. Fisher reader/edited by Dominique Gioia; with
a preface by Ruth Reichl.
p. cm.
ISBN: 1-58243-104-3
1. Fisher, M. F. K. (Mary Frances Kennedy), 1908- 2. Authors, American–20th century–Biography.
3. Women food writers–United States–Biography. 4. Gastronomy. 5. Cookery
I. Gioia, Dominique. II. Title.

PS3511.I7428 A6 1999
641'.092–dc21

The trustees of the literary trust of M. F. K. Fisher would like to thank and acknowledge
the publishers of her books from which these selections were drawn.

FIRST PRINTING

Jacket and text design by David Bullen

Printed in the United States of America on acid-free paper
that meets the American National Standards Institute z39-48 Standard.

COUNTERPOINT
P.O. Box 65793
Washington, D.C. 20035-5793

A member of the Perseus Books Group

10 9 8 7 6 5 4 3 2 1

CONTENTS

GASTEREA, LOVELIEST OF MUSES

S IS FOR SURVIVAL

PLACES ON A MAP

THE ART OF AGING

INTRODUCTION BY RUTH REICHL

America was another country in the fifties.

Spaghetti came in cans. Cheese mainly meant Velveeta. Nobody had ever heard of cappuccino. Most fancy restaurants were serving something called Continental Cuisine, and the only Chinese dish anyone knew was chop suey. W. H. Auden said that he could not think of anyone in the United States who wrote better prose than Mary Frances Kennedy Fisher, but having chosen food as her subject her audience was extremely limited. Americans, in fact, were so disinterested in the whole idea of eating that M. F. K. Fisher said, with some dismay, that the nation was "taste-blind."

Things changed very slowly. A few Americans began to be famous for their fascination with food in the sixties, but what they had to offer was practical advice. Julia Child and James Beard were intent on teaching us to cook; Craig Claiborne was busy telling us where, and what, to eat. Mary Frances Fisher, on the other hand, believed "the first condition of learning how to eat is learning how to talk about it," and she wanted us to read about eating for sheer pleasure. She still did not have a lot of takers.

By the seventies things were starting to look up: A fledgling food movement had formed. For those who were part of it, M. F. K. Fisher was an icon, a person you read because she understood your dreams. "There is a communion of more than our bodies when bread is broken and wine is drunk," she wrote, answering critics who wondered why she had chosen food as her subject. We whispered the words like a mantra. It was comforting to know that the world contained at least one other person who believed we could learn by studying our appetites. Especially a person who wrote so well.

This is where I come in. By the mid-seventies I had reread *The Art of Eating* so many times that the tattered pages fell from my paperback copy each time I picked it up. You can imagine how thrilled I was when *Ms.* magazine called to ask if I would be interested in interviewing M. F. K. Fisher. Actually, the way the editor put it was, "Have you ever heard of M. F. K. Fisher?"

I was simultaneously elated and terrified. The editor had given me Mrs. Fisher's number, but I did not have the courage to make the call. After days of agonizing over it I took the coward's way: I wrote to ask if I might come for an interview.

"Dear Ruth Reichl," she wrote back in her fine, spidery hand. "Thanks for your very nice note. It will not be 'an imposition.' Come at 10 on Friday and stay for lunch." It was the first of many such invitations, for the pattern had been set: Never, in all the years I knew her, did I telephone Mary Frances. Writing seemed so much her natural form that I was always surprised when the serenity of her house was shattered by the ringing telephone.

"Go 6½ miles from Sonoma," she directed, "until you see a fire ranger station on the left. Directly across the street is an abrupt right-hand turn. Take it." I had her note next to me in the battered old Volvo as I drove, slowly, trying not to miss the sign for Bouverie Ranch. I found the lane to her house, a narrow, bumpy gravel path that ended abruptly at a small cottage. I got out and discovered a bell—a real one, the kind you pull a rope to ring—and a gate with a bronze plaque bearing the name, Mary Frances KFisher. "Sounds like a sneeze, doesn't it?" were the first words I heard the silver-haired woman say. "It was a mistake, but I like it."

I followed her into the house, so nervous I had to remind myself to look around and note the cool darkness of the hallway, and the jumble of paintings hanging everywhere. The living room was large and airy, with a kitchen along one wall. I made myself stare at Mary Frances—the movie star good looks of her youth had matured into a more impressive beauty—as she introduced me to the large cat occupying most of the sofa. Charlie gave me the disdainful look I had expected from his mistress, licked himself once, jumped down and stalked off. I plunked myself down in his recently vacated spot, turned on my tape recorder, and began asking questions.

Mary Frances would later encounter many obsessed fans, but I may have been the first who had memorized practically everything she had ever written. I had come, armed with questions about books she hadn't thought about in forty years, expecting detailed answers. How was I to know she was a person who was incapable of rereading a single word she had ever written? She did her best, but after an hour of "Did I say that?" and "I don't know," she asked if I wouldn't like some lunch.

What had I expected? Caviar, I guess, and foie gras. Something exotic. Instead it was split pea soup and what she called "a modest local wine." I was still hoping for something rare and exciting but when she pulled the bottle from the small white refrigerator I saw that it was Sebastiani's *Eye of the Partridge,* a wine sold in supermarkets. Even more shocking: Mary Frances Kennedy Fisher cooked on the very same electric stove that my mother used.

Thinking of my mother I blurted out, "Most people are very bad cooks. It doesn't matter much." She nodded, not seeming to recognize the quote. I blushed, suddenly afraid she would think I was saying the meal wasn't very good. But she graciously jumped into the silence, saying, "I did write that. And meant it. You know, a lot of my dearest friends don't care about food. I think it's so sad. I think they're missing such a lot."

I agreed, and the ice, finally, was broken. We started talking, then, like two people with a great deal in common. Aside from our passion for food we discovered that we were both burdened with relatives with mental illness. And, even better, we both *hated* honey. With that I really relaxed, turned off the tape recorder and settled in for the afternoon.

At some point I asked to use the bathroom. Did I imagine that Mary Frances had a smug little grin on her face as I left the room? Perhaps. I closed the door and discovered that I was in the nicest bathroom I'd ever seen. The walls were red, I think, and there were carpets on the floor and oil paintings on the walls. Right in the middle of the room was a large bathtub. If you were in it you would be facing a long, low, uncurtained window and you would be able to see the trees outside. Great piles of towels were stacked against the tub and books were heaped around the room. Shelves held an astonishing assortment of jars filled with unfathomable potions. "Sometimes," said Mary Frances when I was back in the living room, "my friends disappear into my bathroom for hours." At that moment I wanted, desperately, to be one of those people.

The editors weren't thrilled with the article I turned in. It was, after all, *Ms.* magazine, and it turned out that what they had really wanted were the writer's opinions on women's liberation. I went back to have another conversation with Mary Frances, who threw out a few controversial opinions like "Men wear out quicker than women. That's why there are so many old widows," and "Women are more subtle than men, more practical than men, and they live more intensely." None of that interested me very much, but I obediently included it all, and when the article finally appeared we were both disappointed. "You and I," she wrote, "know what it could have been." What she meant, of course, was that once again the metaphor she had chosen, food, had been shunted to the sidelines.

But it was the last time that would happen: The world was finally catching up to Mary Frances. Suddenly food writers were important, and M. F. K. Fisher, who had been focusing on human hungers for half a century, was thrust into the limelight.

Writers of all sorts began beating a path to her door, soliciting her opinions. She took it all with a grain of salt. When I mentioned how strange it must be, after writing into a void all those years, to suddenly become so popular she replied practically, "When you write you have no idea if you'll ever be read by any human being."

"So," I said, "you write for yourself?"

Mary Frances looked horrified. "Write to yourself?" she said. "It's like kissing yourself, don't you think?" She had a habit of dismissing things she considered silly by simply saying, "Oh, ridiculous!" and I half expected her to say that now. But she didn't. Turning suddenly thoughtful she said, "I have to write towards somebody I love."

AWE AND
INNOCENCE

THE PREDILECTION
FOR LAME DUCKS

Time makes it easier to trace hereditary influences than it does environmental, I am almost certain, although I do not want to be. It is fortunate that much that we grow aware of in our later years was a fine mystery to us for a period of bliss. I, for instance, was supposed to have many of my father's points of behavior, although I was a girl. When I was intelligent, generous, nicely behaved, I was told that I was just like him. When I was impatient, rude, bitter-tongued, I was just like him too. There was plainly some resemblance, temperamentally and of course genetically, since it was unthinkable even to this child who would like to be a foundling princess left on the doorstep that she was anything but the result of lawful mating of Edith and Rex Kennedy.

One thing I began to hope for at an early age was that I would inherit my father's nose. It was a noble racy beak, touched with divinity by a football break which grew leftward when nobody was around to set it, and divinely sizable in proportion to his very tall body. I cannot know what it would have looked like on a soft female face, for it never happened, to my knowledge, and certainly not to me. I got, through the genes again, a nondescript thing called retroussé by the merciful or coy, and snub or turned-up otherwise. Rex let me down in other ways too, and I turned out to be the midget of the family, a bare five feet eight to this day. I scuttled around underfoot, always looking upupup.

One thing I did get from my father, though, and loud and clear: his predilection for Lame Ducks. I still claim it jauntily.

Charles Somerville, a withdrawn, gentle man from Edinburgh, our best tramp of them all, was proof positive of Rex Kennedy's need for such drifters. There were others: Little Ears, Chucka-da-Noos, Buck the Rough Rider, mostly men but now and then a female waif. He was drawn like a moth to their flickering flames: the torch of the alcoholic, the phosphorescence of an evil refugee, the glitter of a broken gambler.

In the early teens of the century there were thousands of men roaming this enormous country. They drifted in unpredictable patterns, so that for a time there would be two or three a day at our back door, asking for food or perhaps a little work, and then there would be none for a week. They were called bums, mostly, or hobos. My

Anglomaniac mother called them tramps, so we did too. The ones I remember were very old, which to a child means anywhere over the age of being able to shave, probably. I did not wonder about them, for they were part of the way life was for me then.

Only once did I face their oldness: for some reason I was alone at the back of the house, and a man came to the door and asked for something to do so that he could eat. I was about six, I think. Instead of calling the cook as I'd been told to, I decided for myself that since our own tramp Charles was with us there would be nothing for this man to do, and I never opened the icebox unless told to, so I quickly gave him a couple of big fat pears ripening on the window ledge, and he went off. I felt a new twinge in my stomach, at the way he was so sad and quiet. I told what I had done at lunch, and Mother said that I must always call the cook even if she was upstairs, and that I must not give away things without asking. Then she added, "And those pears are still as bitter as gall. Poor devil!"

I felt mixed about all this. There was no denying that Charles was with us, and supposed to cope with all the things like kindling and paths and weeds that the other roamers suggested doing . . . but to give a hungry man bad food!

The way Charles Somerville came to us was through a project Father started with the minister of our Episcopal mission and some friends who were fellow vestrymen there, Peter MacLaren, whom we called Uncle Mac, and Matty Matteson, and probably others. They rented an old building down near the railroad tracks where the tramps rolled off the freight trains. Under the bridge, they had a couple of "jungles," wretched mucky pits during the spring rains, and always hazardous in the tinderbox times between them. Word was spread; from all over town came cots, clean blankets, help to install showers and washtubs and a big cookstove. And I was carefully taught to tell all the men who came to our back door to go down to the hostel, on South Greenleaf, I think. They could sleep and get clean and eat there, and not have to pray for it first, or at all.

Charles Somerville, I think, first lived at the shelter, which was down at the other end of town. Then next thing we knew, he was living in our garage. But before that I must, as a woman who loved him, tell how he looked. (As I think on it, I believe he came like all the others to our back door, and then came again from the shelter, and we were so aware of him that we asked him to stay. . . .)

He was a frail thin man, with delicate bones, but still tall. He had a fine face under silky white hair which was long but not straggly, and was always clean-shaven, which may be one good reason Edith accepted him . . . she had a neurotic dislike of hair on faces, male or female. He had blue eyes, and I know they were large and steady and far back under his brows. His voice was low, and he spoke with the soft accent of a man from Edinburgh, well bred and well taught but always a Scot. (One of the first things he told me in his little room was how to pronounce the name of his town, and not to put a hard *g* on its end, as Americans did with Pittsburgh. . . .) I think he brought in wood for our big fireplace, and tidied the back yard and mowed the meaningless front, and swept the paths. But I never saw him sit down in either kitchen or front rooms, and I doubt that my mother ever set foot in his small hole that Father managed to carve out of the side of the garage, once he knew (probably from the first encounter) that Charles should stop roaming and stay with us.

The room had been meant for tools, I assume. It was big enough for a cot, which was always tidy, and an old Morris chair, and a decrepit office desk. The walls were part of the garage, with newspaper darkening on them to keep out the drafts. There was a small round kerosene stove, the kind we sometimes used in our Laguna summer place, with a murky glow through its window and a good warm smell. There was a soft light from an overhead bulb. There was a shelf of books, but what they were I never knew. From the roof beams hung slowly twirling bundles of half-cured tobacco leaves, which Charles got through some strange dealings from Kentucky. He dried them, and every night ground their most brittle leaves into a pipe mixture in the palm of his hand. He would reach up, snap off a leaf, and then sit back in his old chair and talk to us, my sister Anne and the new one Norah and me, until it was time to puff out more delicious fumes.

I still cannot imagine where Charles washed himself, or defecated. Both he and Rex were healthy decent men, and I am sure some provision had been made for continuance of such attributes, but where and how I do not know. To us children he always smelled wonderful. . . .

In the same way, I cannot remember where he cooked. There must have been a gas plate in the room? At first he ate at the shelter . . . really was it called a Mission? . . . but I never remember any smells of cooking in his room, and I spent at least an hour a day there for several fine years, after he came home from his work as janitor at the *News*. Probably, once he started regular work, he went to one of the few dismal hash houses in the town.

Soon after he came, he told Father that at one point in his wanderings he had been a master candymaker, and would like to make something for the little girls. Mother had a compulsive and almost suicidal love for sweets, and while Grandmother frowned on exotics like chocolate-covered cherries, which might have a foreign liquor in them, she admitted to keeping an occasional small bag of salt-water taffy in her desk drawer. Could this new tenant, this latest example of Rex's misguided quixotism, possibly prove his origins by making a batch of real butterscotch? He could, and did, and it was pronounced flawless.

This must have been when Anne was about four and I six, for I remember clearly the whole sequence of our sessions in the kitchen. Anne sat on the high stool, near enough the stove to watch, but out of the paths between it and the sink and the table. I stood nearer, on my little dictionary stool. Charles left his hat on the back porch as he came in, and the dangling kitchen light shone on his white hair as he bent over the pot and moved about in the late afternoon shadows. He talked along as he worked, telling us what he was doing and what would happen. The smells were beautiful.

At exactly the right moment he tipped out the pale brown syrup onto buttered cookie sheets, to let it spread evenly, magically, like glass, and he cut a knife across it to make little squares. Then we had to wait, and his voice went on softly, with his Scottish accent so like Uncle Mac's and yet different. Finally it was time for him to crack off a sliver of the glass, and if it was set enough he would break more for Anne and me to sample. Deftly he picked up the panes of colored crystal, and broke them into neat patties along the knife marks, and placed them in fancy pyramids on two or three plates, for Mother to put away as she saw fit. Just as deftly he washed off every sign that we had spent a good afternoon in the kitchen, and he went out the back door.

Once there was a slight hitch in the satisfaction from the front of the house, when he changed our private pattern a little and told Anne and me that we were going to make lollipops. Sure enough, he had perhaps fifty proper sticks for them in a little bag, and that day he made only half of the butterscotch into squares for Mother and Grandmother, and with the rest he created dozens of what we called all-day suckers at school. It seems to me now that they were shaped like stars, like strawberries, like sunbursts, but I think they may have been plain blobs. They were artfully done, though: the sticks never fell out too soon from the last licks, which to any connoisseur of such sweetmeats is a proof of superior workmanship, and very rewarding. I think Charles was as pleased and excited as we were by the beautiful gleaming things, and he arranged them in an elaborate whorl on a platter, and as he disappeared told us to show them first to Mrs. Kennedy, before the regular candies.

The trouble came when Mother, as admiring as we, asked where he could have bought the sticks in Whittier. I told her proudly, for it was one more proof of his general wizardry, that he had found them all himself, and had picked up every one of them around the Bailey Street School grounds on his way home from work. It took him a long time. They were of different sizes, but all as good as new.

We were allowed to eat that whole batch of supernacular lollipops, after Mother talked with Father and he talked with Charles, who assured him that he had boiled the sticks in water for a long time (. . . so he *must* have had a gas burner in his room!). But he never made them again for us, and when we begged him to, he said that nobody seemed to throw sticks into the weeds any more. . . .

The dim delicious afternoons, with the three of us alone in the kitchen, peaceably murmuring and tasting, stopped forever not long after that. By now I cannot know which of us children innocently blasted them, so I shall share the honors with Anne. It was after dinner, and for a treat all of us there got a little patty of the beautiful tawny-clear butterscotch we had watched Charles create that afternoon. (It must have been on Sundays that we collaborated, because he was not at the *News* and the cook was never around. . . .) Before we left the table, we tucked a sweet into our cheeks, and Mother said, "How does that old man do it? The best I ever ate, *ever!* And always the same! How can he possibly know, I wonder, just when to take it off the stove?"

As I remember, Anne and I were so proud of Charles that we almost burst to tell of his artistry and his incredible courage, and we talked together:

She: He puts his hand right into the boiling candy . . .

I: He puts his thumb and finger right down into the candy, and pulls them out and . . .

She: . . . he snaps them together, just once very fast, and if they sound right . . .

I: He just snaps them once, and if they come apart right, it is time, and he never gets burned.

She: And it never even hurts him. It would hurt us, he says.

I: Oh, Charles says we must never try it. You have to know how. It is a special . . .

She: . . . trick, a secret.

I: It's a secret. But he told it to us.

And of course when we were gently prodded into disclosing it, we did, probably in unison: All you need is a whole lot of real spit on your thumb and your finger, plenty of it. Then if you do it fast, you won't get burned.

Mother and Grandmother were plainly if quietly upset, disgusted, repelled, put out. Father said that the high temperature of the boiling candy no doubt changed the . . . uh . . . saliva in many ways, but admitted on further complaints that the casual introduction of cast-off sucker sticks was . . . uh . . . perhaps part of the picture of shiftless and wanton irresponsibility of a confirmed vagabond. Mr. Somerville *spoke* like a gentleman, the ladies also admitted fairly, but hygienically he was not up to American standards. Granted, he made the best butterscotch ever tasted. But he never made it again for us.

Every afternoon on the way home from his job he passed the bakery, and picked up a leftover bun or doughnut. Anne and I always got a good piece of whatever he had scavenged or been given (he was a distinguished man, and sensitive people were proud to know him . . .). And after Norah began to walk, while Mother was readying herself for David, he splurged and bought or otherwise acquired so many dreadful sweet rolls and cream puffs and suchlike that finally a halt was called. Anne and I, and our darling little sister, would stagger up the back steps when the cook called us in for supper, so sated that we could hardly lift our eyelids. Edith talked to Rex, and Rex talked to his friend Mr. Somerville, and from then on the three of us got one tobacco-flavored sliver of chocolate-frosted greasy doughnut, and no more, and because Charles was a gentleman he never murmured sly destructive comments to us about our thinning rations and their reasons.

He changed and grew warmer than at first, after Norah started trotting down the back stairs to his room. Mother knew that the little girl was safe there, and concentrated on other matters, and the cook was glad because Norah was out from under, and Anne and I were glad because we knew we would find the new sister there, safe in the grey-blue stench of Charles's castle, a princess in his loving gaze.

Charles did honestly love her. He taught us a new way to be gentle and as if awestruck by her innocent beauty. Anne and I would sit on his cot, and the little golden-colored girl would perch like a plump bird on his bony old knees, and slowly he would divide one leftover bran muffin or a withered doughnut into four even pieces with his tobacco-blacked pocketknife, and we would commune.

After David was born and well established, Mother became aware that her three older children were invisible from the time Old Charles came home from the *News* until they were called for supper, which we ate together, but often hurriedly because Father almost always had to get to a meeting by 7:30 and it was too complicated to arrange otherwise about table settings, what with the Help one could get. . . .

Charles was an unknown (certainly to Mother). He was the Hired Man . . . or at least a temporary lodger of mysterious origin (here he qualified as the first of my father's endless string of what we later came to call Rex's Lame Ducks . . .), who smoked too much vile tobacco. Anne and I were getting too old to sit in a man's bedroom. What was worst, he probably filled little Norah *secretly* with cheap bakery pastry, on which she seemed to thrive (Charles *never* cheated!).

Mother put her foot down, and Norah was kept indoors at the one time of day when she wanted to head for the Garage and Mr. Somerville's gas chamber, and Anne gradually tapered off too, and finally I was the only Faithful to the 5:15 call to arms, complete with slow tobacco mixing and courtesy bite of a sweet roll. I know that Rex sometimes went out to the Garage after dinner, and I suspect that he took along a little flask of Scotch. I hope so. But not long after Charles was made out of bounds (Norah would head down the back stairs right on the dot, and the cook would pull her back and say gently, "Not tonight, honey . . . ") he moved upstairs in the new *News* Building on North Greenleaf.

Until then Father had been running the whole daily operation in one big store building, with no more than a low fence separating Business from Editorial, and the presses right there at the back, with the two linotype machines a nervous barricade against their mighty whopping sound. Now there was our own building! On the ground floor, back of Business and Editorial (where Rex had his own office with walls made half of cloudy glass and half of plyboard, very impressive), were the linotypes and the presses, a small room with a special smell where paper was kept for the job work, a big garage-type door on the alley where classmates of mine rolled papers for their delivery routes. . . . It was a palace of a place! And upstairs was a room, like the Captain's Quarters on a tight little freighter, that belonged to Charles Somerville.

My heart swelled with pride and happiness for him. He had everything there from his room at home, but more space for books, which I still do not remember: the bed, two chairs now, the old desk, and of course the tobacco twirling slowly in bunches from the rafters.

Then he broke his leg, and when he came back from the hospital everybody at the *News* gave some money for a party for him and there was a noble armchair as the present, the kind that tips and revolves. It was colored a good blue, too, like his fading eyes. I went after the formal "office" presentation to see it, and he seemed quite shaken, so we did not stay. Later Mother told me he had cried at the party, in front of everybody, which of course we had all been taught not to do.

The way he broke his leg was that he fell off the Electric, on his way to a dinner party.

There was a lanky attractive freight agent in town, a friend of Rex's of course, whom Mother did not "know": he was not a Quaker, which made him unimportant professionally, and he was not an Episcopalian, which excluded him from our inner circle. He and his wife "adopted" Charles Somerville, as my poor mother never failed to put it icily when the relationship was mentioned. She would ask Anne and me if Charles was getting into his party clothes when we last saw him, to go to be spoiled and flattered by people who thought they *appreciated* him . . . that sort of thing. It was really an odd antagonism for such a nice woman to feel. But I think Mother always resented the Lame Ducks. There was jealousy there. . . . Why did not her husband, the simple Iowa newspaper reporter she had given her hand to, know the bankers, the lawyers? Why did he pick up people like Charles?

She was at an impasse, of course, in Whittier: bankers and lawyers in that tight fortress of brotherly love had no need for Rex or for her, except as he could run their advertisements, and would play some of their political games. The *News* was a public commodity, and the people running it were part of the machine. This isolation may be one reason why my father became more and more prone to Lame Ducks, and my mother to her couch and the English Novel. . . .

It is probable that the people Charles was going to visit the night he slipped off the Electric and landed with a broken leg were unusually nice people. They had the same recognition of a fine man that we did. It is too bad that we were not friends, drawn together by him. And they invited him often to their house, for meals at their own table, and he went there for Christmases.

On that holiday, while he lived with us, Anne and then Norah and I would always take out to his room, when he sat alone in the garage under his twirling bundles of tobacco by his kerosene stove, a pipe and some tobacco and a sweater or a muffler. If Norah was there he would put her on his knee in a close gentle embrace. But he never came into our house, festival or not, after the Butterscotch Period.

This seems *impossible*, too painful, as I remember it. Why was it this way? Why did Father not change things more? Was he a weak man really? Why was Mother so detached from any lives but those sharing her own blood? Why was I so stupid and docile, not to kick like a sick fawn at the ice forming? Perhaps Father was right, to rescue tramps and even to bring them to the edge of his own campfire, and then to let them stay there if they wanted to, but never come in any further. Was that because he was afraid of his own inner need to join them? Did I have to join *him?*

The nearest I got to this possible explanation of Charles and many other people was one day when I was almost twelve, and Rex was taking a carload of his own and neighbor children to something or other, along what used to be called Whittier Boulevard. There was one house I always looked out for, because it had a gazing globe in a little square of lawn edged by box hedge and gravel. At first I had thought this stylish, but soon it became only a visual tease to me. As we neared it, and I peered for the concave flash of it, there was a hobo walking against the thin traffic, with his bindle. I said something trite about being sorry for him, for there were not as many as in my earlier life and I was more aware of their dusty search. Rex said, in a quiet way, something that still rocks me, and that day left me hanging on a thin silver wire of puzzlement, twirling like Charles Somerville's tobacco high above a room that I thought was there forever but had almost disappeared. He said, "I envy him." It may have been the first time that I asked why to him, and he said, "He has nothing. He is a free man."

Now, I do not think Father was being bitter. Perhaps he was desperate, with a carful of sprats, but he was not a man to feel sorry for himself, at least consciously. He gave me an honest answer, and I said something about the hobo's probably having a toothbrush anyway, and Rex snorted and the talk ended. But I wondered how a man like my father, with Mother and a newspaper and us four children and a ranch with the beans growing between the rows of orange trees, could think a poor lurching dusty hobo was free. The more I wondered, the more I came to conclusions about not only freedom but Father. Mother. Myself. Charles.

Charles hopped around the *News* for several years. People liked him deeply, and the girls from the Front Room gave him little parties with homemade cookies, and the Back Room kept him fairly well supplied with a gentleman's ration of potables, and sometimes we did walk up to his room and have a rather formal shy meeting with him. After his accident he used a cane, and finally, for better or worse, a crutch. Then he could not get in and out of the fine blue swivel chair. The tobacco fell from his hand.

Father and the freight agent got him into the County Farm. Mother remained apart from all this, as far as I know. It was as if a leaf had drifted across her path and then on into the forest. Two times at least I went with Rex to the impressive hospital, but by now I do not remember Charles there at all. It did not worry me much. He was part of my life, and I was just beginning. . . .

Other wanderers came from far lands, speaking other tongues, and I came to understand without question that this was like honey to Rex, or perhaps more like a spiritual physicking to his pot-bound restlessness. They had known lives forbidden to him, lives of waste and recklessness and derring-do, and his own nature plainly drew some vicarious satisfaction from being able to talk with them and feed them and then, more often than not, send them stumbling along again on the paths he secretly dreamed of treading.

That is surely one reason, perhaps unsuspected, why he dove with all his heart into that quixotic "mission." Nobody interfered, as far as I know. Mother condoned it because it was tacitly sponsored by the St. Matthias Church: what other attitude was there, with the minister and two vestrymen acting like schoolboys over it? The businessmen in Whittier remained aloof, for the most part, unless they were religious mavericks. The Quakers had their own quiet charities, and this was a dangerous kind of sport, a variation from their normal and established procedures in rescuing men's souls from their bodies.

And business was good, at the hostel. Those were lean years, before and during the First World War, and most of the men who drifted back and forth across the American continent like lemmings with no place to head for death rode the rails, so the little mission next to the tracks and an overhead bridge was a good location. I like to think that it was Rex who chose it. As a latent frustrated bindle stiff he would know. . . .

It would be easy to trace the development of the place into the present Salvation Army branch in Whittier, but better people have done it, and I prefer to leave it lay where Jesus has flang it, in the convolutions of my wishful memory. It is enough that slowly it became important to everyone with what is called a Civic Mind, and that while this was happening (small-town people, especially if they are temperate judicious members of the Society of Friends, move without undue or overemotional haste), my father spent a lot of his vigorous hungry nature on the Lame Ducks who fluttered in and out of his unwitting blind.

He needed them. Part of his nature was fiery and impatient. The larger part was timid, at least to the point of believing in predestination as outlined to him by the people he respected and loved, including his wife and her family. He had been *meant*, they told him, to be taller, stronger, better equipped to stay respectable and honored, than many people he knew secretly to be much braver and more privileged than himself. His absorbing interest in hungry broken transients was proof positive of this inner doubt and quarrel, I think.

My mother accepted Rex's compulsive brotherliness, but with scoffing tosses of her head, and a fairly successful withdrawal from any direct involvement with the steady parade of his pets, both male and female, through our lives. Actually she liked only people related to her; they were her reality, and the rest of her inner landscape was filled but dimly by "the others." Members of the Episcopal Church were less shadowy, but seldom did she part the veils and let them into her warm loving presence. As an Anglomaniac, she was helplessly swayed by any scoundrel with an upper-class English accent, but fortunately the only people in Whittier who spoke that way were members of St. Matthias, which made life simpler for her, socially.

When Father might mention, which he did rarely, an interesting fellow who had come into the office that morning, Mother would shrug scornfully and say, "Of course he *wanted* something! You're too soft, Rex. You're an easy mark . . . you and Mac too!" Rex would agree quietly, and say, "He seemed like a decent enough fellow. Has a wife and some children in South Dakota, and . . . "

"Naturally," Edith would interrupt, tapping her right foot vibrato under the table. "South Dakota! Who would live there? No wonder he's a tramp! *Escape!* And please don't send him around here. Four men this morning, all saying you'd told them there might be something to do. Not a slice of bread left in the house. . . ."

This firm and continued antagonism from Mother finally forced Father underground. Gradually, little was said, in front of Anne and me anyway, about my father's increasingly sub rosa friends, transient and otherwise. Granted, Charles Somerville was a fine man and had once been a gentleman. As for the rest, they were not Episcopalians nor were they good solid respectable Friends. They were not businessmen, and therefore not advertisers in the *News* and therefore not to be patronized for meats and toothpaste and such. . . . They were not of Edith's chosen and circumvented world, and Rex learned how to see that they remained so.

He consorted enjoyably, and for many years, with people like the Catholic priest, the secretly radical high school principal, a renegade Mormon who ran a garage for a time, a two-bit orange rancher with a French wife who pickled olives with garlic, very good with his home-pressed red ink. . . . None of these people ever set foot in our house, any more than we did in the "nice" Quaker homes in Whittier, but they were indefinably within our awareness of the lives we all led in our own ways, and not Edith's.

One man we always stopped to salute, as we left Laguna after a weekend there, was a short Dutchman who got out a weekly sheet when he felt like it. Rex saw at once that he was a peculiar character, and was drawn helplessly to the smell of ink in the little building, and to the sound of the foreigner's talk. Here was another newspaperman . . . and here was one who had come from a great town in Holland to sit quietly waiting to die in a deserted wintry Pacific village redolent of rain and eucalyptus buds.

I think the man was named Harry Hansen. He was short and white-haired, and I can see him standing thick and solid against the light in his dingy little building, waving to us like a priest and bowing silently to Mother in the front seat of the Ford. She never got out. He seldom came to greet her.

When we slowed down on the late Sunday afternoons in front of the newspaper office she would sigh and say nothing. Then when Rex jumped back into the car she would sigh again, and ask him if he had the last issue of the Laguna paper. She liked it, but could not help being sarcastic about a typo ("He sets it all himself," Rex would say as we tore along through the Canyon at a good thirty-mile clip . . .), or a lapse in syntax ("He speaks five languages," Rex would say, and she would add, "Four of them better than English, let us hope"). All this went on nicely, with no bickering: Rex was in love with the *idea* of a man's leaving his own land and starting a new life in a far country, alone; Edith was resigned to her husband's need for this strange un-Holbrook hunger in him, and protested almost dutifully.

Somehow Rex told us of the picture on the shabby desk in Laguna, of a beautiful woman and several smiling children: they had all died in the fire that burned the best newspaper in Holland. "Why didn't you tell me?" Mother cried out with true anguish, but there was no answer, for it was something between men, beyond female compassion.

This removal from the woman's sphere was a part of Rex's whole Lame Duck Syndrome, of course. The reasons for his adoption of misfits and underdogs and human rats and crippled gentlemen were separate from his wife's own ways, and it was a good thing for everyone concerned that for the most part she seemed willing to confine herself to her family, her Church, and the British Empire as represented in fiction. He went right on rubbing himself in the dust of other men's spiritual shoes, much as another man would keep a mistress or two, or study Swahili.

The difficulty of keeping a mistress has too often been considered, as it relates to living in a small American town in the early twentieth century. It was done, of course, but not by a cautious and aspiring young newspaper editor with a highly respectable wife and a growing family. Fortunately I was able to discuss this peculiarly Yankee dilemma at length with my father, long after there was any immediate need to remedy the situation. It was a sad-but-true picture he sketched for me. . . . As for studying Swahili, he settled for Spanish, an unheard-of whim in Whittier then among the white citizens. This enabled him to travel occasionally to Mexico, where perhaps he found answers to other questions.

Only once did Edith permit herself to lend a hand with one of her husband's continuing involvements with the seamier side of Whittier society, and it was, as she well knew from the start, a great mistake.

We began to acquire some pieces of beautiful ancient Spanish brass: flat shaving bowls like Don Quixote's helmet, an exquisite ewer which could well have been Greek. Mother loved brass. It was everywhere at home (the first test of a new Hired Man was how well he handled the polishing kit), and it is probable that Rex used the fine foreign pieces deliberately as bribes or foils, in what turned out to be one of the wildest of his crusades.

It seems that there was, flying through our staid town like an exotic tropical bird, a family straight from South America, Peru, I think. There were several little children, a nurse, a couple of maids, the invisible lady of the house. The father spoke excellent English. He was a very nice fellow, Rex gradually reported, a mining engineer down on his luck, looking hard for work with one of the California oil companies. They were crowded into a miserable little house (this detail was ignored blandly by Edith, as he surely knew it would be, for in spite of the first desirable gifts of Spanish brass, she could see that her husband was helplessly involved with another Lame Duck . . .), and we never met any of them, except Anita.

Gradually we acquired several more really lovely objects, which are still part of the family holdings: a big Talavera jar, a rare embroidery made of beads, two rugs from the tent of a sheik, things like that.

And gradually the rare bird of passage collected enough of Father's money to fly on, hopefully to a richer jungle. He left one last thing for us, the only gift Father did not pay him for, at least directly: Anita. He would send soon for her, he promised Rex, who was by then completely hypnotized: such adventure, such exciting glamorous strangers, such noble courage. . . .

Anita was a tiny woman, a bag of bones with fuzzy black hair, a face snow white with powder but dark in the wrinkles, and a shocking use of make-up around her sunken beady eyes. She would learn English with us, and Father would study Spanish with her on the rare nights he had no meetings. She would help in the house . . . cook, sew, anything.

The first thing we learned, by a kind of Esperanto, I suppose, was that she had never been a *servant*. She had lived all her life with the unseen señora's family, as a kind of maid-duenna-nanny. This meant that she was incapable of admitting any familiarity with things like carpet sweepers, mops, garbage pails, beds, wastebaskets. . . . She and Mother were oddly alike in this great talent of ignoring anything too dull or unpleasant to admit recognition. Anita simply did not *see* what she preferred not to do, and early in her stay with us Mother took to her bed, her own answer to every dismay, her solution to any problem. (Grandmother was on a lengthy series of visits to her Eastern relatives, and by the time she got back everything was in order, except perhaps for a sore but hidden spot in Father's ego.)

The second thing we found out about Anita was that she could not cook. She loved to tell Anne and me, in growing detail as we got used to hearing real Spanish instead of our border-Mex, that she had once taken a course of lessons from the former chef of the King of Spain, and it is true that she could make two dishes superbly: a vanilla flan, and an elegant version of chicken enchiladas. That was all. She did not even know how to make toast!

It was easier with Mother out of the way, and Anne and I got Anita so that she would present decent coffee and eggs for Father's breakfast, and apparently none of us starved. And at least twice a week she would spend most of the day crashing around in the kitchen ("How can any human being make that much noise?" Mother would ask irritably from her chaise longue upstairs . . .), baking her famous flan. It was a perfect *crème renversée*, made always in the big Custard Dish reserved for special feastings, and then turned out at the last, with never a crack in it, never a flaw, and the brown subtle liquid running at just the proper speed over its flat surface and down its impeccably sloping sides. On flan nights Mother always dined with us.

It was when we ate the chicken enchiladas that she stayed immured for the two or three days it took to assemble them. Her basic resentment of the whole business was that it not only involved Anne and me in precise demanding assistance in the kitchen, but it actually got Rex to leave his desk and drive clear in to Los Angeles to a tortilla factory, a special one near the Plaza, and to an herb shop on the edge of the Chinese quarter, and to a ranch on the way home where Anita felt the best possible chickens were to be found (for twice what they cost in Whittier, Mother would manage to add sarcastically . . .).

My little sister Anne soon tired of all the skillful mashings and choppings and so on, but I stayed as much as I could in the kitchen with the weird bird of a woman, working contentedly to her directions and listening to her chirps and twitters. She measured as precisely as if she were filling a dangerous pharmaceutical prescription. She let some things stand for three hours, some for overnight. She cooked this and that, and set little dishes aside. Always she checked and rechecked her pages of lacy

Spanish-convent writing. When it was the normal time for us to eat during this pageant, nothing would be ready for a plain American meal, and I would scramble eggs, or invent a hash of sorts. . . .

Anita's chicken enchiladas were like nothing I have ever tasted. Except that they were made of superfine tortillas instead of crêpes, they perhaps most resembled the elegant cannelloni served on an Italian luxury liner at the captain's request, to a prime minister traveling incognito, two international movie stars, and the Prince and Princess Sostenuto Klein-Ragazzi. They were not Mexican, although they did have the herbs from the little "native" shop in them. They were not bland, but neither were they like the enchiladas we knew in Southern California, crudely heady with peppers and tomatoes. The lightly stewed chicken was pulled off the breast-bones (usually by me) in long tender pieces, and laid precisely on the warm tortillas before they were rolled. The sauce was smooth and yellow-creamy, but it had authority. The dish was a masterpiece . . . and like the flan, it was infallibly so.

It would have been a strange sight, there in the Whittier dining room, to see the Kennedys eating slowly, in a kind of rapture, a dish so foreign to everything they had been raised to consider good food. Father and Mother talked softly between their bites, and she forgot her real antagonism toward the strange woman hovering in the kitchen door to watch her accustomed triumph. Edith, like any true gourmande, sensed always that she must live for the moment, and told Rex firmly that she would like some dry sherry. He was a little shocked, the first time: sherry was for when the minister came, and to be drunk before a meal. It was the perfect wine for that dish, of course, as I taste it now on my mind's tongue. Anne and I found that cool fresh milk was the right tipple for our own palates. We ate and sipped happily, and it was not until the next day that poor Mother returned to her toe-tapping on the chaise longue upstairs.

"I suppose our Spanish *Lady* is exhausted today?" she would ask me in a mildly furious way, looking up from a new novel from the Public Library as I set a tray across her knees. "Three days on nothing but that one dish! And this time your father drove *twice* to town, because our Spanish *Lady* decided the tortillas should be fresh the day she put the whole concoction together! And I don't like to have the *cook* open the kitchen door and watch me eat."

I soon realized that my poor mother was uncomfortable. That was why she stayed in bed more than usual, and had her meals in her room. She was basically ill at ease, with people saying things all around her that she could not even guess at. Perhaps she felt they might be mocking her? She was a shy woman, strangely insecure behind her regal manner. She was superbly Nordic as Caucasians go, even with her large brown eyes and dark hair, and maybe small wiry people, especially females, made her feel tall and heavy and clumsy. (I surmise this because I myself, as an adult, often feel like a great pink Anglo-Saxon cow when I am with Japanese women. . . .) Yes, it may have been the contrasting sizes of the two females that made the real trouble.

I am not sure about Anita. It seems strange now that her probable loneliness, abandoned in a foreign country, did not affect me in any way. I did not like her. Her affectations, her little gesturings and twitterings, her strange smell of rice powder like a stale marshmallow: all this bored me. But I loved to help her work on the enchiladas, and watch her whisk eggs for the flan and tip the melting sugar in the Custard Dish. She did not matter to me as a human being, nor apparently to any of us except perhaps Father.

The clue, as I now see it, to Mother's resentment of this strange jungle bird's insolent and unprecedented perching on our sacrosanct fruit tree was a realization of what happened when one night Rex said casually at the table that he was going to work a little later on his Spanish, with Anita Patita. There was a bad silence. Then Mother asked whom he meant, with that crazy name, and when he said he meant Anita, she asked casually something like Ah, the cook? and then said something like What does the new name Patita mean? Perhaps Patata?

It was just about the coldest I had ever seen my mother, at dinner or anywhere. Anne and I sat in a kind of daze, knowing something mean was going from the smiling woman at one end of the table to the casually unsmiling man at the other.

He said, "I think it is funny: Anita Patita. It sounds funny, that's all. And there is the French word *petite*, but of course it doesn't rhyme in Spanish, and anyway it doesn't mean anything either. In Spanish, that is."

"And what do you imagine it means in French?" Mother's nonchalant smiling voice made it clear that *she* knew what it meant, having traveled in France, but that Father, a backwoods semiliterate journalist, could not possibly understand any foreign words except perhaps a few in lower-class Mexican. Her right-foot toes were vibrating like a snake's tongue at the end of her long leg. She pushed back her soft dark hair from her forehead, to show her admirable forearm, very white and silky. (All this is straight fantasy, of course, but from my memory of my own shock I think it was about thus. . . .)

"That's it," Father said easily. "*Petite* means tiny, little, in French. And Anita is tiny, and so I call her Anita Patita to rhyme."

He seemed pleased, and Anne and I thought it was a nice little joke and laughed one relieved laugh with him. But Mother backed out her chair roughly from the table and swept to the stairs to her room. Her eyes were flashing with tears and an outraged dignity, and she looked about ten feet tall instead of only six.

I don't remember anything more. Perhaps the jobless engineer sent for Anita to live with his family again and see to the First Communion dresses of his numerous little daughters. Probably Father gently paid her to rejoin her own people . . . and the faster the better. Things took on a jauntier look after she left, anyway. There *had* been something spidery about her . . . and the house was hung with the real cobwebs she never saw, and the dust Anne and I never quite stayed ahead of. We got a new maid-of-all-work, of course, the kind who cleaned cheerfully, put three hearty meals a day on the table, and did not come home too drunk from her Thursdays off.

Gradually Mother began to insinuate the term Anita-Patita into our family vocabulary, and if Father winced a little at first, he came to understand it to mean something indefinably meaningless, silly, laughable . . . not *personal* at all. "Well! AnitaPatita!" we would say, for the next fifty-odd years, and then go off into cryptic titters if someone took to bed to avoid a domestic crisis, or on the other hand spent hours making an exquisite soufflé when some quick plain scrambled eggs were indicated. . . .

As far as I can remember, Father was the only one who never said his own pretty little words again, even teasingly, and I think there was a wound in him about them. He did not mind at all being gently twitted about all the other Lame Ducks on his list, but that tropical bird left fluttering in his hand, on his hands, was different in ways we need not ponder. She was a woman, although too wee and skinny to count as such in my young eyes, accustomed as they were to giant goddesses like Mother and Aunt Gwen. She was alone in a strange land, and that was incomprehensible to me, who had not yet wandered. She had been entrusted to my father, and whether the reasons for that had been dishonest or not, he was not one to forswear his obligations. Yes, it must have left a wound. I am sorry, and I wonder if my mother ever was.

Meanwhile I wish I had the two recipes from the King of Spain's cook and that tiny woman, whose name, right now, I have no wish to say again . . . or for a while at least. I resemble Rex Kennedy more than is comfortable, in some ways.

THE MEASURE OF MY POWERS
1919—1927

The first thing I cooked was pure poison. I made it for Mother, after my little brother David was born, and within twenty minutes of the first swallow she was covered with great itching red welts. The doctor came, soda compresses were laid on, sedatives and mild physic were scattered about, and all subsided safely . . . except my feeling of deep shock and hurt professional pride. As the nurse, Miss Faulck, pointed out, I should have been content to let well enough alone.

The pudding was safe enough: a little round white shuddering milky thing I had made that morning under the stern eye of Miss Faulck and whoever it was that succeeded mad Ora in the kitchen. It had "set" correctly. It was made according to the directions for Invalid Cookery in Mother's best recipe book, and I had cleaned my fingernails until tears filled my eyes before I touched so much as the box of cornstarch.

Then, in the middle of the afternoon, when the pudding slid with a chill plop into the saucer, I knew that I could not stand to present it, my first culinary triumph, in its naked state. It was obscenely pure, obscenely colorless.

A kind of loyalty to Ora rose in me, and without telling Miss Faulck I ran into the back yard and picked ten soft ripe blackberries. I blew off the alley-dust, and placed them gently in a perfect circle around the little pudding. Its cool perfection leaped into sudden prettiness, like Miss America when the winning ribbon is hung across her high-breasted symmetry.

And even a little while later, when Mother lay covered with compresses and Miss Faulck pursed her lips and David howled for a meal he couldn't have because he might drink hive-juice, Mother smiled at my shocked anxious confusion, and said, "Don't worry, sweet . . . it was the loveliest pudding I have ever seen."

I agreed with her in spite of the despair.

I can't remember ever learning anything, that is, I don't hear Mother's voice saying to me, "Now this is a teaspoon, and this is the way you sift flour, and warm eggs won't make mayonnaise . . ." But evidently I loved to cook, and she taught me several things without making them into lessons, because in the next few years I knew how to make white sauce, and cup cakes with grated orange rind in them. (Father was always very complimentary about them, and Anne and I loved to save ours until the rest of the family had left the table, and then cover them with cream and sugar and eat them with a spoon.)

I could make jelly rolls, too, which seems odd now; I don't think I've even tasted one since I was about ten, much less had any interest in putting one together.

I loved to read cookbooks (unlike my feeling for jelly roll that passion has grown stronger with the years), and inevitably I soon started to improve on what I had read. Once I made poor Anne share my proud misery with something I called Hindu Eggs. I was sure I had read about it in Fanny Farmer; all you did was add curry powder to a white sauce and pour it over sliced hardboiled eggs.

When Mother said she and Father would be away one night, and I might get supper alone, I hid the gleam in my eye when she told me to put the sauce and the eggs in a casserole, and be sure to drink milk, and open a jar of plums or something for dessert.

"Yes, Mother, I know I can do it," I said smoothly, and the word *Hindu* danced sensuously in my mind, safely unsaid until Mother was out of the house.

The casserole was handsome, too, when Anne and I sat down to it in exciting solitude at the big table. Anne admired me, there was no doubt of it . . . and I admired myself. The rich brown sauce bubbled and sent out puffs of purely Oriental splendor. I sat in Father's place, and served each of us generously.

The first bite, and perhaps the next two or three, were all right; we were hungry, and in a hurry to feel the first warmth in our little bellies. Then Anne put down her fork. She beat me to it, so I continued to hold mine, determined like any honest cook to support my product.

"It's too hot, it burns," my little sister said, and gulped at her milk.

"Blow on it," I instructed. "Mother's not here."

We blew, and I ate three more bites to Anne's dutiful one. The heat seemed to increase. My influence over Anne must have been persuasive as well as autocratic in those far days, because she ate most of what was on her plate before the tears started rolling down her round brown cheeks.

I ate all mine, proudly, but inside I was cold with the new knowledge that I had been stupid. I had thought I remembered a recipe when I didn't, and I had used curry without knowing anything about it, and when the sauce looked boringly white I had proceeded to make it richly darker with probably five tablespoonfuls of the exotic powder.

I ate all I could, for fear Father would see how much we threw into the garbage pail, and then after my sweet forgiving little sister helped me straighten the kitchen we went upstairs and, with the desperate intuition of burned animals, sat on the edge of the bathtub for a long time with our mouths full of mineral oil. She never said anything more about it, either; and the next morning there were only a few blisters, just inside our lips.

When I was eleven we all moved to the country. We had a cow, and chickens, and partly because of that and partly because Grandmother had died we began to eat more richly.

We had chocolate puddings with chopped nuts and heavy cream. The thought of them makes me dizzy now, but we loved them. And lots of butter: I was good at churning, and learned very well how to sterilize the wooden churn and make the butter and then roll it into fine balls and press it into molds. I liked that. And we could have mayonnaise, rich yellow with eggs and oil, instead of the boiled dressing Grandmother's despotic bowels and stern palate called for.

Mother, in an orgy of baking brought on probably by all the beautiful eggs and butter lying around, spent every Saturday morning making cakes. They were piled high with icings. They were filled with crushed almonds, chopped currants, and an outrageous number of calories. They were beautiful. Saturday afternoons they sat cooling, along with Mother and the kitchen after the hectic morning, and by Sunday night they were already a pleasant if somewhat bilious memory.

After about a year of this luscious routine, Mother retired more or less permanently to the front part of the house, perhaps with half an eye on the bathroom scales, but before she gave up cooking, I learned a lot about cakes from her. The fact that I have never made one since then—at least, the kind with many layers and fillings and icings and all that—has little to do with the gratitude I have often felt for knowing how to measure and sift and be patient and not be daunted by disappointment.

Mother, like all artists, was one-sided. She only cooked what she herself liked. She knew very little about meats, so I gradually learned all that myself. She hated gravies, and any sauces but "white sauce" (probably a hangover from Grandmother's training), so I made some hideous mistakes with them. And there was always an element of surprise, if not actual danger, in my meals; the Hindu eggs had warned me but not curbed my helpless love of anything rare or racy.

But in spite of all that, I was the one who got dinner on the cook's off-night. I improved, there is no doubt about it, and it was taken for granted that I would step into the kitchen at the drop of a hat.

Perhaps Anne would have liked a chance at having all the family's attention for those few hours. If so she never got it. The stove, the bins, the cupboards, I had learned forever, make an inviolable throne room. From them I ruled; temporarily I controlled. I felt powerful, and I loved that feeling.

I am more modest now, but I still think that one of the pleasantest of all emotions is to know that I, I with my brain and my hands, have nourished my beloved few, that I have concocted a stew or a story, a rarity or a plain dish, to sustain them truly against the hungers of the world.

from LOVE BLEMISHED
BUT ABIDING

Soon after we moved to Whittier, in 1912, Anne and I climbed onto the high back seat of the Model T, on a fine summer evening, and drove with Father and Mother down Philadelphia, past the place where Greenleaf intersected it, and on toward the State School for bad boys. We turned to the left, farther down a street I forget the name of, although I could still go to it, and finally stopped in front of a shabby small house under old eucalyptus trees. There were no sidewalks, but lush bushes of oleander grew taller than a man, and I know now that all the houses there were ones built hastily by the less privileged camp followers of the first Quaker settlers, in a kind of slum. The air was probably sweet and cool.

Out from the cottage and then down to us in the car came a tall fine young woman, and it seems to me now that my heart opened at that first view of her, as did my sister Anne's. It was our Aunt Gwen, related by love alone.

My parents *were,* the way the sky is, or a great tree. My trust in them was unquestioning, I never thought about things like love or hatred or insecurity. I was almost eleven before I said a flat and very unsuccessful *No* to them. I was much older, perhaps into the comparative senility of seventeen or so, before I heard them have a real row. They were young and beautiful and intelligent when I first knew them, and I accepted them as my father and mother without the slightest need to question their being so.

I early knew some of their moods, as when Mother felt a little nervous during the Sunday afternoon "drives" Rex would take us on, to let Grandmother have a quiet house for her weekly letters to Pittsburgh and Ireland. Edith would turn her face from the cliff edge we were skirting jauntily in Turnbull Canyon, Father's favorite place to practice high curves, and press a fine handkerchief to her lips, and I would feel my breathing chopped off in sympathy, although the wild road really did not scare me at all. Sometimes in downtown Whittier when we were allowed to sit in the back seat while Father drove Edith here and there, I am sure proudly, she would push her foot frantically against the floorboard when he nudged the back of a farm wagon or another car, and I remember hearing him ask sarcastically, "If you can't drive, why use the brake?"

That was as near to bickering as they got, as far as I know. There was one argument, about how to pronounce "allies" (this was in 1917 when the word was suddenly important . . .): Grandmother won it as usual by sending me to the dictionary stand in the corner of the dining room. Now and then Edith would weep, but never as much as she would have enjoyed doing, when Rex was sharp-tongued . . . "Your father is like his mother, very quick-tempered," she would say. "But have you noticed that his eyes turn absolutely black when he is a little put out? So handsome!" (He had the kind of eyes that were normally grey-green, and I do too, but I no more inherited this flashing change of coloration than I did his big bony nose, to my lifelong regret.)

So I lived wrapped in the unquestioned love of those two people. They *were,* and I was their pup, taking everything they gave me because it was mine.

Aunt Gwen was a different matter. She flowed through my life, all our lives, like a gusty river bringing food and excitement and adventure. She was strong. She was loving, but no nonsense there . . . strictly stiff-upper-lip, with strong doses of *Uncle Remus* and *Stalky and Company* . . . and of course *The Jungle Books:* "Go down without a whimper. Never be a tattletale. Protect the weak. Do what you are asked to do and a bit more. Be polite. Don't lie, or cheat at parcheesi. Don't grouse." All this sounds awful, but it was not, for she accepted the rules she taught us as part of herself, and we wanted only to be part of her too.

My mother leaned upon her, and surely gave her courage and strength in return. Edith needed security, above all except perhaps love, it now seems clear to me, and Aunt Gwen was even taller than she, and more firmly if not as heavily built. She possessed an enormous energy in her strong body, and gave of it eagerly to anyone who would accept it: her dog Pat, her parents and brothers, the St. Matthias choir and refreshment committees, *us.* For a long time *we* were the lake into which most of her flowed, from all her generous springs and sources. It was an awesome gift, and we accepted it as our due, much as dry ground accepts fresh water. We *used* her.

She spoke always with a weirdly British accent, thanks to her missionary beginnings in the New Zealand bush and then the most isolated northern islands of Japan, and finally adolescence in a kind of asylum-orphanage run by the Church of England for its more hapless dependents, somewhere near Brighton, I think. Mother, always so Anglomanic, would put up with any reasonable facsimile of British linguistics, which to her automatically meant noble-cultured-educated-charming as long as all the aitches were in place. It is only by the Grace of God that the few people in Whittier who said "cahn't" and pronounced "aunt" as if it were not an insect were perforce members of the Episcopal Church and therefore available to us as friends . . . people like Uncle Mac and his tiny quiet wife Barnie, their girl Isobel, Gwendolyn Nettleship. If Aunt Gwen had been a Quaker, we would never have known her, an impossible thought. . . .

Her accent in Whittier was firmly enunciated, unchanging, and almost unintelligible to many of our misplaced Midwesterners, and I think the greatest tribute to it is that while I still slip now and then and say Bean instead of Bin, and even Agayn for Agen, and occasionally Tomahto instead of Tomayto, I listened for years to her

when she read Uncle Remus' tall tales and never once laughed at her peculiar interpretation of that equally strange dialect spelled out by Joel Chandler Harris. It all
seemed right to me, and I can still smile when I think of Aunt Gwen repeating Br'er
Fox's insistence that "it *is* Sparrygrahs. . . ." Ah, yes: "*looks* lahk sparrygrahs, *tase* lahk
sparrygrahs . . . ," and off I go chuckling. Much later, when I got to live with Negroes
who were supposed to talk that way, it never occurred to me that there was any connection between them and Uncle Remus, and indeed there could not possibly have
been.

Fortunately she never forgot the jungle ways of her first days: when she was not a
week old she had been slung in a hammock and trotted through the bush, ahead of
her mother, in a long line of aborigines carrying the woman doctor to a sick village.
During the years I myself trotted alongside her, with Anne only a step or two behind,
she taught us a thousand things too intangible to report, as well as how to roast kelp
leaves, steam mussels, tease a rattlesnake away from a frightened saddle horse, skin
an eel after sundown, stay quiet while a night-blooming cereus unfolds . . . things like
that.

I never wondered or asked how Aunt Gwen came to the same place we did, and
at the same time. Perhaps it was because her father knew a great deal about bugs and
such, and had some kind of job in the laboratories of the local Citrus Association?
Her mother was often far away, or else invisibly at home, a frail beautiful woman
who was said to write for newspapers Down Under and "at home," which meant
England of course. Then there were three younger brothers, all handsome and, like
their parents and many other English people who lived in America in those days,
aloof and seemingly disdainful of everyone. The two older boys soon fled the nest
for marriage and like adventures, and Raymond, our favorite, stayed within our worshipping reach until he had graduated from high school and enlisted, in 1917 or so.

And not long after the Nettleships all moved to the little cottage in Whittier, Aunt
Gwen married. This rocked the Episcopalian enclave almost as violently as it must
have her own family: she seemed cut out to be the spine, the provider, the classical
Devoted Daughter, and not the flighty victim of a quick romance. (I was of course
unaware of all this at the time, but lived in its widening ripples for many years. . . .)
And that daughter, dutiful and devoted, may really have been what she was meant to
be, for the wedding lasted only one night.

Lieutenant Shaw was, according to a picture I vaguely remember, a delicate
young man about half or a third the size of his bride ("She would have made three
of him," my mother said almost maliciously), a lonely Englishman who had shyly
presented a letter of introduction to Mr. Nettleship . . . something about a common
interest in fruit flies. A week or so later there was a hasty marriage ceremony, and he
and Aunt Gwen spent one night in a moderately priced hotel in Los Angeles and
then she saw him off at the station and went back to Whittier on the Electric, in time
for her job at the packing house, where she wrapped oranges. Her husband went
straight to France, where he was killed immediately. How sad that they did not make

a child! It might have robbed me of much of my own full happiness, but I love Aunt Gwen enough to wish it for her.

Not long after that, she moved bag and baggage and complete with her parents and her brothers to a shabby house on the corner of Painter and Philadelphia. I think there must have been some arranging and discussing between her and my father and mother, and perhaps between them and her own parents. But any such finaglings were never mentioned in the next decades.

The house, although plainly falling apart, was better than the wreck of a cottage the Nettleships had been living in. It was probably an old farmhouse, and there was the remnant of a fruit orchard on its big lot . . . peaches, no-good apples, a wonderful apricot tree. Our house came next, at the southmost edge of the "nice" Quaker area.

Edith was a few years older than Gwen, and more polished and experienced as a female, and in spite of her naïve respect for anything remotely connected with the Anglo-Saxon persuasion she dominated the strange couple they made. She had a natural but imperious daintiness about her, in spite of her increasing bulk, and of course she did indeed need help and comfort as she dawdled through her dangerous pregnancies; she was largely ignored by both Rex, who disliked ailing women, and Grandmother, who found every aspect of reproduction distasteful, in spite of her own Victorian brood of nine. Aunt Gwen seemed to love Edith without cavil, especially after Mrs. Nettleship died, and Mr. Nettleship remarried, and even Raymond flew off. More and more Mother handed over large pieces of her whole matronly existence to the big red-faced Englishwoman, and devoted herself to herself, and of course to the next child. And more and more Anne and I came to recognize Aunt Gwen as the core of our lives.

Part of Mother's voluptuous acceptance of all of Aunt Gwen's devotion and energy (I am sure Edith believed unquestioningly that she was rescuing her friend from a drab existence, being nothing but kind and supremely generous to her . . .) was based on the convenient fact that while she lay waiting for parturition her husband was healthily active in correct chaste pastures, which indeed he was. Rex soon began to feel, in his male way, a little like my sister and me about our large loving goddess. With lesser people this could have turned into the classical sex game, but Rex seemed simply to enjoy the way she was always ready to fry a mess of fresh sea bass, or swim out with him to Mussel Rock at dangerous low tide and help him pry off a couple of bucketfuls of the delicious shellfish, or make a powerful if heavy-footed fourth at tennis. She played a passable card hand, and she laughed well. Mother never seemed to question the real enjoyment Rex showed in doing things with Aunt Gwen that she herself neither could nor would attempt, and, in spite of her real affection, it was partly because she could not have got along without the other woman, so quickly and fully had she and all of us come to depend on her. How fortunate this was! I really think that if Aunt Gwen had been forced to leave us when

I was between four and about ten years old, I might have pined and withered into death . . . and Anne too.

After we moved to the Ranch, in the second decade of life in Whittier, my mother no longer needed Aunt Gwen, and there was a strong cooling, at least on Edith's part. It is too painful for me to discuss with myself, but one thing I remember Edith's telling me, in a gabby moment, which showed that *all the time* there had been a latent resentment of the other woman, not in the children's lives, apparently, but in Father's. Mother said that before Norah was born, when she was supposed to be dying, she discussed with her husband what he should do without her, and asked him to marry Aunt Gwen, to take care of the children. And there was a small vicious smile on her sweet mouth when she said he had recoiled, yes *recoiled* from the thought. "But she's not a woman to me," he had protested. Mother went on about how foolish and blind even the best of men can be, but I wished she would smile differently and talk about something else. . . .

Her open love for everything English did not quite cover the rest of the Nettleship family, and as far as I know there was no kind of friendship between my parents and Aunt Gwen's. I think Mrs. Nettleship may have upstaged Edith a little, with her obvious refinement and her fluty voice, so different from her worshipping daughter in every way. Like many displaced English ladies she hated America, and made no attempt to change her views. And while she was alive, Anne and I never went upstairs in the old farmhouse, where she had her "study," and we tiptoed when she might be writing or resting.

Her three sons resembled her in their fine bones and their aloofness, and contrary to Aunt Gwen were almost pretty. They were like the father in their womanizing, and there was usually a little quiet buzz going on at home about their escapades, to which Anne and I paid no attention. All three were in the Army during The War, and I can remember some shocked astonishment when Raymond, the youngest, brought home a German wife called Hanni, indecently soon after the Armistice . . . strange behavior in a good American doughboy! And Aunt Gwen was the only person in Whittier, or at least the only one we knew, who could have three blue stars, and a gold one for the dead husband, on the red-bordered cotton flag hanging in her window. This dubious honor was only one more proof to us of her grandeur, and Anne and I looked proudly up at it as we passed her house toward school.

Raymond was a nice fellow, a kindly faun. When he was finishing high school he wanted to go right away into the Army, which he managed with some chronological connivance with the Draft Board, and to prove his virile aptness he grew a little golden moustache. It made my heart quicken, for he had the kind of skin that turns very brown in the summer, and it was almost too beautiful to see that crinkly badge on it, even though it meant that he was no longer a boy we could punch and hug and try new riddles on.

In the summers, until he went into the Army, he earned money by collecting rattlesnake venom in the Laguna hills. He wore high leather boots that laced tightly up his legs, and Anne and I loved to have him show us little scars on them where the snakes had struck at him. He killed them by jumping on them, mostly, just three or four inches back of the head, and once he missed and all the color came off his boot where the poison had sprayed onto it as the snake struck. My father was strangely angered by this story, and called Raymond a damned cub, but Aunt Gwen laughed proudly with us.

Mr. Nettleship was largely invisible. My mother could not stand him, a courteous handsome man, because he wore a short grizzled beard which Anne and I found quite lovely. (This was our first intimation that Mother was almost unhinged by the sight of a beard. She was the youngest in a family with several older teasing brothers who grew them as soon as possible and cultivated them foppishly, and her dearly loved father was of course bearded all his life. Her favorite of them all was her brother Evans, who, to his chagrin, could never grow more than a dollar-sized spot of silky whisker on his smooth pink face. And when the one living boy in our own family, David, planned to come home for Christmas with fine curly whiskers he had grown at art school in Colorado, my mother bit back fierce sobs and refused flatly to see him unless he shaved first. He was the pride of her life, but she so clearly meant what she said that young David bowed to her, one more time a child and not a man.)

Mother saw Mrs. Nettleship now and then in the tiny parlor of the farmhouse, and reported somewhat maliciously to Grandmother that Aunt Gwen waited on the lady hand and foot, and kept her as dainty as a princess. A few times Father and Mr. Nettleship went deep-sea fishing with a group of local heathens like Sam Jackson, foreman of the Back Room at the *News*, but that ended when the old Englishman got very sick and lost both his upper and lower teeth overboard. At Christmas Anne and I dutifully took him a small tin of his favorite pipe tobacco, and a necktie for Raymond. But never, as far as I can remember, did any of that family but Aunt Gwen ever come into our house. It seems impossible to me that such a warm good place could have stayed cold when Mother wanted it that way, but such was the case.

Not long after the Nettleships moved next door, perhaps in a couple of years, the mother vanished even more permanently than before. I knew nothing about it until I came home from school and told Mother that on Aunt Gwen's front door there was a lavender silk scarf of Grandmother's, tied in a big bow. Mother said that Mrs. Nettleship had died, and that we would not see Aunt Gwen for a day or two and that we should not bother her if she sometimes cried. She said that Aunt Gwen had loved Mrs. Nettleship very much. This all seemed natural, and Anne and I probably thought nothing more about it. I cannot remember ever mentioning it again, although I do know that Grandmother sometimes wore the lavender scarf. And soon after Mrs. Nettleship's death the widower married a tall thin spinster named something like Hutzenpiller, or Seegmiller, the town's librarian, and was summarily dismissed by my mother, although I cannot see from what, as a nasty old rake.

Perhaps my sister and I were a little more loving than usual with our goddess after her bereavement, but I can remember no difference in her straightforward no-nonsense stiff-upper-lip wholeness to us. She went on doing odd jobs in the community, always admitted to the best non-Quaker homes, because she had what sounded like an English accent to the Americans. And she sang contralto in the Episcopal choir. Sly people of today might have hinted it was more a low baritone, to match her rather whiskery face as she settled into an apparent spinsterdom, and it is true that she and Uncle Peter MacLaren did a very good male-trio arrangement of "On the Road to Mandalay," about once a year on a good picnic in Laguna, because he could sing both tenor and bass.

One time, before Christmas, Aunt Gwen spent days nailing layers of old newspaper to the inside of a little shed behind the Nettleship house, where tools had been stored when a small farm stood there, and she installed a borrowed sewing machine and started a little studio, as she called it. She made really dreadful things, like cotton flannel nightgowns. But they hung against the walls, which she had pasted with magazine covers over the newspapers, on dainty wooden hangers covered with puckered satin ribbon, and usually they had a little bow somewhere around the neck. They looked nice, to us. There were also potholders made from scraps of bright material she had got from the ladies of St. Matthias: she sewed them together zigzag, and I was allowed to stitch a bone ring on one corner of each. Little Anne, probably, got the more infantile privilege of picking up pins and thread. The tiny room was warm and bright and stuffy, with a wonderful smell of newsprint and burning kerosene from the stove and cheap fuzzy flannelette and ribbon, and Aunt Gwen hummed along loudly at the sewing machine, which ran with a foot pumper like the church organ. Mother was a bit scoffing of the venture, but saw to it that all her acquaintances helped deplete the jaunty supplies by Christmas, and as I recall it, Aunt Gwen felt successful: although no richer, she was hardly much poorer, and it had been fun. . . .

Mainly, though, as time went on, she devoted herself to *us*. I assume she was "helped" with this, financially, but have never known. I do know that once during the War, when sugar was scarce, rather a fuss was made at home about Father's giving her a hundred pounds of it. Or perhaps it was a barrel. There was Conversation about such foolish generosity, and what is left from it makes me feel that the sugar was more or less black market, of inferior quality, relatively cheap, and that Aunt Gwen would do some of our summer canning anyway, so who was being generous? This sounds niggling, and perhaps it was. Meanwhile Anne and I spent more time every day in the wretched old farmhouse with Aunt Gwen, and liked nothing better than to be asked to stay to supper, although Mr. Nettleship was not too friendly about that. It became much easier, however, as he began to court the town librarian and then moved to her house on the west side of town.

I have no idea of how all six of the Nettleships fitted into the house when they were together, in the first year or months of it. I would be willing to wager that it was Aunt Gwen who slept on the living room couch, or even on the floor. . . . Downstairs, as one entered, there was a tiny parlor with a silk-covered love seat in it, and I think a little marble fireplace, neither ever used. Next to it down a dark narrow hall with a peculiar smell which I now recognize from English novels, there was a little room where Raymond slept and studied, never entered by Anne and me of course, and then a primitive bathroom. And on the right side as one entered, there was a dingy living room, dark and comfortable, where Mr. Nettleship sat and read and smoked his pipe, and then an even darker kitchen where I spent many fine hours of gluttony and general escape.

Upstairs in the narrow rickety house the best room, the only one with light and air, looked east to the hills and south into a tall tree, perhaps a magnolia. There were probably two other little rooms, but that is the one I remember. It belonged to Mrs. Nettleship. I suppose her husband slept in one of the two beds, but there was no sign of anyone there but the tall frail lady. There were pretty white curtains billowing gently in front of the four windows, and the wallpaper was striped with wide bands of blue and ivory, different from any we had seen. (Mother went in for very British cretonnes, and lots of sprigs of things on the wallpaper . . . impossible flowers and leaves. . . .)

And there was a dainty dressing table made of pale bamboo bent and fixed into lacy patterns. It was unforgettable. Aunt Gwen let us look at it now and then, and told us that it had gone everywhere in the world with her mother, from long ago in Japan. It was a symbol of regal femininity to me, and later when I knew all the queens and princesses in and around the Wonderful Land of Oz, I always saw such an elegantly fastidious piece of furniture in their most intimate closets, in the palaces made of emerald, of ruby. . . .

In the kitchen there was a big black stove with a trash burner, so I suppose it used wood. Certainly it was much more interesting than the one at home. In the middle of the shabby room a generous table was covered with oilcloth, which I still have a weakness for, and on a long shelf covered with the same bright stuff there was a beautiful set of china freckled with small pink carnations, which Aunt Gwen had collected gradually by using a canned milk that gave prizes.

From such drab cheap china, those bowls and cups and plates still as clear to my mind's eye as any Wedgwood or Sèvres I have seen, I ate happily and whenever I could, for several years. I ate things we never had at home, and of course a few we did, but not with the pungency and savor they had in that farmhouse kitchen, and at Laguna when Aunt Gwen and Anne and I were down there.

And we were down there as much as we could be, on bright chilly Sundays in winter and all summer long. In winter Rex drove us from Whittier at a reckless speed, and we ate a shivering picnic and watched the angry waves from clifftops, full of anticipation for summer. In summer we were *there*, Anne and I, because we were alone with Aunt Gwen except for the family Sundays, always a pleasurable invasion but basically something to be tolerated until we could be alone again.

We walked a lot, because Aunt Gwen had almost literally been born on her feet, like any self-respecting Englishwoman. And we never went anywhere, along the cliffs or up into the hills, without a hefty fried-egg sandwich or two in our pockets . . . and time for the fruit when we got home again. There and in her Whittier kitchen we knew that if the moon and stars were right, we would have deep rich floating puddles of hot cocoa for supper, with buttered toast sogging deliciously in them. . . .

I do not think my mother ever knew of our gastronomical treats: she was deliberately bland about "what went on," secure in the knowledge that we were safe while she carried on with other duties like reproduction.

In Whittier we walked too, everywhere, because it was the way Aunt Gwen moved best from place to place, and always for an exciting reason. We walked in the rain, and in the scorching heat, to Bailey Park, to the hills behind the College, best of all to the hills back of the town reservoir, where occasionally a motor would start coughing in the little shed and make us laugh. There was a big wooden cover over the round pool of water, and we could look through the fence and see black glints and now and then hear a rippling sound, as if perhaps a mouse had jumped in. We would walk through eucalyptus groves and in the springtime pick wild flowers, and then settle our backs against a fallen tree and look down upon the rooftops of our town, and across brown plains to the occasional shimmer of the ocean, many miles away. On fine days we learned to study the horizon and find the long blue line of Catalina Island. This always pleased Aunt Gwen, to agree with us that indeed it was that far place, where I finally went when I was eleven.

Aunt Gwen was a wonder with flowers. I learned how to put them in a "garden bunch" as if they were growing, not head against head but at different levels. She taught me how to take care of them, once in the house and the vase. (She called a vase a vahz, which always irked Mother when we did too.) She also taught us respect for growing things, so that we never pulled up the tiny garlicky buds of the *Brodiaea*, which grew in sweeps of blue in the springtime, or broke stems with our feet unless we had to. And she knew resounding names, always with a reason, like Indian Paintbrush which is indeed dipped in color, and Monkey Face which makes a monkey face, especially when it is pinched gently in the right place, which she always knew too.

Aunt Gwen never lived with us. Often after her mother died, Anne and I stayed with her overnight, and of course we were together for several long heavenly-beautiful summers in Laguna, and for the miserable-but-marvelous-and-merry months of May–June in 1917, when we both had thoroughgoing measles and Mother had Norah. After the first miseries it was exciting to be in the defunct Mrs. Nettleship's own room, with her elegant fluty dressing table. Father came to stand in the doorway every day, to tell us a poem he had composed for us, and one night Raymond, the only one of Aunt Gwen's brothers still at home, appeared there to show himself to us, dressed as Monsieur Beaucaire for the high school Senior Play. We could have swooned at his silken beauty, had we not been prone, and as I remember the ugly smell of measles, and the pathetic *sick* look of little children who are in its clutches, I wonder at Raymond's real gallantry. However, perhaps sometime in his life he understood that never again would two females let out that same moan of delight at the sight of him. . . .

We looked at Norah through the front screen door of our house, in the nurse's arms, while we were getting onto our pins again after this bout, and although the prospect of living with a third sibling in the family was vaguely delightful, we would have chosen, I am quite sure, to stay forever at Aunt Gwen's if it had been left to us.

As far as I can remember, nobody ever marveled at her cheerful acceptance of us for that month when she was so fully occupied with helping Mother bear the baby, helping Father run the house, helping Raymond into his pink satin costume, helping us go to the toilet and all that. But we loved her, and she loved us.

Although we never really lived in the Nettleship house after that blissful accident in Time, we often ate there in the big dark smelly kitchen, thank God. It seems never to have been when Raymond was home from school, or Mr. Nettleship's new wife was visiting her relatives and he needed a cook. Aunt Gwen made large meals for the men, and served them deftly . . . and I doubt that she often sat down while they ate. But when the coast was clear, Anne and I would set three places on the glamorous checked oilcloth, and help carry the cups and bowls and plates that Aunt Gwen would fill before she joined us. Occasionally she said Grace, as much to teach us how to behave when Grandmother's missionaries were at our table at home as from any religious effort. We always ate nicely if with unconcealed heartiness, and talked a lot, and then washed the dishes together.

By now I wonder a lot about the inner life of this goddess, the one we never were aware of. I feel sure that she was happy for several years, to have us love her so much, but it is painful to know, now in my own life, that she was a young vital woman cut off firmly from things she must have longed for: a world of her own, children of her own, a good man. I sigh and stretch with sadness for her position in her own family *and then ours:* the kind cheerful drudge, adoring her fragile princess of a mother so totally unlike her, and serving her autocratic father and spoiled handsome brothers *and then us,* like a big ruddy Cinderella, day and night for too many years. Yes, how did it happen?

It is dangerously easy for me to think that my parents, and especially Edith, kept Aunt Gwen under their thumbs as long as they really needed her: that is, while Mother was busy with the second batch of children. This is not quite fair to any of them. The truth is that some time after the War, Rex and Edith both did everything in their power to encourage Gwendolyn to become a trained nurse, and they used all the pull they had in Bishop Johnson's hierarchy to brush aside a few rules and encourage her to enter training at Good Samaritan in Los Angeles.

Aunt Gwen was too old for the requirements, and thanks to her Church "education" in England she was abysmally ignorant of almost every subject on the list of the precurriculum. But she had proved to be a brilliant student in the Red Cross classes given in Whittier at the last of the War, and everybody in the little Episcopalian colony rallied loudly enough to be heard, and she was accepted at the hospital for several years of what must have been straight Hell. She had to work four times as hard as any of the slim young students who brushed past her big thick middle-aging body, girls who knew secrets about mathematics and chemistry she had never dreamed of, girls who went out with boys. . . .

Gradually there was less of her in our lives, perforce. She stayed friends with Iso-bel MacLaren, Uncle Mac's daughter, and formed a strong and lasting relationship with—perhaps not too oddly in that town where the circles outside of Quakerdom were so restricted—the spinster-companion of the town librarian, who had taken Mrs. Nettleship's place in her widower's heart, if never her daughter's.

Mother disdained this new friendship as unworthy, although I am not sure of what, since the two women understood and liked each other, and even indulged in a few lady-like capers such as starting a small flower-and-gift shop which soon went broke, and taking little trips together which must have made Edith Kennedy's sub-conscious grit its teeth in frustrated rage. I think the reasoning, if such it could be called, was that if Aunt Gwen was to know any real happiness it should be with us, not with "other people," even though there was obviously no room for her in our own home. Still, Edith corresponded once a year or so until Aunt Gwen died, and I don't know when that was, now . . . sometime after World War II.

They wrote letters twenty pages long to each other. I have no idea what the sick lonely woman in California said to the big eccentric woman on Molokai, where she was running a hospital for everybody but the lepers, but Aunt Gwen's letters are somewhere in my boxes of family detritus, and although Edith read parts of them aloud to us with less than her usual mockery, I prefer not to dig them up again for myself.

But I did find out from my mother once, after I had written two or three books on the pains and pleasures of our basic need to eat in order to live, that Aunt Gwen had expressed a sad note about me in one of her annual screeds. It was uncharacteristic. Her reports were usually factual and vivid, but dealt little with her own or other people's emotional involvements. She still believed in a stiff upper lip and no whim-pering and all that, just as she had decades earlier when she was my goddess-mentor-pillar. She never hid troubles, but she considered it poor taste perhaps, or boring, to talk much about them.

For instance, when my sister Anne found herself at twenty-five or so a spoiled beautiful brat with a little son to raise alone, she reverted instinctively to the ruler of her infancy and childhood, and wrote often and fully to Aunt Gwen about becoming a nurse. It might have been salvation for her, but Aunt Gwen apparently advised her against it, or at least made clear to her the quarrels such a profession would cause in Anne's nature. Anne said nothing to Mother about this deep correspondence with the Islands, perhaps feeling it might hurt Edith Kennedy to have advice asked from anyone else. But Aunt Gwen wrote to Mother something as simple as, "Our Annie seems to be in a bit of a pickle, doesn't she? But everything will straighten out. She is a fine brave girl, and will land on her feet. You are all made of good stout stuff, you know. . . ." This implied tactfully that Edith knew about Annie's questing, which I doubt that she ever did, probably with secret relief.

When I heard that Aunt Gwen had let down her guard, and written sadly about me, I was shocked, and although much time has passed since then, I often feel a stabbing, poignant regret that I hurt her by never once mentioning her, in whatever I had written about "the gastronomical me," while she was still alive. She had read my books with great pleasure, she told my mother, but she wondered why I did not remember some of the good things we ate together when I was little. . . . (It pains me even to write about this now, but I think I should.)

I tried to explain to my mother that I was not mature enough, that my focus was not yet right, that Aunt Gwen and the things she cooked for us and taught me to make were still either too immediate or too removed from whatever life I was then leading. Someday I would do it, I said. "Don't wait too long," she said. But I did. I was not yet enough of a *person* to write straight to Molokai and say, "I am not ready. . . ."

All I could now say about Aunt Gwen will never be said, but it is sure that much of my enjoyment of the art of living, as well as of eating, comes from her . . . as well as my certainty that the two are, or can be, synonymous. [. . .]

A Palace Incident

My first intimations of both elegance and sorrow came early in the American part of The War, perhaps in 1917. They seemed to belong together, for a while anyway.

In the beginnings of our life in Whittier there was a strong need among small religious groups to band tightly into themselves, and we felt it as a good solid clannishness at St. Matthias for want of anything better . . . like community importance, perhaps. We had a commendable choir, thanks to my mother's drawing-room contralto and Uncle Mac's barrack-room bass, with Mrs. Emory always making the altar bloom with scavenged flowers, and old Mrs. Atkinson, valiantly and slowly dying of bronchial cancer, at her companionably wheezing organ. We had excellent parties, with thin Jack Swain or plumper Matty Matteson being a well-stuffed Santa Claus, and then the annual Sunday school picnics in summer, with exactly three ice cream cones for every child: one chocolate, one strawberry, and one vanilla. On Easters, after we had made our best manners to the current minister at the door, there was a big chocolate egg for each of us. Of course people like my father were very seldom serious about their duties as vestrymen, but that had nothing to do with anyone under twelve. . . .

Aunt Gwen, of course, was an Episcopalian. How could she be anything else, since we knew her and she knew us, and we probably would not have met otherwise? And who else could be her dearest friend, not counting Mother of course, but Isobel MacLaren, Uncle Mac's only daughter? Both young women sang in the choir, Isobel in a small firm soprano, Aunt Gwen the female counterpart of Uncle Mac's spur-of-the-moment mingling of low baritone and basso profundo.

It was a fine sight to see the vested choir march ponderously into the little shack of a church, especially if we had watched some of their vestments being ironed frantically in our kitchen the night before. The people who were our lives were beautifully changed into near-angels, as they rocked a little from side to side behind the boy carrying the crucifix. Anne and I stared respectfully at them all, knowing warmly that under the flowing black and white lived Mother, Uncle Mac, Aunt Gwen and Isobel, and then groundlings like Mrs. Emory and other kind willing people. We always hoped that Uncle Mac would have forgotten to switch off the ship's bells in his handsome pocket watch, presented to him when he retired as Chief Engineer on a British shipping line to the far reaches of the Empire. It was lovely to hear that little bell ringing so sweetly and irrevocably from his surpliced middle, while not the twitch of a smile showed anywhere, and the service rolled on and his face turned a deeper purple.

His daughter Isobel was a Lovely Lady, Anne and I knew. I suppose that she was in her early twenties when we first met her. I was, and still am, caught in the sound of her name, Isobel MacLaren. Mother, the Anglomaniac, would have been happier if Isobel was not a name so blatantly from north of the Border, but she taught us right away how to say it: *Eye*-zo-bell, and not the ugly *Izz*-uh-bell we were used to in America.

Isobel was built in a compact way, and bit off her words with a near-snap of her firm jaw. She and Aunt Gwen were a good pair: both with Anglican accents that made them socially desirable in our tiny enclave of ethical behavior, and both well respected as Dutiful Daughters.

Isobel lived with her father (Uncle Mac) and her mother Barnie. We knew this birdlike dignified little woman was called that, even by her daughter, but we never addressed her as such, although as time passed we *referred* to her sometimes as Aunt Barnie. (Isobel had her soft lilting voice, but with more insistence in it.) Barnie must have led a largely self-sufficient life as the wife of a master seaman. She always stayed in the background, but it was fine to hear Uncle Mac say her name, rolling it out with the tenderness of a loyal if roaming lover over so long and rough a marriage.

The MacLarens seemed to coast always on rather thin times. I suppose there was a kind of pension . . . but they lived within a block of her younger brother Mr. Chaffee, and apparently she had often stayed in his other houses when Uncle Mac was at sea. All her brothers had left Scotland for Australia, it seems, and Down Under had made enormous fortunes. They had stables of famous horses. They had yachts. They were big spenders and knew how to be. And Old George held onto Barnie, and brought her to Whittier with him not long before we got there in 1912. He *needed* her.

I cannot know if he actually paid her and Uncle Mac for what they did to keep his whimsical investment in an elegant villa functioning as he wished. I hope so. There was a kind of jaunty subservience and mockery in Uncle Mac about it all, which used to make my parents snort impatiently. I do not even know if Mr. Chaffee brought them to Whittier or came there to be near their loyal help, the rich man following beloved and penniless immigrants from too many years of wandering, secure now in the close ghetto of Low Church Episcopalian retirement which he never touched except with his munificent yearly dues. How could I know about all this? The important thing is that the MacLarens were *there*.

I was always aware, in a disinterested way, that my family treated the Chaffees with a remoteness that was perhaps because of their economic differences, but more probably because they loved Uncle Mac and did not like to see him bend with such courteous good humor to the autocratic whims of the Australian brother, and see Barnie at Mrs. Chaffee's beck and nod, and see Isobel used as a substitute nurse and lady's maid for her fragile aunt. That is to say, the Chaffees, pronounced Chay-fees, were a different cut from ours.

The MacLarens lived in a small brown shingle house a minute's walk from the low but imposing palace Old George had built for his wife. This was on the beginning of the foothills north of Whittier, on steep streets named for the plain Quaker fathers and still lived on by the plainer citizens, down on the flats, but suddenly desirable to rich newcomers able to pay for pumping water and building retaining walls, and all that unnecessary display and frippery frowned upon by the first dedicated founders of the little religious settlement. If people like this Australian foreigner wanted to spend their money on a sprawling villa designed to coddle the mysterious invalidism of his invisible wife, let them! Let him with his gambling and his ill-begotten riches throw up the conceits of tropical plantings in a glass-covered loggia in the center of the house, like a heathen! The Friends withdrew from all this as if it were the Black Pox, or simply ignored it. I cannot know if the Chaffees were ever aware of their local isolation, nor if our indirect association with them, through the MacLarens, may have added to our own tacit enislement by the locals.

Tropical plants did flourish under the glass ceiling of the center loggia, and on its four sides glamorous dim rooms lay silently behind closed doors, with such a plenitude of bathrooms pretty and not plain like ours, and silky boudoirs with little curvy chairs in them, as Anne and I had never dreamed of seeing, even though we were already caught in the web of princesses in the Green and Red and Brown Fairy Books and in the spicy derring-do of King Arthur's knights.

The most astounding of all the empty languorous purlieux of the Chaffee House, which we often tiptoed through as Father grew more devoted to Uncle Mac and Aunt Gwen to Isobel and therefore we could all go into the place when the owners were away, and Uncle Mac was supposed to be keeping his eye on the elaborate plumbing and the exotic planting and so on, and the most elegant of anything a princess could ever have, was Mrs. Chaffee's bathroom.

Anne and I wandered through it, probably holding hands in solidarity, as if we were in the most intimate secret apartment of Queen Glinda Esmeraldina, which perhaps we were, for we saw Mrs. Chaffee herself only one time, and then she was as if made of cobwebs on an enormous bed, nourished perhaps by three peeled grapes a day and a sip of yellow wine. She smiled faintly and waved at us, with a grey-white hand so thin it was like a filament or tentacle pushing out from the froth of lace she lay in, and then Isobel led us deftly from the dim room.

Later, when the lady left, to die somewhere from whatever it was that had slowly changed her into such a strange shadow, we went oftener and more freely into the house, and it was always first to her bathroom, which of course we never used for anything as carnal as our own relievings.

It was bigger than our generous living room at home. The creamy skins of polar bears lay everywhere. Perhaps eight or a dozen different kinds of tubs sat around its edges, all running hot and cold water from golden spigots and sprays and douches and such. (This was one reason why Uncle Mac was such a jewel of a brother-in-law, after his life in the bowels of a hundred ships: he knew *pipes!*) Mrs. Chaffee needed all these tubs, to help comfort whatever it was that for ages had been wrong with her. Mr. Chaffee obviously loved her, and wanted to be good to her. He kept nurses there night and day, and they must have spent hours picking up the tiny colorless body and dipping it like an egg being poached into this perfumed water or that, while he had to be away almost all the time on business.

On good days her chair would be pushed into the loggia, to give her a fleeting look at the luxuriant jungle plants thrusting and twining steamily under the opaque roof (another useful accomplishment of Uncle Mac's, thanks to his years in tropical hinterlands: he knew *orchids!*). Usually, though, the poor lady lay alone in her great bed, between baths, while nurses slipped in and out of the cautious gloom in her chamber, and tested the waters in her many tubs.

Across the house from this shadowy apartment was a jolly room with a good smell, meant for men, for The Man. Father and Uncle Mac would sit there whenever the Chaffees were away. It was my first view of the leathery easiness of a small warm place where males, at least Anglo-Saxons, like to get away from females. It was cosy, comfortable. . . . I went in several times, then out, having observed sharply the books on the walls, the fine smell of tobacco and leather, not as bitter (nor as fine, I added loyally) as that in Charles Somerville's room in our garage . . . and my first seltzer-water bottle with its powerful silver squirter on the top of the bluish heavy glass. The two men would be sitting the way I never saw them at home, with their legs out, and big tumblers in their slow hands. Their voices were idle, and plainly different from other ways they talked. From the door Isobel might beckon to me, and I would leave unnoticed, an invisible and as yet unbothersome woman.

At the far end of the big flat house, carefully built so that Mrs. Chaffee could go almost anywhere in it when she felt able to sit in her enormous silent wheelchair as a nurse pushed her from one empty room to another, there was a Sun Parlor, as glassed rooms were called in California when I was little. It was long and big and bright, with a generous table where perhaps someone had dreamed that a dozen lusty eaters and drinkers might sit. It had an air of waiting and waste, but I liked it because its glass walls went to the floor, instead of nose-high to me in our own such room, and because on the tiles in the dusty glare were succulents in pots, occasionally vivid with strange flowers which Uncle Mac knew how to make spring from their dead-looking fingers and stems. To me they were part of the palatial elegance everywhere. (Mother and Grandmother rejected "house plants" as a part of the prairie life they preferred to dismiss as undistinguished, or at least forgettable: Iowa farm wives kept geraniums and ferns blooming in empty tin cans on their kitchen windowsills, but the nearest the Holbrooks came to that was a pair of impressive cacti on the front steps of their village mansion . . . and once an impudent and rebellious offspring of the banker and his dowager, my Uncle Evans, stuck a red apple on every long cruel needle. . . .)

One bright winter day, in 1917, perhaps, with the sun blasting in through the westerly windows of the Sun Parlor, I roamed almost invisibly here and there while Aunt

Gwen, the giant widow, helped Isobel, oh, Eye-zo-bell, unpack and do away with and distribute all the earthly belongings of her younger brother Fred MacLaren. He had been blown up or something—as, it was said to me later, Aunt Gwen's frail little homesick husband had been—on a beach or in a trench in France. He was still a British citizen, although later most of the MacLarens became Americans.

The young women moved slowly through the bright air. I watched them, from this and that position, and it did not seem to bother them. They went on quietly folding and sighing, and occasionally held each other in a silent passionless embrace, as they dug through the two or three lockers the Crown had forwarded to Uncle Mac, last of kin and no doubt thankful to have womenfolk handy, to do this job for him. I knew a little of how they were protecting him, and Barnie too: strong sturdy girls there, raised to cope with life, to ignore any weak nonsense of whimpering and all that! Good British stock, both of them! They kept on almost wordlessly, in the best tradition of Empire, and pulled out mildewed uniforms and a few books and things, and then a gas mask.

I was shocked by its almost beautiful ugliness, which of course I had seen on posters, and I came in from my permitted edge of the action and asked about it. It was like a desiccated animal, with the strange tubes and stiff flaps that barnacles make on more helpless shells. It was colored a dull fecal brown (which was called khaki by the time the Yankees got into the War, and caused me some trouble at Penn Street School since I said *kah-ki* because Aunt Gwen did, but which was pronounced *kaa-ki* by the other kids . . .).

Then I crashed innocently through and into the intense controlled circuit of emotions and sorrows. When I asked about the hideous mask, and was told something or other, I suddenly pulled it on over my head, for I knew that I would seem to turn into a bug of some kind and amuse Aunt Gwen and Isobel, and get them out of their silence. Instead, those two greatest of all the giants in my life, goddesses of tenderness and gentle shapings, burst into huge undisciplined sobs and wails, and rushed out of the Sun Parlor and into the farthest part of the great pretentious hopeless house, like thundering wild horses.

I stood there in the waning sunlight. I did not know why I was alone, or what had happened. The straps of the dead boy's mask caught over my ears as I managed to pull it off me.

And that is the last about the Chaffee House, I think, except for a kind of footnote: the invisible lady did die, although when and even why I do not know, and then Old George stayed more in Whittier, and when a cousin of mine was "let out" of the U.S. Army and joined forces with another one of Uncle Mac's equally wearied sons, in about 1918, the two of them, mechanically inspired and for the time being somewhat manic-neurotic-nutty, materialized a dream of George Chaffee's, of carrying around behind him on his compulsive jauntings a fully equipped little house, what an English gypsy would call a caravan, in which he could sleep and eat and otherwise live.

My cousin stayed with us. George MacLaren lived with his young wife and oncoming children. The two men were refugees from concerted violence, and in silent companionship they built the rich old Australian a beautifully engineered and designed behemoth which was, as far as I can discover, the father of all "mobile homes." He would take it out, either with only his chauffeur-houseboy or with the builders too, and they would get stuck on narrow mountain curves or in Death Valley sand dunes, and come back to Whittier and revamp the whole wheelbase, or the wiring or plumbing.

So . . . perhaps Mr. Chaffee was a good man. I think of his frail wife there in the faery-tower (through whose wish?), with all the soft waters flowing (but what else?). I think of his warm heady "office," with his jolly kowtowing brother-in-law, my Uncle Mac, using his elegant seltzer bottle in the whiskey my father undoubtedly took there and shared happily, away from us women like Mother and Grandmother and Barnie, even Aunt Gwen and Isobel and my little sister Anne and . . . yes, and me. Mr. Chaffee was perhaps all the things whispered about him in Whittier: a high liver, a gambler, a racing man . . . and he got those two shaky younger men through a peculiarly hard time, when they came back from the far shores of France. He saved them, by handing them an idea to perfect.

It is possible that I too helped release some war casualties from their immediate travail, the time I put Fred's gas mask over my little head and drove the brave young women sobbing out of the bright Sun Porch and into the dim elegance of the Chaffee House. I know now that their growing friendship entrusted them to that shared storm of grief, for they remained firm and loving all their lives.

And I remember getting the mask off. It was slower than pulling it on had been, perhaps because of my astonishment at what wearing it had caused, and it was horridly stuffy inside. Once out of it, I looked at all of Uncle Mac's weird blossoms against the glass walls of the empty room, and wondered for at least a few minutes what had really happened so suddenly in the palace.

FROM LIGHTENED HEART AND QUICKENED ENERGIES

[. . .] And where is the organ grinder? There was one, for at least a few years, in Whittier. I know this because I was four when we went there, and when I was in the second grade, a good four years later, I could compare notes with my friend Gracie about him. Then he stopped coming.

He came always at twilight. Anne and I would hear him down at the corner, approaching slowly from Philadelphia around to Painter. It was a magical sound, and my heart still falters when I hear it with my spiritual ear. Whoever was in command of the house at that moment would understand, and put a nickel or perhaps some pennies in our hands, and we would go out alone and wait at the edge of the sidewalk. Up toward us (I see all this now in light flickering from the overhead lamp at the intersection, and long shadows, but that is fantasy pure and simple, for we would not have been allowed to stand outside alone in the real dark . . .) would come the small bent man with an organ strapped in front of him, and on his shoulder his little monkey. The man wore a soft pointed green hat, very dirty but with a feather in it, and the monkey wore a red coat with buttons, baggy pants, and a little round flat cap with gold braid, which he took off when he asked us for our coins. Sometimes the man would tell him to shake hands with us, and his fingers were cold and like bird bones.

First the little shadowy man would crank out a tune or two, depending on the time of day, how tired he probably was, and what our money might add up to. I know they were Italian, because afterward Mother would laugh a little about the way "O Sole Mio" or "La Donn' è Mobile" had sounded (she pretended to hold her ears when the organ grinder came, but always knew what he had played!). Then, for a year or two, he would go slowly on up the street. But it was the wrong time of day: people were closing their doors, pulling down their blinds. And he was really not in the right part of town for sidewalk frolicking. He found that he would have more luck down along the south and west edges, where the houses were small and shacky, and the people were more open than the respectable Quakers who lived on North Painter. Anne and I waved sadly as he turned away.

He would find my friend Gracie, though, and she was enough to cheer him and his monkey too. She was a stalwart mixture of her big Mexican mother, who still wore her hair in a long braid down her back, and her white father, who was said to be an itinerant butcher. She compared notes with me about the organ grinder, which it never occurred to me to do with my more proper friends, all of whom were Friends as well. The morning after the organ grinder had come, she would ask me tauntingly if he had been to our house, and I felt quite proud and jaunty that of course he had. We told how much we had put into the monkey's hat, and whether he had shaken hands with us. He always shook Gracie's. . . . She told me that one time the monkey jumped right into her arms, wearing all his clothes. That never happened to me, and I admitted it to her, but if one of the girls from the north of town had vaunted such a triumph, I might well have lied a little, at least by implication, and said nonchalantly, "Of course . . . me too . . . *twice* . . . of course. . . ."

Once when I did not have a single penny, and the house seemed empty of adult bankers, I left Anne on the sidewalk as hostage and ran to the house to grab a ripe avocado from the sideboard. The little monkey plunged into it, and surfaced like a green plum, with his eyes on top as black and bright as olives. The man laughed, and played another tune, but I know a nickel would have been more use to him.

I have seen pictures of slum children, pale and thin but gay, dancing to the music of an organ grinder in the slums of New York long ago, just about when my little sister and I stood shyly on the edge of our neat lawn and listened without moving to the wheezy music, and then waved good-by. How muted we were! But inwardly we vibrated like twanged cello strings to what the man and his companion had given us. After they left we would go into our warm house again, and Mother would play more music for us sometimes, and we would sing together. There was one book we liked especially, *A Child's Garden of Verses*, with really good accompaniment, the kind Mother could cope with. Snatches from it still slide through my mind at unexpected times: Oh, how I like to go *up* in the air, / *Up* in the air so bluuuuue. . . . I saw three ships a-sailing. . . .

But it was the organ grinder we still thought of, and perhaps sang to in our own ways . . . and perhaps still do. Where did he come from . . . and why did he come to such a tightly closed place as Whittier then was? After he withdrew into the shadows toward the lower part of the little town, did he find something to eat? There was the electric tramway which ran between us and Los Angeles. It cost more than the pennies he could ever earn on our street. Our family had a pass on it because of the *News*, but Anne and I knew he did not. And once into the big city, where would the tiny monkey stay, in all that dark noise? We discussed adopting him and his friend, but in a hopeless way. I talked with Gracie about the plan, and she laughed loudly and told me to forget it. All we could do was keep our ears open, and hope for the return.

It had nothing to do, then anyway, with the music classes with Mrs. Graham, in either three-four or four-four time but all sung at the same volume, the way young sheep blat, well fed, almost ready for the market. It had nothing to do with groups singing together as I knew them: church choirs, a wandering quartet intoning hymns in the Friends' church for foreign missions, even what I heard alone and more rarely together at home. Certainly it was far from Spain and Mexico and Italy. It was far from the Lower East Side. It was the piper's tune, played from the shadows of Whittier, and the tiny cold hand of the monkey still reaches toward me.

FROM THE MEASURE OF MY POWERS
1929—1930

III

The dining room at the Biarnets' was just large enough for the round table, six or eight chairs, and a shallow kind of cupboard with a deerhead over it and two empty shell-cases marked *Souvenir de Verdun* on the top. It was an ugly little room, spotted and stuffy, with a cluster of mustard and spice pots on the dirty checked tablecloth. But it was pleasant while Madame was in it. Her wonderful honest vulgarity made us alive too, and after a meal, when she finally stopped pestering the cook and stretched her tired piano-teacher hands out across the cloth, her talk was good.

She was always late for meals; her pupils were for the most part young or stupid, and she was too much interested in even the dullest of them to send them off at the strike of the hour. Instead, she pounded out do-re-mis on the big piano under our rooms so long and so violently that from pure exhaustion the children grasped their rhythmic monotony before she let them go home. Then she came running down to the dining room, the lines deep in her red face.

She was usually two courses behind us, but caught up with our comparatively ponderous eating almost before we could wipe our lips or drink a little wine, which on her instruction Monsieur Biarnet kept well watered in our tumblers. She ate like a mad woman, crumbs falling from her mouth, her cheeks bulging, her eyes glistening and darting about the plates and cups and her hands tearing at chunks of meat and crusts of bread. Occasionally she stopped long enough to put a tiny bite between the wet delicate lips of her little terrier Tango, who sat silently on her knees through every meal.

Under and around and over the food came her voice, high and deliberately coarse, to mock her prissy husband's Parisian affectations. She told jokes at which her own lusty laughter sounded in the hot air before ours did, or proved that Beethoven and Bach were really Frenchmen kidnapped at birth by the Boches. She became excited about the last war, or the lying-in of a step-daughter by one of her three other marriages, or the rising prices, and talked in a frantic stream of words that verged on hysteria and kept us tense and pleasurably horrified.

We were hypnotized, Al and I and any other transient diners whose extra francs were so irresistible. Madame glanced at our faces as if we were her puppets, her idiotic but profitable puppets. Her eyes, amicably scornful, appraised us, felt the stuff of our clothes, weighed the gold in our rings, and all the time she saw to it that we ate better than any other *pensionnaires* in town, even if she did make more money out of us than any other landlady.

Her reputation was a strange one, and everyone in Dijon knew her as the shrewdest bargainer, the toughest customer who ever set foot in the markets. One of her husbands had been a pawn-broker . . . but gossip said that she taught him everything he ever knew. She was supposed to be wealthy, of course, and I think she was.

She drove herself cruelly, and looked younger than many women half her age, except for the hardness in her finely modeled mouth when it was still. She supervised the cooking, gave music lessons, played in the pit for visiting musical shows, and if the leading man pleased her slept with him . . . gossip again . . . and did all the marketing.

I was to learn, a couple of years later, that collecting enough food for even two people in a town the size of Dijon meant spending two or three days a week scuttling, heavily laden, from the big market to the *charcuterie* around the block, to the *primeur's*, to the milk-shop. And Madame's system was even more complicated by her passion for economizing.

Storekeepers automatically lowered their prices when they saw her coming, but even so she would poke sneeringly at the best bananas, say, and then demand to be shown what was in reserve. Up would come the trapdoor to the cellar, and down Madame would climb, with the poor little fruit man after her. She would tap and sniff knowingly at the bunches hanging in the coolness, and then, on her hands and knees, pull off the greenish midgets that grow along the step at the bottom of the great clusters.

They were worthless: the man had to admit he gave them to his children to play house with. Into the black string bag they went, for a magnanimous twenty centimes or so . . . and in a few days we would have them fixed somehow with cream (at half-price because it was souring) and kirsch (bought cheaply because it was not properly stamped and Madame already knew too much about the wine merchant's private life). They would be delicious.

And while she was in the cellar she would pick up a handful of bruised oranges, a coconut with a crack in it, perhaps even some sprouting potatoes.

The little fruit man shook his head in an admiring daze, when she finally dashed out of the shop.

She sometimes wore several diamond rings left to her by her late husbands, and when she was playing at the music hall she had her hair freshly tinted and waved. The rest of the time, in the daily hysterical routine, her appearance meant nothing to her if it involved spending money. She had an old but respectable fur coat, but scuttled around town in two or three or four heavy sweaters rather than wear it out, and when even they did not hold off the dank Dijon cold, she simply added more layers of underwear.

"Eugénie," her husband said one day, in his precise pettish voice, rolling his eyes waggishly, "it is hardly seemly that a woman of your age go around looking as if she were about to produce twins."

Jo, his gentle effeminate son, flushed at the ugly reference to human reproduction. He was used to enduring in stiff silence his stepmother's vulgarities, but could usually trust his father to behave like a member of the upper classes to which they both so earnestly aspired.

Madame looked quickly at them. Two men, her eyes seemed to say, but neither one a man. . . .

She screamed with laughter. "Twins! No fear, Paul! The Dijonnais would never blame *you* for twins. If anything but a little gas should raise my belly, there would be more horns in this room than those on the deer's head!"

Her eyes were screwed into little points, very bright and blue under the tangled hair. She was cruel, but we had to laugh too, and even Monsieur Biarnet grinned and stroked his little moustache.

He accepted his advancing years grudgingly, and floated from one unmentioned birthday to the next on an expensive flood of "virility" tonics. Of course, the labels said Rheumatism, Grippe, Gout, but we saw around him an aura of alarm: Eugénie stayed so *young*. . . . In spite of his Royalist leanings and his patent embarrassment at her robust vulgarity, he knew she had more life in her eyelashes than he in his whole timid snobbish body. He took refuge in wincing at her Burgundian accent, and raising his dainty son to be a gentleman.

Madame had a hard time keeping cooks in the house. They found it impossible to work with her, impossible to work at all. She was quite unable to trust anyone else's intelligence, and very frank in commenting on the lack of it, always in her highest, most fish-wifish shriek. Her meals were a series of dashes to the kitchen to see if the latest slavey had basted the meat or put the coffee on to filter.

She could keep her eyes on the bottle that way, too. All her cooks drank, sooner or later, in soggy desperation. Madame took it philosophically; instead of hiding the supply of wine, she filled up the bottles with water as they grew empty, and told us about it loudly at the table, as one more proof of human imbecility.

"Poor fools," she said, her strong flushed face reflective and almost tender. "I myself . . . what would I be if I'd spent my life in other people's swill? The only cook I ever had that didn't take to the bottle ate so much good food that her feet finally bent under when she walked. I'd rather have them stagger than stuff."

Madame herself drank only in Lent, for some deeply hidden reason. Then she grew uproarious and affectionate and finally tearful on hot spiced *Moulin à Vent,* in which she sopped fried pastries called *Friandises de Carême.* They immediately became very limp and noisy to eat, and she loved them: a way to make long soughings which irritated her husband and satisfied her bitter insistence that we are all beasts.

She let the little dog Tango chew soft bits from the dripping crullers in her big fine hands, and they both grew more loving, until finally poor Biarnet flounced from the room, *L'Action Française* tucked under his arm.

Madame loved boarders; they amused her, and brought in regular money which became with her magnificent scrimpings a fat profit every month. When Al and I came we were the only ones, but in the next few months, before she had rented the house with us in it to the Rigagniers, there were probably twenty people who came and went, most of them foreigners.

Monsieur Biarnet, who resented having paying strangers at his table, but had little to say about it in the face of his wife's pecuniary delight in them, only put his foot down, and then lightly, about Germans. He loathed them. They made him choke. He would starve himself rather than be polite to them, he said.

Madame shrugged. "We all must eat. Who knows? Someday they may come to Dijon as bosses, and then we'll be glad we were decent to them."

So there were a few who ate with us now and then. They never stayed long. Paul Biarnet really won, because he was so loathsomely, so suavely polite, so overpoweringly the tight-lipped French courtier, that the poor baby-Boches soon found other places to eat. Madame grinned affectionately and rather proudly, and soon refilled the empty chairs with pretty Rumanian girls, or large heavy Czechs.

She liked to have at least one safely attractive female at the table; it kept Paul's small pretentious mind off his various aches and grouses, and made it easier for her to continue her own robust and often ribald life. I did very well . . . I was young and amusing, and at the same time safely and obviously in love with my husband. Monsieur Biarnet made himself truly charming to me, and even Jo, now and then, would flutter from his sexless dream world long enough to make a timid joke with me. It was good for my French, and pleased Madame. Life would have been hell if it hadn't.

We used to sit there at the table, after the noon dinner or on Sundays, and talk about the private lives of ghosts and archbishops and such. Occasionally, the cook would hiccup.

"You hear that?" Madame would interrupt herself. Then she would shout toward the kitchen, *"Imbécile!!"*

We would go on talking, cracking little wizened delicious nuts that had been picked up off the cellar floor of some helplessly hypnotized merchant. We would be pleasantly full of good food, well cooked, and seasoned with a kind of avaricious genius that could have made boiled shoe taste like milk-fed lamb *à la mode printanière*.

Maybe it *was* boiled shoe . . . but by the time Madame got through with it, it was nourishing and full of heavenly flavor, and so were all the other courses that she wrung daily, in a kind of maniacal game, from the third-rate shops of Dijon and her own ingenuity.

She would look at us, as we sat there cozily in the odorous little room, and while she told us the strange story of one of her pupils who ran off with a priest, her mind was figuring what each of us had paid her for the good meal, and how much profit she had made.

"*Imbécile!*" she would scream ferociously at another helpless hiccup from the kitchen. And when we finally left, she would dart to the sink, and we would hear her say, gently, "Girl, you're tired. Here's enough cash for a seat at the movie. Finish the dishes and then go there and rest your feet. And don't bring home any soldiers."

Then Madame would laugh loudly and, if it were Sunday, go to her little salon and play parts of a great many things by Chopin . . . all tenderness and involuted passion.

THE MEASURE
OF MY POWERS
1931

When I went back to Dijon, after the summer spent with my family, it was plain that the time had come for Al and me to live by ourselves. For two years we had eaten all our meals with good, interesting, even affectionate people, and lived in their house. We had learned much from them and accepted a thousand courtesies. Now, suddenly, they were intolerable, they and their sad quarrels and their gay generosities, they and their fine feathery omelets and their shared meats and vintages. We loved them, and we fled them like the black pox.

Even after so long in an army town, I still could not always tell a *"gros numéro"* from a reputable house, and managed to interrupt several business transactions and even exchange a few embarrassed salutations with unbuttoned University friends before I found the little apartment we were to live in.

It was in a "low quarter," everyone assured us with horror. The tram ran past it, and it looked down on a little square that once had held the guillotine and now, under the shade of thick plantains, housed two or three *pissoirs* and an occasional wandering sideshow, with small shops all around.

Indeed, the quarter was so low that several Dijonnais who had been friendly with us stopped seeing us altogether. What had been an amusing social pastime in the fairly dull town life, coming to tea with us in the Rue du Petit-Potet safely surrounded as we were there by mayors and bishops and the smell of thirteenth-century cellars, became an impossibility when it meant walking through streets that were obviously inhabited by nothing but artisans and laborers. We basked in the new freedom, and absorbed sounds and vapors never met in a politer life.

Our apartment was two floors above a pastry shop, Au Fin Gourmet, and was very clean and airy, with a nice smell. The smell was what made me decide to take it, after days of backing confusedly out of brothels and looking at rooms dark and noisome and as lewdly suggestive as the old crones who showed them to me.

We signed several official certificates, bending over peach tarts and a row of soggy *babas* to reach the ink bottle. The proprietor looked at our signatures, and asked, "Married?"

"Yes," Al said, raising one eyebrow almost invisibly in a way that meant, in those days at least, that in spite of his politely innocent manner his words carried a tremendous reprimand or correction or general social commentary. "Yes. You see we have the same name, and I have marked us as Monsieur and Madame."

"Well," the man said, "it is less than nothing to me, you understand. But the police must be satisfied." He looked amicably at us, wiped his hands again on his sugary apron, and marked out Madame and my profession as student. In place of it he wrote, "Monsieur Fisher, and woman."

His wife, a snappish-looking small woman with pink eyebrows and tight mouth, gave us our keys and warned us again that the chambers were now in perfect condition and were expected to remain that way, and we went up the stairs to our own private home for the first time in our lives.

There was a big room with a shiny but uneven tiled floor and two wide windows looking down on the dusty little square. The bed, half-in–half-out a little alcove, did not keep everything from looking spacious and pleasant, especially when we pushed the round table into the corner and put books on the fake mantelpiece under the wavy old mirror. There was a kind of cupboard, which Madame the owner had called *"la chambre noire"*; we got some candles for it, and turned one of our trunk tops into a washstand, and it was very matter-of-fact in spite of its melodramatic name.

Outside our front door, on the landing, was a little faucet, where we got water for washing and cooking. It was a chore to carry it, and even more of one to empty the pail from the Black Chamber and the dish water and what I washed vegetables in, but it was something so new that I did not much mind it. There was a fountain in the square, of course, and I soon learned to take my lettuces and such down there and let the spout run over them, like the other women in the quarter.

The kitchen was astonishing to me, because I had never lived in a place like New York, where people cook on stoves hidden in their bureau drawers, I've heard. It was perhaps five feet long, perhaps three wide, and I had to keep the door open into the other room when I stood at the two burner gas-plate. There was a little tin oven, the kind to be set on top of a stove, and a kind of box with two shelves in it, for storage and instead of a table.

And there was the window, one whole wall, which opened wide and looked down into the green odorous square, and out over the twisted chimney pots to the skies of the Côte d'Or. It was a wonderful window, one of the best I can remember, and what I saw and thought and felt as I stood in it with my hands on the food for us, those months, will always be a good part of me.

Of course, we celebrated, the first night in the new place, and dined well and late at Ribaudot's, so that in the morning it was fun to lie in our niched bed and listen to the new noises.

They made a pattern we soon knew: the workers in their hard shoes, then the luckier ones with bicycles, and all the bells ringing; the shop-shutters being unhooked and folded back by sleepy apprentices; a great beating of pillows and mattresses, so that now and then brown feathers floated past our windows; and always the clanging of the little trams going up into the center of things.

That first morning there was something more, something we were to hear every Wednesday and Saturday, a kind of whispering pattering rush of women's feet, all pointed one way. I should have listened harder and learned.

When we finally got up, and went to the little café on the corner for our first breakfast, we saw that the soft rushing came from hundreds of women, all hurrying silently, all dressed in black and carrying black strings or pushing little carts and empty baby buggies. And while we were sitting there in the sun, two easy-going foreigners, some of the women started coming back against the stream, and I knew that they came from the big market, *les Halles*.

Their bags and carts were heavy now, so that the hands that held and pushed them were puffed and red. I saw the crooked curls of green beans and squashes, the bruised outer leaves of lettuces, stiff yellow chicken-legs . . . and I saw that the women were tired but full of a kind of peace, too. I had no black-string bag, no old perambulator. But I had a husband who enjoyed the dark necessity of eating, as I did myself. And I had a little stove. . . .

I stood up. It was almost noon, and too late now to go to the market. I planned innocently to pick up enough food at local stores to last until the next regular day, and headed for a store I'd often passed, where pans hung in rows in the window, and on the sidewalk clay casseroles and pots lay piled.

The first week I tried to feed us was almost too difficult. I learned a hundred things, all the hard way: how to keep butter without ice, how to have good salads every day when they could only be bought twice a week and there was no place to keep them cool (no place to keep them at all, really), how to buy milk and eggs and cheeses and when and where. I learned that *les Halles* were literally the only place to get fresh vegetables and that two heads of cauliflower and a kilo of potatoes and some endives weighed about forty pounds after I'd spent half an hour walking to market and an hour there and missed three crowded trams home again.

I learned that you bought meat and hard cheese and such by the kilo, but that butter and grated cheese, no matter how much you wanted, always were measured in grams. I learned that the stall-keepers in the market were tough loud-mouthed people who loved to mock you and collect a little crowd, and that they were very friendly and kind too, if you did not mind their teasing.

I learned always to take my own supply of old newspapers for wrapping things, and my own bowls and cans for cream and milk and such. I learned, with the tiredest feet of my life, that feeding people in a town like Dijon meant walking endless cobbled miles from one little shop to another . . . butter here, sausage there, bananas someplace again, and rice and sugar and coffee in still another place.

It was the longest, most discouraging, most exciting and satisfying week I could remember, and I look back on it now with an envy that is no less real for being nostalgic. I don't think I could or would ever do it again; I'm too old. But then, in the town I loved and with the man I loved, it was fine.

We ate well, too. It was the first real day-to-day meal-after-meal cooking I'd ever done, and was only a little less complicated than performing an appendectomy on a life-raft, but after I got used to hauling water and putting together three courses on a table the size of a bandana and lighting the portable oven without blowing myself clear into the living room instead of only halfway, it was fun.

We bought four plates and four forks, instead of two, so that we could entertain! Several of the people we knew found it impossible to condone our new address even with the words "whimsical" and "utterly mad," and very conveniently arranged to meet us in restaurants when they wanted to see us. The faithful ones who picked their way through the crowded streets and up our immaculately clean tenement steps were few, and they were welcome.

I wanted to invite the Rigagniers, but even if we could have asked them to bring their own plates and forks, I did not think the little stove would be able to cook anything they would honestly or even politely call a meal. And by then I was already beginning to have theories about what and how I would serve in my home.

I was beginning to believe, timidly I admit, that no matter how much I respected my friends' gastronomic prejudices, I had at least an equal right to indulge my own in my own kitchen. (I am no longer timid, but not always adamant, when it is a question of religion or old age or illness.)

I was beginning to believe that it is foolish and perhaps pretentious and often boring, as well as damnably expensive, to make a meal of six or eight courses just because the guests who are to eat it have always been used to that many. Let them try eating two or three things, I said, so plentiful and so interesting and so well cooked that they will be satisfied. And if they aren't satisfied, let them stay away from our table, and our leisurely comfortable friendship at that table.

I talked like that, and it worried Al a little, because he had been raised in a minister's family and taught that the most courteous way to treat guests was to make them feel as if they were in their own homes. I, to his well-controlled embarrassment, was beginning to feel quite sure that one of the best things I could do for nine tenths of the people I knew was to give them something that would make them forget Home and all it stood for, for a few blessed moments at least.

I still believe this, and have found that it makes cooking for people exciting and amusing for me, and often astonishingly stimulating for them. My meals shake them from their routines, not only of meat-potatoes-gravy, but of thought, of behavior. Occasionally I am fond enough of a person to realize that any such spiritual upset brought about by my serving an exotic or eccentric dish would do more harm than good, and I bow. It is usually women past middle age who thus confound me, and I have to be very fond of them indeed. They are few fortunately, and in spite of my solicitude I still think sometimes I am betraying them and myself too.

Perhaps it is not too late for them, I think; perhaps next time they come I will blast their safe tidy little lives with a big tureen of hot borscht and some garlic-toast and salad, instead of the "fruit cocktail," fish, meat, vegetable, salad, dessert, and coffee they tuck daintily away seven times a week and expect me to provide for them.

Perhaps they *should* feel this safe sand blow away so that their heads are uncovered for a time, so that they will have to taste not only the solid honesty of my red borscht, but the new flavor of the changing world. But when they come, they are so polite, so dazed, so genteelly dead already. . . .

The people who came oftenest to our room above the Fin Gourmet were Norah, on her free Thursday afternoons away from the convent, and the American student Lawrence, who was like our brother. They were both simple people, and reassuring. For Norah I would get a pitcher of milk and a pot of honey. I'd put them with the pat of sweet butter on the table, and a big square block of the plain kind of Dijon ginger-bread that was called *pavé de santé*. There would be late grapes and pears in a big bowl.

Norah and I would sit by the open window, listening to the street sounds and play-ing Bach and Debussy and Josephine Baker on the tinny portable phonograph. The food was full of enchantment to my sister, after her gray meals in the convent, and she ate with the slow voluptuous concentration of a *dévouée*.

Lawrence was as satisfactory. He came for real meals, of course, and always brought a bottle of red wine, cheap but good. There would be candles on the table, because the one light-bulb in the room was far in the opposite corner, by the bed.

We would have a big salad always, and something I had made in one of the clay casseroles. I invented with gusto, and after the first days of experimenting with stoves, pots, and the markets, I turned out some fine odorous dishes that were a far cry, thank God, from the Hindu eggs that tortured my little sister Anne, the first time I ever let my imagination conquer over the printed recipe.

Our long stay with the Rigagniers, where Lawrence still lived, had given all of us a lust for simplicity after Madame's heady sauces. As I remember, the thing we all liked best, with the salad and Lawrence's wine, was a casserole of cauliflower, and bread and fruit afterwards. I made it so often that it became as natural as sneezing to me, and I was put off the track completely when I got back to America and found how different it was . . . the manner of doing it, the flavor, everything.

There in Dijon, the cauliflowers were small and very succulent, grown in that ancient soil. I separated the flowerlets and dropped them in boiling water for just a few minutes. Then I drained them and put them in a wide shallow casserole, and covered them with heavy cream and a thick sprinkling of freshly grated Gruyère, the nice rubbery kind that didn't come from Switzerland at all, but from the Jura. It was called *râpé* in the market, and was grated while you watched, in a soft cloudy pile, onto your piece of paper.

I put some fresh pepper over the top, and in a way I can't remember now the lit-tle tin oven heated the whole thing and melted the cheese and browned it. As soon as that had happened we ate it.

The cream and cheese had come together into a perfect sauce, and the little flowers were tender and fresh. We cleaned our plates with bits of crisp bread crust and drank the wine, and Al and Lawrence planned to write books about Aristotle and Robinson Jeffers and probably themselves, and I planned a few things, too.

And as I say, once back in California, after so many of those casseroles, I found I could never make one. The vegetable was watery, and there was no cream thick enough or unpasteurized and fresh. The cheese was dry and oily, not soft and light. I had to make a sauce with flour in it. I could concoct a good dish, still . . . but it was never so *innocent*, so simple . . . and then where was the crisp bread, where the honest wine? And where were our young uncomplicated hungers, too?

Quite often Jean Matruchot would come at noon.

He never went anywhere at night, and of course at the Lycée and the University where he taught there were a hundred stories about his licentious nocturnals. The truth was, I think, that the state of his poor popping eyes, which made it almost impossible for him to read large print in daylight, turned nights into a complete blackness which his pride would never let him confess. He was a misanthrope, and like most such men had fifty friends who would have been glad of a chance to walk with him along the dim crooked streets; but instead, he sat alone in his hideously furnished "bachelor suite" and went about only in daylight.

He ate his meals in the *pensionnaires'* room at Ribaudot's, and when he came to us for lunch he was like a man breathing after being almost too long without air.

"No rich dark-brown gaudy sauces," he would mutter, bending over his plate and sniffing what he could hardly see. "No ancient meats mummified with spices, exhumed and made to walk again like zombies! My God, no dead birds, rotting from their bones, and hiding under a crust five men have spent their lives learning how to put together so my guts will fall apart!"

"Madame," Jean would say, rising gallantly and spilling all the red wine in our glasses, which he did not see, and putting his napkin carefully on top of the salad, which was two feet away and therefore invisible to him, "chère Madame, a true victim of gastronomy, a fugitive from the world-famed Three Pheasants, a starved soul released temporarily from the purgatory of la Cuisine Bourguignonne, salutes you!"

Jean would bow, I would thank him, Al and I would whisk the more obvious damage from the table, and we would sit back to a somewhat heavy but enjoyable noon dinner.

Jean liked potatoes, so there would be a casserole of them fixed in the cauliflower routine, and quite often a watercress salad and steaks broiled somehow on the top of the stove. Then we would eat some good cheese . . . the Brie from the shop across the square was wonderful in that autumn weather, with the hot days, and the chilly nights to keep it from ripening too fast . . . and drink some more wine.

He had been an interpreter for the Americans in the last war, and on his good days he would tell us fantastic stories about the peaceful occupation of Beaune and all the homesick generals who called him Johnny. On his middling days he would tease me masterfully, like a fat Voltaire, for my class translations of "Gilpin's Ride." And on his bad days he would mutter such cynicisms as we had never heard, in French as rich and ripe as the cheese he loved, about the world and his honest hatred of it.

He was a strange passionately cold man, the kind who wants to be disliked and has true friends like us to refute all his intellectual desires. I think often of him, and of the hunger he showed for our food, and of the half-blind way his eyes would watch our faces, as if behind all the smug youthful foolishness he saw something he was looking for.

He was very different from Miss Lyse. She came often to eat with us, too, and I don't think she ever looked once at us. If she did, we were simply a part of all the sixty or so years of people who had fed her. She was charming to us; she sang for her supper, as life had taught her to, and she ate with the same ferocious voracity of any little bird while she kept us entertained.

She was about eighty then, I think, with a small pyramid of a body, and a fine proud little head with dark eyes and an ivory skin inherited from her Portuguese father. She had lived in Dijon since she was a girl, teaching English to the upper families. She still knew some conversation, all of it in simple words for the children she was used to talking to, but it was plain the French was more comfortable for her. She spoke it with a rank British accent, which she had promised her Devonshire mother never to abandon, and in spite of all the decades she had spent in the nurseries and drawing rooms of Burgundy, she sounded like a schoolgirl on a month's holiday from London, except for her volubility.

For years now, since her tyrannical dam breathed one last command and folded her hands in the death-grip over her cut jet locket, Miss Lyse had been cadging meals. She did it charmingly, amusingly.

She knew everybody, and all of the provincial gossip. She went to all the weddings of her former pupils, and then the christenings and the weddings of their children . . . and when the season was slack, and they remembered, they sent baskets of wine and cakes and butter to her attic room, as if in apology for the lack of festivals.

She was a character, everyone in Dijon said. She had followed the Bishop up the bloody steps of Saint Jacques, during the great troubles between Church and State, and had been stoned for it. Sadi Carnot had lain dying in her arms, assassinated. She had been a child in India where her father was ambassador and she knew how to charm snakes. That was the way the Dijonnais felt about her.

Myself, I was more than interested; there was something so indomitable about the set of her head and the fine flash of her old, old eyes. But it was the hunger that held me.

I don't know how she ate so much at one time. It was the result of years of practice, surely, years of not knowing just when another good meal would come her way. She was like a squirrel, with hidden pouches for the future. Norah and Lawrence and Jean Matruchot were as spindly ghosts compared with her, and meals big enough for six of us melted to a few crumbs almost before I had the time to serve them. Her manners were good, and she talked constantly in her funny mixture of nursery-English and London-French, and yet the lunch would be liquidated in the time Al and I usually spent on a salad or a tart.

I tried sometimes to see if I could stump her; I would make a bowl of two whole kilos of Belgian endive, cut into chunks and mixed with marinated green beans and sweet red peppers and chives. There would be a big casserole of fish and mushrooms and such in cream. I'd buy rich tarts at Michelin's.

Halfway through the meal Al and I would lie back in our chairs, listening and watching in a kind of daze. Miss Lyse was like something in a Disney film . . . nibble bite chew nibble nibble . . . through everything on the table, until it would not have surprised us at all to have her start conversationally, daintily, with a flick of her bright dark eyes and a quirk of her white head, on the plates themselves and then the books, right down the mantelpiece, Shakespeare, Confucius, *Claudine à l'Ecole* . . . *les Croix de Bois, The Methodist Faun* . . . nibble nibble crunch.

"That was so delicious, my dear," she would say at the end, wiping her mouth nicely and getting up with a brisk bob. "You are most kind to an old lady. And now I must thank you and be off. The Countess Malinet de Rinche is in from the country and I am having tea with her. This was *such* a nice little lunch together! Shall we say for the same day next week? Then I can tell you all about the dear Countess! Her sons! *Mon Dieu!*"

And Miss Lyse would give me a dry sweet-smelling peck on both cheeks and be out of the door before we could even get to our feet.

Would she really have tea with the unknown Countess What's-her-name, whose sons were less interesting than dead sea-fruit to us? Would she eat again until we next saw her? Did she really have *sous* enough for bread? We never knew.

It worried me, and I resolved to buy nine caramel tarts, instead of six, for the "little lunch" we knew she would not forget to take with us in exactly a week. . . .

I had one letter from her after the invasion. It was vigorous and amusing, although by then she must have been almost a hundred years old. She had been evacuated to a wretched little village near Clermont-Ferrand, and she had organized all the children into a band, to be ready to greet the Tommies in their own tongue when they came marching in. She said nothing about herself . . . but I have a belief that as long as there was life in that proud-headed little body, she would find crumbs.

from THE MEASURE
OF MY POWERS
1931–1932

I

One night about ten o'clock, perhaps a week after Al was awarded his doctorate at the Faculté, we stopped on our way home from a dinner party and stood looking at each other for a minute on the cold street.

Then, without a word, we headed for the station. We bought two tickets for Strasbourg on the midnight train, *that* midnight, not the one a week away when we had planned to go.

Most of our things were ready to be shipped. We arranged with the station master to have them brought from our apartment in a day or two. Then we ran down the back streets to our flat, routed out the saw-faced cake-maker who lived just below us in his libelously named shop, Au Fin Gourmet, and arranged in five minutes all such questions of refunds, taxes, rental papers as he would have preferred to spend five hours on. We threw what wasn't already packed into suitcases.

We left the door open on our dear little apartment without one backward glance of regret or even gratitude, and when we were finally sitting in the Buffet de la Gare, drinking a last coffee with a porter who had become our friend in the past years, we breathed again.

We were fleeing. We were refugees from the far-famed Burgundian cuisine. We were sneaking away from a round of dinner parties that, we both felt calmly sure, would kill us before another week was over.

Ever since Al's masterly and amusing public oral defense of his thesis, which drew almost as big a crowd in the Faculté amphitheatre as had the last visit from a footloose Balkan regent, we had been deluged with invitations. Most of them were from lawyers, viscounts, and even professors who, in spite of the obvious cordiality of the Faculté Dean and the Rector toward us, had peered suspiciously at us over the tops of their newspapers and waited until now to bestow the accolade of their social recognition.

For almost two and a half years they had watched us, and observed to their cynical amazement that we were breaking every precedent established by former American students: we stayed; we didn't get drunk; Al actually worked hard enough to be awarded a degree, and I actually let other men alone, in spite of wearing the same color lipstick as the upper-bracket broads. And now we were guaranteed safe. Al had earned a right to wear a little round bonnet edged with rabbit fur and I, fortunate among all women, could now look forward to being the wife of a full professor some day, instead of an instructor.

"They really seem charming," people whispered about us in the discreetest drawing rooms of Dijon. "Lunch? A small dinner?"

Suddenly we were like catnip, after all those blessed months of being stinkweed. The closed doors swung open, and we found ourselves drowning in a sea of Burgundy's proudest vintages, Rheims' sparkle, Cognac's fire. Snails, pâtés, *quenelles de brochet;* always a great chilled fish *in toto* on a platter; venison and pheasants in a dozen rich brown odorous baths; intricate ices and well-laced beaten creams . . . and all of them served to the weighty tune of polite conversation, part condescending and part awed: it was too much for us.

The unsuspected strain of getting ready for the doctorate and then this well-meant deluge of hospitable curiosity made us feel that "we must press lettuce leaves upon our brows," or die.

And that is why we were hiding in the Buffet, that cold November night. We suddenly felt rested, knowing the train was almost there for us. We would send telegrams . . . I would write letters. . . .

Our friend the porter piled us into the compartment. We shook hands. The train shivered for a minute, and then started slowly to pull northward.

We heard a shout outside.

The porter was running along beside our window, and with him was Paul de Torcy, little hunchbacked Paul who adored Al, Paul who was rich and spent all his money publishing volumes of dreadfully poor poems for bankrupt provincial welshers. Paul loved Al more than any of them, and showed him his most private room, hung with black velvet and with . . . yes, it is true . . . with a skull on the carved oak desk. Paul wore a flowing tie. Paul hated me. Paul's drunken father had thrown him down the château steps when he was little.

And there he was running desperately along the platform, his great head with its sunken temples rolled back against his hump. How had he learned that we were fleeing? What suspicions hissed behind his wild pleading eyes?

He was weeping, glaring up at Al. And without wanting to, God knows, we began to laugh, there in the hastening train, in our own safety and warmth. We stood in the window looking down at Paul and *laughing,* because his eyes, so enormous and hopeless, looked like the eyes of a planked turbot we had been served so few hours before at dinner.

The turbot lay regally on its linen couch, bedecked with citrons and fresh herbs.

Paul, more alive, ran crazily along the gray platform, unadorned. But their eyes, their great deep glassy eyes, were the same eyes, wild and full of a mute adoration and a terrible humility.

We kept on laughing, in a kind of sickness. And as the porter grabbed Paul's arm to stop his running, Al raised his fingers in a queer gesture that was half kiss, half salute.

BORDERLAND

Almost every person has something secret he likes to eat. He is downright furtive about it usually, or mentions it only in a kind of conscious self-amusement, as one who admits too quickly, "It is rather strange, yes — and I'll laugh with you."

Do you remember how Claudine used to crouch by the fire, turning a hatpin just fast enough to keep the toasting nubbin of chocolate from dripping off? Sometimes she did it on a hairpin over a candle. But candles have a fat taste that would taint the burnt chocolate, so clean and blunt and hot. It would be like drinking a Martini from silver.

Hard bitter chocolate is best, in a lump not bigger than a big raisin. It matters very little about the shape, for if you're nimble enough you'll keep it rolling hot on the pin, as shapely as an opium bead.

When it is round and bubbling and giving out a dark blue smell, it is done. Then, without some blowing all about, you'll burn your tongue. But it is delicious.

However, it is not my secret delight. Mine seems to me less decadent than Claudine's somehow. Perhaps I am mistaken. I remember that Al looked at me very strangely when he first saw the little sections lying on the radiator.

That February in Strasbourg was too cold for us. Out on the Boulevard de l'Orangerie, in a cramped dirty apartment across from the sad zoo half full of animals and birds frozen too stiff even to make smells, we grew quite morbid.

Finally we counted all our money, decided we could not possibly afford to move, and next day went bag and baggage to the most expensive pension in the city.

It was wonderful — big room, windows, clean white billows of curtain, central heating. We basked like lizards. Finally Al went back to work, but I could not bear to walk into the bitter blowing streets from our warm room.

It was then that I discovered how to eat little dried sections of tangerine. My pleasure in them is subtle and voluptuous and quite inexplicable. I can only write how they are prepared.

In the morning, in the soft sultry chamber, sit in the window peeling tangerines, three or four. Peel them gently; do not bruise them, as you watch soldiers pour past and past the corner and over the canal towards the watched Rhine. Separate each plump little pregnant crescent. If you find the Kiss, the secret section, save it for Al.

Listen to the chambermaid thumping up the pillows, and murmur encouragement to her thick Alsatian tales of *l'intérieur*. That is Paris, the interior, Paris or anywhere west of Strasbourg or maybe the Vosges. While she mutters of seduction and French bicyclists who ride more than wheels, tear delicately from the soft pile of sections each velvet string. You know those white pulpy strings that hold tangerines into their skins? Tear them off. Be careful.

Take yesterday's paper (when we were in Strasbourg *L'Ami du Peuple* was best, because when it got hot the ink stayed on it) and spread it on top of the radiator. The maid has gone, of course — it might be hard to ignore her belligerent Alsatian glare of astonishment.

After you have put the pieces of tangerine on the paper on the hot radiator, it is best to forget about them. Al comes home, you go to a long noon dinner in the brown dining room, afterwards maybe you have a little nip of *quetsch* from the bottle on the armoire. Finally he goes. Of course you are sorry, but——

On the radiator the sections of tangerine have grown even plumper, hot and full. You carry them to the window, pull it open, and leave them for a few minutes on the packed snow of the sill. They are ready.

All afternoon you can sit, then, looking down on the corner. Afternoon papers are delivered to the kiosk. Children come home from school just as three lovely whores mince smartly into the pension's chic tearoom. A basketful of Dutch tulips stations itself by the tram-stop, ready to tempt tired clerks at six o'clock. Finally the soldiers stump back from the Rhine. It is dark.

The sections of tangerine are gone, and I cannot tell you why they are so magical. Perhaps it is that little shell, thin as one layer of enamel on a Chinese bowl, that crackles so tinily, so ultimately under your teeth. Or the rush of cold pulp just after it. Or the perfume. I cannot tell.

There must be some one, though, who knows what I mean. Probably everyone does, because of his own secret eatings.

HUNGERS FED AND UNFED

From Laguna Journal

25.vii.34

Once a young woman walked every afternoon along a stretch of beach. She was tall, with a slender tanned body, and her bathing suit was very short and tight and of a soft gay green yarn.

Every afternoon as she crossed the warm sand to the steps up the cliff, she passed close by a rug, on which sat two people. She was conscious that they both noticed her and waited for her. Especially she knew that the man watched her. She walked very straight and stuck out her two small round breasts a little.

It surprised her that the man and woman were together. He was a tall rather soft man, a few years away from being very handsome. He wore bathing trunks and was busy tanning his skin. The woman rubbed oil on him, and even with her strong hands rubbing him, he watched the young girl pass by. His eyes were spoiled and laughing, the slightly moist brown eyes of an attractive middle-aged man.

That was what surprised the girl, his blatant charm and the woman he was with. There were so many lone lovely women to be with him, but he was always with the plain, gray, strong woman who never spoke but sat watching over him and rubbing his skin when he wanted it rubbed.

The girl thought they were probably the same age. But the man was still boyish and his eyes roved, and the woman was a stocky middle-aged person, blunt looking and never dressed in anything but a white apronlike dress and a coarse misshapen sweater of dull gray.

Every day the girl grew more conscious of the man. She knew he waited for her to pass. She could feel him watching the rise and fall of her little round buttocks, and she was glad that her legs were straight and firm. She stuck her breasts out proudly and wondered about his staying always with an old stubby woman.

One day she walked past them. The man half-lay against the woman's shoulder, and she was humped strongly like a rock to support him. His hand dropped lax beyond a raised knee.

He watched the girl. The woman seemed not to. The girl was very conscious. Just before she got to the steps, she turned and for the first time looked at the two people. Her head was up, very triumphant, because she knew she would catch the man finally with his bright roving look and hold him.

He smiled confidently into her eyes. Then the woman leaned slowly around, and with her white clean teeth she caught hold of the soft sidepiece of the man's hand, the piece from the base of the little finger to the wrist, and she bit it. Probably she did not bite very hard, but it was a stern, an authoritative bite. And it told the girl suddenly of a deep real passion she had not known yet nor even thought about.

The woman looked at the girl. Her eyes were clear and impersonal and swung from the young face out to the ocean. The girl turned and walked quickly away, and for a long time felt very young and humiliated.

YOUNG HUNGER

It is very hard for people who have passed the age of, say, fifty to remember with any charity the hunger of their own puberty and adolescence when they are dealing with the young human animals who may be frolicking about them. Too often I have seen good people helpless with exasperation and real anger upon finding in the morning that cupboards and iceboxes have been stripped of their supplies by two or three youths—or even *one*—who apparently could have eaten four times their planned share at the dinner table the night before.

Such avidity is revolting, once past. But I can recall its intensity still; I am not yet too far from it to understand its ferocious demands when I see a fifteen-year-old boy wince and whiten at the prospect of waiting politely a few more hours for food, when his guts are howling for meat-bread-candy-fruit-cheese-milkmilkmilk-ANYTHING IN THE WORLD TO EAT.

I can still remember my almost insane desperation when I was about eighteen and was staying overnight with my comparatively aged godparents. I had come home alone from France in a bad continuous storm and was literally concave with solitude and hunger. The one night on the train seemed even rougher than those on board ship, and by the time I reached my godparents' home I was almost lightheaded.

I got there just in time for lunch. It is clear as ice in my mind: a little cup of very weak chicken broth, one salted cracker, one-half piece of thinly sliced toast, and then, ah then, a whole waffle, crisp and brown and with a piece of beautiful butter melting in its middle—which the maid deftly cut into four sections! One section she put on my godmother's plate. The next *two*, after a nod of approval from her mistress, she put on mine. My godfather ate the fourth.

There was a tiny pot of honey, and I dutifully put a dab of it on my piggish portion, and we all nibbled away and drank one cup apiece of tea with lemon. Both my godparents left part of their waffles.

It was simply that they were old and sedentary and quite out of the habit of eating amply with younger people: a good thing for them, but pure hell for me. I did not have the sense to explain to them how starved I was—which I would not hesitate to do now. Instead I prowled around my bedroom while the house slumbered through its afternoon siesta, wondering if I dared sneak to the strange kitchen for something, anything, to eat, and knowing I would rather die than meet the silent, stern maid or my nice, gentle little hostess.

Later we walked slowly down to the village, and I was thinking sensuously of double malted ice-cream sodas at the corner drugstore, but there was no possibility of such heaven. When we got back to the quiet house, the maid brought my godfather a tall glass of exquisitely rich milk, with a handful of dried fruit on the saucer under it, because he had been ill; but as we sat and watched him unwillingly down it, his wife said softly that it was such a short time until dinner that she was sure I did not want to spoil my appetite, and I agreed with her because I was young and shy.

When I dressed, I noticed that the front of my pelvic basin jutted out like two bricks under my skirt: I looked like a scarecrow.

Dinner was very long, but all I can remember is that it had, as *pièce de résistance,* half of the tiny chicken previously boiled for broth at luncheon, which my godmother carved carefully so that we should each have a bit of the breast and I, as guest, should have the leg, after a snippet had been sliced from it for her husband, who liked dark meat too.

There were hot biscuits, yes, the smallest I have ever seen, two apiece under a napkin on a silver dish. Because of them we had no dessert: it would be too rich, my godmother said.

We drank little cups of decaffeinized coffee on the screened porch in the hot Midwestern night, and when I went up to my room I saw that the maid had left a large glass of rich malted milk beside my poor godfather's bed.

My train would leave before five in the morning, and I slept little and unhappily, dreaming of the breakfast I would order on it. Of course when I finally saw it all before me, twinkling on the Pullman silver dishes, I could eat very little, from too much hunger and a sense of outrage.

I felt that my hosts had been indescribably rude to me, and selfish and conceited and stupid. Now I know that they were none of these things. They had simply forgotten about any but their own dwindling and cautious needs for nourishment. They had forgotten about being hungry, being young, being . . .

In an essay by Max Beerbohm about hosts and guests, the tyrants and the tyrannized, there is a story of what happened to him once when he was a schoolboy and someone sent him a hamper that held, not the usual collection of marmalade, sardines, and potted tongue, but twelve whole sausage-rolls.

"Of sausage-rolls I was particularly fond," he says. He could have dominated all his friends with them, of course, but "I carried the box up to my cubicle, and, having eaten two of the sausage-rolls, said nothing that day about the other ten, nor anything about them when, three days later, I had eaten them all—all, up there, alone."

What strange secret memories such a tale evokes! Is there a grown-up person anywhere who cannot remember some such shameful, almost insane act of greediness of his childhood? In recollection his scalp will prickle, and his palms will sweat, at the thought of the murderous risk he may have run from his outraged companions.

When I was about sixteen, and in boarding-school, we were allowed one bar of chocolate a day, which we were supposed to eat sometime between the sale of them at the little school bookstore at four-thirty and the seven o'clock dinner gong. I felt an almost unbearable hunger for them—not for one, but for three or four or five at a time, so that I should have *enough*, for once, in my yawning stomach.

I hid my own purchases for several days, no mean trick in a school where every drawer and cupboard was inspected, openly and snoopingly too, at least twice a week. I cannot remember now how I managed it, with such lack of privacy and my own almost insurmountable hunger every afternoon, but by Saturday I had probably ten chocolate bars—my own and a few I had bribed my friends who were trying to lose weight to buy for me.

I did not sign up for any of the usual weekend debauchery such as a walk to the village drugstore for a well-chaperoned double butterscotch and pecan sundae. Instead I lay languidly on my bed, trying to look as if I had a headache and pretending to read a very fancy book called, I think, *Martin Pippin in the Apple Orchard*, until the halls quieted.

Then I arranged all my own and my roommate's pillows in a voluptuous pile, placed so that I could see whether a silent housemotherly foot stood outside the swaying monk's-cloth curtain that served as a door (to cut down our libidinous chitchat, the school board believed), and I put my hoard of Hersheys discreetly under a fold of the bedspread.

I unwrapped their rich brown covers and their tinfoil as silently as any prisoner chipping his way through a granite wall, and lay there breaking off the rather warm, rubbery, delicious pieces and feeling them melt down my gullet, and reading the lush symbolism of the book; and all the time I was hot and almost panting with the fear that people would suddenly walk in and see me there. And the strange thing is that nothing would have happened if they had!

It is true that I had more than my allotted share of candy, but that was not a crime. And my friends, full of their Saturday delights, would not have wanted ordinary chocolate. And anyway I had much more than I could eat, and was basically what Beerbohm calls, somewhat scornfully, "a host" and not "a guest": I loved to entertain people and dominate them with my generosity.

Then why was I breathless and nervous all during that solitary and not particularly enjoyable orgy? I suppose there is a Freudian explanation for it, or some other kind. Certainly the experience does not make me sound very attractive to myself. Even the certainty of being in good company is no real solace.

Whittier, 1946

THE FIRST OYSTER

The intramural complexities of the faculty at Miss Huntingdon's School for Girls have become much clearer to me since I left there, but even at sixteen I knew that Mrs. Cheever's social position was both uncomfortable and lonely.

She had her own office, which was certainly more than any snobbish Latin teacher could boast. She was listed as part of the school's administration in the discreet buff and sepia catalog; I cannot remember now just what her title was, except that it implied with high-sounding ambiguity that she was the housekeeper without, of course, using that vulgar word itself.

She was a college graduate, even though it was from some domestic-science school instead of Smith or Mount Holyoke.

She was, above all, a lady.

She was almost a super-lady, mainly because it was so obvious that the rest of the faculty, administration as well as teachers, considered her a cook. When she stepped occasionally after dinner into the library, where I as an honor Sophomore was privileged to carry demitasses to the Seniors and the teachers on alternate Wednesday nights, I could see that she was snubbed almost as thoroughly as her well-fed colleagues snubbed the school nurse, one notch below the housekeeper on the social scale but also a colleague as far as the catalog went.

No malicious, inverted, discontented boarding-school teacher on God's earth, however, could snub the poor nurse as much as Mrs. Cheever could. Her coarsely genteel face under its Queen Mary coiffure expressed with shocking clarity the loathing she felt for that gentle ninny who dealt out pills and sticking plasters, and all the loneliness and bitter social insecurity of her own position showed in the way Mrs. Cheever stood proudly alone in the crowded library, smiling with delicacy and frightful pleasure at the nurse, whose hand trembled clumsily as she sipped at her little coffee cup and tried to look like a college graduate.

The two women studiously spoke to no one, mainly because no one spoke to them. Perhaps once or twice, long since, the nurse may have said a timid nothing to the housekeeper, but Mrs. Cheever would have bitten out her own tongue before loosening it in charity toward a sister outcast.

Once it almost looked as if she would have a friend on the faculty, when a new gym teacher came. So often athletic people were not exactly . . . that is, they seldom had M.A.'s, even if they seemed really quite ladylike at times. And Mrs. Cheever felt sure that the new colleague would be as scornful as she was herself of all the pretentious schoolma'ams, with their airs and graces.

But after the first week, during which the little gym teacher stood shyly by the housekeeper for coffee, or nibbled in her room on the pink grapes and small frosted cakes that Mrs. Cheever sent her, the other women discovered that not only was she from Barnard . . . *summa cum laude, parbleu!* . . . but that she had the most adorable little cracked voice, almost like a boy's. It was perfect with her hair, so short and boyish too, and by the end of the second week three of the teachers were writing passionate notes to her, and Mrs. Cheever once more stood magnificently alone on her occasional visits to the library after dinner.

Perhaps loneliness made her own food bitter to her, because Mrs. Cheever was an obvious dyspeptic. The rest of us, however: Miss Huntingdon herself, remote and saint-like; Miss Blake, her shadow, devoted, bewigged, a skin-and-bone edition of Krafft-Ebing; all the white women of the school, fat, thin, frantic or calm, and all the Filipino servants, pretty little men-dolls as mercurial as monkeys, and as lewd; all the girls, who felt like victims but were really the raison d'être of this strange collection within the high walls . . . Mrs. Cheever fed us four times a day with probably the best institutional food in America.

She ran her kitchens with such skill that in spite of ordinary domestic troubles like flooded basements and soured cream, and even an occasional extraordinary thing like the double murder and hara-kiri committed by the head-boy one Good Friday, our meals were never late and never bad.

There were about seventy boarders and twenty-five women, and for morning-recess lunch a pack of day-girls, and most of us ate with the delicacy and appreciation of half-starved animals. It must have been sickening to Mrs. Cheever to see us literally wolfing her well-planned, well-cooked, well-served dishes. For in spite of doing things wholesale, which some gastronomers say is impossible with any finesse, the things we ate at Miss Huntingdon's were savory and interesting.

Mrs. Cheever, for instance, would get a consignment of strange honey from the Torrey pine trees, honey which only a few people in the world were supposed to have eaten. I remember it now with some excitement, as a grainy greenish stuff like some I once ate near Adelboden in the Bernese Alps, but then it was to most of us just something sweet and rather queer to put on hot biscuits. Tinned orange marmalade would have done as well.

At Thanksgiving she would let the Filipinos cover the breakfast tables with dozens of odd, beautiful little beasts they had made from vegetables and fruits and nuts, so that the dining room became for a while amazingly funny to us, and we were allowed to make almost as much noise as we wanted while we ate forbidden things like broiled sausage and played with the crazy toys. The boys would try not to laugh too, and even Mrs. Cheever would incline her queenly topknot less scornfully than usual when spoken to.

Saturday noons we could eat sandwiches and cocoa or pink punch on the hockey field, and have ice cream from the soda fountain in the village if we told Mrs. Cheever between eight and nine that morning. I sometimes went without it, or got another girl to order for me, simply because I could not bear to go into the little office and have the housekeeper look at me. She made me feel completely unattractive, which is even worse at sixteen than later.

She would sit stiffly at her desk, waiting for orders with an expression of such cold impersonal nausea on her face that I could hardly believe the gossip that she had made a fat sum weekly by charging us almost double what the drug store got for its cartons of ice cream and its incredibly sweet sauces.

She would make precise notations on a sheet of paper while we mumbled our orders, and sometimes even suggested in her flat clear voice that salted pecans might be better than strawberry syrup on chocolate-ice-cream-with-butterscotch-sauce. Her expression of remote anguish never changed, even when she reminded us, with her eyes resting coldly on a bulging behind or a spotty chin, that we were limited to one pint apiece.

It was for festivals like Easter and Old Girls' Day, though, that she really exercised her talents. Now I can see that she must have filled many hours of snubbed isolation in plans for our pleasure, but then I only knew that parties at Miss Huntingdon's School for Girls were really fun, mostly because the food was so good. Mrs. Cheever, callously ignored by the girls except for a few minutes each Saturday morning, and smiled at condescendingly by her unwilling colleagues with university degrees, turned our rare bats into what could truly be called small gastronomic triumphs . . . and the more so because they were what they were within high walls.

Old Girls' Day, for instance, meant to all but the Seniors, who had to be nice to the returning alumnae, that we spent a long gray warm June day on the sand and the rocks, and that we could wear our full pleated gym bloomers and *no stockings*, and take pictures of each other with our Brownies, and, best of all, that at half past noon a procession of house-boys would come down the cliffs from the school with our lunch for us in big baskets.

There would be various things, of course, like pickles and napkins and knives and probably sandwiches and fruit, although how Mrs. Cheever managed it with the school full of hungry shrieking postgraduates is more than I can guess. Perhaps she even sent down devilled eggs to make it a real picnic.

I don't remember, because all that we thought about then, or could recall now if we ever dared to think at all of those days, were the hot crisp fried halves of young chickens, stiff and tempting. We could have all we wanted, even three or four, and we could eat with our fingers, and yell, and gobble. It was wonderful.

There must have been chaperones, but they seemed not to exist down there in the warmth and the silly freedom, and when a stately figure stood for an instant on the cliff top, wrapped fussily in an afternoon gown for the Old Girls, and looked down at us with her face set in a sour chill smile, we waved our greasy drumsticks hilariously up at her, and cried,

Miss-is Chee-ver
Miss-is Chee-ver
Miss-is Chee-ver
Rah-ah-ah-ah,

almost as if she were a whole basketball game between the Golds and the Purples. For one moment, at least, in the year, we were grateful to her for our deliciously full mouths.

She did her conscientious best to be sensible in her menus, and fed us better garden things and fresher cream and milk than most of us have eaten since, but there must have been a dreadful impatience in her for such pap, so that occasionally she would give us the Torrey pine-honey for breakfast, or have the Chinese cook put chives over the Friday fish instead of a cream sauce.

Once, for the Christmas Party, she served Eastern oysters, fresh oysters, oysters still in their shells.

Nothing could have been more exotic in the early twenties in Southern California. The climate was still considered tropical, so that shellfish imported alive from the East were part of an oilmagnate's dream, or perhaps something to be served once or twice a year at Victor Hugo's, in a private room with pink candleshades and a canary. And of course any local molluscs were automatically deemed inedible, at least by *nice* people.

The people, that Christmas Party night, were indeed nice. We wore our formals: skirts not less than eight nor more than fifteen inches from the floor, dresses of light but not bright colors and of materials semi-transparent or opaque, neck-lines not more than three inches below the collar bone and sleeves long or elbowlength. We all passed the requirements of the catalog, but with such delectable additions as long chiffon scarves twined about our necks in the best Nita-Naldi-bronchitic manner, or great artificial flowers pinned with holiday abandon on our left shoulders. Two or three of the Seniors had fox furs slung nonchalantly about them, with the puffy tails dangling down over their firmly flattened young breasts in a most fashionable way.

There may even have been a certain amount of timid make-up in honor of Kris Kringle and the approaching libertinage of Christmas vacation, real or devoutly to be hoped for, but fortunately the dining room was lighted that night by candles only.

Mrs. Cheever had outdone herself, although all we thought then was that the old barn had never looked so pretty. The oblong tables, usually in ranks like dominoes in their box, were pushed into a great horseshoe, with a little table for Miss Huntingdon and Miss Blake and the minister and the president of the trustees in the middle, and a sparkling Christmas tree, and . . . yes! . . . a space for dancing! And there were candles, and the smells of pine branches and hot wax, and place cards all along the outer edge of the horseshoe so that the Freshmen would not sit in one clot and the other groups in theirs.

We marched once around the beautiful room in the flickering odorous candlelight, singing, "God Rest You Merry, Gentlemen" or some such thing to the scrapings of the assistant violin instructor and two other musicians, who in spite of their trousers had been accurately judged unable to arouse unseemly longings in our cloistered hearts.

Then we stood by the chairs marked with our names, and waited for the music to stop and Miss Huntingdon and the minister to ask the blessings in their fluty voices. It was all very exciting.

When I saw that I was to sit between a Senior and a Junior, with not a Freshman in sight, I felt almost uplifted with Christmas joy. It must mean that I was Somebody, to be thus honored, that perhaps I would even be elected to the Altar Guild next semester. . . .

I knew enough not to speak first, but could not help looking sideways at the enormous proud nose of Olmsted, who sat at my left. She was president of the Seniors, and moved about the school in a loose-limbed dreamy way that seemed to me seraphic. Inez, the Junior, was less impressive, but still had her own string of horses in Santa Barbara and could curse with great concentration, so many words that I only recognized *damn* and one or two others. Usually she had no use for me, but tonight she smiled, and the candlelight made her beady eyes look almost friendly.

The grace done with, we pulled our chairs in under the unaccustomed silkiness of our party-dress bottoms with less noise than usual, and the orchestra flung itself into a march. The pantry doors opened, and the dapper little house-boys pranced in, their smooth faces pulled straight and their eyes snapping with excitement.

They put a plate in front of each of us. We all looked mazily at what we saw, and waited with mixed feelings until Miss Huntingdon had picked up her fork (where, I wonder now, did Mrs. Cheever even find one hundred oyster forks in a California boarding school?), before we even thought of eating. I heard Inez mutter under her breath, several more words I did not recognize except as such, and then Olmsted said casually, "How charming! Blue Points!"

There was a quiet buzz . . . we were being extremely well-bred, all of us, for the party . . . and I know now that I was not the only Westerner who was scared shaky at the immediate prospect of eating her first raw oyster, and was putting it off for as long as possible.

I remembered hearing Mother say that it was vulgar as well as extremely unpleasant to do anything with an oyster but swallow it as quickly as possible, without *thinking*, but that the after-taste was rather nice. Of course it was different with tinned oysters in turkey dressing: they could be chewed with impunity, both social and hygienic, for some reason or other. But raw, they must be swallowed whole, and rapidly.

And alive.

With the unreasoning and terrible persnicketiness of a sixteen-year-old I knew that I would be sick if I had to swallow anything in the world alive, but especially a live oyster.

The Gastronomical Me

Olmsted picked up one deftly on the prongs of her little fork, tucked it under her enormous nose, and gulped. "Delicious," she murmured.

"Jesus," Inez said softly. "Well, here goes. The honor of the old school. Oi!" And she swallowed noisily. A look of smug surprise crept into her face, and she said in my ear, "Try one, Baby-face. It ain't the heat, it's the humidity. Try one. Slip and go easy." She cackled suddenly, watching me with sly bright eyes.

"Yes, do," Olmsted said.

I laughed lightly, tinklingly, like Helen in *Helen and Warren*, said, "Oh, I *love* Blue Points!" and got one with surprising neatness into my mouth.

At that moment the orchestra began to play, with sexless abandon, a popular number called, I think, "Horses." It sounded funny in Miss Huntingdon's dining room. Olmsted laughed, and said to me, "Come on, Kennedy. Let's start the ball rolling, shall we?"

The fact that she, the most wonderful girl in the whole school, and the most intelligent, and the most revered, should ask me to dance when she knew very well that I was only a Sophomore, was so overwhelming that it made even the dreamlike reality that she had called me Kennedy, instead of Mary Frances, seem unimportant.

The oyster was still in my mouth. I smiled with care, and stood up, reeling at the thought of dancing the first dance of the evening with the senior-class president.

The oyster seemed larger. I knew that I must down it, and was equally sure that I could not. Then, as Olmsted put her thin hand on my shoulder blades, I swallowed once, and felt light and attractive and daring, to know what I had done. We danced stiffly around the room, and as soon as a few other pairs of timid girls came into the cleared space by the tree, headed toward Miss Huntingdon's table.

Miss Huntingdon herself spoke to me by name, and Miss Blake laughed silently so that her black wig bobbled, and cracked her knuckles as she always did when she was having a good time, and the minister and Olmsted made a little joke about Silent Sophomores and Solemn Seniors, and I did not make a sound, and nobody seemed to think it strange. I was dumb with pleasure at my own importance . . . practically the Belle of the Ball I was! . . . and with a dawning gastronomic hunger. Oysters, my delicate taste buds were telling me, oysters are *simply marvelous!* More, more!

I floated on, figuratively at least, in Olmsted's arms. The dance ended with a squeaky but cheerful flourish, and the girls went back to their seats almost as flushed as if they were returning from the arms of the most passionate West Point cadets in white gloves and coats.

The plates had been changed. I felt flattened, dismayed, as only children can about such things.

Olmsted said, "You're a funny kid, Kennedy. Oh, green olives!" when I mumbled how wonderful it had been to dance with her, and Inez murmured in my ear, "Dance with me next, will you, Baby-face? There are a couple of things boys can do I can't, but I can dance with you a damn sight better than that bitch Olmsted."

I nodded gently, and smiled a tight smile at her, and thought that she was the most horrible creature I had ever known. Perhaps I might kill her some day. I was going to be sick.

I pushed back my chair.

"Hey, Baby-face!" The music started with a crash, and Inez put her arms surely about me, and led me with expert grace around and around the Christmas tree, while all the candles fluttered in time with my stomach.

"Why don't you talk?" she asked once. "You have the cutest little ears I ever saw, Baby-face . . . like a pony I had, when I was in Colorado. How do you like the way I dance with you?"

Her arm tightened against my back. She was getting a crush on me, I thought, and here it was only Christmas and I was only a Sophomore! What would it be by April, the big month for them? I felt somewhat flattered, because Inez was a Junior and had those horses in Santa Barbara, but I hated her. My stomach felt better.

Miss Huntingdon was watching me again, while she held her water glass in her white thin fingers as if it had wine in it, or the Holy Communion. She leaned over and said something to Miss Blake, who laughed silently like a gargoyle and cracked her knuckles with delight, not at what Miss Huntingdon was saying but that she was saying anything at all. Perhaps they were talking about me, saying that I was nice and dependable and would be a good Senior president in two more years, or that I had the cutest ears. . . .

"Relax, kid," Inez murmured. "Just pretend . . . "

The pantry door swung shut on a quick flash of gray chiffon and pearls, almost at my elbow, and before I knew it myself I was out of Inez' skillful arms and after it. I had to escape from her; and the delightful taste of oyster in my mouth, my new-born gourmandise, sent me toward an unknown rather than a known sensuality.

The thick door shut out almost all the sound from the flickering, noisy dining room. The coolness of the pantry was shocking, and Mrs. Cheever was even more so. She stood, queenly indeed in her beautiful gray evening dress and her pearls and her snowy hair done in the same lumpy rhythm as Mary of England's, and her face was all soft and formless with weeping.

Tears trickled like colorless blood from her eyes, which had always been so stony and now looked at me without seeing me at all. Her mouth, puckered from years of dyspepsia and disapproval, was loose and tender suddenly, and she sniffed with vulgar abandon.

She stood with one arm laid gently over the scarlet shoulders of the fat old nurse, who was dressed fantastically in the ancient costume of Saint Nicholas. It became her well, for her formless body was as generous as his, and her ninny-simple face, pink-cheeked and sweet, was kind like his and neither male nor female. The ratty white wig sat almost tidily on her head, which looked as if it hardly missed its neat black-ribboned nurse's cap, and beside her on the pantry serving table lay the beard, silky and monstrous, ready to be pulled snug against her chins when it was time to give us all our presents under the Christmas tree.

She looked through me without knowing that I stood staring at her like a paralyzed rabbit. I was terrified, of her the costumed nurse and of Mrs. Cheever so hideously weeping and of all old women.

Mrs. Cheever did not see me either. For the first time I did not feel unattractive in her presence, but rather completely unnecessary. She put out one hand, and for a fearful moment I thought perhaps she was going to kiss me: her face was so tender. Then I saw that she was putting oysters carefully on a big platter that sat before the nurse, and that as she watched the old biddy eat them, tears kept running bloodlessly down her soft ravaged cheeks, while she spoke not a word.

I backed toward the door, hot as fire with shock and the dread confusion of adolescence, and said breathlessly, "Oh, excuse me, Mrs. Cheever! But I . . . that is, *all* the Sophomores . . . on behalf of the Sophomore Class I want to thank you for this beautiful, this *simply marvelous* party! Oysters . . . and . . . and everything . . . It's all *so* nice!"

But Mrs. Cheever did not hear me. She stood with one hand still on the wide red shoulders of the nurse, and with the other she put the oysters left from the Christmas Party on a platter. Her eyes were smeared so that they no longer looked hard and hateful, and as she watched the old woman eat steadily, voluptuously, of the fat cold molluscs, she looked so tender that I turned anxiously toward the sureness and stability of such small passions as lay in the dining room.

The pantry door closed behind me. The orchestra was whipping through "Tales from the Vienna Woods," with the assistant violin instructor doubling on the artificial mocking bird. A flock of little Filipino boys skimmed like monkeys into the candlelight, with great trays of cranberry sauce and salted nuts and white curled celery held above their heads, and I could tell by their faces that whatever they had seen in the pantry was already tucked far back behind their eyes, perhaps forever.

If I could still taste my first oyster, if my tongue still felt fresh and excited, it was perhaps too bad. Although things are different now, I hoped then, suddenly and violently, that I would never see one again.

To Feed Such Hunger

After Christmas the foreign students changed, at the University in Dijon. The hungry Poles with too-bright eyes, who lived through the warmer months on international fellowships and pride in unlisted attics, went back to Warsaw. The few pretty American girls who bothered to come to such a stuffy little town stopped baffling Frenchmen by their bold naïveté, and left the tea shops and the cafés for Evanston, Illinois. The cool long-limbed Swedes smelled snow, and hurried back to their own ski slopes.

Now, instead of a dozen accents in the halls of the Faculté, you heard only one, and it was German. There were Lithuanians and Danes and Czechs, but German was the tongue.

The girls all looked much alike, thick and solemn. They walked silently about the streets, reading guidebooks, in flat broad shoes and a kind of uniform of badly tailored gray-brown suits.

The men, most of them, were young and pink-cheeked and oddly eager. They sat lonesomely in the cafés, and seldom spoke to one another, as if they had been told not to. The Dijonnais students, who were still fighting the war of '71, when the Boches had besieged the town, were politely rude to them, and they seemed to be scattered like timid sheep, longing for a leader. It was only at the University that they dared band together, and almost before the first class of the new semester, they elected a Prussian the president, as if to prove that there at least they were united and strong.

I had not much to do with the student body as such; my own life with Al was too absorbing and complete. But I couldn't help feeling surprised to learn that Klorr was our new leader.

He was quite unlike any of the other young Germans, who seemed to dislike and almost fear him, in spite of their votes. He was as tall as they, probably, but there was something about the set of his bones that made him seem slight and weak. He wore his brownish hair rather long and slicked back against his head, not in a fair brush; and he dressed in bags and tweed jacket like an Englishman, not in a stiff short coat that showed his hips, and narrow trousers, as his compatriots did.

He had a thin sneering face, too, all of a color with his pale slick hair, and it stuck forward on his neck, instead of being solid between his shoulders.

He was, I think, the most rat-like human I have ever seen, and at the same time he was tall, well set-up, intelligent looking . . . a contradictory person. I dismissed him from my thoughts, as someone I would not care to know, and most surely never would.

I noticed him, though, because he and a girl distracted me several times in class before I knew who she was. I was surprised to see him with her. She was one of the big pallid ones, and I'd have thought him the type who would marry her finally but spend his "student days" with someone small, light, exciting.

The two of them always seemed to be sitting right in front of me in classes, and always very close together, so that her thigh pressed hard against his and her large face almost touched him. They would whisper all through the lectures. It annoyed me. I found it hard enough to keep my mind on the professorial drone about the preposition "à" without having to sort it out from their moist Germanic hissings.

Usually they were reading parts of letters to each other, and usually Klorr sneered coldly at the girl, who seemed to be defending what they read.

Then at the end of class they would go silently out of the room, she carrying all his books as well as her own. Often she carried his thick topcoat, too.

I found myself interested enough in them to tell Al about them. They seemed such a strange pair to be so intimate, and I was very naïve then about the many visages of love.

One night at supper Madame Biarnet tore through her meal faster than ever, pushed her plate away and the dog Tango off her lap as if she had come to a great decision, and in her slowest, richest Burgundian accent asked us to make up our minds. At once, she said. There and then.

Her voice rose like a general's. Her long nose whitened. Her beautiful hard shrewd eyes, deep in wrinkles but young, looked at us with infinite enjoyment of the comedy she was playing.

"The time has arrived," she said harshly, and we wondered in a kind of stupor what joke she would tell, how soon she would burst into a great gust of laughter and release us from her teasing. We were used to her by now, but constantly fascinated, like a magician's petted nervous rabbits.

Monsieur Biarnet stirred fussily, and popped a vigor pill under his little waxed gray moustache. "Eugénie," he murmured. "Enough. Don't shout so, please! My nerves tonight . . . "

She slapped, absently, fondly, at his shoulder. "Make up your minds! You Americans are all dreamers! Are you going to stay or go?"

"Go where? Why? Do you want us to go, Madame?" We were stammering, just as she planned us to, and we must have looked quite flabbergasted at the thought that we might want to leave our snug small home at the top of the house.

She shrieked, delighted with her game, and then wiped her eyes with her napkin and said softly, almost affectionately, "Calm yourselves! It's about renting the rooms. We'll have a new guest tomorrow, and if you plan to stay she shall have the third floor room on the street, next to Jo's. And if you . . . "

"But of course we plan to stay . . . as long as you want us."

"That's the ticket, then," she said in pure gutter-French, with a malicious grin at her husband.

And as always, as if to prove to himself or someone that he at least was a man of the world, the *upper* world, he murmured in his most affected way, "Charming! Charming children!"

Madame whispered to us before noon dinner the next day that the new boarder was in the dining room. She was Czech, a ravishing beauty, daughter of a high official, someone completely sympathetic and destined to be my undying confidante.

Of course, it was Klorr's friend. Her name was Maritza Nankova, and she spoke when spoken to, in French somewhat better than mine was then. She was very shy for many days, but I could tell that she was lonely and envied me for being gay and happy and in love. I was almost completely uninterested in her.

She spent much of her time alone in her room when she was not at the Faculté. Now and then we would hear her solid shoes climbing the stairs late at night, and I would feel a little ashamed of my own fullness, and think I should go pay her a visit, talk with her about her country and her family and clothes . . . things girls are supposed to talk about together.

A few weeks after she came, there was a minor drama going on in the Biarnet ménage. We could only guess about it. Madame's voice was more hysterically high than ever, and her nose whiter in her red face; and quite often her husband and Jo did not eat at home, or sat icily silent through a meal. Finally one day Maritza was not there for lunch, and as if she had pulled a cork out of the situation when she went through the little door into the street, all three Biarnets started talking at once to us. We felt flattered, of course, and somewhat dazed. Even Jo waved his delicate hands excitedly, and shook back his silky hair with dainty fire.

Madame, they all told us, had been asked by La Nankova to make a place at the table for her friend Klorr. "No, no, and again no," the two men thundered in their small ways.

"But he will pay well," Madame said. "Even filthy Boches must eat."

"Not here. Not with us. The food would choke us," they answered.

"But," she said, "La Nankova says he is very powerful, and important already in Germany . . . and what if someday he comes here the way they came in '71? *Then*," she went on triumphantly before they could interrupt, "then we will be glad to have a friend in him."

The enormity, the basically female realism of it, floored us all for a minute.

Then Monsieur, with a flattering little bow to me, and a slight twist of his moustache with two fingers to prove himself not only masculine but always the *boulevardier*, said, "It is bad enough, Eugénie, my dear, to have to see that well-behaved but clod-like peasant virgin twice a day, sitting in the same room with you and Madame Fischer. The addition of a yearning Prussian swain is more than I could bear."

Madame laughed delightedly. "Virgin, yes," she agreed shrilly. "Swain, definitely not. Klorr is much more interested in finding a good meal than exploring Maritza's possibilities. She has the appeal of a potato."

Jo flushed. "Papa is right," he said, and I thought that at last he had expressed himself, even so circumspectly, on a sexual matter. But he went on, "Mademoiselle Nankova is dull enough. No Boches, please, Belle-mère."

Madame looked gently at him. He usually called her Madame. It was as if anything more intimate to this coarsely vital woman who had taken his dead mother's place would betray him and his father too, and he was endlessly cruel to her, the way a young person can be.

She laughed again, then, and banged on the table. "I give up," she cried. "You are all against me . . . yes, you two smug American lovers too. No Boche. If we starve, we starve together. But," and she looked maliciously at her husband, "when Paul is away on business this Klorr can eat here. My stomach is not so delicate as some, and Klorr may not be bad-looking, even if he is a German."

So she won, after all. We celebrated the ambiguous victory with a little glass of *marc* all 'round. It was the nicest lunch Al and I had eaten with them, because we felt that we were no longer well-mannered paid-up boarders, but confidants of the family. We wished Maritza would stay away oftener, or always.

The cold winter dragged into Lent. Klorr came a few times to the dining room, always when Monsieur was away, and if Jo was caught there he ate almost nothing and excused himself. The German sensed it, I think. He was very charming to Madame, and was an entertaining talker, except for his lisp. He had a way of leaning across the table after a meal, rolling bread crumbs between his white knobby fingers, with his small strange eyes fixed almost hypnotically on his listener's.

He paid little attention to me, and none at all to Maritza, but seemed much attracted to Jo when he was there, and to Al. Al met him a few times in cafés, and told me Klorr talked mostly of the coming renaissance in Germany. Klorr said it would be based on a Uranic form of life.

I looked up the word Uranism. I *think* it was Uranism. It seemed to agree with what I had seen of Klorr, at least in his attitude toward Maritza. She never spoke at the table when he was there unless he addressed her by name, and then she flushed and seemed almost to tremble. It was a strange kind of love affair, I thought.

I grew more curious about her, and determined, tomorrow or tomorrow, to see more of her, go chat with her in her room. She never looked either happy or unhappy, except now and then after a meal, when she and the Madame would go into a kind of orgy of ghost stories.

Then Maritza's face would flush under her white skin, and her large dull eyes would be full of light and almost beautiful. She would talk rapidly in her up-and-down Czech accent, and laugh and clasp her big strong hands in front of her.

Madame loved it, and sometimes matched her, tale for tale, and sometimes let her go on alone, with her strange village stories of ghouls and charms and lost cats miraculously found, and of what it meant to sneeze three times . . . that sort of thing.

Maritza's eyes would stare into the steamy air, and sometimes they almost frightened me with their mute superstitious mysticism. There was the same thing about them that I have never been able to accept in some Wagnerian music, a kind of religious lewdness, maybe.

One night Al and I came through the silent streets quite late, midnight or so. We had gone to a movie and then sat drinking *café-crème* and listening to the exhausted music at the Miroir, hating to go out into the raw cold Dijon air.

We saw that Maritza's two windows were brightly lighted, with the curtains not drawn. It was strange; always before, ever since she came, they had been dark when we unlocked the little door. We both spoke of it, and then went on tiptoe up the stairs, forgetting her for ourselves.

Much later, I opened our windows. There, across the deep silent courtyard, her inner window still shone, beside Jo's dark one. The curtains were not pulled.

It upset me a little. I stood watching for a minute, but I could see nothing. I got back into bed. I would surely go see her tomorrow, I thought . . . maybe ask her to have tea with me.

I was asleep when the knock came on the door. We both sat up sharply, like startled children; it was the first time anyone had ever come to our door at night. Al clambered out, and ran on his bare brown feet to open it, with his heart probably pounding like mine, from sleep and bewilderment.

It was Jo. He stood there in a mauve woolen bathrobe, carefully not looking toward me in the bed, and asked softly, "Is Madame here? I beg her pardon a thousand times, and Monsieur Fischer's . . . but if Madame would perhaps come." He was stammering, speaking very softly with his eyes cast down.

"What's wrong?" Al asked bluntly, taking him by the arm. I don't know what he thought had happened.

"It's Mademoiselle la Nankova. She still has the light on in her room, and I can hear her. But I don't know whether she is laughing or crying. It is very soft. But it is late. I'm worried. I thought Madame Fischer, as a woman . . . "

"I'll come, Monsieur Jo," I said, and he bowed without looking at me. We heard his light steps down and up the zigzag stairs, and then the firm closing of his door on the landing across the courtyard.

Al looked upset. "Why not ask Madame Biarnet?" he said. "I don't like your being called this way. It's cold tonight. It's . . . it's an imposition."

"You're jealous," I said, while I put his warm bathrobe over my pajamas. "You'd like to go yourself."

"That pudding!" he said, and we both had to laugh, even while I hurried, and his eyes blinked at me with curiosity in them as well as sleep and crossness and love.

The light was on over the top zigzag of the wide stone staircase. I went quickly, wondering what was wrong with the girl. She seemed such a dull lump. Probably she was homesick, or had cramps . . . I knocked on her door, and while I listened I could hear a little rustling in Jo's room; he was listening too, close there behind the safety of his wall. There was no sound at all in Maritza's room. I knocked again. Finally a chair was pushed back, and I heard what I thought were her firm steps across the room.

But when the lock turned and the door opened, deliberately, it was Klorr who stood there, with a white napkin held to his mouth.

I don't know what I thought: I was not embarrassed for either of us, and for some reason not surprised. We stood looking at each other, and I could see that his eyes were not pale at all, as I had thought, but very dark above the napkin. He kept patting his lips. In the room behind him I could hear Maritza breathing in long soft moaning breaths, monotonously.

I started to say why I had come, but he interrupted me in a smooth courtly flow . . . I was so kind to worry . . . just about to call me . . . our little Czech friend seemed upset . . . he had stopped for a few minutes in passing . . . undoubtedly a small indisposition that I, a sister creature, would comprehend . . . a thousand thanks, goodnight, goodnight. And he was off down the stairs, silent and unruffled as a rat, with the napkin in his hand.

I went reluctantly inside. The room was bright with light from an enormous bulb that hung, unshaded, over the middle of the big bed. I went quickly to the curtains, and covered all the windows, like a fussy old nursemaid or like a mother protecting her daughter's modesty, for Maritza was lying there in that light, naked except for a few crumbs and grapeskins on her belly.

When I had with my instinctive gesture made things more seemly, I looked full at her.

The bed was covered with a big white sheet, as if it were a smooth table, and she motionless in the middle, lying with her arms at her sides. I was surprised at how beautiful her body was, so white and clean, with high firm breasts and a clear triangle of golden hair, like an autumn leaf. There were no pillows on the bed, so that her head tilted back and I could see pulses beating hard in her throat. Her eyes were closed, and she kept on breathing in those low soft moans.

I leaned over her. "It's Madame Fischer, Maritza."

She did not answer or open her eyes, but at the sound of my voice she started to tremble, in long small shudders that went all over her, the way a dead snake does. I spoke again, and when I picked up one heavy arm it fell softly back. Still, I felt she knew everything that was going on.

I was not exactly puzzled . . . in fact, I seemed at the time to take the whole thing as a matter of course, almost . . . but for a minute I stood there, wondering what to do. Maritza's face was very hot, but the rest of her was cold, and shaking now with the long shuddering ripples, so I covered her with a coat from her armoire, after I had pushed the grapeskins and crumbs off her.

They were only on her belly. There were several crumbs down in her navel, and I blew at them, without thinking it funny at all. I put them all in my hand, and then onto a plate on the little table, before I realized how strange it was.

It was set up by the fireplace, with a linen tablecloth, and placed precisely on it were a plate of beautiful grapes with dark pink skins, an empty champagne bottle and a fine glass, and a little round cake with a piece out of it. It looked like the kind of table a butler arranges in the second act of an old-fashioned bedroom comedy, except that there was only one glass, one plate, one fork.

I knew Klorr had been supping there, while Maritza lay naked on the bed and moaned for him. And I knew that he had put the empty grapeskins on her unprotesting flesh without ever touching her.

My hands felt foul from them. I went to the armoire, to look for some alcohol or toilet water to rub on them, but I could see none in the neat bareness of the shelves.

I ran silently as I could to our rooms. Al was lying in bed, reading, and when he asked me mildly what was going on, I suddenly felt a strange kind of antagonism toward him, toward all men. It was as if Maritza had been ashamed in some way that only women could know about. It was as if I must protect her, because we were both females, fighting all the males.

"Nothing . . . it's all right," I said crossly. "She's got the jitters."

"Oh," Al said, and went on with his book.

I ran down the stairs with a bottle of eau de Cologne. I thought I would rub Maritza with it. I closed her door, and pulled the coat gently off her.

"It's Madame Fischer," I said, because her eyes were still closed.

I rubbed in long slow motions up her arms, and up her legs from her ankles, the way I remembered being massaged in a Swedish bath when I was younger. Gradually she stopped making the moan with every breath, and the unnatural shudders almost ceased. Her face was cooler, too.

"You are better, now, Maritza," I kept saying as I rubbed the toilet water into her fine white skin. "You are all right now."

It was like quieting an animal, and had the same rhythm about it, so that I don't know how long it was before I saw that the door had opened silently, and Klorr stood there watching me.

Maritza's eyes were still shut, but she felt something in my hands, although I did not feel it myself, and she began the long hard shuddering again.

Klorr was staring at me with jet-bead eyes, and hate seemed to crackle out of him in little flashes, like electricity in a cat's fur. I glared back at him. I must have looked fierce, because as I got up slowly and approached him, he backed away and out into the hall by Jo's door. He had the napkin in his hand, and he held it out to me. I closed the door into the girl's room.

"What do you want?" I asked, speaking very distinctly. I could hear my own voice, and impersonally I admired my accent. I am in a rage, a real rage, I thought, and rage is very good for the French accent.

Klorr smiled weakly at me, and wiped his lips again.

"I was just passing by," he said for the second time that night. "I . . . how is our little Czech friend? I appreciate your unusual interest in her. How is she, if I may be so bold as to enquire? Tell me, dear Madame . . . what is wrong with her?"

His smile was stronger now, and he was speaking smoothly, with his eyes staring scornfully, sneeringly at me.

Then I drew myself up. It sounds funny even to write about now, or think about, but I actually did draw myself up, until I seemed much taller than he. And very distinctly, in the most carefully enunciated and completely pompous French that has ever been spoken outside a national theatre, I said, "What is wrong with her? Mademoiselle Nankova, Monsieur Klorr, is suffering from an extreme sexual overexcitement!"

Those were my words, which sprang unsought for into my furious brain. Yes . . . they rolled out magnificently . . . *une sur-ex-ci-ta-tion se-xu-el-le* . . . syllable by mighty syllable, even to the final "le," like a quotation from Racine.

Klorr looked away. He bowed stiffly, and then as if he could not stand it any longer he threw the napkin at me and ran again down the stairs, as silent as a rat.

When I went back into the room, Maritza was curled up like a child in the middle of the bed, crying peacefully into her hands. She was rosy and warm, and I put the coat over her and turned out the light and went home. I felt terribly tired.

Al was asleep. He never asked me anything about it, and I never told him.

The next day Maritza was the same as always, shy and dull as if she did not know me, and in about a week she left, without saying goodbye to any of us. Madame said that she and Klorr, by a very odd coincidence, were going to be in Venice together for the Easter celebrations.

"Love is hair-raising," Madame said. "Imagine that great lump in a gondola."

"I for one am thankful," Monsieur said, rolling his eyes first toward the good God in heaven and then toward me. "Now we can resume our old chats, without having to wait for La Nankova to keep up with us, and without having to escape her questionable Prussian acquaintance. It will be excellent for practice, for perfecting the accent."

Jo looked at me, and before he lowered his soft eyes in their deep curling lashes, he smiled in an abashed way at me, and murmured, "But Madame's accent is already excellent at times, Papa."

And I burst out laughing, and could tell nobody why. Whenever I say those words in my mind, I must laugh now, in spite of the feminine shame I feel to think of that table laid in the bright room, and the strange ways of satisfying hunger.

FROM LONG AGO IN FRANCE

[. . .] Probably the most orgiastic eating we did while we lived [in Dijon] was with the Club Alpin. Monsieur Ollangnier proposed us for membership soon after he had decided for himself, over the dinner table in his stuffy little dining room, that we were amusing and moderately civilized. It was supposed to be an honor, as well as making it possible for the club to get better rates on its feasts by having a large number of members, and certainly it was a fine although somewhat wearing experience for us.

We heard good French from the lawyers and retired army officers and fuddy-duddy architects like our friend Ollangnier who belonged, for one reason or another, but mostly gastronomic. We saw castles and convents and wine *caves* that were seldom bared to public eyes. We walked and crawled and slithered and puffed over all that corner of France, in the cold March rains, the winy gold-leafed days of autumn, April's first tantalizing softness.

We all had to wear properly stiff heavy boots, and on almost every one of the bimonthly promenades we managed to find a small safe grotto or gully to explore, so that the Alpin part of our club's name would not be too much of a joke, even in the heart of smooth-rolling Burgundy. The club's rooms in Dijon, on the ancient rue des Forges, were in one of the most perfect and beautiful fourteenth-century town houses in Europe, and we often listened solemnly to lectures there about the places we would visit in the future.

The real reason, though, for submitting to these often boring duties was that every time we spent half a day plugging doggedly across muddy fields and shivering in bat-filled slimy ruins, we spent an equal amount of time sitting warmly, winily, in the best local restaurant, eating specialties of the village or the region more ardently than ever peak was scaled or Gothic arch gazed on.

The schedule was always the same: a brisk walk from the station and the little train that had brought us from Dijon, four or five hours of eating and drinking, and then the long promenade, the climbing, the viewing of monuments and fallen temples. Al and I were probably the youngest in the club by some thirty years, but more than once pure bravado was all that kept us from tumbling right into the nearest ditch in a digestive coma. The colonels and counselors slapped their aged chests enthusiastically as the air struck them after the long hours in the restaurants, and they surged like a flock of young colts out into the country. We trotted mazily after them, two thin little American shadows convinced for a time at least that they were cousins of Gargantua.

The meals went on for hours, in spite of the length of the walk planned for later, and as a matter of pure research, based of course on our interest in folkways as well as culture, we arranged to taste not only the most noted dishes of the cook of the house, but also the Widow LeBlanc's way of pickling venison, and Monsieur le Curé's favorite recipe for little whole trout marinated in white wine and served chilled with green sour grapes.

The chef and his family would come in to enjoy our enjoyment, and then Widow LeBlanc and the Curé and the Curé's cook, and all of us would compare, with well-selected examples, the best local and district wines for each course. We always paid due homage to the ordinaries first, and then gradually lifted ourselves toward the heights of local pride, the crowned bottles known to every connoisseur alive, but never treated more respectfully than in their own birthplaces.

Sometimes the mayor or the lord of the *château*, knowing the Club Alpin of Dijon for what it really was, would send with his compliments a few bottles of such wines as I can only dream of now, wines unlabeled, never tired by travels, inviolate from the prying palates of commercial tasters. Then the gabble would die down, and Monsieur le Curé would bend his head over his goblet as if he were praying, and finally one or two of the old warhorses would murmur reverently, with his eyes focused far inward, *"Epatant . . . é-pa-tant!"*

The club secretary always tried to arrange our sorties so that after we had studied a regional cuisine with the thoroughness it deserved, and had made solemn notes both physical and spiritual on the vintages that flourished there, or there, or there, we could devote ourselves with equally undivided zeal to the promenade itself.

More often than not, though, we would quite by accident find that along with the *château* in a little village some two hours walk past dinner, there was also a tiny pastry shop where a certain ancient *dame* made sour-cream *fantaisies* the like of none other in all France.

"My God," Monsieur Vaillant, the retired advocate, would cry, halfway through our tour of a private country house where one of Maintenon's exiled lovers had spent twenty leisurely years painting Chinese pagodas on the wainscoting. "My God and double-zut!! This is infamous! Here we are within ten minutes' delightful promenade from one of the great, the *great* pastry makers of all time! She is modest, yes. She is content with a small fame. She made her *fantaisies* for my dear mother's First Communion. They came in a wooden trunk, packed in layers of silk-paper and dead leaves to survive the trip.

"Stop the tour!" Monsieur Vaillant would snort, his face flushed with inspiration, and a dawning appetite in his rheumy old eyes. And he would send a boy ahead, to warn the old witch to start up her fire and bestir her bones.

And then after we had looked dutifully at the rest of the wall-paintings, and some of the more erudite had identified classical symbolism in the obscure little scenes, and some of the more lecherous had identified with equal pleasure a few neoclassical positions among the slant-eyed nymphs and mandarins, we would head for the pastry shop. Even Al and I would forget our surfeit, whipped by the clean air and Monsieur Vaillant's jubilant memoirs into a fresh hunger.

Sure enough, the toothless village heroine's sour-cream *fantaisies,* light, delicate, fried in pure butter to a color clearer than gold, paler than Josephine Baker but as vital, would be the most delicious pastry in all of France, and Monsieur Vaillant the proudest member of our club.

We'd drink hot wine . . . "Nothing better against these November winds," we agreed with Vaillant valiantly . . . and then climb up perhaps only three of the four hills planned on by the optimistic secretary, before we caught the stuffy train back to Dijon. We'd smoke and talk and doze, in that intimacy peculiar to a third-class French "local" on Sunday night, and never once did we regret in any way, digestive or moral, the day's licentious prodigality of tastes and sensuous pleasure.

Once a year, on Ascension Day, the club left all such energetic ideas of rising above the earth-level strictly to the church, and held its annual banquet without benefit of sortie, promenade, or appreciation of any well-preserved ruins other than the fellow members.

The only year I went to the Ascension Day banquet we dined for six hours at the Hôtel de la Poste in Beaune. That was long before the old place had its face lifted, and we ate in the dark odorous room where generations of coachmen and carriage drivers and chauffeurs had nourished themselves as well as their masters did "up front."

There was a long table for us, and an even longer one for the wines. Piles of the last year's grapes, kept carefully in straw, made the air tingle with a kind of decadent promise, but there were no flowers to interrupt our senses.

We toasted many things, and at first the guests and some of the old judges and officers busied themselves being important. But gradually, over the measured progress of the courses and the impressive changing beauty of the wines, snobberies and even politics dwindled in our hearts, and the wit and the laughing awareness that is France made all of us alive.

It seems strange, though, that of all the fastuous dining that we learned to take for granted on the Sundays with the Club Alpin, one of the meals I remember most clearly was early on in our membership. One bitter February Sunday when I stood panting on a hill near Les Laumes-Alésia, the earth was hard as granite beneath me, and air drawn into my tired lungs felt like heavy fire before it thawed. I broke a twig clumsily between my mittened fingers.

"Here!" a voice said, roughly. I looked with surprise at the old general, who stood, shaggy and immense, beside me. He had never done more than bow to me, and listen now and then with a face of stony suffering to my accent, which always grew ten times as thick when he was near. What did he want now?

"Here! Try some of this, young lady!" And he held out a piece of chocolate, pale brown with cold. I smiled and took it, resolving to say as little as possible.

He cleared his throat grumpily and shifted his eyes to the far thunderous horizon.

In my mouth the chocolate broke at first like gravel into many separate, disagreeable bits. I began to wonder if I could swallow them. Then they grew soft, and melted voluptuously into a warm stream down my throat.

The little doctor came bustling up, his proudly displayed alpenstock tucked under one short arm.

"Here! Wait, wait!" he cried. "Never eat chocolate without bread, young lady! Very bad for the interior, very bad. My General, you are remiss!"

The soldier peered down at him like a horse looking at a cheeky little dog, and then rumbled, "Give us some, then, old fellow. Trade two pieces (and big ones, mind) for some of our chocolate?"

And in two minutes my mouth was full of fresh bread, and melting chocolate, and as we sat gingerly, the three of us, on the frozen hill, looking down into the valley where Vercingetorix had fought so splendidly, we peered shyly and silently at each other and smiled and chewed at one of the most satisfying things I have ever eaten. I thought vaguely of the metamorphosis of wine and bread.

Stay Me, Oh Comfort Me

There is an urgency, an insistent beauty, about words written while they are hot in the mind, soon after something has happened to make them burn there. I wrote that way the morning after my last meal with Rina. I sat in the gentle sunlight, just inside the great open window of a *brasserie* on the Champs Elysées, and the words flowed onto the letter paper like melted stone, swirling in strange shapes and mysterious shadowy meanings that I can never find again. I kept the sheets of paper for a long time, without reading them. I knew that what I had written could not yet be talked about or even looked at. And now that I feel it is all right, the paper is gone. I shall have to tell this from recollection, and it is a kind of consolation to admit to myself that I can do it in tranquillity, the way the poet said it might be.

That was the summer of an exposition in Paris. It was supposed to open in June, but there were strikes. At least, that is what the reactionary newspapers said . . . and it is true that when you went on the riverboats past the autoworks on the little island, the men leaned from the windows and yelled and raised their hands in the clenched worker's salute.

Some of the exhibits were ready to open, incredibly neat and even beautiful behind the rubble in the half-finished pathways, and the cafés were full of foreigners come to Paris to work in the fair or to see it. They sat gaily in the June sun, drinking their native drinks, or *citron pressé*, or even champagne, waiting for things to begin.

I was in Paris because my father and mother were coming from California. I was excited about that, but I had used them as an excuse to be by myself. Nobody knew this but me, and I was not ashamed of it. I had to be by myself for a few hours, so I lied a little, where I lived in Vevey, and came a day earlier than the boat was to arrive.

I do not think I knew, on the way to Paris, that I was going to see Rina, but as soon as everything was in order at the hotel, I called her.

The next morning, as I sat in the sun and wrote about it, I still felt sickish. It was almost like a hangover, but I knew I had not drunk much the night before.

When the waiter first came, and I asked for paper and a pen, I told him I would order later. I felt a little strange, alone in the big place. There were only a few people at that hour, and although the tiny tables and the trim wicker chairs on the sidewalk were in twenty neatly impenetrable rows, the back part of the *brasserie* was still dark and smelled dankly of Javelle water from its late scrubbings.

There were a lot of places like that then, high priced and badly served, along the Elysées: big tawdry rooms, usually with balconies at the back and windows that slid away so that the wide *trottoir* and the interior of the café could be one establishment on any sunny day or warm lovely night. There was always either a "gypsy" orchestra or a "ladies'" orchestra. Sometimes it was called *"orchestre de dames tsiganes,"* to be thorough. They were usually pretty good, too, in spite of the contortions of Romany abandon that their contracts apparently called for. The leader, always a violinist, was the prettiest, and winked and wiggled her way through night after night of Liszt and Enesco without ever quite forgetting that she had almost been first at the conservatory in Lyon or Clermont or maybe even Paris.

And there were the beautiful German girls that summer. There had been a few for three or four years, but that summer they were in full strength. I had noticed it at Easter time, when I went to Paris to decide a few things, but now that the fair was to begin, it was even plainer.

I sat at my table, writing fast and then resting, watching people, and as the chairs on the terrace filled, I thought that I had never seen so many beautiful German girls. I knew, without much surprise, that they were there for a reason—to show all the hungry, thirsty, excited tourists that they were the most beautiful in the world and the happiest, being the most German.

It seemed like a dirty trick to play. I remembered the fat girls from little Prussian villages, and their dowdy muckle-dun suits, and the way their eyes squinted and their hair smelled, in the classrooms when I was going to the university in Dijon. Those girls had won scholarships and worked like slaves at their lessons. After 1933 you didn't see them anymore. And now Hitler's machine was sending these lovelies . . .

They were tall, slender with the lithe flatness of youth. Their skin was firm and beautifully gilded—not burned brown enough to look un-Aryan but gilded to show what you knew anyway, that they could sail and ski and dance. They all had rather shaggy hair, bleached a little in streaks so that you were to be sure the sun had done it. It was startling and lovely, after the neat tourist hairdos and the elaborate whorls of the French women, and the girls would stand hatless, tall and young, beside the tables of their acquaintances and shake back their hair softly against their shoulders, like sensual colts. And they all wore beautifully tailored gray flannel suits, casual but as artfully revealing as any Hollywood extra's, and white shirtwaists open at the throat.

They never worked together, but there was at least one at every big café in Paris that summer. They would stand up and call out to people they knew or stride from table to table—anything to make people see them and know by their accents that they were German. They all used that seemingly childlike, voluptuous soft way of speaking that is supposed to be Viennese, so that the French would not possibly think of them as Boches.

An Alsatian *brasserie* was just across the street. I knew it was supposed to be a Nazi hangout. I saw two or three of the girls come out of it and then head for their next jobs, up and down the boulevard. I felt very bitter suddenly, and when my waiter came slapping and scowling toward me, I asked him to bring me a double porto-flip. He looked sourly at me and probably was about to tell me that the barman was not yet on duty, but I said very firmly, "Double, please, with two egg yolks . . . and the best red port."

I loathed port, and raw eggs, too. But I had left the hotel without breakfast, and I knew that it would be silly to drink an aperitif and then feel even stranger than I did already. Soon my dear parents would be in Paris. . . . I must meet their train and be young and happy and untouched by evil.

After I drank resolutely at the sweetish, creamy eggnog, I felt steadier in spite of my resentment of it and began to write as fast and as impersonally as I could about the night before. I wish I had not lost those papers. This would be much easier. . . .

It doesn't matter whether I meant to see Rina or not when I went to Paris early: I did see her. I kept saying to myself, or rather my mind kept saying, the way a mind does when a person is trying to ignore too many facts at once, Flagons and apples, flagons and apples. My mind would also say things like, Involution, convolution, trivo-intro-spinolution.

But as I sat in the hotel bedroom and knew that flowers were in vases and mineral water was ordered and English novels were on the bedside tables for my parents and that all was in order at least a day too soon, my mind was saying, Flagons and apples . . . oh, stay me with flagons, stay me with flagons and comfort me with apples, for I am tired of love.

Was that it? It was in the Bible. Did it say tired or sick? I was tired. I wanted love, but I was tired of it, wearied by its involutions, convolutions, its complex intraplexities. I had fled from it, leaving there in Vevey the husk and the bud, the empty and the refilled, renewed, revived, recrucified. . . .

When I tried to write a letter to tell my husband that I was well and happy, I knew that running away had not helped us at all. I loved him too much to lie, although not enough to live with him . . . and it was the same thing again: Stay me with flagons, for I am tired, sick, tired, tired of love.

It was then that I decided to call Rina. She was the answer. She would be like cool water, I knew it. I felt younger and suddenly freed from all the wordy anguish of the last weeks. Rina knew everything about love. She knew so much and for so long that she had left it all behind. I felt sure of that, convinced of it.

Rina had known every kind of love in the world, and by now she must have left it all behind, she must have. By now she must be a woman beyond purchase, dispassionate at last because she had known all passion, cool at last after all the fires. I wanted terribly to be with her for a while, to rest my weary self with her. I knew now why I had come so resolutely, so slyly, a day early.

It was five years since I had last seen her, perhaps, but everywhere she went she sent me her new address, as if I would be likely to find myself, or her either, in Berlin, or Minorca, or a Baltic fishing town. Now I even had her telephone number in Paris.

My heart was beating hard, partly from the nervousness that telephoning always brings to me and partly from a strange physical reaction, the way it might if I had been lost in a dark cave and had suddenly found the exit.

A maid answered, and then I was talking with Rina. Her voice sounded low one moment and then high and foolish the next, and I realized quickly that she was saying things to me, the usual things two women say after a long separation, but that through me she was talking to someone in the room with her. She was trying to impress someone.

It annoyed me. She must know that after so many years she could not impress me, but doing it to another person was important enough to her to risk my scorn before two minutes had passed. I listened to her voice, lush with affectation and little laughs and murmurs, and wished that I had stayed in Vevey.

There was some nonsense going on about a Packard. "What do *you* think of them?" she demanded lightly, and then before I could answer, she said, "But that's exactly what I say! You've never driven anything else! That long gray roadster . . . "

There was a lot more like that, and I kept thinking, Oh, to hell with it! I've never had a Packard in my life. Long gray roadster!

Rina's accent grew more and more British, and I felt cold and bored. She . . . they . . . just leaving for the Riviera . . . she must see me . . .

I looked around the sterile little room and thought of eating alone: any table in Paris would be one at which my husband or my own true love and I had sat . . .

"I'm leaving, myself, early tomorrow," I said politely. "But I'd so like to see you. Can you have supper with me tonight?" I heard my voice, almost as silly and affected as hers. There was more chatter: I was to come first for a cocktail. . . . I said yes and hung up, bone weary, almost empty of the fine hopes that had leapt in me.

It was a charming afternoon, though, light and limpid, the way Paris can be. There was a big chestnut tree in the courtyard, and a few of its white candles, nearly burned out by now, moved in the pure trembling light against my balcony. The walls looked silvery, not gray, and the dingy mustard plush curtains were golden. I took a long bath and lay on my bed drinking slowly at some brandy and water, and when I finally got up, I dressed almost as carefully as if I were meeting a man I loved very much, instead of a woman who by now should be past such things.

I remembered that I had always dressed with extra care for Rina. She wore very conventional clothes herself, like a rather horsey Junior Leaguer from Pasadena or Milwaukee, but she always made other people want to be extraordinary, to tie a scarf as it had never been tied before or wear one pink glove and one black one. I was satisfied with myself, Rina or not: my dress, the color of a green almond, was like a good dressmaker's idea of what human skin should be, with all the tucks and gores just so instead of as God put them. That was two or three years before women began to wear veils, and I had a big green net that held on my black priest's hat and tied under my chin.

I gazed at myself coolly for a few minutes with great pleasure, as I put on my black gloves in the sweetly dying light. I was slender, chic, with a face as smooth and almost as meaningless as a doll's, and my mind felt quiet again. The bath and the brandy and then this agreeable vision of myself made me put far out of my mind the weariness after my talk with Rina.

By the time I was in the taxi I was excited again, thinking that perhaps she would be as I wanted her to be, wise and rich and dispassionate. I needed someone like that, someone far past sexual wonderings, like a mountain, like a true priest. I needed to withdraw from the lists, to stand for a few minutes away from the battle.

Rina's name was printed on a card for the sixth floor. The apartment house was quietly swanky, somewhere off the Étoile, and I went up in a tiny elevator. A middle-aged maid with a mean face opened the door, and then I was standing in a big room at the top of the building, meant for a studio. Light still glared hotly in through the huge tilted window so that I was dazzled. Rina always liked darkness, I thought. She must hate this.

There was a pleasant fragrance in the air, like full-blown roses.

It seemed as if I waited several minutes. I stood motionless near the door, notic-ing and thinking several things at once, like any animal in a new place. I still heard the maid saying, "The young lady will be here soon." That sounded queerly insolent when I repeated it to myself; she should have said Rina's name, she should have asked me to sit down. Something rang false as hell.

The room was attractive, surely, in a way that had been made banal by French decorators: white plastered walls, several good pieces of peasant furniture, hand-blocked heavy cloth on the low couches and the chairs. The floor was darkened to look "provincial," and there were good rugs. It is queer . . . I don't believe there were any pictures at all—the walls must have been quite blank.

But it was a pleasant place, except for the loud glare of light—and, except for that, completely characterless. I felt surprised; Rina always took possession of wher-ever she lived, and I could see nothing of her here. I began to feel very curious about her, in a detached way—what she would be like, after so long.

I took off my gloves and then started slowly to put them on again, knowing with-out caring that she was going to make an entrance. That at least would be in the right tradition, I thought, not maliciously but almost with relief to find something still left.

The last time I saw her, what did she look like? It was in the rain, in the station at Dijon. I was catching the midnight train for Paris, to go back to California for a few weeks. She stood with her arm through my husband's, and I thought he would prob-ably fall in love with her. Men always did, helplessly. She would do him good, I thought.

I stood in the train window, watching the wet lamplight on their faces turned mutely up to me, and probably I felt a little noble to be so fatalistic. Rina was beautiful, so thin from China and fevers and Leningrad that the bones showed everywhere in her, yet she still looked strong. Yes, it would do them good, I thought, looking down at them as if I were already a thousand miles at sea.

(But he did not fall in love with her. Instead, she gave a disease to our best friend, and when she found out about it, two years later in Berlin when she was having an abortion, she wanted to kill herself. She wrote to me, but by then there was not much I could say.)

I thought of all these things and probably more, and when Rina finally came through a door at the other end of the room, down near the big glaring window, I stood without speaking for a moment.

She put her hands behind her, in a strange childish gesture, and said, "Don't look at me that way. Don't, don't!"

Now, I was not looking at her in any way at all, unless maybe past her, and her low violent pleading was planned. It was a deliberate command to look at her and to be shocked and speechless. I know that my face, which can be very stolid, showed nothing. That was to reprove her for trying to make me gasp or turn away, as she wanted me to do so that she could suffer more.

I sat down on a couch and took off my gloves again without touching her. "Hello, Rina," I said, and she began to talk in a high affected voice, twitching all over the room, moving ashtrays and pillows and such, asking questions too fast and too silly to be answered: how was I, how was the trip up from Vevey, did I like Gitanes or Gold Flakes?

She seemed much shorter, probably because she was so fat and because she wore beautifully cobbled brogues. Her stockings were exquisite, and she still had fine legs, and her tailored suit and shirt and necktie were fine, too, as I had known they would be. But it is true that I never would have known her.

I had met several women who looked almost exactly as she did now, in Hollywood mostly, but it had never occurred to me that Rina would ever resemble them. I suppose it is a glandular condition. She was fat in a certain way, with compact hips and very heavy, almost bull-like shoulders. Her head stuck forward, making her neck look shorter still, and there was a roll at the back, like a caricature of a German burgher, so that the close-cropped hair made unattractive bristles. It was thin at the temples, like a middle-aging man's.

Her face was the strangest, yet I knew it well . . . on other women. It was dead white, with the close-pored vaguely dirty whiteness of an alcoholic's. Her eyes had grown very small, it seemed, and were timid now, instead of large and deep blue and gravely intelligent. She had no eyebrows left at all but only a thin silly penciled line above each puffy socket. And her mouth was small and carefully made up. It looked like a baby's, covered with lipstick, meaningless and nasty.

Perhaps I was less stolid than I thought, for Rina suddenly stopped fussing at the books on the big oak table and came over and took my gloves away.

"Don't put them on again," she said quietly. "You're nervous, too, aren't you? Let's have a drink." Her voice was natural, the low almost harsh voice I remembered. I could smell a heavy scent—she had always liked them.

She pushed an electric button in an elaborate little cloisonné thing on the table in front of my couch, and because neither of us had anything to say, we waited silently. She rang it again. She ran her fingers back over her thinning hair. "It's because *I'm* ringing it," she muttered, not looking at me. "She knows I'm ringing it. She hates me." Then she pushed crankily at the little bell several times and said in the affected English voice, "Servants are so difficult, what with the Exposition . . . I'll simply have to do it myself."

She laughed like something in a drawing room comedy. "A sidecar. You do want a sidecar, don't you?"

"No, thank you, Rina. May I have some brandy and water, please?"

"Oh, but I make such heavenly sidecars . . . Well . . ." She put her hand on my shoulder, the first time we touched, and said, still in that foolish voice, "Just like a little boarding school girl: please . . . thank you, no; thank you, yes . . . "

Then she went hurriedly out of the room. I could hear her heavy flat footsteps go down a long hall.

I was shaking a little all over. I didn't know why, then, but now I think it was the same way a cat shakes after she gives birth to a kitten. I had got rid of something, some burden inside me, and it was a physical shock. For fifteen years I had known Rina and, without words, had believed that she sometime would be my comfort, my very present help in time of trouble. I had lied for her and condoned her eccentricities, her cruelties to people who loved her, without ever loving her myself but because I believed that someday she would save me. And now I knew that she never would. I pushed all that trust away from me, and it was like relieving myself of a great burden, like a birthing of something I had thought was dependence and was really my own freedom. That is why I trembled, but I did not know it then. I just wondered a little.

She came back soon with two tall lovely glasses, the kind that should have flowers in them and are too heavy full of drink. My highball was thin but good. Rina was drinking barley water.

She sat down at the other end of my couch and began to talk rapidly, as if she wanted to tell me everything before it was too late. I listened without speaking, very coolly, as to a tactless stranger.

There was almost nothing I recognized: she was still a snob, but her old small references to social position had become crude boasting about titles and hunting lodges; she was still conscious of money, but her old mannerism of pretending that it was too base, too vulgar to talk about, had turned into a long financial whine.

She seemed to feel misunderstood now and persecuted: Tanya the Polish cook sneered at her, her uncles had cut down her share of her rightful inheritance from a sixth to a thirty-sixth of the estate, Moira always rented places with studio windows when she knew what torture the light was, she went to doctor after doctor and they deliberately hoaxed her into taking medicines that did no good, Moira was wonderful but wouldn't let her help in any way so that she simply felt *kept*. . . .

"Who is Moira?" I asked politely, knowing that she must be Rina's mistress.

She looked oddly embarrassed, as if I were too young to be told. I grinned to myself, thinking of when we were in boarding school together and in college and of all the girls who had hated me or tried to hurt me or wept in my arms because Rina was cruel to them and loved me better. "Do you love her?" I asked as if it didn't matter, which was true.

Rina frowned peevishly. "We . . . I live with her, if that's what you mean," she said in a stiff way. "Her name is Moira Bentley-Wivers, *Lady* Bentley-Wivers. She is an exquisite Irishwoman. She will be here soon."

And then she was off again on her monologue: Moira's dog was more important in the ménage than she, the doctors took her money and laughed at her behind her back, Tanya did, too, and told Moira lies about her. . . .

Rina got up two or three times to get more barley water for herself, and when she came back, she smelled more strongly of the heavy perfume, so I guessed that she was drinking brandy or whiskey and trying to hide it. She asked me each time if I wouldn't change and let her make a wonderful sidecar, but I said no and nursed my glass. I did not feel like drinking anything at all, or even breathing.

"I fixed those flowers for you," she said, interrupting herself is if she could no longer stand the sound of the high silly voice. She sounded like my old friend again but pleading, not proud. "Do you like them? They remind me of you."

I saw that behind me, almost hidden in the angle the couch made with the wall, was a copper kettle filled with pink peonies, the pale bruised gray-pink color that only peonies can have. It was their subtle roselike fragrance I had first smelled. Now it was lost in Rina's crude perfume.

"They are lovely," I said politely. They were, but I felt bored and mean.

"I fixed them for you . . . that color against the copper . . . I knew you would like it . . . "

"I think pewter would be better," I said, and as if my small cruelty had broken open a wound, she cried out harshly, "Oh!"

And she called me a name that only my husbands and my family have ever called me. It is a short ugly little name, but nobody else has ever dared call me by it because it is completely private. Rina had heard my sisters say it, of course, and my brother, too. Now it was more shocking than I can say to hear her use it. It was past impertinence, past importunity, like seeing a father show his idiot son for money, and it was sad in the same ignoble way.

"Oh!" Rina cried again, again calling me by that name, and she was like someone in hell, praying to the last god on the list, beating on the last closed door.

I put down my glass on the low table and thought as coldly as I could, This is probably a game she has often played, often rehearsed. It is the usual masochistic whine of a once proud, once strong and beautiful human seeing herself, whimpering in self-pity for her perversities.

But when I looked at her, I saw in her blinking pale little eyes that she was there, the old intelligent Rina, perhaps for a few seconds but truly, and I had to answer.

"What can I do, Rina?"

"You are the same. You haven't changed." She turned her head away as if she could not stand to have me look at her eyes and said, very low, "Take off your hat. Take the pins out of your hair. Let it down so that it will be the way it used to be just once."

I had to, I felt so full of pity for her. I put my handsome little hat and the fine green veil beside me on the couch and took out the pins so that my hair fell softly down my back.

Rina looked at me without smiling, but I could see that she felt better. She leaned a little toward me, and I tried not to smell the heavy perfume on her breath.

"Oh," she said, using my private name again, "is there anyone who can help me? Do you know anyone? Look at my hands!" She held them in front of her as if they stank: pale, puffy, trembling, with bitten nails. "You know how I used to be! Is there anyone to help me?"

I remembered her firm strong body, and the way she could always do anything, *anything* at school better than we could, and how she was more exciting and brilliant than any student had ever been so that the professors feared her and girls wept for her and men stopped breathing for wanting her. All that grace and wit, all that strange electricity had been mine for the taking. But I had taken nothing. I had waited too long, and now I felt a deepening remorse in me. Perhaps if I had been more generous . . . it was too late now to tell anything but the truth.

"Rina," I said, beginning to shake again a little, "there is a man in California, an endocrinologist. It might kill you, though. You're rotten. There'd be no liquor, no love . . . no drugs. . . . I don't know whether you have the guts."

But she did not hear me. The little elevator was humming. The doorbell sounded, and then Moira and her dog were in the room, and me with my hair down and my fine hat on the couch. Tanya half-followed Moira, her hard sly face full of pleasure, and then pulled back like a snail when she saw my disarray.

Rina stood up and began fussing at ashtrays and books as she had when I first came, but I sat still, not knowing what else to do, while the tiny dog sniffed circumspectly at me and Moira stood in the middle of the room, as I had stood, slowly drawing off her gloves. I liked her, and she liked me, but we were wary. We recognized a mutual knowledge of what time could do and of our fleeting unimportance to each other.

She was a tall woman, about our age or perhaps a little older. Her torso was solid and mature, and she had lovely legs and a small head rather like mine. She wore very high heels and a subtle hat, and although her suit was tailored like Rina's, it looked female, not male. And she did not wear a shirt and cravat, but a soft silk blouse with a cairngorm shawl pin at the throat. Her hair was short, too, but not like Rina's. It was tawny, and all her clothes were the soft colors of toasted bread, warm and clear.

I cannot remember anything about her face except that it was all right—good bones, noncommittal—and that the corners of her wide mouth were as pointed as an adder's tongue and as sensitive.

All this time Rina was fidgeting. I left my hair the way it was, and I knew Moira was looking coldly at my hat and veil there on the couch. Rina had introduced us in her incredibly affected voice, and then she said, "Oh, darling . . . the embassy has been calling frantically . . . and there are flowers for you from the *vicomte* in the kitchen. Tanya wouldn't let me open them. And did you get the Packard, Moira, darling?" Like that, on and on.

Moira pulled her hat off and threw it with her gloves on the big table. "Let's have a drink, shall we?"

She smiled at me and began to talk politely about the weather and what a pity it was that the Exposition was late and weren't the peonies exquisite this year. I felt back in school again, taking a deportment lesson and saying, Yes, Miss Moira, No, Miss Moira, with my ankles crossed. And yet, as I say, we liked each other.

Rina came back in a few minutes with a shaker and three glasses, and the perfume in a cloud about her.

Moira said, "But, Rina . . . I always drink whiskey."

Rina laughed shrilly, as if Moira had made a great joke. "Darling! But it's all gone . . . I hate to say this, but Tanya looks . . . Oh, well, for once, Moira, drink one of my sidecars. You *know* how good they are . . . and we love them, don't we?"

She leered archly at me from under her crazy penciled eyebrows. She was a stranger, and an unpleasant one. I took one of the cocktails. I never tasted it, but I knew Moira did not care, any more than she cared when Rina clinked glasses elaborately with both of us and said, "First drink today! I've been a good girl today, Moira . . . nothing but barley water. Of course, Tanya would love to tell you another tale!"

"How did you two get along today, dear?" Moira spoke dutifully, like a nice husband home from the office.

Rina laughed again, like a parrot. "Beautifully," she cried. Then she turned to me. "As Tanya so aptly puts it, Moira got all three of us the same week. We all get our pay, too. Tanya cooks for her, and the Pekingese amuses her, and I——her."

And she used a word that I have never been able to say. I had never in my life heard Rina say anything like it. In school, she had never even goshed and helled and gollied, like the rest of us.

Moira went on sipping at her drink, and I started to put the pins back in my hair.

"M'ing!" Rina called. The little dog raised his head. He looked like a Chinese carving, there in his basket under the table. He stared for a cold second at her and then closed his eyes.

She laughed again and said gaily to me, "Do you remember those wonderful hunting dogs your father used to have? I've told Moira about them."

Of course, my father never had any hunting dogs . . . just one old broken-down hound that wandered to the Ranch and stayed there until he died. But I murmured yes to that and some other equally outrageous things that Rina knew I knew for lies, and then said I must put on my hat. I stood up.

Moira said quickly, warmly, "Oh, but we're having supper together, aren't we? You *must* have supper with us!"

I was surprised at her urgency. And I had forgotten my invitation. I wanted more than anything in the world to go back to my hotel: I felt sleepy, the way you do when you go up a high mountain and then come down again all in one day, or one hour.

"Oh," I said, "I had hoped that you and Rina would have supper with me. We could go to Michaud's or Daniel's—they're nice—"

I saw Moira look strangely at me. "No, no," she said. She sounded almost cross. "No, we insist, don't we, Rina? You *must* have supper with us. We have a favorite little place . . . so quiet . . . and tonight is Tanya's free night or we'd all stay here . . . but I know you'll love this little place. It's very near here." It was queer to have Moira suddenly so eager. The room was almost dark, but I could see her looking at me, insisting with her whole body that I stay, that I be their guest.

"Thank you . . . I should love to." There was nothing else I felt able to say. After all, it was my own fault. I would leave early. . . .

"Rina!" Moira's voice was sharp, and Rina spilled some of her drink as she stood up heavily, clumsily, from the chair she had finally settled in. "Rina, I must call the ambassador—no, I'll write him a note, and we can post it on our way out. Will you please show Mrs. Fisher our room? She wants to rearrange her hair, I'm sure."

She's a smooth one, I thought admiringly, as Moira sat down at the desk and switched on a light beside her, and Rina went ahead of me into the shadows under the big window.

I fixed myself in the bathroom and then went into the bedroom, where Rina stood quietly by an enormous mirror. It was like the window in the other room, except that now the light on it was very delicate and somber. Rina turned her back to me, and we stood looking at each other in that glass for a long moment, not really saying anything but feeling the only peace we were ever to feel again together.

Then she laughed shrilly, and turned back, and said like a boastful little girl, "This is *my* dressing table."

It was covered with large bottles of very expensive perfume, and there were boxes of powder and several lipsticks, more like a movie star's than this pathetic woman's.

"And this is my armoire. See?" She pulled open the doors, and there were more beautifully cut suits and piles of fine silk and linen. It was like a finicky man's wardrobe, and yet not like it. "And there," we turned about-face, "are Moira's dressing table and armoire. And there is our bed."

How narrow it was, I thought. It seemed impossible that two such large people could sleep together in it, night after night, every night.

The room was like a big setting, like a sardonic Ziegfeld parody of a boarding school bedroom: matching furniture stage right and stage left, bed upstage center

. . . and then the great mirror where the audience would be. Perhaps there were chairs and such . . . oh, certainly there were . . . but I really remember only that ridiculous little bed and the mirror.

We went back into the studio. Moira was writing busily under the light at the far end. Rina and I stood for a minute looking out into the soft beautiful Paris night. The horizon behind the chimney pots was like Venetian glass, lemon clear, but stars showed, and underneath there were lights, more and more.

Rina was talking, not too loud but loud enough for Moira to hear if she wished. "Now I can live. It is dark now. This window hurts me, kills me. She knows it. Everywhere we go we live in a glare like this. It tortures me . . . "

"Oh," I cried, and at my voice Rina stopped breathing, just as I had, to see flaming against the dark glassy sky a kind of torch. It was gold, and it glowed but was solid, too. Suddenly it had leapt into the night there, perhaps a half mile away from us across the roofs, and it stayed, instead of flickering away again as such strange things should rightly do.

"Rina! What is it?"

"What does it look like?" Her voice was low, impatient. "It's the statue at the Soviet pavilion—a man and a woman on a pillar."

"A man and a woman!" I laughed. "But it looks like a seal from here, with a ball on his nose. Yes, I can see it better now. It's a seal with a ball on his nose." I felt silly and almost happy, like a child. The golden thing there in the sky was magical.

Rina said something very distinctly about balls. She said it the way an old man will murmur a rhyme to a little boy, watching him to see how many of the words he knows.

"You don't think that's funny, do you?" she asked softly.

I could see by the way she swayed that she was abruptly drunk. I have watched that happen to other people who drink the way Rina did: they stay coldly, deliberately steady for almost any length of time they want to. Then, perhaps because they cannot fight their own secret demons any longer, or because they are bored, or because it is dusk or high noon or they hear someone singing in the street, they are drunk. They are drunk in the middle of a sentence. This is how it was with Rina. She was all right, in a pinched hard way, and then, standing there beside me watching the golden torch, she was suddenly very drunk.

"You don't think that's funny, do you?" she said again, loudly.

"No."

Moira came quickly to us and put her arm through Rina's. For the first time she sounded Irish when she spoke, soft and cajoling.

"Supper! Forgive me, both of you! I've kept you, and it's time for supper, surely now."

She led Rina into the bedroom. In a minute they came out, Rina in an awful hat not quite a man's but never meant for a woman, Moira smooth and cool looking, with only a finger or two on Rina's elbow to guide her.

When we got to the elevator and held open the door, it looked too small for even one of us. I said, "Please let me walk down. I hate elevators." I wasn't being polite; it was the truth.

Rina lurched away from us. "No," she said violently. "*I* hate elevators. *I'*ll walk down."

Moira tried to seize her arm. "No, Rina," she cried, and her voice was full of anguish. It was the only time I heard her talk with any love. "Rina, please! It will be bad for you. You aren't well . . . your heart . . . "

I thought what a pity it was that this fine tender woman, so full of compassion, should not have her own children.

Rina laughed sneeringly, like a man who is mean drunk. She pushed Moira hard into the tiny elevator and then, without touching me, started down the first flight of curving stairs.

I got in as quickly as I could, closed the door, and pushed the button. Moira stood leaning away from me, all drooping, like the leaves on a broken branch in the hot sun. She said, "Oh, God," quietly.

"Are you unhappy?" I asked it without thought and then knew that I had been wrong: she raised her head, and her eyes were cold and the fine thin corners of her mouth trembled like adders' tongues.

"Why should I be?"

"Is she . . . are you used to this then?" I felt impertinent, like a brash child, and glad that there was no more time to be rebuffed, for we were down already.

The elevator door rolled open. Rina stood there, trying not to pant. Her face was an ugly red. She must have run all the way. It made me shudder to think of it.

"Rina! That's wonderful," Moira said warmly, and Rina's face lit up. She laughed and pulled off her horrible hat, and we went out and got into a taxi, and Moira gave an address.

Rina sat next to me. I thought for a few minutes that she had stopped being drunk, but when Moira got out to post her letter, I could tell that she was perhaps worse. She leaned against me a little, needlessly, and breathed in an excited way. It was mechanical, like a prostitute pretending, or an old man.

It was as if Rina did it because all women that close to her expected her to, but I was not all women—I was me, her longtime friend, who knew her too well ever to love her.

I made no sign of anything, and when Moira came back and saw Rina so close to me, she looked sharply at me, but I still made no sign of anything. You should go along the Elysées, I thought furiously, and get yourself one of the German girls. Yes, go along the Elysées, with some of Moira's money. Go anywhere. But *I* am *me*—

The restaurant was small, the kind that is a café during the day, with a little bar beside the cash desk and wavy mirrors behind the marble-topped tables around the walls. It was like the Roy Gourmet, if you remember that, except that it was just one room instead of two, and it was mediocre instead of good. There were waitresses, big taciturn girls. The patrons were big, too, perhaps young lawyers and functionaries and store people, with their wives and a few middle-class whores. When we came in past the row of tables under the open windows on the sidewalk, everybody stopped eating and talking and looked at us.

Now, every woman who holds her head up and looks as if she has known good love has at times made a room quiet when she has walked into it. There is something silencing, even for a few seconds, about her. It is not because of beauty or her vestments or the people with her; it is a kind of invisible music, or perfume, or color that surrounds her and makes people stop their usual thoughts and motions. When they pick up their forks, they may not even know why they put them down and may never think of the woman again, but for a time she has touched their lives, usually without meaning to.

This had often happened to me, of course, because of my bony structure and the fortunes of my years, but I had never been made either comfortable or uncomfortable by it. I had probably taken it as part of being human.

When we walked into the little restaurant, though, and all the heavy people in their black office clothes looked at us, I felt as if my skin were being pulled off. I saw their eyes slide with amazement over us: Moira so cool and disdainful, with her mouth thin and tight and her mature body tight, too, under her beautiful clothes; Rina all puffed and bullish, like a monstrous caricature of a creature neither man nor woman; and I so obviously not a partner to either, I like a slim and modish cuckoo in this ex-normal nest. They looked most at me, wondering about my green dress and my green veil probably, trying to place me in their vocabularies of behavior.

Moira and I sat against the wall at the last small table, with Rina facing us. A waitress brought us the usual blurred menus and then with a smirk took Rina's hat and hung it on the rack by the cash desk with all the other heavy dark fedoras and straws.

I was ravenously hungry—I had only eaten some cold chicken and salad that day on the early train from Vevey—and besides being empty, I felt a sort of hectic need in me, as if I had rid myself of something enormous, and all my bones were now crying for new nourishment. I wanted a meal to satisfy me, a real meal chosen with thought, a long good meal with the right wine or two.

The menu looked fairly promising. But Moira was already ordering for the three of us. She spoke French correctly but with a rather scornful flatness, as if it were a language not worth sounding out, which reminded me more of an English than an Irish person. The waitress stood looking down at us, her face blank and her eyes wearily entertained.

"The day's specialty . . . that sounds all right," Moira said. "It's too hot for anything first, of course . . . or would you like something first, Mrs. Fisher?"

I felt annoyed that such a seemingly well-bred person could be so careless, and I was disappointed, too: I had thought Moira would be more intelligent. So I said, "Yes, I would, thank you. I am awfully hungry. I'd like some pâté . . . it says *pâté d'été* here . . . that will taste good."

"Madame will take the *pâté d'été*," Moira said to the waitress in her flat insensitive

French. "We will have the entrée at once and . . . and a bottle of the restaurant's *champagne nature.*"

"No salad, no vegetable for the young ladies?" the waitress's voice was subtly insolent, the way Tanya's had been when she told me Rina would come in a minute.

"No. And hurry, please."

I looked at Moira, and suddenly I realized that she was terribly anxious about Rina. She wanted to get food into her as soon as possible; Rina was swaying in her chair, and her poor pale eyes were glassy. I felt ashamed of myself for changing her orders, for interrupting the quick functional flow of food into belly that this meal must be. How stupid of me to think that with a person like Rina at the table a meal could have any grace or ease or pleasure in it. It must be a feeding, that was all—a sort of sponge for extra alcohol, which was to be swallowed as quickly as possible.

Why do people like this ever eat in public? I wondered. They should take food as they take physics, in the privacy of their bathrooms.

I looked at the menu: the specialty of the day was *coq au Chambertin.* It would be ghastly with *champagne nature.* It would not be made with Chambertin either. I could tell by the looks of the place. The pâté might be all right . . . probably veal and spices with a little cubed ham discreetly through it, but cold and savory.

"Rina, some bread? Here, split it with me." I held out a big piece to her. She pushed it away.

"Rina hates bread," Moira said, "Don't you, darling?" But Rina did not answer.

Moira sat stiffly against the cheap cloth seat, and I felt that she was forcing Rina with every muscle in her body to stay conscious, to sit up, not to fall over or be sick. Her face was almost as expressionless as mine.

The waitress brought the unlabeled bottle of wine. It was very crude, but we all drank it thirstily. It seemed strange to me not to click glasses, no matter how perfunctorily, the way we always did in Vevey. It was very sour with the bread, but I felt starved.

The people, except for an occasional shrug and almost surreptitious look at us, had gone back to their own problems. Rina sat without speaking. She held her glass in both hands and drank in small rapid sips, as if the wine were hot consommé. Moira was talking to me about her house on the Riviera. She and Rina were joining her parents there, she said politely, as if either of us could be interested. There would be other people there. Did I love to swim?

"Tell her about Raoul," Rina said suddenly. Her words were almost impossible to separate one from another.

Moira looked upset for a second. "Oh, Mrs. Fisher doesn't know Raoul," she said. Then as she saw Rina open her mouth again and scowl, she went on, "Raoul is our dearest friend, our . . . father confessor, really."

"Show her his picture," Rina commanded brusquely.

Moira shrugged and without saying anything took a little leather folder from her purse. There was an old-fashioned photograph of a man in it, a slender delicate face, the hair long, the eyes rolled up, one finger of his bony hand pressed against his temple. It looked like a cruel parody of an 1890 aesthete. There was nothing to say about it, except perhaps "Oh," which I did.

"We are very fond of Raoul," Moira stated flatly. "He spends a great deal of his time with us."

"Moira keeps him. Moira keeps Tanya and M'ing and Rina and Raoul. Moira is kind, isn't she?" Rina muttered.

I could feel Moira praying desperately for the day's specialty to come. I looked at the picture facing Raoul's. One of the women was Moira, in a bathing suit. Her figure was beautiful. The other woman, sitting at her feet on a beach, was in slacks and had a heavy long mop of bright blonde hair, and for a minute I did not see that it was Rina. She looked very beautiful, too, the way I remembered her except for the hair.

"Let me see," Rina said, and pulled the folder out of my hand. She shut it after a quick look. "That's me. That was last summer. I dyed my hair. I thought it would change things." She pushed the folder back toward Moira, and I sat wondering how any human could be so different within so few months. I didn't look anywhere but ate little pieces of bread and drank my wine.

Then the waitress came with our plates piled up her arm. "Messieurs-'dames," she said insolently, and put down a casserole, and then my pâté, and the serving spoons in front of Moira. "Or does Madame prefer me to serve?" she asked. Moira picked up the spoons quickly.

"What's that?" Rina asked loudly, and looked up at the girl.

"*Coq au Chambertin*, as ordered."

"Coq?" And very distinctly, without smiling at all, Rina said something completely obscene about a cock in clear and perfect French. The waitress drew back, frightened, I think, and then flushing, and people around us stopped everything, the words heavy in their ears.

"Thank you, Mademoiselle . . . I can serve," Moira said, and there was something so dignified and suppliant about her voice that the girl hurried away, instead of screaming or striking Rina as she might have.

Moira put quite a lot of the chicken stew, for that is what it was, on a plate for Rina and filled her glass again. She began to eat, too, watching Rina all the time.

Rina ate a little, but she was dreadfully clumsy and kept getting bits onto her fork and then watching them fall slowly off again, the way I had seen old drunks do in hash houses on skid row in Los Angeles. There were already several smears of the dark sauce on her suit. She looked as if swallowing hurt her.

I was still very hungry, in a detached way, but I couldn't eat. The pâté, as I had thought, was far from disreputable. It was simple and savory, just what I had wanted. But now I couldn't. I tried to eat the chicken. It was fairly well made but too heavy for such a summery night. I wanted a salad—but I knew that if I had one it would not go down my throat. I drank some more wine.

Moira was talking, and perhaps I was, too, when Rina suddenly stood up. Her chair squealed against the floor, and people looked at us again, a kind of alarm now on their faces.

"Shall I come with you?" Moira asked softly.

Rina shook her head without speaking and walked unsteadily out the door and past the sidewalk babies.

We all watched her—all of us, even the waitress. The men shrugged, and the women leaned over the tables toward them to whisper strangely excited little questions, and I kept seeing long after she had disappeared down the dark street the heavy shoulders, the thin black hair on her temples, the neat hips and slender legs.

But more clearly I saw the other Rina, the proud sure one, the reckless handsome woman who had gone like a flash of lightning through so many hearts and bodies.

"The water closet is down the street," Moira said casually. "It is really too hot to eat anyway, isn't it? We should have stayed home and raided Tanya's kitchen. But sometimes Rina thinks Tanya is trying to poison her."

"And I leave so early in the morning," I lied. "I should really go back to my hotel and pack."

It seemed silly to keep up that kind of bluff, but we both did it. Rina came back. She looked a little soberer and ate some of the cold sauce on her plate with a piece of bread. She drained her glass and then said, "Pay the bill, Moira."

"I wish you'd let me," I said. "You know I asked you this afternoon, Rina . . . "

"No. Moira always pays the bill, don't you, Moira?" And Rina laughed shrilly, like a parrot again, without looking at either of us.

In the taxi we sat without talking, after I had told the driver my address. It was as if we were too tired to say anything. Moira sat up straight, but Rina was bent and sagging, like an old person. We had to stop often: the crossings were crowded with people strolling slowly, the way they always used to in Paris on warm summer nights. I felt an almost violent impatience to hurry, to end all this.

Moira shook my hand in a polite, detached way when I finally got out. "Mrs. Fisher is going now," she said to Rina.

Rina roused herself. "Good-bye," she said, and she used the name that nobody ever uses but my family and my husbands. This time it did not sound importunate or brash but only final, so that I could not resent her.

"Good-bye," I said, and went into the hotel without thanking them.

I took another bath and went to bed as fast as I could. It was as if I had a rendezvous with something in my sleep. I rushed to meet it.

And this is where I regret the lost pages I wrote the next morning in the *brasserie*, because I wrote mostly about the dream. It was a long dream, one of the most vivid I had ever had, and I woke from it panting and shaking with a kind of abysmal horror such as I had never felt before.

This is all I can remember now: I was on a high wall, watching a long stretch of beach where little blue waves edged with white curled symmetrically, as in a Chinese embroidery. And down the beach raced a great roan horse with a golden mane. He reared back at the wall, and then, time after agonizing time, he hurled himself at it in an orgy of self-destruction. It was terrible. Time after time he leapt straight at the wall with all his strength, and there was a sound of breaking sinews and flesh, and everywhere there was his blood, bright imperial yellow blood, while the little waves rolled silently, symmetrically . . .

I awoke, and it was as if I were drowning in horror. Then I went to the bathroom and was sick, and put cold water on my face and brushed my hair very hard. I went to sleep again, and everything was all right, as if I were a little child.

In the morning, as I have said, I felt strange. It was as if I had been poisoned and then violently washed clean of the poison. The porto-flip finished the job and made me feel warmed and fed again. I drank it dutifully, not liking it but knowing its reason, and paid my bill and put all the sheets of paper in my purse and walked out into the sunlight, past the filled noontime tables on the sidewalk.

People looked casually at me as I went by, as I would have done in their places, and suddenly, because of last night and the stares and shrugs there in the little restaurant, I felt as shy and ill at ease as a young girl. The thought of going alone to lunch, *anywhere*, was impossible.

But my father and mother would not be in Paris until late afternoon. . . .

I walked slowly toward the Tuileries, gradually getting used to humanity again, like a soul sent back to earth. I stood in the sun for a long time by one of the round fountains with the fat glass pigeons.

In the gardens under the plane trees I bought a ham sandwich and sat on a chair eating it and watching some little boys sail their boats across the pond.

By the time I had to go back to the hotel I was young, untouched by evil. I was ready to be with my dear parents, and I was ready to meet love alone again, not asking for another person's comfort, nevermore to thirst for any flagon but my own.

Paris, 1937

FROM P IS FOR PEAS

. . . naturally! and for a few reasons why the best peas I ever ate in my life were, in truth, the best peas I ever ate in my life.

Every good cook, from Fanny Farmer to Escoffier, agrees on three things about these delicate messengers to our palates from the kind earth mother: they must be very green, they must be freshly gathered, and they must be shelled at the very last second of the very last minute.

My peas, that is, the ones that reached an almost unbelievable summit of perfection, an occasion that most probably never would happen again, met these three gastronomical requirements to a point of near-ridiculous exactitude. It is possible, however, that even this technical impeccability would not have been enough without the mysterious blending, that one time, of weather, place, other hungers than my own. After all, I can compare bliss with near bliss, for I have often, blessèd me, eaten superlative green peas.

Once, for instance, my grandmother ran out into her garden, filled her apron with the fattest pods, sat rocking jerkily with a kind of nervous merriment for a very few minutes as she shelled them—and before we knew it she had put down upon the white-covered table a round dish of peas in cream. We ate them with our spoons, something we never could have done at home! Perhaps that added to their fragile, poignant flavor, but not much: they were truly *good*.

And then once in Paris, in June (what a hackneyed but wonderful combination of the somewhat overrated time-and-place motif!), I lunched at Foyot's, and in the dim room where hot-house roses stood on all the tables the very month roses climbed crazily outside on every trellis, I watched the headwaiter, as skilled as a magician, dry peas over a flame in a generous pan, add what looked like an equal weight of butter, which almost visibly sent out a cloud of sweet-smelling hay and meadow air, and then swirl the whole.

At the end he did a showy trick, more to amuse himself than me, but I sat openmouthed, and I can still see the arc of little green vegetables flow up into the air and then fall, with a satisfying shush, back into the pan some three or four feet below and at least a yard from where they took off. I gasped, the headwaiter bowed faintly but with pride, and then we went about the comparatively mundane procedure of serving, tasting, and eating.

Those petits pois au beurre were, like my grandmother's, à la crème mode d'Iowa, good—*very* good. They made me think of paraphrasing Sidney Smith's remark about strawberries and saying, "Doubtless God could have made a better green pea, but doubtless He never did."

That was, however, before the year I started out, on a spring date set by strict local custom, to grow peas in a steep terraced garden among the vineyards between Montreux and Lausanne, on the Lake of Geneva.

The weather seemed perfect for planting by May Day, and I had the earth ready, the dry peas ready, the poles ready to set up. But Otto and Jules, my mentors, said no so sternly that I promised to wait until May 15, which could easily be labeled Pea-Planting Day in Swiss almanacs. They were right, of course: we had a cold snap that would have blackened any sprout about May 10. As I remember, the moon, its rising, and a dash of hailstones came into the picture too.

And then on May 15, a balmy sweet day if ever I saw one, my seeds went into the warm, welcoming earth, and I could agree with an old gardening manual which said understandingly, "Perhaps no vegetable is set out in greater expectancy . . . for the early planting fever is impatient."

A week later I put in another row, and so on for a month, and they did as they were meant to, which is one of the most satisfying things that can possibly happen to a gardener, whether greenhorn and eager or professional and weatherworn.

Then came the day with stars on it: time for what my grandmother would have called "the first mess of peas."

The house at Le Pâquis was still a-building, shapes of rooms but no roof, no windows, trestles everywhere on the wide terrace high above the lake, the ancient apple tree heavily laden with button-sized green fruit, plums coloring on the branches at the far end near the little meadow, set so surprisingly among the vineyards that gave Le Pâquis its name.

We put a clean cloth, red and white, over one of the carpenters' tables, and we kicked wood curls aside to make room for our feet under the chairs brought up from the apartment in Vevey. I set out tumblers, plates, silver, smooth, unironed napkins sweet from the meadow grass where they had dried.

While some of us bent over the dwarf-pea bushes and tossed the crisp pods into baskets, others built a hearth from stones and a couple of roof tiles lying about and made a lively little fire. I had a big kettle with spring water in the bottom of it, just off simmering, and salt and pepper and a pat of fine butter to hand. Then I put the bottles of Dézelay in the fountain, under the timeless spurt of icy mountain water, and ran down to be the liaison between the harvesters and my mother, who sat shelling peas from the basket on her lap into the pot between her feet, her fingers as intent and nimble as a lacemaker's.

I dashed up and down the steep terraces with the baskets, and my mother would groan and then hum happily when another one appeared, and below I could hear my father and our friends cursing just as happily at their wry backs and their aching thighs, while the peas came off their stems and into the baskets with a small sound audible in that still high air, so many hundred feet above the distant and completely silent Léman. It was suddenly almost twilight. The last sunlight on the Dents du Midi was fire-rosy, with immeasurable coldness in it.

"Time, gentlemen, time," my mother called in an unrehearsed and astonishing imitation of a Cornish barmaid.

They came in grateful hurry up the steep paths, almost nothing now in their baskets, and looks of smug success upon their faces. We raced through the rest of the shelling, and then while we ate rolled prosciutto and drank Swiss bitters or brandy and soda or sherry, according to our various habits, I dashed like an eighteenth-century courier on a secret mission of utmost military importance, the pot cautiously braced in front of me, to the little hearth.

I stirred up the fire. When the scant half-inch of water boiled, I tossed in the peas, a good six quarts or more, and slapped on the heavy lid as if a devil might get out. The minute steam showed I shook the whole like mad. Someone brought me a curl of thin pink ham and a glass of wine cold from the fountain. Revivified, if that were any more possible, I shook the pot again.

I looked up at the terrace, a shambles of sawed beams, cement mixers, and empty sardine tins left from the workmen's lunches. There sat most of the people in the world I loved, in a thin light that was pink with Alpen glow, blue with a veil of pine smoke from the hearth. Their voices sang with a certain remoteness into the clear air, and suddenly from across the curve of the Lower Corniche a cow in Monsieur Rogivue's orchard moved her head among the meadow flowers and shook her bell in a slow, melodious rhythm, a kind of hymn. My father lifted up his face at the sweet sound and, his fists all stained with green-pea juice, said passionately, "God, but I feel good!" I felt near to tears.

The peas were now done. After one more shake I whipped off the lid and threw in the big pat of butter, which had a bas-relief of William Tell upon it. I shook in salt, ground in pepper, and then swirled the pot over the low flames until Tell had disappeared. Then I ran like hell, up the path lined with candytuft and pinks, past the fountain where bottles shone promisingly through the crystal water, to the table.

Small brown roasted chickens lay on every plate, the best ones I have ever eaten, done for me that afternoon by Madam Doellenbach of the Vieux Vevey and not chilled since but cooled in their own intangibly delicate juices. There was a salad of mountain lettuces. There was honest bread. There was plenty of limpid wine, the kind Brillat-Savarin said was like rock-water, tempting enough to make a hydrophobic drink. Later there was cheese, an Emmenthaler and a smuggled Reblochon . . .

. . . And later still we walked dreamily away, along the Upper Corniche to a café terrace, where we sat watching fireworks far across the lake at Evian, and drinking café noir and a very fine *fine*.

But what really mattered, what piped the high unforgettable tune of perfection, were the peas, which came from their hot pot onto our thick china plates in a cloud, a kind of miasma, of everything that anyone could ever want from them, even in a dream. I recalled the three basic requisites, according to Fanny Farmer and Escoffier . . . and again I recalled Sidney Smith, who once said that his idea of Heaven (and he was a cleric!) was pâté de foie gras to the sound of trumpets. Mine, that night and this night too, is fresh green garden peas, picked and shelled by my friends, to the sound of a cowbell. [. . .]

FROM SEA CHANGE
1929—1931

In 1929 the stock market crashed, and I got married for the first time and traveled into a foreign land across an ocean. All those things affected me, and the voyage perhaps most.

Everyone knows, from books or experience, that living out of sight of any shore does rich and powerfully strange things to humans. Captains and stewards know it, and come after a few trips to watch all passengers with a veiled wariness.

On land, the tuggings of the moons can somewhat safely be ignored by men, and left to the more pliant senses of women and seeds and an occasional warlock. But at sea even males are victims of the rise and fall, the twice-daily surge of the waters they float on, and willy-nilly the planetary rhythm stirs them and all the other voyagers.

They do things calmly that would be inconceivable with earth beneath them: they fall into bed and even into love with a poignant desperate relish and a complete disregard for the land-bound proprieties; they weep after one small beer, not knowing why; they sometimes jump overboard the night before making port. And always they eat and drink with a kind of concentration which, according to their natures, can be gluttonous, inspired, or merely beneficent.

Sometimes, if people make only one short voyage, or are unusually dull, they are not conscious of sea change, except as a feeling of puzzlement that comes over them when they are remembering something that happened, or almost happened, on board ship. Then for a few seconds, they will look like children listening to an old dream.

Often, though, and with as little volition, people will become ship addicts, and perjure themselves with trumpery excuses for their trips. I have watched many of them, men and women too, drifting in their drugged ways about the corridors of peacetime liners, their faces full of a contentment never to be found elsewhere.

(I know only one person who ever crossed the ocean without feeling it, either spiritually or physically. His name is Spittin Stringer, because he spits so much, and he went from Oklahoma to France and back again, in 1918, without ever getting off dry land. He remembers several places I remember too, and several French words, but he says firmly, "We must of went different ways. I don't rightly recollect no water, never.")

The sea change in me was slow, and it continues still. The first trip, I was a bride of some eleven nights, and I can blame on the ocean only two of the many physical changes in me: my smallest fingers and toes went numb a few hours after we sailed, and stayed so for several days after we landed, which still happens always; and I ·developed a place on the sole of my left foot about as big as a penny, which has to be scratched firmly about five times a week, a few minutes after I have gone to bed, whether I am on land or sea. The other changes were less obvious, and many of them I do not know, or have forgotten.

For a while, several years later, I mistrusted myself alone at sea. I found myself doing, or perhaps only considering doing, many things I did not quite approve of. I think that may be true of most women voyaging alone; I have seen them misbehave, subtly or coarsely, not wanting to, as if for a few days more than the decks beneath them had grown unstable. Then, as land approached and they felt nearer to something they loved, or at least recognized, their eyes cleared, as if they were throwing off an opiate, coming into focus again.

Yes, I have been conscious of that, and mistrusted it, so that I usually acted so stiffly virginal as to frighten even myself when for many reasons I had to go alone to America or back to France or Switzerland. I think that by now I am old enough, though, to know why such things happen, or at least how to cope with the ramifications and complexities of loneliness, which is by now my intimate and, I believe, my friend. [. . .]

THE LEMMING TO THE SEA

More often than not people who see me on trains and in ships, or in restaurants, feel a kind of resentment of me since I taught myself to enjoy being alone. Women are puzzled, which they hate to be, and jealous of the way I am served, with such agreeable courtesy, and of what I am eating and drinking, which is almost never the sort of thing they order for themselves. And men are puzzled too, in a more personal way. I anger them as males.

I am sorry. I do not like to do that, or puzzle the women either. But if I must be alone, I refuse to be alone as if it were something weak and distasteful, like convalescence. Men see me eating in public, and I look as if I "knew my way around"; and yet I make it plain that I know my way around without them, and that upsets them.

I know what I want, and I usually get it because I am adaptable to locales. I order meals that are more typically masculine than feminine, if feminine means whipped-cream-and-cherries. I like good wines, or good drinkin'-likka, and beers and ales. I like waiters; I think the woman who said that waiters are much nicer than people was right, and quite often waitresses are too. So they are always nice to me, which is a sure way to annoy other diners whose soup, quite often, they would like to spit in.

And all these reasons, and probably a thousand others, like the way I wear my hair and what shade my lipstick is, make people look strangely at me, resentfully, with a kind of hurt bafflement, when I dine alone.

Sometimes the results are more tangible. I think now of Jacques.

He was on the *Ile de France* when I went back to Switzerland. By then I had fairly well developed my system of public behavior, but the ship was a hard test, bleak, rattling, stuffy in Second, and heart-breakingly pretentious in First. Jacques and I were in Second.

I saw him soon, and enjoyed the way he moved quietly about the decks and halls, like a Spanish dancer, very self-contained. He was small and dark, and made me think of a fox, not because of the cunning a fox is supposed to have, but because of a smooth fine brown-eyed potency about him.

He was looking at me, and admiring me too, but I did not realize it: my whole reason for being lay ahead of me, on the lake near Vevey in the canton of Vaud, and I was hurrying there as irrevocably as an Arctic lemming hurries to the sea cliff, through poisoned fields and fire and flood to what he longs for.

Jacques watched me in the dining room, where I sat alone and ate judiciously, with amiable concentration. And he watched me in the Smoking Room, which was the only warm place to sit. I read, and drank without ever showing anything but a self-contained enjoyment, and seemed not to want better company than my own. All this was puzzling to Jacques, and because he was a man it was annoying too.

Finally we met, and when he told me his name and asked me teasingly if I could spell it, I amazed him by doing so, because I had learned it in a history course in Dijon, years before.

He was a Norman. There were seven sons and six daughters in his family. Some of the boys went to the colonies or to Canada, like Jacques, and some of the girls went into nunneries. There were a few of each sex in private insane asylums. The rest were very important in Paris, or the Foreign Service. Jacques showed me pictures of his home, a great grim place with its own church, its own village, and of his stubborn handsome mother.

He was a very simple man, almost childish, and did not talk much at a time. Sometimes we drank cognac together after dinner, and once he ate at my table, with a kind of charmed jealousy at the good meal we had, and the good wine.

He was very modest, but always there was in his bones, in every hair on his fine dark head, the assurance of his great name, so that one night when he was trembling with nervousness at having to officiate at the ship's concert, and I said, "Why not get someone else to, then?" he dismissed the idea and me with it by saying, very simply, "But it is expected of me."

That night, in honor of the concert and perhaps of taking me up to dine in First with the captain, he wore a beautiful little satin waistcoat, I remember, of the most delicate shell-pink, with flowers embroidered on it in petit-point. It was perfect on him, for some reason I cannot tell.

Only twice did he ever say anything personal to me. Once he said he liked to look across the dining room and watch me eating there, so thoughtfully and voluptuously, because I was the only woman he had ever seen except a Chinese, the wife of a great leader, who could do it. I knew very little about her, but I asked if it might not be our smooth hair. No, he said, and did not have words for more.

And another time, just before we landed, he stood twirling his beret on one finger, not confusedly but with real grace, and asked me if I had ever thought what it would be like to marry a trapper and live in the Canadian forests. I never had, but when I looked at him I realized he was planning something in his slow simple brain, and I said, "It would take strength."

"Yes," he said, looking impersonally at me, as if I were a horse.

I don't know how or why I told him what hotel I would stop at in Paris, on my way to Switzerland. Certainly I never thought to see him again. My mind was fixed on tomorrow, on being once more with Chexbres.

The boat train was late, and by the time I had tidied myself for dinner and got to Michaud's, a boy was putting up the shutters. I felt depressed and tired, and went past him anyway, thinking I could get a good glass of sherry, and then go to bed. But when Madame Rollo saw me she shrieked for her brother, and a dash to the kitchen proved that there was enough heat left in the ranges to make me a little omelet, and would I consider eating a few spiced mushrooms first, and yes, by God, there was one portion of *crème au kirsch* left, after a little salad . . . and for this time of night and this cold month a small bottle of Montrachet '23, with my permission. . . .

It all made me feel warm and human, sitting there with those kind voluble quarrelsome people behind the shutters, knowing that tomorrow I would be with Chexbres again, and my long journey over.

When I got back to the hotel and saw Jacques sitting by the desk, I could hardly remember who he was. He was very nice, and asked me to forgive him for being importunate . . . but two of his brothers were in Paris, and anxious to meet me, and . . . and he looked so fine-boned and simple and honest that I left my key on its hook, and went out with him to a waiting car.

We went to the little upstairs-bar at Weber's. It was the first time I had been there. People were sitting quietly, drinking champagne and eating vanilla ice cream, which one of Jacques' brothers told me was chic at the moment.

They were taller than he, and handsomer, but they did not have his *good* look. They were much more intelligent, and treated him with a kind of affectionate scorn that older members of a large family often seem to feel for the young ones. He was a yokel home from Canada, and they were Paris diplomats, and even if he had been articulate he would have said very little.

They were politely startled when I ordered a very good cognac. One of them drank scotch, and the other champagne, and Jacques ordered a bottle of Perrier water.

I had told them when I first met them that I was very tired and must go back soon to the hotel, but as I listened to them I wanted to go even sooner. I was speaking good French that night, probably because their accents were so perfect, but very quickly I knew there was nothing I could say that would be truthful. They were the most cynically weary men I had ever met, like the young officers on the *Ile*, but with more force . . . not physically or religiously or sexually, but in their patriotism. They were complete defeatists.

I sat there listening to them, hardly able to swallow for the revolt and horror I felt. They were betraying France, two men as old as France herself, and strong and intelligent enough to fight for her. They were selling her, there in Weber's little bar, as surely as they were selling her on the Bourse and in the embassies.

I looked at Jacques, to see if he understood what had happened to his brothers, but it was impossible to tell. He was tired and obviously bored by them.

They kept on talking, charmingly, wittily, and I realized that all around me there was the same kind of conversation. Hitler and Tardieu and Laval: these aristocratic Frenchmen were discussing them blandly, as if they were unpleasant but humble menials, to be handled puppet-like at their own discretion.

I could stand no more of it, and asked to be taken to my hotel. I was shocked, so that I could hardly keep from shaking.

Jacques took me to the desk from their car, and when he kissed my hand he looked at me and said, "I should have stayed in Canada. I understand trapping animals better."

His poor simple mind was full of misery, I could tell, and I said goodnight gently, as if I would see him tomorrow, to comfort him.

A few weeks later I got a strange letter from him. "I am just back in Paris for a couple of days," he wrote. "I find the country place most depressing, dreary, and terribly damp. I can hardly tell you how much unpleasant it was to stay there, in consequence of the wet and my sister who has returned to the château after twenty-one years in a convent, to expect the world to have been stopped during that time. However, my dear, I shan't bother you with all that . . . how are you getting on, working hard, do you?"

Here Chexbres, who knew as much as I did about Jacques, said rather stuffily, "I thought you told me his English was good." I could only laugh. I thought the letter was funny.

He wrote about going south. He wanted to go to Corsica and buy an old farm. "I don't want to stay home too long. I will feel too depressed. Do you know Marie Françoise how happy I will be if it were possible for you to take that trip with me?"

"The bastard," Chexbres said softly.

The letter told me that it might help my writing to go on such a trip in that interesting island, and then, "Please let me know how foolish it all sound to you. I won't get *fâché*. Excuse this awful writing. The pen is a poem! Hoping to read you soon and have my life worth living, *à bientôt*."

I felt confused, to have to read this in front of Chexbres. He would think I had flirted. . . . Then I began to laugh again. It was such a simple proposition, just like Jacques.

But Chexbres, for a time, was almost hateful toward me, feeling a kind of brotherhood with Jacques against all women. "You can't do things like that to men," he said resentfully.

"But what?"

"Whatever it is that makes them write letters like that," he muttered, hating me. "That chap's suffering. . . ."

How could I say it was because I ate in a dark cold miserable ship as if I enjoyed myself, and drank without getting silly . . . because I behaved myself in public?

I wrote to Jacques and thanked him for his invitation, and told him that if ever he was near Lausanne, Chexbres and I would be so glad to see him. It was a very polite letter.

And in a few days I was called up to the village (it was before we had a telephone), to reverse a call to Evian from the Café de la Grappe, and it was Jacques. I had sat trembling, thinking awful thoughts of runaway relatives and such, and when it was only Jacques, so matter of fact, I felt almost glad to hear him. He wanted to stop to see us on his way south.

I was rather ungracious, and told him our houseman had influenza, which was true, but he ignored that. I knew Chexbres would look grim, and he did.

Jacques came that afternoon, and that night we went to dinner at Cully and ate piles of perch filets on a big platter in the café. I don't think Jacques had ever eaten so simply that way, with a lady and gentleman in a common-man's place.

Later we dressed and went dancing at Montreux, and drank a lot of champagne. Jacques danced almost as well as Chexbres. And that night his only personal remark was, very close to my ear in a tango, "But who is Chexbres?"

I told him, as well as anyone could ever tell who that strange man was, and he said, "Oh."

The next day we went all over the neighboring vineyards with Jules, our own *vigneron,* and it was wonderful to see Jacques with those cautious careful Swiss.

They had always been cordial with us, and seemed to like us, but with him it was different. They frisked about like stiff colts in the spring, and I have never heard such delight and laughter from them. They boasted and sang, and brought out bottles of wine that we had only learned about in whispers, and invited us all to festivals months away. It was fun, although Chexbres and I felt a little jealous of what we had thought was our own solid friendship with the vineyardists.

That night we drove up through the snow to Châtel, and ate trout at the Treize Cantons. We had a nice enough time, but Jacques was really hard to be with for very long, because he was too simple. He had only a few reactions to things, and almost no words to describe them. And besides, there was the feeling underneath that he had written asking me to go to Corsica with him. . . .

We were glad when he said that he must leave the next day at two o'clock. He told us that a sister-in-law was staying at Glion, and that he was very anxious to have her meet me. Would that be all right with Chexbres? Chexbres looked strangely at me, and said of course.

So I drove Jacques up the winding road behind Montreux, and was presented to his sister-in-law, who as wife of the oldest son was representing the mother of the tribe. She was a beautiful thin English woman, resting while her husband took one of his periodic vacations in a private asylum. She inspected me in a completely cold-blooded and charming way.

And then we drove down the mountain again. Jacques looked depressed.

"Denise is enchanted by you," he said glumly. "My mother will be enchanted by you too. It is very important that you go see her. She is old, and hates Paris now, or she would be glad to meet you in Paris."

I felt a little hysterical.

"Jacques, we have time before your train," I said. "Let's go eat something. We need some lunch."

"Undoubtedly you know just where you want to go," he said politely, and if I had not known his denseness I'd have suspected him of sarcasm.

We sat in the station restaurant, and ordered a fondue, because it was a cold day and Jacques said he had never tasted one.

It was not very good: too thin, and then suddenly stringy like cool rubber. Jacques ate two or three polite bites of it, and drank a little of the Dézaley and ate some bread crumbs.

We made conversation about regional dishes, and all the time he looked glummer and sadder. He wrote out his mother's address for me, and said, "I have showed you her picture, haven't I?"

"Yes, yes," I said. I didn't think I could stand much more.

"She will be enchanted by you," he said again.

We still had twenty minutes or so. I picked up a piece of bread, and dabbed at the cold gluey fondue on my plate. Suddenly Jacques began to speak very rapidly, standing up and reaching for his hat and coat on the station rack behind the table.

"Go on eating. Go on sitting there with your food and your wine. I saw you first that way, alone, so goddamned sure of yourself. This is right. I'll leave now. Do this last thing and stay as you are, here at the table with the wine in your hand."

"Oh, Jacques, I'm so sorry," I said. I looked up at him, and his eyes were very black. Then he moved swiftly among the tables, like a dancer, and the door swung behind him.

I must get home, I thought. I feel awful, like crying or being sick. I must get back to Chexbres.

I drove as fast as I could. I didn't know what I would do when I got there, but I must get home. I wanted never to be alone again, in a restaurant or anywhere.

The house was full of a fine smell. Chexbres was in the kitchen.

"Hello," he said. "Did that poor bastard give you his address? He left his pajamas. I've invented a new way to make fondue. It's absolutely foolproof. Here . . . "

We sat by the fire for a long time, and the fondue was indeed delicious, and by the time we had finished it and the bottle of wine and written the new recipe, Jacques was well on his way to Corsica, and I felt all right—sorry, but all right.

THE STANDING
AND THE WAITING

It was at the top of the stairs that I first felt something wrong. Until then all had been as I last knew it: the archway, the irregular honey-coloured courtyard, the rounded trees in tubs. The stairs, too, were the same, bending round and back over themselves in several shallow flights; and at the top was the familiar glass box with trout, a plate of mushrooms, and some steaks laid carelessly across the cold-pipes that made its bottom.

We looked for a moment into the box, Chexbres with the hurried, timid appraisal of a man who is in a strange place and conscious of being watched for his reactions to it by another person to whom it is familiar, I with the proud worry of a woman who fears she has too much boasted.

Would the dishes be as exciting, as satisfying? Would the wine still be the best wine? And I, would I be accepted, a loving admirer, or would I now be long forgotten?

Well, the glass box was the same. Chexbres flipped me a quick smile of reassurance. We went along the ugly tiled corridor, past the water closets where I felt a sudden hilarious memory of my mother's consternation when she had first entered them and found them full of men all chatting, easing themselves, belching appreciatively.

I started to tell Chexbres of her face, puckered in an effort to look broad-minded. We turned the first abrupt corner of the hall, the corner where the kitchens started.

One of the doors opened. A rat-like boy darted out, ducking his head and grinning shyly as he passed us. I refused to look at Chexbres, for I knew that he had smelled, as I had, as alas! I had, that faint trail of bad air following after the scullion like the silver of a snail, bad air rising noxiously from the hidden dirty corners of the kitchens.

I finished the story of my mother's dauntless face, as we hurried on down the long dim corridor.

"There are two dining rooms for the *pensionnaires*," I chattered foolishly, "and the *pensionnaires* are everybody—like the mayor and the rich brothel-keepers and carpenters and Chinese students.

"And here is Ribaudot's office."

I was trying to sound casual, but I felt very nervous. Oh, to have talked so much of the restaurant, to have boasted! And then that little ominous whiff! Or had Chexbres noticed it?

I tapped nonchalantly on the half-open glass door of the small, incredibly disordered room.

"Come in, then!" The voice was cross and muffled.

We pushed into the office. By the dim window two cooks in very tall hats sat with their bare arms leaning on a table covered with empty dishes. A cradled bottle lay in front of them. They smiled impersonally.

Ribaudot stood clumsily with one leg still half under the table, his hands leaning on his tall desk.

"Come in, come in," he said, more pleasantly. He wiped his mouth, and peered politely at us.

"How do you do—good afternoon, Monsieur Ribaudot. I am sure you don't remember me: Madame Fischer, who used so often to dine here? I used to come here with——"

"Oh, of course! Why of course!" He smiled warmly, but I could see that he did not remember. I shrugged inside, and while I introduced Chexbres as a fervent student of gastronomy, and we all chattered and assured each other of remembrance and good will, I looked for change.

If the whiff, the faint bad trail, had caught Ribaudot, it was not yet evident. His office was filled with the conglomerate cooling odours of a good meal, and he himself with the first leisurely torpor of perfect digestion. Yes, of course he looked older, perhaps thinner, uncombed as ever, though, and still modestly sure of being a great *restaurateur.*

"And Charles, little Charles?" I asked, suddenly.

Several looks crossed in the air. Chexbres looked at me, warmly, smiling at my nostalgic probings and at what I had told him of the waiter Charles. I looked first at Chexbres, thanking him for recognizing the name, and assuring him that even if Charles were long dead, he had still been the ultimate, the impeccable peak of all waiters. Then I saw Ribaudot look swiftly at the two silent cooks and they at him, a look—a look—I felt very sad and puzzled.

Ribaudot interrupted me.

"The little Charles?" he asked, blandly. "Ah, you remember the little old Charles?" His voice was noncommittal. "But certainly he is here. We will call him."

Through my halfhearted protestations he walked majestically the three paces to the door, and disappeared. The air was still full of crossed meaningful looks. I wondered very much, and watched Chexbres' impassive interest in the framed diplomas on the walls. I tried to feel impassive, too.

Chexbres turned. Charles stood in the doorway, breathing quickly, a rumpled napkin over one arm. Oh, I had forgotten how small—but hadn't he been fatter? Yes, old, the little *old* Charles.

I went quickly toward him, watching his pouchy face lighten quickly from peevish bewilderment to pleasure.

"Howdedo, Charles. I don't know if you remember——"

"O my God! Oh, pardon, pardon, but it is the little American student, the little lady!"

Behind me, Chexbres laughed to hear me called little as I peered down on Charles, he up at me, timidly still, but recognizing me.

"And you, Madame? And how long is it? And you, are you well? Has it been two years? *Six?* Impossible! But it is good, pardon me for saying so, but it is good to see you!"

He stopped suddenly, looking confusedly at the two silent cooks, and then at Ribaudot. He seemed to shrink even smaller.

"Monsieur Ribaudot," I said, "would it be possible to command a dinner for this evening, and ask for the services of Charles?"

"But certainly, certainly!" He pulled a pad of paper toward him, and started to make squiggles on it.

"Until eight tonight, then, Charles. And the old table in the corner—was it Number Four?"

I turned to Ribaudot again. He seemed to know me at last, and to be trying to comfort me, to soften life for me. And all the time we discussed food so pleasantly I wondered at Charles' quick, poignant, wet look of—of gratitude—as he hurried back to his work.

I felt sad, but said nothing to Chexbres. Instead, we talked of Burgundian architecture, not even mentioning the Burgundian meal we had so long planned.

At eight o'clock the small dining room was full, except for our waiting table. As we sat down I saw in one easy glance that the people were no different after six years. There was the old woman with a dog and a dancing boy on her way to Cannes, and the table of American schoolteachers eating from a guidebook. And there were the two big young Englishmen in brown and grey, looking embarrassed before their larks on toast.

At the table under the mirror sat a college professor; the College Professor, twirling a glass of Corton, the pedagogic connoisseur, sipping alone in solemn appreciation, sure that his accent was as refined as his taste.

There were two tables of French people, gay and hungry. I remembered that their faces would grow red, later on.

A Chinese eating truffled pâté in a trance of philosophical nausea, two Lesbians drinking Vichy, three silent *pensionnaires*, a priest—the hard white lights burned down on all of us, the mirror reflected our monotonous gestures, the grey walls picked out our pale natures and the warmth of colour and odour and taste before us on the white tables.

"This is a good room," Chexbres murmured, lowering his eyelids and straightening a straight fork. "I like small rooms. Small rooms, for eating—or mountainsides."

"Good evening! Ah, 'sieur-'dame, you are here!"

Charles stood by the table, breathing fast. His minute moustache was newly stiff with wax, and his hair was plastered in a thin replica of the debonair curlicues he used to wear. He beamed anxiously at us.

"Does—is everything as you wished?"

"Everything is perfect, Charles!" I wondered if my voice were too fervent. "Now we will start with a little glass of Dubonnet, please."

When he had gone, Chexbres said: "You are known, my dear! You should be much flattered—or I for being with you."

He smiled, the sweet-tongued self-mocker, at me and at the table, and I looked with less haste at the tall crystal tulips to hold wine, at the napkins folded like pheasants, at the inky menu big as a newspaper, and our own little typewritten one on top of it, at the flowers——

Flowers *chez* Ribaudot, Ribaudot who hated any foreign odours near his plates? Never before—no, we were the only diners with flowers on our table.

On the little serving-board beside us, Charles fussed clumsily with a new bottle of Dubonnet. Finally it was open. He poured it with a misjudged flourish. Purple spread on the cloth. I looked quickly, without meaning to, at Chexbres, but he was watching the quiet colour in his glass. Perhaps he had not seen, had not realized, the fumblings of my perfect waiter?

He raised his *apéritif*. His eyes were wide and candid.

"I drink to our pasts—to yours and mine. And to ours. The wine is strong. Time is strong, too." He bowed slightly. "I grow solemn—or sententious."

I laughed at him. "I'm not afraid of time."

"Don't boast."

"I'm not boasting. Really, I'm glad six years—oh, it's too complicated. But this tastes good. I'm hungry."

"And this will be a good meal, worth waiting even longer than six years for. Do you know," he asked naïvely, "that I've never before had a menu written just for me? It's very exciting."

I felt my self-confidence sweep back, as he meant it to.

"And flowers," he went on. "I've had flowers on my table, but never the only ones, in a room of such important people."

We looked vaguely, amicably, at the stiff little bouquet, mimosa and a purplish rosebud and a short twig of cypress.

Charles steamed beside us, with a tall pitcher of soup. While he served it, it spilled from the trembling cups into the saucers. I felt a flash of intense irritation: wet saucers, God! how they irritate me! I looked straight into his eyes.

They were not wet and grateful now. They were desperate eyes, bloodshot, frantic, desperate. I cringed away.

"Oh, Chexbres," I whispered, "don't mind the spilling! Don't! It's that he's nervous. His hand's shaking because of that, I know."

You are lying to save your own boastful face, too, I said inside. You know Charles is drunk. Yes, Charles, the perfect waiter, spilling soup and drunk, and it hurts your pride.

"Maybe his feet hurt him," I went on very fast. "I know you hate soup in saucers. But you know I've heard that waiters do stranger things than most criminals, simply because their feet hurt."

"Yes, I'm sure," Chexbres agreed, vaguely. "This is really delicious, my dear."

"You know," he said, in a suddenly direct voice, "I can't understand why most people are put off at first by the coloured tiles on the roofs of Burgundy. It seems to me they're a definite outcropping of the plebeian in architecture, like the frescoes of Swiss interiors during the same period."

For a moment I felt rebuffed. But almost at once I knew he was right. Six years— six hundred years . . . architecture was better.

We talked, and well, and all the dinner was most excellent, and the wine was like music on our tongues. Time was forgotten, and its signals, too. But I noticed, with a kind of fifth eye, that Charles' hand grew steady, and his own eye clear, until by the end of the meal I dared preen myself upon his delicate sure touch.

"Have you ever seen that better done?" I asked Chexbres.

"No. No, he is wonderful. He is an artist."

We watched as in a blissful dream the small fat hands moving like magic among bottles and small bowls and spoons and plates, stirring, pouring, turning the pan over the flame just so, just so, with the face bent keen and intent above.

"It's like a brain operation," Chexbres said, "—the hard light, the excitement, the great surgeon. Thank you for bringing me here. It's worth——"

It was done. We tasted. We nodded silently, and smiled at Charles, and he looked almost like the old Charles again, very self-sure. I felt happy.

After coffee, I laughed to think of us sitting there almost the last, and at what I was going to do.

"Chexbres, you think I've shown off, but that was only the beginning! Now I really do show off, and all for your benefit."

We smiled at each other, very effortless and calm.

"Charles," I called, warning Chexbres quickly, "You have never tasted the local *marc*, remember!"

"Charles, what do you think has been the sad experience—but first, are we keeping you too late?"

I waved my hand at the now empty room, dim in every corner but ours, and at a scullery boy scrubbing the hall. I felt expansive, warm from the wine, at ease in Time.

"Oh, but what an idea!" Charles exploded. "Excuse me for chiding you, Madame, but what an idea! Madame, you must know that for you to have another good meal *chez* Ribaudot, and go away remembering it and me, I would gladly stay here until morning—no, until tomorrow night, by God!"

Chexbres and I bowed courteously. Charles did, too.

"And the sad experience, Madame?"

"Oh, thank you for recalling me. I had almost forgotten. Charles, last night we had a stroke of luck that was unfortunate—I should say almost desolating. I, who wished to introduce our good friend Monsieur Chexbres to the famous *marc* of Burgundy, was served with a glass of some strange liquid—thank God I had the good sense to taste it before letting Monsieur come near it!—some strange liquid, pale, cut, rank, which could never——"

"Ah, but I know! I know where!" Charles beamed, flourishing his napkin with glee.

"Oh, but naturally I would not be so indiscreet as to mention the name of the miserable restaurant," I protested, rhetorically. I glanced at Chexbres exultantly: the scene was beautiful.

"No need, no need, Madame! A restaurant serving the good *marc* so insultingly, and to you, a connoisseur" (here I bowed graciously) "and to this poor gentleman a sure amateur having his first taste" (here Chexbres lowered his eyes modestly)—"ah, such poisonous conduct, my God! could only be at" (and here Charles leaned very close to us in the empty room and hissed) "could only be at *La Tour!*"

He stood off, triumphant. I pressed a little line into the table-cloth with my thumb nail, smirking, murmuring, "Of course I say nothing, no names!" in complete agreement. I could feel Chexbres' appreciation all around me.

"But, but 'dame, we must rectify that infected, that—pardon me—that stinking behaviour!"

I sighed faintly. It had worked!

"Yes, my idea, too. But no ordinary *marc*, Charles, no liqueur served on anyone's order. This must be——"

"Yes, very special," he finished for me. "Trust me, Madame. It may take a few extra minutes. A little more *filtre*, perhaps, while I am gone?"

Chexbres and I sat wordless, looking mildly and somnolently at each other. We sipped at the bitter black coffee. A rickety old ventilator whirred in the ceiling, and the boy cleaning the hall bumped his bucket against the tiles. Lights went out, except over our table.

Charles tiptoed back, wheezing, but his face full of life. He held a filthy old green bottle, not picturesquely crusted, but filthy. Silently he poured a little dark brown liquid into a large glass. He swirled it round. Chexbres reached for it.

"Permit me, sir," Charles halted him, "permit me to suggest that Madame taste it."

I winked slightly at Chexbres, and took up the glass. I tried to look like a connoisseur, a little pompous probably. I sipped, and then I could only look beatifically delighted, for it was the cleanest, smoothest distillation that I had ever met.

"Ah!"

Charles sighed. I had told him. He poured the glass almost half full, at least twice as full as he should have, and with a jubilant look disappeared into the wet dark hall.

"Chexbres, now *I* shall be solemn. But I have never been served such *marc!* Not even Ribaudot would serve that to his best friends, to anyone less than the mayor or maybe the Holy Ghost. Where did Charles get it?"

Chexbres let it run under his tongue, and sat nodding ecstatically at me. I could almost see it seeping through his head, in and around in a hot tonic tide, and then down his throat.

"Dear sweet gentle Jesus!" he remarked, softly.

"Oh, I'm glad we came, Chexbres. After all, I mean."

We both drank at the one glass, and talked peacefully under the one white light. Finally the *marc* was gone. Charles appeared, carrying the filthy bottle.

"Oh, no more, no more! Really, we couldn't——"

He stopped very still, and looked at me.

"Madame, you must drink one glass. Please!" he said, in a quiet voice, almost muttering. "Please drink this glass from me. It is I, Charles, who offer it to you and to Monsieur Chexbres."

"But—it is so late, and—" The thought of swallowing one more mouthful closed my throat, almost.

"I have said I would stay until tomorrow for you. I would stay until the end of the world, truly." He looked at me calmly, standing between us and the dark doorway. Beyond him I could see nothing, and there was not a sound anywhere, except the three of us breathing rather cautiously.

"Thank you," Chexbres said, warmly. "Madame was afraid only of detaining you too long, Charles. Otherwise we could sit forever, too, drinking this miraculous liqueur."

He held out the glass. With a hand steady as oak, Charles poured it to the brim, a good half-pint of strong *marc*.

"Thank you, Charles," I said. "I want never to leave, here where I have so often been happy. It may be six years again. Will you prepare the bill, please?"

We knew we must drink it all. It was like smouldering fire, wonderful still, but hard now to swallow. We sat without moving, conscious suddenly of exhaustion, and of being perhaps too full of food, with all the heady wine-life gone out of us.

Charles came back, with the little sheet of flimsy paper on a plate. I wondered about the tip: in a way I felt like not leaving one, because he seemed more than a waiter now. But when he brought back change, I left it all on the plate.

"Thank you, Madame," he said, and did not pick it up. He stood watching us sip resolutely at the *marc*. Finally I looked up at him.

"Madame, thank you, thank you for coming again."

I wanted not to be personal, so I said, "But why not? All people who love good food come to Ribaudot's again."

"Yes," he stuttered slightly, "but—pardon me—but I mean thank you for asking for me. You don't know——"

"Oh, Charles, it is we who are fortunate, to have your services." I felt very polished and diplomatic, but at the same time sincere, sincere as hell under the weariness and all the *marc*.

"No, no—I mean, you will never know what it meant, tonight, to have you ask for me, little old Charles. And now, good evening."

Chexbres asked, quickly, "But we will pass this way again, and soon we hope, and then of course——?"

"Ah, who knows?" Charles raised his eyebrows toward his thinning curlicue of hair, restrained a gesture to stroke his little whiff of moustache, smiled debonairly at us, and disappeared finally into the black corridor.

"I thought he said he would wait until tomorrow night," I murmured, flippantly. Then I felt rather ashamed, and apologized. "He'll probably be waiting at the end of the hall, the top of the stairs, to help us with our coats."

Chexbres said nothing, but slowly drank down the rest of the *marc*.

The chairs squawked wildly as we stood up. The sound was almost good in that silent room.

In the corridor we saw a dim light, and as we went by Ribaudot's office, his silhouette was sharp against the frosted glass, bent over his high desk.

"I know where the coats are," I whispered, and we tiptoed down the hall.

"Is it Madame Fischer?" His voice came muffled through the door. He opened it, blinking at us, with his hair mussed.

"Oh, I'm sorry! I do hope we haven't kept you," I said, in confusion.

He looked very tenderly at us. "No. And have you dined well? I am glad. I have your coats in here."

We stood awkwardly in the doorway while he crossed the little room to the table where the two cooks had sat in the afternoon. Our coats were piled on it, to one side, and a stiff ugly bouquet of mimosa and two purplish rosebuds and a twig of cypress stood by them. I looked dully at it, wishing I were home in bed, very tired.

"It was good of you to remember Ribaudot," he said.

"It was very natural. Who does not?"

"Ah, things nowadays—the affairs—" but he bowed, acceptance calm on his face.

"And the poor old Charles. It was especially good for him. I see you and I shared the honour of flowers from him." He looked impersonally at the ugly bouquet. "Yes, I fired Charles today, just before your first visit. He is on his way to the South by now.

"Permit me to help you with your scarf. It was sad—a fine waiter once, a brave little man always—but what will you do? Everything changes. Everything passes."

"Good night. Good night, sir, and Madame, and thank you. And good-bye."

"Au revoir, we hope," I called as we walked away from him towards the dark.

"Who knows?" He shrugged, and closed the glass door.

In the long hall corruption hung faint and weakly foul on the still air. The stairs were deep, with the empty glass box like a dark ice cube, and we breathed freely once out in the courtyard.

It was filled with moonlight. The trees in tubs were black, and through the archway the tower of the palace gleamed and glowed against the black sky.

Chexbres took my hand gently, and pointed to the roofs, coloured tiles, Burgundian, drained of their colour now, but plainly patterned. I began to cry.

LEFTOVERS

One reason that they are disdained is that usually they can never happen again. They can never taste the same, and good eaters do not wish to form any addictions that are hopeless from the start.

Another trouble with them is that their recipes are almost impossible to write. There is no way to capture again the taste of a cupful of yesterday's sautéed mushrooms put at the last minute into a spinach soup because two more people turned up for supper.

Glen Ellen, California, 1985

SPIRITS OF THE VALLEY

Some people believe that it is a fortunate thing if a person can live in a real valley instead of on flat open land, and they may well be right. For some sixteen years, from 1940 on, I lived most of the time on ninety acres of worthless land southeast of the little town of Hemet in Southern California, and they were fine magical ones, important in the shaping of many people besides me, perhaps because Hemet Valley was a true one in every sense. At its far eastern end rose the high mountains that separated coastal land from desert, and our little town lay almost as near their base as Palm Springs did on their other side. Mount San Jacinto loomed on the north; to the south, high rocky hills rolled toward the Mexican border, and westward the valley opened gently, as any proper valley should, toward broad coastal flats and the far Pacific Ocean.

My husband, Dillwyn Parrish, and I bought our land for almost nothing: it was haunted, for one thing, and completely untillable. And we lived there intensely until he died three years later, according to medical schedule, of Buerger's disease. Then I stayed on, through another marriage and two little daughters, who spent their first years there with me after I divorced their father. When the oldest was going on six, we moved to my family ranch near Whittier to live with Father after Mother died. I worked half-time on his newspaper and ran the household, and as often as possible (weekends, vacations) we went back to Hemet to the little ranch house in the wild rocky hills.

It became clear that I could not raise two growing females there alone, where I had decided to remain. Now and then I found someone to repair storm damage and so on, but finally it seemed wise to sell the place. I felt thankful for everything I had learned there, and when I said it was no longer mine, I withdrew forever from it, even though ashes of my love and my mother may still blow from under some of its great rocks. I know the wind still sings over the Rim of the World and always will.

Tim (my husband was always called that by people who loved him, which meant everyone) named our ranch Bareacres, after a character in *Vanity Fair* who had several marriageable daughters and countless acres of barren land. He managed to sell the land, bought a string of pearls and a husband for each girl, and he and Lady Bareacres lived penniless but happy ever after, as I remember.

Certainly our land was bare! It rose in rough steep hills, with one deep canyon that split it down from the Rim of the World, its horizon, to the wide dead riverbed that was its northern boundary. A thin little road track went up from the valley floor, past our house and on up past the trickle of our only spring, to a deserted old ranch on the Rim of the World. There was a big sturdy redwood tank at the spring and a handful of stubby cottonwoods, and down nearer our house in the canyon, dry except for an occasional mud puddle from the underground trickle, stood a few tall eucalyptus trees. The rest of the place was covered with great harsh boulders, some of them bigger than a house. On the flat top of an enormous rock above the spring, two oblong tubs had been chipped out centuries ago, and we were told that sick Indians were brought there to lie in the hot sun while soothing water was poured over them, water that we found was heavy with lithium.

In front of the house, which stood about a thousand feet up off the wide dry riverbed that separated us from Hemet Valley, the land was steep but with fewer big rocks, almost like a meadow, covered with sage and mesquite and low cactus. Across the riverbed, northward, between us and Mount San Jacinto, lay the flat valley land, rich with apricot orchards. It was neatly laid out with roads and little houses here and there, but we could see only a general kind of lush carpet, flowery in spring, then green, and then winter-silver. Hemet was westward, invisible.

Our narrow dirt road went straight across the riverbed and up to the valley floor to meet Crest Drive, which curved the whole length of the valley. Directly opposite us, a small grove of eucalyptus trees grew down the slope where Fredrika van Benschoten had a little orange orchard along Crest, and in that grove the Squawman, who had left his land for us to find, had a correct Navaho house built for his bride. It was of adobe, one room and a wide closet and a corner hearth, and it was so heavily plastered that there were no hard corners or lines but a softness to everything under the thick whitewash, as if it were a robe to be worn, firm and protecting but with no part of it to cut or hurt or rub against. The floor was of dark crude tile. The beams across the low ceiling were slender eucalyptus trunks. There was a kind of kitchen in the closet whose wall came up only eye height, and Freda had piped cold water to a small sink. There was no toilet, and since the Squawman had not made an outhouse, I decided the grove was answer enough.

I spent much time in the squaw house, mostly after Tim died. I wrote a couple of books there. I never slept there, strange to say, but would go down from Bareacres in the mornings. I always took a thermos of broth or a cool drink, and about 11:00 I'd go out and look up across the riverbed and see my home there, sometimes with my two little girls waving from the west terrace, with a neighbor to watch them until I got back. The trees Tim and I had planted back of the house and down into the canyon were thriving: sycamores, eucalyptus, tough cottonwoods.

When Tim and I bought the place, with a veteran's bonus of $2,000 plus $225 we borrowed (we were dead broke after his illness made us leave Switzerland in 1938 when World War II got under way), it was flatly undesirable, even according to the realtor who showed it to us. It had been owned by a shady fellow said to be a degraded government Indian trader, an army officer, whose Navaho woman followed him to

Hemet Valley. He bought what we called Bareacres twenty years later, but she, of course, did not live there, so her relatives unwillingly came from New Mexico and built her a decent house across the riverbed in Freda's grove.

Because of strict caste laws, the Navaho was not only called a lost member of her own tribe but could not have anything to do with the local Indians, the Sobobans, who were beneath her social level. It must have been very lonely for her. The Squawman, as he was always scornfully called, had a lot or some or a few valuable Indian artifacts, depending on who was talking about him to us, and most of them were gone when his body was found in the house and a clean bullet hole showed in the south window. Perhaps it was robbery? Navaho are good shots, we were told. The little house in Freda's grove was empty, with not even a blanket or cup left. Nobody knew "anything." Up on the hill across the dead riverbed the air blew through the unlocked door of the Squawman's house. Everything in it was stolen, gradually and without real harm . . . no vandalism, no ugly dirt, no mischievous fires. It was haunted, for sure.

It looked empty and welcoming when Tim and I first saw it in the kind January sunlight, and we stepped into it past the bullet hole as if it had been waiting. We rented an airy little house near Moreno, toward Riverside, and came every day over the Jack Rabbit Trail around the base of the mountain with two old carpenters Tim found. We shifted a few walls around and screened the long front porch that was held up by six trunks of cedar trees that Indians had brought from Mexico, it was said, for the Squawman.

His rock foundations were good. The porch floors across the north and east sides of the little U-shaped house were of well-poured smooth cement, and there was a big fireplace of rough brownish stone in the living room. We made one room and its porch into a fine studio, and put in another little toilet and lavatory there, and slept on the porch outside, looking east. The kitchen spread out to the east, too, over the old cement porch. Down in the canyon we built a big doghouse, with a fenced yard to fool the coyotes and the occasional lynx. On the west side of the U was an entry and office for me and a bedroom and bath for anybody we liked enough. (Hemet had no motels then, but there was a small adobe hotel behind a half circle of fine palm trees in town.) And in the hollow of the U was the patio, the most delightful one I have ever known—indeed, the heart of the place. French doors opened onto it on all three sides. We paved it with flat stones from the canyon. Tim devised a series of strips of bright canvas on slanted wires that pulled across it at will, so the air and light would stay filtered. We pulled them back and forth according to wind, weather, the time of day.

There were low tables and chairs, all-weather stuff, and two chaise longues that could be beds. A wide Dutch door opened into the kitchen. The south side of the patio was a stone wall perhaps four feet high, and on the terrace above it were cottonwood trees and some sycamores, so that always there was the sound of leaves growing, blowing, falling. The Squawman had started the wall, and we carried it on past the house to make a fine terrace of sandy earth. Tim and I kept native succulents and cacti growing in the wall crevices, and when my girls were small, they played out there in the warm dry winter days, and now and then we put out a croquet set for the long hot summer twilights. And often we pulled the chairbeds out to the terrace in the brilliant August nights and lay naked in the silky air, watching the meteors shoot and tumble in the pure black sky.

Bareacres bordered the Ramona Bowl on the west, where the pageant based on Helen Hunt Jackson's book about Indians was given every year in a lovely little open-air theater. Tim helped rewrite some of the new script, and we maintained an aloof cordiality with the cast every year. The Indian hero was played by a skillful actor from Hollywood, much as summer theater on Long Island is now held together by stage stars who need fresh air and a nice piece of pocket money, and we knew a few visitors like Victor Jory who came to Hemet. Ramona the Beautiful Indian Maiden was always played by a local girl. And the finale of the long afternoon performance was when a posse of thirty or forty of the valley's best horsemen thundered through the amphitheater and up over the eastern horizon and down onto our land! We always had bottles of cold ale, open and ready, for the excited riders on their panting prancing horses. It was fun. . . . We waited to hear the guns sound to the west and then opened bottles as fast as we could. And they would come pouring over, a thunder of hooves, wild yahoo yells. We forgot that they were hunting the Indian Alessandro, poor devil, every afternoon at precisely 4:54 for three weekends. (He, or some other reasonable facsimile, was safely panting in a hidden bunker up the theater hill.)

We stayed aloof from active life in Hemet while Tim was there, because we knew his time was short and he had a lot of painting to do. We made fine firm friends, though, and some of them still live. And later I made many more, when my little girls were starting there. Of course, they don't remember much about people, but they still know how to walk away smoothly and quickly when they meet a rattlesnake and how to listen to what the wild quail mothers say.

Freda stayed my dear friend until she died, a very old woman, the last of all her group of strange witty people who seemed to take Tim and me for granted as a part of their own very private lives. And there was Spittin Stringer, who lived in the cottage at our turn off Crest Drive down into the riverbed and on up homeward. Spittin was called that, of course, because he spat a lot. He was the only man we ever met who had gone to France in World War I and then back to Oklahoma without setting foot off dry land. He knew this was a fact because he had just gone with his buddies into a big dark room that had bumped along the road a long time and then they had gotten off and started fighting. There was no arguing about a fact like that. What's more, nobody in his whole family could rightly remember how many kids there were. He said around thirteen. His wife couldn't rightly recall either, and if she had ever counted she would not admit it in front of Spittin. But the oldest boy, J.B., said flatly it was fourteen.

J.B. used to pose for Tim, once he and his mother had walked up the hot hill together so that she could see if we were decent. When I met her at the door, she had on a store-bought dress and shoes, but she took off the killers when she saw I was barefoot and went back with them in her hand, satisfied that J.B. would be all right. Though I never saw her smile, the next time I passed she called out, "Hi ya! Still got mah bar' feet!" and stuck one big muddy toe out from behind the washtub by the door.

When J.B. enlisted, Spittin could not think of what the initials might be for. J.B. was simply his oldest boy's name. And on second thought, maybe his, too. So Tim suggested putting Joseph Benjamin on his papers to satisfy the army, and perhaps he is still alive to remember that J.B. might as well stand for that as anything else. Tim painted one unforgettable picture of him, a thick young boy sitting dully, vacantly, with one hand on his knee holding a green Coke bottle. Tim called it *Kola High*.

On the other side of our turnoff, up on a knoll in a grove of trees, was the Lee house. It was something of a palace, at least compared with Spittin's place or Bare-acres or even Freda's prim little white house behind the orange trees on Crest Drive. The younger son of its owners lived there with his wife and a burgeoning family, and they raised turkeys and a few noisy beautiful peacocks and stayed pretty much to themselves, the way we did. Later, though, my girls and theirs were peers, and their mother Isabel became a quietly true-forever person in my life.

And over all of us rose proud San Jacinto Mountain, sacred to many Indians of its own and other tribes. The Jack Rabbit Trail snaked around its west side, between Hemet and Moreno, and it seemed to hold the raw steep slopes up almost like an invisible wall. The Indians called it a hot mountain, and steaming water burst out of it, more or less controlled for human bathing, in places like Gilman Springs and Soboba Springs and even downtown in the little town of San Jacinto just outside the Indian reservation. Once when I was about ten, relatives came from the Midwest to spend the winter at the Vosburg Inn so that an uncle could "take the baths," and I was embarrassed to have my aunt tell us how Mrs. Vosburg cut up her very fat husband's worn trousers to make clothes for all her small children. Years later one of the Vosburgs was a very beautiful Ramona in the pageant, and I helped with her makeup and never told her what I knew about her father's pants.

A man named Leonardo came often to help us. He was a Pala Indian from the agrarian tribe farther south, but had lost caste by taking up with a Soboban girl. He was cut off from his tribe, and gradually I watched him turn heavy and morose. He was always courteous to me but did not really see me, the way one does not see every leaf on a tree. He loved Tim but would not pose for him. Now and then he drove his girl and their little son Cowboy over to see us in his shabby truck. Cowboy was a dimpled brown nugget, but we only smiled at each other. The girl was silent, unsmiling but not hostile. Leonardo and Tim talked in his studio. Then they would go away, without any words to me but a quick wave and a smile between the two men.

After Tim died, Leonardo returned a few times and cut back some branches in the cottonwoods and made the little tool shed outside the kitchen very tidy. But he grew heavier, and I knew that he was drinking much of the time instead of only for the few religious retreats that the Sobobans were allowed to mix in with their Catholic celebrations at Saint Hyacinth's Chapel on the reservation. And, of course, every year it was almost as ritualistic to round up him and a few other gifted braves for fire fighting. They were sold or perhaps given spiked gallons of sweet muscatel wine, fixed with a half pint of straight alcohol to fill the drained tops. A friend who ran the local bar showed us how this was done.

The men got drunk very fast, and the one cop and the judge who was also the bartender knew when to move in. I felt as shocked as I ever have in my life, and as disgusted. But it was considered fair play there in those days, when good fire fighters were as much a need as water itself and the best ones could be had for a gallon of spiked wine and a couple of nights in jail to make their indenture legal. The awful thing was that every time it happened, it got easier for the men to *stay* drunk, of course, so that after several seasons Leonardo was half lit most of the time, with a fat body and a bitter dull face, no more the lithe man who ran up our road with a flashing smile when he saw Tim wave from the big studio window.

Another fine friend was Arnold. He was always thin, although I am sure he had drunk his fair share of rotgut all over the world. He had been a desert rat for many years, the kind of shadowy drifting loner who becomes almost dust colored—protective coloration, it is called in toads and mice and serpents, and the few real desert rats I have met were the same. By the time he came to be our friend and protector, he had married a little round brown girl named Lena and they had two little round brown daughters, but he still wore dust-colored cotton clothes, and his eyes were as hard and colorless as stone, except when they smiled at Tim and now and then toward me.

Arnold knew more about native desert plants than anyone I ever heard of, and while he was the caretaker up at the Ramona Bowl, it was a kind of secret paradise for botanists and crackpot gardeners who came to watch him plant the unplantables and whom he in turn watched like a hawk, because they almost always tried to steal some of his cuttings. It was a game they all played, and Arnold reported every sneaky trick, every artful dodge, of this unending tournament of trickery among the famous people who came to watch him. He turned weeds into jewels, for sure.

After Tim died, Arnold buried the little tin box of clinkers [Tim's ashes] under an enormous hanging rock. I said, "Let's go up to the Rim of the World and let the winds catch them," but he said, "Nope," and simply walked off. I knew it was all right, and went back to Bareacres and waited, and when he came back, we had a good nip of whiskey.

Arnold did a hitch with the Seabees, and I felt responsible for Lena and the little dumplings, for a time anyway. Then they met him someplace up north, and I never heard from him again, except that he is still clear and strong in my heart.

That is the way Bareacres is, of course. I am told that the fine pure air that first drew us there, half mountain and half desert, is now foul with smog and that the rich carpet of fruit trees we looked down on is solid with RVs and trailer parks. One block on Main Street is now in the *Guinness Book of World Records,* or maybe it is *Ripley's Believe It or Not:* something like 182 banks and savings-and-loan offices on that sleepy little stretch of sidewalk! And there are almost a hundred doctors, most of them connected with "convalescent homes" of varying status and opulence. And Crest Drive is lined with million-dollar villas, with the subdivision where Bareacres was (a "ninety-acre hell of red-hot rocks and rattlesnakes," as one New Yorker described it to us after a lost weekend there) the most snobbish and stylish area between Palm Springs and Los Angeles.

That is the way it is, I say, and I do not grieve or even care, any more than I did when Arnold went up the hill with the little box. I have taken and been given more than can ever be known that is heartwarming and fulfilling forever from that piece of wild haunted untillable land we named Bareacres for a time. No doubt roads have been cut into it and rocks have been blasted away, but I know that the contours cannot change much in a few hundred years in that country. And meanwhile the ghosts are there, even of the sick sad Indians who went to lie in the magic lithium waters of the spring, and even of the poor Squawman with a bullet in his heart, and of my own mother who loved the place . . . they are all there to cleanse and watch over it. They, and many more of us, keep an eye on things so that time itself can stay largely unheeded, as anyone will know who spends more than a few minutes in country like Bareacres.

There are many pockets of comfort and healing on this planet, and I have touched a few of them, but only once have I been able to stay as long and learn and be told as much as there on the southeast edge of Hemet Valley.

When I decided I could not stay there alone with my young girls and then had to decide further that I could not pretend to be an absentee owner, it did not hurt me at all to sell it. I felt serene about it then, and I do now. I had found what I needed there, and now other people will. I do not care how many millions of dollars Bareacres is now worth, nor how many days of smog alert there are each month in the little valley. I do not have any of that money, but I still breathe sweet fine air. My mind and my heart are bursting with unsuspected scents and notions and strange whiffs from other places, and I would like to write ten thousand times more than any human could about that one spot in my own tiny cosmos! All I dare hope, with perhaps some embarrassment for this unabashed gluttony, is that other people can open long-locked doors in their memories and enjoy some such rediscoveries of bliss and pain and beauty and foolishness and general enjoyment of our human condition.

Glen Ellen, California, 1984

ANSWER IN THE AFFIRMATIVE

Yesterday I thought about Mr. Ardamanian and the time I let him make love to me.

I say "make love," but it was not that, exactly. It was quite beyond maleness and femaleness. It was a strange thing, one I seldom think of, not because I am ashamed but because it never bothers me. When I do think back upon it, I am filled with a kind of passive wonder that I should have let it happen and that it never bothered me, for I am not the kind of woman who stands still under the hands of an unloved man, nor am I in any way the kind who willy-nilly invites such treatment.

There is a novel by Somerset Maugham in which an actress lets a stranger sleep with her for one night in a train. As I recall it, she never manages to call up any native shame about this queer adventure but instead comes to recollect it with a certain smugness, pleased with her own wild daring. I do not feel smug about Mr. Ardamanian's caresses; until yesterday, I believed myself merely puzzled by their happening, or at least their happening to *me*.

Yesterday, I had to make a long drive alone in the car. It was a hundred miles or so. I was tired before I started, and filled with a bleak solitariness that gradually became self-conscious, so that before I had passed through the first big town and got out into the vineyards again I was, in spite of myself, thinking of my large bones, my greying hair, my occasional deep weariness at being forty years old and harassed as most forty-year-old women are by overwork, too many bills, outmoded clothes. I thought of ordering something extravagant for myself, like a new suit—black, or perhaps even dark red. Then I thought that I had gained some pounds lately, as always when I am a little miserable, and I began to reproach myself: I was turning slothful, I was slumping, I was neglecting my fine femaleness in a martyr-like and indulgent mood of hyperwifeliness, supermotherliness. I was a fool, I said bitterly, despondently, as I sped with caution through another town.

I began to think about myself younger, slimmer, less harried, and less warped by the world's weight. I thought with a kind of tolerant amusement that when I was in my twenties I never noticed my poundage, taking for granted that it was right. Now, I reminded myself as I shot doggedly through the vineyards and then a little town and then the peach orchards near Ontario—now I shuddered, no matter how gluttonously, from every pat of butter, and winced away from every encouraging Martini as if it held snake venom. Still I was fat, and I was tired and old, and when had it happened? Just those few years ago, I had been slender, eager, untwisted by fatigue.

I had been a good woman, too. I had never lusted for any man but the one I loved. That was why it was so strange, the time Mr. Ardamanian came to the house with my rug.

We were living near a college where my husband taught, in a beautiful shack held together by layers of paint. I was alone much of the time, and I buzzed like a happy bee through the three rooms, straightening and polishing them. I was never ill at ease or wistful for company, being young, healthy, and well-loved.

We were very poor, and my mother said, "Jane, why don't you have Mr. Ardamanian take a few of these old rugs of mine and make them into one of his nice hash-rugs for your living room? It wouldn't cost much, and anything he can do for our family he will love to do."

I thought of Mr. Ardamanian, and of the twenty years or so of seeing him come, with great dignity, to roll up this rug and that rug in our house—for my mother had a great many—and then walk down to his car lightly under the balanced load. He knew us all, first me and my little sister, then the two younger siblings, and my grandmother and the various cooks we had, and even Father. He came in and out of the house, and watched us grow, year after year, while he cleaned and mended rugs for us. Mother told us his name was that of a great family in Armenia, and, true enough, every time since then when I have seen it in books or on shopfronts, mostly for rugs, I have known it to be part of his pride.

He was small, very old and grey, it seemed, when I was a little girl. He had a high but quiet voice, deep flashing eyes, and strong, white, even teeth. He called my mother Lady. That always pleased me. He did not say Missus, or even Madam, or Lady So-and-So. He said *Lady*. He dressed in good grey suits, and although he rolled up big rugs and carried them lightly to his car, he was never dusty.

Mother went ahead with her generous plan, and Mr. Ardamanian did come to the little house near the college, bearing upon his old shoulders a fairly handsome hash-rug made of scraps. He stood at the door under the small pink roses that climbed everywhere, and he looked as he had always looked to me over those twenty years.

He bowed, said, "Your lady mother has sent me," and came in.

I felt warm and friendly toward him, this strange familiar from my earliest days, and as the two of us silently laid the good solid rug upon the painted floor, under my sparse furniture, I was pleased to be with him. We finished the moving, and the rug looked fine, very rich and thick, if not what I was used to at home—the big, worn Baluchistans, the glowing Bokharas.

Then—I do not quite remember, but I think it started by his saying, in his rather high, courteous voice, the one I knew over so many years, "You are married now. You look very happy. You look like a woman at last, and you have grown a little here . . . not yet enough here . . ." and he began very delicately, very surely, to touch me on my waist, my shoulder, my small young breasts.

It was, and I know it even now, a wonderful feeling. It was as if he were a sculptor.

He had the most fastidiously intelligent hands I had ever met with, and he used them with the instinct of an artist moving over something he understood creatively, something alive, deathless, pulsating with beauty but beyond desire.

I stood, silent and entranced, for I do not know how long, while Mr. Ardamanian seemed to mold my outlines into classical loveliness. I looked with a kind of adoration at his remote, aged face, and felt his mysteriously knowing hands move, calm as God's, over my body. I was, for those moments of complete easy-breathing silence, as beautiful as any statue ever carved in stone or wood or jade. I was beyond reproach.

I heard my husband come up the path through the mimosa trees. The old man's hands dropped away. I went to the door, unruffled, and I introduced the two men. Then Mr. Ardamanian went gracefully away, and it was not until an hour or so later that I began to remember the strange scene and to wonder what would have happened if he had led me gently to the wide couch and made love to me in the way I, because of my youngness, most easily understood. I felt a vague shame, perhaps, because of my upbringing and my limited spiritual vocabulary, and the whole thing puzzled me in a very minor and peripheral way. There had been no faintest spark of lust between us, no fast urgent breath, no need. . . .

So I found myself thinking of all this yesterday, alone in the car. I felt bitter, seeing myself, toward the end of the tiring trip, as a thickening exhausted lump without desire or desirability. I thought fleetingly of the tall, slim, ripe woman who had stood under those ancient hands.

When I got to my mother's house, I needed quiet and a glass of sherry and reassuring family talk to jolt me out of a voluptuous depression. Mind you, it was not being forty that really puzzled and hurt me; it was simply that I had got that far along without realizing that I could indeed grow thicker and careless, and let myself eat and drink too much, and wear white gloves with a hole in them, and in general become slovenly.

Almost the first thing my mother said was that she was waiting for Mr. Ardamanian. I jerked in my chair. It seemed too strange, to have thought about him that morning for the first time in many years. Suddenly I was very upset, for of all things in the world I did not want that old man who had once found me worth touching to see me tired, mopish, middle-aged. I felt cruelly cheated at this twist and I cried out, "But he can't be alive still! Mother, he must be a hundred years old."

She looked at me with some surprise at my loud protest and said, "Almost. But he is still a good rug man."

I was stunned. It seemed a proof to me of all my dour thoughts during the long ride. Oh, the hell with it, I thought; what can it matter to an old ghost that I'm no longer young and beautiful, if once I was, to his peculiar vision? "That hideous hash-rug fell apart," I said ungraciously, and paid no heed to my mother's enigmatic gaze.

When he came, he did look somewhat older—or, rather, drier—but certainly not fifteen or eighteen years so. His temples had sunk a little, and his bright, even teeth were too big for his mouth, but his dark eyes flashed politely, and he insisted on moving furniture and carrying in the clean rolls of Oriental carpet without any help. He performed neatly, a graceful old body indeed.

"Do not move, Lady," he said to my mother, and he whisked a small rug under her footstool without seeming to lift it. I stood about aimlessly, watching him and thinking about him and myself, in a kind of misery.

At the end, when he had carried the dirty rugs out to his car and had told my mother when he would come back, he looked at me, and then stepped quite close.

"Which one are you?" he asked.

"I'm the oldest," I said, wondering what he would remember of me.

And immediately I saw that it was everything, everything—not of me as a little growing child but of me his creation. His eyes blazed, and fell in an indescribable pattern from my cheeks to my shoulders to my breasts to the hidden cave of my navel, and then up over the bones of my ribs and down again to the softened hollows of my waist. We were back in the silent little house near the college, and I was filled with a sense of complete relaxation, to have this old man still recognize me, and to have him do with his eyes what once he had so strangely and purely done with his hands. I knew that it was something that would never happen again. What is more, I knew that when I was an old woman it would strengthen me, as it strengthened me that very minute when I was tired and forty and thick, that once Mr. Ardamanian had made me into a statue.

The question about seduction still remains, of course, in an academic way. Would he have done any more to me than what he did, and, indeed, would anything more have been possible—not from the standpoint of his indubitable virility, no matter what his age, but from that of our spiritual capacity to pile nectar into the brimming cup? I can never know, nor do I care.

I was filled with relief, standing passively there before my mother in the familiar room. I felt strong and fresh.

He smiled his gleaming smile, bowed to my mother, and then said directly to me, "Lady, it is good that I met you again. Goodbye."

When he had gone, as poised as a praying mantis under his last roll of rugs, my mother said, pretending to be cross, "I thought *I* was his Lady, not you!" She smiled remotely.

Mother and I talked together through the afternoon, about children and bills and such, but not about Mr. Ardamanian. There seemed no need to, then or ever.

FROM IN THE BEGINNING

By the time a story five thousand years old, or three thousand, comes to our ears, it has lost its trappings. It is as simple as any story can possibly be, because it is like a piece of driftwood that once has been a tree, with all its boughs and twiglets—a silvery noble fragment now, with faint carvings on it from the long-dead sea worms, but no other outward sign of its illimitable travel.

The Bible is like that, perhaps more so than any other collection of the stories of man. Every old language, though, has its revered lot of them. One mouth after another has discarded ornamentation in the telling; one hurried or persecuted scribe after another has cut off this little descriptive phrase and that little prettiness. What is left for us to read is as straightforward as Genesis, as direct as a Chinese poem.

The problem, then, is whether we are ready to read it. The sins and omissions of everything we have learned about it, from our devout grandmothers to our glib professors, tend to push us away from it into the safe void of disinterest and boredom. Through all our young years we learn the emasculated legends of Joseph's coat and baby Moses floating in the bulrushes, and we shun the hints of pain and awfulness in the stories of Jesus Christ. Then we retreat angrily, from what we have been told by our elders, or have read dutifully in the family Bible; we laugh in resentment, and call ourselves agnostic with all the enthusiasm of adolescence. That makes it easy and delightful to ape our teachers, a little later, and to agree, with only a sneaked glance over our shoulder at Grandmother's patient ghost, that the Bible is indeed "literature," a fascinating collection of myths and fairy tales.

How good it is to be free of the intellectual restrictions of Sunday School! And how disturbing we find it, a little later, to discover a sincere wistfulness, a wish confessed half-mockingly that we could feel devout, credulous, stupid enough to read the Book as some older people seem to! We hate to confess such a lacuna in our chain of culture.

Many people, like me, content themselves with the surety that one day, soon or late, they will be able to read, and mark, and inwardly digest the great feast that awaits. They will hardly suspect, as I did not, that the awaited realization of a true wish may come through some such a thing as the printed word *gluttony*.

It happened to me when I decided to make a collection of feasts that I had read about. I knew that I must include the first one, about the Apple on the Tree. I could find it, in the Bible I unthinkingly include among my other reference books because of my early and my later educations: easy, because I went to a school where we were taught more about the tribes of Israel and their battles than we ever suspected about Napoleon, or Sherman's march through Georgia, or Bismarck. I found the passages I wanted, and then, in the New Testament, the ones about the miracles of the loaves and fishes, the water changed to wine, all of those. . . .

And it grew clear to me that the priests and the storytellers, the great singers and the teachers, everywhere and always showed their people real food, real wine, to prove to them the truths of spiritual nourishment. A great catch of fishes from an empty sea, or water springing from a dry stone: such things were told of over and over to sustain men whose hope of Heaven dwindled and grew faint as their stomachs cried out.

I read more, excited at last to have found for myself a thread to follow through the long books. Then I remembered about concordances, on a hot gray day in July, 1945, an important day for me, in the New York Public Library, with the dim roar of a rainstorm outside the enormous room and all about me the rustle and squint and faint sour smell of reading. I found two thick black books on the reference shelves, and sat looking at them for several minutes, timid and inept. Finally I decided to search for the word Gluttony. And that was the beginning of pleasure and joy and great strength for me, because suddenly I was able, after long waiting, to read the Bible and know why and how, without duty to my grandmother or my professor or anything in the world but my own awakened understanding.

It was dark in the wet streets when I went away that night, but I was not tired, and the next days I came back and feasted more, as after a long fast. [. . .]

GASTEREA, LOVELIEST OF MUSES

THE BROTHERS

Once there were two brothers. They were twins, but their nine closed months were all they had in common.

One brother, the elder by some minutes, was a big fellow, red-faced and hairy. He spent all his days afield and swiftly grew into a great hunter, and at night he made into savoury stews the day's killing. His father loved the stews and his elder son who made them.

The younger brother was his mother's love. In him she admired her own sly, clever ways. He stayed by her side and learned from her to make lentil pottage, which he could sell each day, and profitably, to the workers.

One day the hunting was very bad, and the sun too hot. Then chill came suddenly into the darkening air, and the older brother, still far afield and very tired, turned empty-handed homeward. No fine stew tonight to cheer him and to warm his old man's innards! Afterwards no rest by the fire for the two of them! He sighed and longed to be home, full and warm.

The younger brother sat by a great pot of his steaming soup, with hard sour bread in a pile beside him. The day was almost over, with no more labourers to buy food from him. But he sat on, quiet and sure, waiting for what he knew must happen sometime, and perhaps today.

Suddenly his toes curled under him with scorn and fear, for he saw his elder brother. The great lazy spendthrift lout! He smiled and waited.

And you know what happened. Jacob was the little crafty fellow who sold lentil soup, and Esau was the hungry man who gave his birthright for a bowl of it. And Jacob's mother Rebekah was, like many women, a good cook and a good teacher of cookery for one purpose or another, but never for pleasure. She taught her dear son to be the father of all (almost all) *restaurateurs*.

Her other son she never understood, nor his father Isaac neither, for they would spend all day catching a deer, simply that they might cook it and eat it and then lie by the fire and talk about it. They may have been the first gastronomers.

FROM THE DOWNWARD PATH

What is sauce for the goose is not always the same thing for the gander, and can even finish him off, in one way or another. Once, for me, a potential romance came to a quiet finale when I misjudged the persuasion of an accompaniment to a leg of lamb which I thought would make any further appraising unnecessary. I still believe that the sauce itself was perfection, and that my prospective table mate did not live up to his carefully nurtured promise.

He and three staunch companions, obviously believing in the safety of numbers, came for a weekend of gastronomical frolic to my ranch in the dry rocky hills near Hemet, in California, to gauge me as a possible asset to their dedicated interest in *la bonne table*. They were cultural light-miles away from their home base in San Francisco . . . or perhaps I should say home plate, for they were skilled trenchermen and eminent in the several clubs in the City which, in those days before "gourmet" became a ridiculous term, were temples to food and wine. They arrived laden with ripe cheeses, prosciutto, little round tins of truffles both black and white, flat loaves of sourdough bread from the Wharf, all in case of a probable dearth of viands in my wilderness. They were protective of my intended victim, and of course themselves.

I, meanwhile, had prepared for their first meal a quietly artful rebuttal, in case that was what they were asking for. They were used to several wines and several courses. During my own limit of three very simple sections of dinner we would drink two unknown light beers, one from a small brewery near Anaheim which somehow had survived Prohibition and one from lower California. There was plenty of a respectable dry champagne from Northern California chilling as needed, and of course there was stronger stuff for any lapse from their studied alcoholic grace.

First, as I remember, we would eat chilled marinated green beans and tomato, with a little anchovy somewhere to tease the palate for the meat to follow, for it would be lamb. And after the meat, which I fully intended to be superb, we would eat a refreshing compote of summer fruits, and then some of the cheeses the three musketeers had brought along with their fine d'Artagnan.

The lamb, a curry, was to be eaten with plenty of its sauce and white Indian rice, already rubbed and ready to be steamed dry and pearly. Since the whole course around its dish would be subtle, the classical condiments were limited, and correctly bland and suave: toasted almonds in slivers, currants poached fat in dry vermouth, a green-peach chutney. I took all this in an easy but serious stride, knowing that in some way it was to change my life.

It is almost embarrassing to admit, so many lives later, that I cannot find a recipe for the dish I spent two days preparing and have often made since then. I know I did not invent it. Its principle is to half-roast a chicken or piece of young meat like veal or lamb, meanwhile preparing a strong and ample court-bouillon, and then drown the meat in the soup and simmer it gently until tender but not overdone. Then the broth is strained and made into a thin sauce, with flour and the usual adjusting of salt and so on, and a moderate amount of the best procurable curry powder. The meat is dropped once more into the deep pot of deceptively gentle gravy and is left overnight in its bath. About an hour before it is to be served, it is brought once more to a thorough simmer, in what has become an insidiously pungent sauce. (If for personal reasons of aesthetics one wished to change the rather insipid color of this brew, I suppose turmeric would be the answer, although I know of it only from books. . . .) To serve, the meat is carved and placed nicely either on a bed of hot cooked rice, or on a platter with the rice served apart, and is loused modestly with some of the sauce. The rest of this is served separately, in a generous bowl.

For me, the meat has always been unusually succulent, and the interesting thing about the whole leisurely and comparatively undemanding process is that the flavor of curry, always delicate in spite of its increasing warmth, permeates the whole dish instead of remaining as a kind of mask or coating, a wild conglomeration of textures whose basic natures are completely hidden.

That time in Hemet I felt alarmingly complacent, if not even somewhat triumphant. Before the gentlemen arrived for their picaresque outing, I tasted the thin sauce several times as it waited in its deep pot around and over the leg of lamb, and I found it correctly sophisticated. It was light but tricky, almost elusive in its impact, and with a very fortunate consistency which was the obvious result of my skill at the stove. Irresistible seemed the word.

The four men arrived on time, relaxed and laden with the goodies which subconsciously served for them as survival kits. Eventually all but the chosen one, aloof and discreetly predatory as always, roamed up to the high lookout in the hills to see if the sun would sink again in the right place. They carried rattlesnake sticks, and some correctly chilled champagne, for emergencies.

My suitor, anxious to play his part for them and perhaps for me, puttered here and there about the kitchen and the big studio where we would dine, checking to see if I had put the right glasses in the right places and if the icebox was properly cold. It was mildly annoying to my vanity to be quizzed so thoroughly and silently, but I told myself that I should grow used to such things. His trained nose told him that curry had been used somewhere lately, and he looked slightly let down at the plainness of the three bowls of condiments he found under a napkin. I smiled happily: his exquisite palate would understand them, once he tasted the lamb, for I knew it would be among the most cunning dishes he had ever been served, in his decades as a well-publicized but honest disciple of the Tenth Muse.

Gradually I found myself irked by his snoopiness, after several more peerings into cupboards and drawers. It is possible at this point that I expected him to seize his few unchaperoned moments to make some sort of attack, no matter how covert, on my availability. By the time he hit his real target, the deep pot of delicate curry simmering, ready for its final drama, I was simmering in rhythm, and when he picked up a big spoon, lifted the lid, and without a by-your-leave cooled and sipped at some of the sauce, murmuring a perfunctory you-don't-mind-do-you, I did mind.

He sipped again.

"This won't do at all, my dear," he said gently, pityingly. "This won't do. Alex and Bob and Armitage . . . well, you know who they are. This is . . . do you call this a curry? I am sorry. Truly. But we still have time."

I remember how I leaned hard on the edge of the pine table. I felt boneless with disappointment. This man, this high priest of hedonism as practiced in a city where I thought I would like to live as one of the handmaidens if not even a subpriestess, this near-god, did not recognize the deliberate confrontation with a subtlety committed to honor him. He was impervious to the insidious magic of the lengthy preparation of it, and the deep gentle ring of it on his vaunted palate. Feet of clay . . . Operation Feet of Clay, I said resignedly.

I said, "You mean there is time to do something?" I did not believe any of it. "There is only an hour or so. I have been making this for two days. It is really quite . . . that is, when we taste the meat . . . "

"Quickly," he commanded, like a surgeon who is stopped on a highway to attend a violent accident. "The curry powder. Veeraswami, of course. Some hot white wine. Dry. Anything. Hurry, for God's sake. They'll be horrified by this. They'll be starved."

And so on, and I watched my muddied idol, the man I had dreamed might eat across from me in my old age or at least sip pabulum somewhere with me in some kind of mutual rhythm, mix a thick paste of raw curry powder which was *not* from London, stir it almost brutally into the beautiful suave sauce I had concocted, and push the leg of lamb impatiently about in the darkening pool of juice.

When Alex and Bob and Armitage thundered down the hill, and we had tidied ourselves in our various ways (they wearing cravats from a far-off dining club in my honor), and when the usual preprandial rituals had been observed and the first course tossed off, we ate the juicy slices of lamb and the excellent rice, all covered with a real tongue-torch of "curry sauce," almost a tear-bringer. I was complimented on the unexpected succulence of the meat, which one of the gentlemen observed had caught a tiny flavor of curry even in its faintly pink interior, for some odd reason. (Lambs are very sensitive, I thought sardonically. Then I took a closer look at him, as a possible successor in my line of *gastronomes manqués*, but it was a short-lived interest. . . .)

The condiments were of course pitiably inadequate in the face of such a blazing assault, and everyone was courteously silent about them, almost abashed: a three-boy curry to men used to a twelve-boy or, for visiting Boston nabobs, an occasional twenty-one-boy! In a kindly way, my choice of light beers was commended.

I played my role as a well-meaning but untutored country ex-lass, and I felt disappointed and lonely. I had been a goose. Alex and Bob and Armitage could take their white-plumed gander home again, unmenaced. But I knew and I still know that the sauce that first lapped gently against the sides of that piece of meat, so tender, so carefully embalmed, was a gem of great worth, something unexpected in the sea of highly flavored disguises and maskings in our prejudiced careless gastronomy.

Perhaps those men lost more than I did, or perhaps we should leave well enough alone . . . forget sauces entirely? I think not. They are a fine challenge, when treated with respect, even at the risk of blasted expectations of future dalliance in digestive, sexual, and related realms.

In my own case, I learned a great deal about other people's natures as well as mine in this one earnest attempt to combine business with pleasure, and even more about the importance of resolute honesty, when my potential swain reacted as he did to that presumptuous sampling. I know now that I should have said, "Put that spoon down! Close that pot! Please, I mean. I have made a beautiful sly smooth curry such as you fat cats from the Golden Gate have never tasted. You will of course understand it, for you are serious and noted gourmets. So go away. Please, I mean. Stop snooping and *trust* me."

By then, of course . . . from that first betrayal to the final fiery denouement when we sat desperately gulping lager . . . it was clear that the three trenchermen would herd their leader homeward, still unfettered, all of them well fed and safe. I myself felt a delicious relief. Men and women being what they are, I might try again, but the next time I would use provisions other than an artful concoction of broths and spices called a sauce. [. . .]

from LET THE SKY
RAIN POTATOES

The Merry Wives of Windsor

———————————

[. . .] Although few realize it, to be complementary is in itself a compliment. It is a subtle pleasure, like the small exaltation of a beautiful dark woman who finds herself unexpectedly in the company of an equally beautiful blonde. It is what a great chef meant once when he repulsed a consolation.

He was a Frenchman, summoned to London when King Edward VII found that his subjects resented his dining more in Paris than at home.

This great cook one day prepared a dish of soles in such a manner that the guests at Edward's table waited assuredly for a kingly compliment. He was summoned. Their mouths hung open in sated expectation.

"The Château Yquem," said Edward VII, "was excellent."

Later the master chef shrugged, a nonchalance denied by every muscle in his pleased face.

"How could my dish have had a greater compliment?" he demanded, calmly. "His Majesty knows, as I do, that when a dish is perfect, as was my sole tonight, the wine is good. If the dish is lower than perfection, the wine, lacking its complement, tastes weak and poor. So—you see?" [. . .]

I WAS REALLY VERY HUNGRY

I

Once I met a young servant in northern Burgundy who was almost frighteningly fanatical about food, like a medieval woman possessed by a devil. Her obsession engulfed even my appreciation of the dishes she served, until I grew uncomfortable.

It was the off season at the old mill which a Parisian chef had bought and turned into one of France's most famous restaurants, and my mad waitress was the only servant. In spite of that she was neatly uniformed, and showed no surprise at my unannounced arrival and my hot dusty walking clothes.

She smiled discreetly at me, said, "Oh, but certainly!" when I asked if I could lunch there, and led me without more words to a dark bedroom bulging with First Empire furniture, and a new white bathroom.

When I went into the dining room it was empty of humans—a cheerful ugly room still showing traces of the petit bourgeois parlor it had been. There were aspidistras on the mantel; several small white tables were laid with those imitation "peasant-ware" plates that one sees in Paris china stores, and very good crystal glasses; a cat folded under some ferns by the window ledge hardly looked at me; and the air was softly hurried with the sound of high waters from the stream outside.

I waited for the maid to come back. I knew I should eat well and slowly, and suddenly the idea of dry sherry, unknown in all the village bistros of the last few days, stung my throat smoothly. I tried not to think of it; it would be impossible to realize. Dubonnet would do. But not as well. I longed for sherry.

The little maid came into the silent room. I looked at her stocky young body, and her butter-colored hair, and noticed her odd pale voluptuous mouth before I said, "Mademoiselle, I shall drink an apéritif. Have you by any chance—"

"Let me suggest," she interrupted firmly, "our special dry sherry. It is chosen in Spain for Monsieur Paul."

And before I could agree she was gone, discreet and smooth.

She's a funny one, I thought, and waited in a pleasant warm tiredness for the wine.

It was good. I smiled approval at her, and she lowered her eyes, and then looked searchingly at me again. I realized suddenly that in this land of trained nonchalant waiters I was to be served by a small waitress who took her duties seriously. I felt much amused, and matched her solemn searching gaze.

"Today, Madame, you may eat shoulder of lamb in the English style, with baked potatoes, green beans, and a sweet."

My heart sank. I felt dismal, and hot and weary, and still grateful for the sherry.

But she was almost grinning at me, her lips curved triumphantly, and her eyes less palely blue.

"Oh, in *that* case," she remarked as if I had spoken, "in *that* case a trout, of course—a *truite au bleu* as only Monsieur Paul can prepare it!"

She glanced hurriedly at my face, and hastened on. "With the trout, one or two young potatoes—oh, very delicately boiled," she added before I could protest, "very light."

I felt better. I agreed. "Perhaps a leaf or two of salad after the fish," I suggested. She almost snapped at me. "Of course, of course! And naturally our hors d'oeuvres to commence." She started away.

"No!" I called, feeling that I must assert myself now or be forever lost. "No!"

She turned back, and spoke to me very gently. "But Madame has never tasted our hors d'oeuvres. I am sure that Madame will be pleased. They are our specialty, made by Monsieur Paul himself. I am sure," and she looked reproachfully at me, her mouth tender and sad, "I am sure that Madame would be very much pleased."

I smiled weakly at her, and she left. A little cloud of hurt gentleness seemed to hang in the air where she had last stood.

I comforted myself with the sherry, feeling increasing irritation with my own feeble self. Hell! I loathed hors d'oeuvres! I conjured disgusting visions of square glass plates of oily fish, of soggy vegetables glued together with cheap mayonnaise, of rank radishes and tasteless butter. No, Monsieur Paul or not, sad young pale-faced waitress or not, I hated hors d'oeuvres.

I glanced victoriously across the room at the cat, whose eyes seemed closed.

II

Several minutes passed. I was really very hungry.

The door banged open, and my girl came in again, less discreet this time. She hurried toward me.

"Madame, the wine! Before Monsieur Paul can go on—" Her eyes watched my face, which I perversely kept rather glum.

"I think," I said ponderously, daring her to interrupt me, "I think that today, since I am in Burgundy and about to eat a trout," and here I hoped she noticed that I did not mention hors d'oeuvres, "I think I shall drink a bottle of Chablis 1929."

For a second her whole face blazed with joy, and then subsided into a trained mask. I knew that I had chosen well, had somehow satisfied her in a secret and incomprehensible way. She nodded politely and scuttled off, only for another second glancing impatiently at me as I called after her, "Well cooled, please, but not iced."

I'm a fool, I thought, to order a whole bottle. I'm a fool, here all alone and with more miles to walk before I reach Avallon and my fresh clothes and a bed. Then I smiled at myself and leaned back in my solid wide-seated chair, looking obliquely at the prints of Gibson girls, English tavern scenes, and hideous countrysides that hung on the papered walls. The room was warm; I could hear my companion cat purring under the ferns.

The girl rushed in, with flat baking dishes piled up her arms like the plates of a Japanese juggler. She slid them off neatly in two rows onto the table, where they lay steaming up at me, darkly and infinitely appetizing.

"*Mon Dieu!* All for me?" I peered at her. She nodded, her discretion quite gone now and a look of ecstatic worry on her pale face and eyes and lips.

There were at least eight dishes. I felt almost embarrassed, and sat for a minute looking weakly at the fork and spoon in my hand.

"Perhaps Madame would care to start with the pickled herring? It is not like any other. Monsieur Paul prepares it himself, in his own vinegar and wines. It is very good."

I dug out two or three brown filets from the dish, and tasted. They were truly unlike any others, truly the best I had ever eaten, mild, pungent, meaty as fresh nuts.

I realized the maid had stopped breathing, and looked up at her. She was watching me, or rather a gastronomic X ray of the herring inside me, with a hypnotized glaze in her eyes.

"Madame is pleased?" she whispered softly.

I said I was. She sighed, and pushed a sizzling plate of broiled endive toward me, and disappeared.

I had put a few dull green lentils on my plate, lentils scattered with minced fresh herbs and probably marinated in tarragon vinegar and walnut oil, when she came into the dining room again with the bottle of Chablis in a wine basket.

"Madame should be eating the little baked onions while they are hot," she remarked over her shoulder as she held the bottle in a napkin and uncorked it. I obeyed meekly, and while I watched her I ate several more than I had meant to. They were delicious, simmered first in strong meat broth, I think, and then drained and broiled with olive oil and new-ground pepper.

I was fascinated by her method of uncorking a vintage wine. Instead of the Burgundian procedure of infinite and often exaggerated precautions against touching or tipping or jarring the bottle, she handled it quite nonchalantly, and seemed to be careful only to keep her hands from the cool bottle itself, holding it sometimes by the basket and sometimes in a napkin. The cork was very tight, and I thought for a minute that she would break it. So did she: her face grew tight, and did not loosen until she had slowly worked out the cork and wiped the lip. Then she poured an inch of wine in a glass, turned her back to me like a priest taking Communion, and drank it down. Finally some was poured for me, and she stood with the bottle in her hand and her full lips drooping until I nodded a satisfied yes. Then she pushed another of the plates toward me, and almost rushed from the room.

I ate slowly, knowing that I should not be as hungry as I ought to be for the trout, but knowing too that I had never tasted such delicate savory morsels. Some were hot, some cold. The wine was light and cool. The room, warm and agreeably empty under the rushing sound of the stream, became smaller as I grew used to it.

My girl hurried in again, with another row of plates up one arm, and a large bucket dragging at the other. She slid the plates deftly onto the table, and drew a deep breath as she let the bucket down against the table leg.

"Your trout, Madame," she said excitedly. I looked down at the gleam of the fish curving through its limited water. "But first a good slice of Monsieur Paul's *pâté*. Oh yes, oh yes, you will be very sorry if you miss this. It is rich, but appetizing, and not at all too heavy. Just this one morsel!"

And willy-nilly I accepted the large gouge she dug from a terrine. I prayed for ten normal appetites and thought with amused nostalgia of my usual lunch of cold milk and fruit as I broke off a crust of bread and patted it smooth with the paste. Then I forgot everything but the exciting faint decadent flavor in my mouth.

I beamed up at the girl. She nodded, but from habit asked if I was satisfied. I beamed again, and asked, simply to please her, "Is there not a faint hint of *marc*, or perhaps cognac?"

"*Marc*, Madame!" And she awarded me the proud look of a teacher whose pupil has showed unexpected intelligence. "Monsieur Paul, after he has taken equal parts of goose breast and the finest pork, and broken a certain number of egg yolks into them, and ground them *very*, very fine, cooks all with seasoning for some three hours. *But*," she pushed her face nearer, and looked with ferocious gloating at the *pâté* inside me, her eyes like X rays, "he never stops stirring it! Figure to yourself the work of it—stir, stir, never stopping!

"Then he grinds in a suspicion of nutmeg, and then adds, very thoroughly, a glass of *marc* for each hundred grams of *pâté*. And is Madame not pleased?"

Again I agreed, rather timidly, that Madame was much pleased, that Madame had never, indeed, tasted such an unctuous and exciting *pâté*. The girl wet her lips delicately, and then started as if she had been pin-stuck.

"But the trout! My God, the trout!" She grabbed the bucket, and her voice grew higher and more rushed.

"Here is the trout, Madame. You are to eat it *au bleu*, and you should never do so if you had not seen it alive. For if the trout were dead when it was plunged into the *court bouillon* it would not turn blue. So, naturally, it must be living."

I knew all this, more or less, but I was fascinated by her absorption in the momentary problem. I felt quite ignorant, and asked her with sincerity, "What about the trout? Do you take out its guts before or after?"

"Oh, the trout!" She sounded scornful. "Any trout is glad, truly glad, to be prepared by Monsieur Paul. His little gills are pinched, with one flash of the knife he is empty, and then he curls in agony in the *bouillon* and all is over. And it is the curl you must judge, Madame. A false *truite au bleu* cannot curl."

She panted triumph at me, and hurried out with the bucket.

III

She *is* a funny one, I thought, and for not more than two or three minutes I drank wine and mused over her. Then she darted in, with the trout correctly blue and agonizingly curled on a platter, and on her crooked arm a plate of tiny boiled potatoes and a bowl.

When I had been served and had cut off her anxious breathings with an assurance that the fish was the best I had ever tasted, she peered again at me and at the sauce in the bowl. I obediently put some of it on the potatoes: no fool I, to ruin *truite au bleu* with a hot concoction! There was more silence.

"Ah!" she sighed at last. "I knew Madame would feel thus! Is it not the most beautiful sauce in the world with the flesh of a trout?"

I nodded incredulous agreement.

"Would you like to know how it is done?"

I remembered all the legends of chefs who guarded favorite recipes with their very lives, and murmured yes.

She wore the exalted look of a believer describing a miracle at Lourdes as she told me, in a rush, how Monsieur Paul threw chopped chives into hot sweet butter and then poured the butter off, how he added another nut of butter and a tablespoonful of thick cream for each person, stirred the mixture for a few minutes over a slow fire, and then rushed it to the table.

"So simple?" I asked softly, watching her lighted eyes and the tender lustful lines of her strange mouth.

"So simple, Madame! But," she shrugged, "you know, with a master—"

I was relieved to see her go: such avid interest in my eating wore on me. I felt released when the door closed behind her, free for a minute or so from her victimization. What would she have done, I wondered, if I had been ignorant or unconscious of any fine flavors?

She was right, though, about Monsieur Paul. Only a master could live in this isolated mill and preserve his gastronomic dignity through loneliness and the sure financial loss of unused butter and addled eggs. Of course there was the stream for his fish, and I knew his *pâtés* would grow even more edible with age; but how could he manage to have a thing like roasted lamb ready for any chance patron? Was the consuming interest of his one maid enough fuel for his flame?

I tasted the last sweet nugget of trout, the one nearest the blued tail, and poked somnolently at the minute white billiard balls that had been eyes. Fate could not harm me, I remembered winily, for I had indeed dined today, and dined well. Now for a leaf of crisp salad, and I'd be on my way.

The girl slid into the room. She asked me again, in a respectful but gossipy manner, how I had liked this and that and the other things, and then talked on as she mixed dressing for the endive.

"And now," she announced, after I had eaten one green sprig and dutifully pronounced it excellent, "now Madame is going to taste Monsieur Paul's special terrine, one that is not even on the summer menu, when a hundred covers are laid here daily and we have a headwaiter and a wine waiter, and cabinet ministers telegraph for tables! Madame will be pleased."

And heedless of my low moans of the walk still before me, of my appreciation and my unhappily human and limited capacity, she cut a thick heady slice from the terrine of meat and stood over me while I ate it, telling me with almost hysterical pleasure of the wild ducks, the spices, the wines that went into it. Even surfeit could not make me deny that it was a rare dish. I ate it all, knowing my luck, and wishing only that I had red wine to drink with it.

I was beginning, though, to feel almost frightened, realizing myself an accidental victim of these stranded gourmets, Monsieur Paul and his handmaiden. I began to feel that they were using me for a safety valve, much as a thwarted woman relieves herself with tantrums or a fit of weeping. I was serving a purpose, and perhaps a noble one, but I resented it in a way approaching panic.

I protested only to myself when one of Monsieur Paul's special cheeses was cut for me, and ate it doggedly, like a slave. When the girl said that Monsieur Paul himself was preparing a special filter of coffee for me, I smiled servile acceptance: wine and the weight of food and my own character could not force me to argue with maniacs. When, before the coffee came, Monsieur Paul presented me, through his idolater, with the most beautiful apple tart I had ever seen, I allowed it to be cut and served to me. Not a wince or a murmur showed the waitress my distressed fearfulness. With a stuffed careful smile on my face, and a clear nightmare in my head of trussed wanderers prepared for his altar by this hermit-priest of gastronomy, I listened to the girl's passionate plea for fresh pastry dough.

"You cannot, you *cannot*, Madame, serve old pastry!" She seemed ready to beat her breast as she leaned across the table. "Look at that delicate crust! You may feel that you have eaten too much." (I nodded idiotic agreement.) "But this pastry is like feathers—it is like snow. It is in fact good for you, a digestive! And why?" She glared sternly at me. "Because Monsieur Paul did not even open the flour bin until he saw you coming! He could not, he *could* not have baked you one of his special apple tarts with old dough!"

She laughed, tossing back her head and curling her mouth voluptuously.

IV

Somehow I managed to refuse a second slice, but I trembled under her surmise that I was ready for my special filter.

The wine and its fortitude had fled me, and I drank the hot coffee as a suffering man gulps ether, deeply and gratefully.

I remember, then, chatting with surprising glibness, and sending to Monsieur Paul flowery compliments, all of them sincere and well won, and I remember feeling only amusement when a vast glass of *marc* appeared before me and then gradually disappeared, like the light in the warm room full of water-sounds. I felt surprise to be alive still, and suddenly very grateful to the wild-lipped waitress, as if her presence had sustained me through duress. We discussed food and wine. I wondered bemusedly why I had been frightened.

The *marc* was gone. I went into the crowded bedroom for my jacket. She met me in the darkening hall when I came out, and I paid my bill, a large one. I started to thank her, but she took my hand, drew me into the dining room, and without words poured more spirits into my glass. I drank to Monsieur Paul while she watched me intently, her pale eyes bulging in the dimness and her lips pressed inward as if she too tasted the hot, aged *marc*.

The cat rose from his ferny bed, and walked contemptuously out of the room.

Suddenly the girl began to laugh, in a soft shy breathless way, and came close to me.

"Permit me!" she said, and I thought she was going to kiss me. But instead she pinned a tiny bunch of snowdrops and dark bruised cyclamens against my stiff jacket, very quickly and deftly, and then ran from the room with her head down.

I waited for a minute. No sounds came from anywhere in the old mill, but the endless rushing of the full stream seemed to strengthen, like the timed blare of an orchestra under a falling curtain.

She's a *funny* one, I thought. I touched the cool blossoms on my coat and went out, like a ghost from ruins, across the courtyard toward the dim road to Avallon.

Vevey, 1937

Love and Death
Among the Mollusks

. . . Secret, and self-contained, and solitary as an oyster.

A Christmas Carol, CHARLES DICKENS

An oyster leads a dreadful but exciting life.

Indeed, his chance to live at all is slim, and if he should survive the arrows of his own outrageous fortune and in the two weeks of his carefree youth find a clean smooth place to fix on, the years afterwards are full of stress, passion, and danger.

He—but why make him a he, except for clarity? Almost any normal oyster never knows from one year to the next whether he is he or she, and may start at any moment, after the first year, to lay eggs where before he spent his sexual energies in being exceptionally masculine. If he is a she, her energies are equally feminine, so that in a single summer, if all goes well, and the temperature of the water is somewhere around or above seventy degrees, she may spawn several hundred million eggs, fifteen to one hundred million at a time, with commendable pride.

American oysters differ as much as American people, so that the Atlantic Coast inhabitants spend their childhood and adolescence floating free and unprotected with the tides, conceived far from their mothers and their fathers too by milt let loose in the water near the eggs, while the Western oysters lie within special brood-chambers of the maternal shell, inseminated and secure, until they are some two weeks old. The Easterners seem more daring.

A little oyster is born, then, in the water. At first, about five to ten hours after he and at least a few hundred thousand of his mother's eggs have been fertilized by his potent and unknown sire, he is merely a larva. He is small, but he is free-swimming . . . and he swims thus freely for about two weeks, wherever the tides and his peculiar whims may lead him. He is called a spat.

It is to be hoped, sentimentally at least, that the spat—*our* spat—enjoys himself. Those two weeks are his one taste of vagabondage, of devil-may-care free roaming. And even they are not quite free, for during all his youth he is busy growing a strong foot and a large supply of sticky cementlike stuff. If he thought, he might wonder why.

The two weeks up, he suddenly attaches himself to the first clean hard object he bumps into. His fifty million brothers who have not been eaten by fish may or may not bump into anything clean and hard, and those who do not, die. But our spat has been lucky, and in great good spirits he clamps himself firmly to his home, probably forever. He is by now about one-seventy-fifth of an inch long, whatever that may be . . . and he is an oyster.

Since he is an Easterner, a Chincoteague or a Lynnhaven maybe, he has found a pleasant, moderately salty bottom, where the tides wash regularly and there is no filth to pollute him and no sand to choke him.

There he rests, tied firmly by his left foot, which seems to have become a valve in the immutable way of all oyster feet. He devotes himself to drinking, and rapidly develops an enviable capacity, so that in good weather, when the temperature stays near seventy-eight degrees, he can easily handle twenty-six or-seven quarts an hour. He manages better than most creatures to combine business with pleasure, and from this stream of water that passes through his gills he strains out all the delicious little diatoms and peridia that are his food.

His home—we are speaking now of domesticated oysters—is a wire bag full of old shells, or perhaps a cement-coated pole planted by a wily oyster-farmer. Or perhaps it is what the government describes winningly as "a particularly efficient collector," which is made from an egg-crate partition coated with a mixture of lime and cement.

Whatever the anchorage (and I hope, sentimentally again, that it is at least another shell, since because he is an Easterner our little spat can never know the esthetic pleasure of finding a bamboo stick in Japan, nor a hollow tile laid out especially for him in France or Portugal), whatever the anchorage, spat-dom is over and done with. The two fine free-swimming weeks are forever gone, maturity with all its cares has come, and an oyster, according to Richard Sheridan's *Critic*, may be crossed in love.

For about a year this oyster—*our* oyster—is a male, fertilizing a few hundred thousand eggs as best he can without ever knowing whether they swim by or not. Then one day, maternal longings surge between his two valves in his cold guts and gills and all his crinkly fringes. Necessity, that well-known mother, makes him one. He is a she.

From then on she, with occasional vacations of being masculine just to keep her hand in, bears her millions yearly. She is in the full bloom of womanhood when she is about seven.

She is a fine plump figure of an oyster, plumper still in the summer when the season and her instincts get the better of her. She has traveled some, thanks to cupidinous farmers who have subjected her to this tide and that, this bed and that, for their own mean ends. She has grown into a gray-white oval shape, with shades of green or ocher or black in her gills and a rudimentary brain in the forepart of her blind deaf body. She can feel shadows as well as the urgency of milt, and her delicate muscles know danger and pull shut her shells with firmness.

Danger is everywhere for her, and extermination lurks. (How do we know with what pains? How can we tell or not tell the sufferings of an oyster? There is a brain . . .) She is the prey of many enemies, and must lie immobile as a fungus while the starfish sucks her and the worm bores.

She has eight enemies, not counting man who is the greatest, since he protects her from the others only to eat her himself.

The first enemy is the starfish, which floats hungrily in all the Eastern tides and at last wraps arms about the oyster like a hideous lover and forces its shells apart steadily and then thrusts his stomach into it and digests it. The picture is ugly. The oyster is left bare as any empty shell, and the starfish floats on, hungry still. (Men try to catch it with things called star-mops.)

The second enemy, almost as dangerous, is a kind of snail called a screw-borer, or an oyster drill. It bores wee round holes in the shells, and apparently worries the poor mollusc enough to make men invent traps for it: wire bags baited with seed-oysters catch it, but none too efficiently, since it remains a menace.

Then there is a boring sponge. It makes tiny tunnels all through the shell like honeycomb, until an oyster becomes thin and weak from trying to stop up all the holes, and then is often smothered by the sponge from the outside, so that you know what Louisa May Alcott meant when she wrote, "Now I am beginning to live a little, and feel less like a sick oyster at low tide."

There are wafers, or leeches, and "Black Drums." And mussels too will smother oysters or starve them by coming to stay on their shells and eating all their food. Out on the Pacific Coast, slipper shells, which are somewhat fancily called *Crepidula fornicata*, will go the mussels one better. And even ducks, flying here and there as ducks must, land long enough to make themselves a disastrously good meal occasionally on an oyster bed.

Life is hard, we say. An oyster's life is worse. She lives motionless, soundless, her own cold ugly shape her only dissipation, and if she escapes the menace of duck-slipper-mussel-Black-Drum-leech-sponge-borer-starfish, it is for man to eat, because of man's own hunger.

Men have enjoyed eating oysters since they were not much more than monkeys, according to the kitchen middens they have left behind them. And thus, in their own one-minded way, they have spent time and thought and money on the problems of how to protect oysters from the suckers and the borers and the starvers, until now it is comparatively easy to eat this two-valved mollusk anywhere, without thought of the dangers it has run in its few years. Its chilly, delicate gray body slips into a stewpan or under a broiler or alive down a red throat, and it is done. Its life has been thoughtless but no less full of danger, and now that it is over we are perhaps the better for it.

FROM X IS FOR XANTHIPPE

. . . and the sure way any shrewish woman can put poison in the pot for her mate, whether or no he be as wise as Socrates and call her Xanthippean or merely Sarah-Jane-ish or Francescan, routinely vituperative or merely undergoing "one of her bad days."

Probably no strychnine has sent as many husbands into their graves as mealtime scolding has, and nothing has driven more men into the arms of other women than the sound of a shrill whine at table. Xanthippe's skill at being ill tempered is largely legendary, and I do not know how much of her nastiness took place over the daily food she served forth to Socrates, but I am convinced that there is no better culture for the quick growth of the germs of marital loathings than the family board. Even the bed must cede position to it, for nighttime and the occasional surcease of physical fatigue and languor can temper mean words there. Nothing alleviates the shock of nagging over an omelet and a salad.[1]

Brillat-Savarin has said as much, and most straightforwardly. But each of us has the right to add his own version of it, and as a two-time widow, both grass and sod, I can vouch for the fact that every man who ever confided in me, as all men eventually

---

[1] . . . and it may be said here that no omelet can withstand the spiritual battering of a bad-tongued shrew. It will look delicious, certainly, but turn to gravel between the teeth no matter what its creamy texture or its fine ingredients.

I know how to make scrambled eggs that to my own mind are, quite frankly, the best I have ever eaten, and they would taste like old minced carpet and stick in my throat if I had to try to swallow them while Xanthippe hacked at Socrates, or anyone else for that matter: a son, a relative of either sex. I have, in public places, watched women suddenly turn a tableful of human beings into scowling tigers and hyenas with their quiet, ferocious nagging, and I have shuddered especially at the signs of pure criminality that then veil children's eyes as they bolt down their poisoned food and flee.

My recipe, guaranteed to gripe a man's vitals if served with hate, and to soothe him like pansy petals if set down before him with gentle love, varies somewhat with the supplies to hand, but is basically this, and, as will be evident, it is quirky:

Scrambled Eggs
  8 fresh eggs
  1½ cups rich cream (more or less)
  salt, freshly ground pepper
  4 tablespoons grated cheese, or finely minced fresh herbs, *if desired*

Break eggs into cold, heavy iron skillet, add cream, and stir gently until fairly well blended. *Never beat.* Heat *very* slowly, stirring occasionally in large curds up from the bottom. *Never let bubble.* Add seasoning (and/or cheese and herbs) just before serving. This takes about half an hour—poky, but worth it.

This concoction is obviously a placid one, never to be attempted by a nervous, harried woman, one anxious to slap something on the table and get it over with. Its very consistency, slow and creamy, is a deterrent to irritation, and if it were attempted by any female who deliberately planned to lean over it, once on its

will to a seemingly lone woman, that he has not been well understood by his wife, has in the end confessed that try as he would to come home patient and kind for dinner, Sarah-Jane or Frances would serve it forth to him with such a mishmash of scowls and scoldings that he must, to save himself, flee from her.

There are, of course, many sides to this problem, as to all, and I can and do understand Xanthippe's. The main thing to do, in my way of thinking, is to strike an amicable if not truly easy relationship, with full admission that the husband may be basically weary of his wife and the wife fed to the teeth with him. I know several such arrangements, questionably right from a moral point of view (or sentimental!) and made for a hundred reasons from the most venal to the vaguest, and if they be done intelligently they can and do succeed.

The reason I advocate this tacit admission of extramural satisfactions and intramural tolerance is that people must eat. It is true that they must also make love, and in order to do so must in one way or another make money. But the most important of these functions, to my mind, is the eating. Neither of the others can be done well without it: an impoverished man is hungry, and a hungry man, as too many dictators have proved, is not a reproductive and perforce sexually keen fellow. That is why I think that food is the most important of our three basic needs, and why I do deplore its poisoning, its deadly contamination, by anything as vicious as bad temper.

Socrates escaped from Xanthippe in ways impossible to modern man, no matter how philosophical. Today a lesser thinker must hide in his Third Avenue pub and snatch a tough steak and worse potatoes to nourish him if he cannot bear to go home and face the sour woman he is commanded by law to live with. Indigestion is the inevitable aftermath, not so much from the rank victuals he has stowed away as from his basic sorrow that he and she have come to such a pass.

But if he does go home, his stomach will curse even louder, thanks to the acids of anger and hatred that he can counteract in the pub with aloneness and a couple of short ryes. He sighs, gulps, and looks over the bar at his own mirrored face, bitterly thankful that he does not see there the pinched, ruined beauty of his woman, the Sarah-Jane, the Frances, who forced him here.

And she? Women have more ways than men for lone survival, so Xanthippe may drink too much, or exhaust herself in a whirl of club meetings with her like, or

---

plates, and whang at her guests (for a lover, a husband, a father, or a child is indeed the guest of any woman who prepares the food they must eat), I would rather have my scrambled eggs turn into hard, fanged snakes and writhe away. I love this recipe, for its very gentleness, and for the demands it makes upon one's patience, and the homage it deserves from its slow tasting.

I can suggest a good recipe for a shrew, to take little time, be very indigestible, and imply frustration, outrage, and great boredom by its general air of hardness and tough, careless preparation:

    4 eggs
    cooking oil or fat
    4 tablespoons water
    salt, pepper

Beat eggs angrily until they froth. Add the water. Season without thought. Heat oil quickly to the smoking point in thin skillet, pour in egg mixture and stir fast. Scrape onto cold plates and slam down on carelessly laid table. [. . .]

An Alphabet for Gourmets

sit weeping and moaning in a darkened movie house. She may long for her husband . . .

. . . and then when he does come home, heavy with fatigue and forced joviality, she forgets her longing and slaps ill-cooked food upon the table, a kind of visual proof of her boredom at his dullness and her hatred of his dwindled lust, which she, poor soul, was genteelly raised to mistake for love. She may even try hard to be patient, and not to mind when in subconscious pain at the sight of her sharp face he hides it from him with a spreadout sheet of news about pugilists and midget auto-racers. She may hope that he will notice the cherry she has, with synthetic optimism fed by radio commercials and monthly magazines, placed upon the top of his canned peach.

But he reads on, with the instinct of a cornered toad pretending courage, and in desperation the woman, who has sworn not to do it again, begins to talk.

The rest is too familiar, a pattern used tastelessly by comicstrip writers, modern literary giants, and psychiatrists: she whangs, he scowls back, suddenly the food in their bellies feels intolerably sour and dreadful, he returns in a furious rush to his pub and she to her bitter, teary pillow, and finally they end according to accidents of time and place and money in the relative asylums of death, insanity, hypochondria, or the law courts.

A good answer to this Xanthippean formula must start practically with the cradle. A child, male or female, who has been raised to eat in peace, and has never gulped to the tune of scolding or anger, stands a better chance of knowing the pleasures of the table when he is full grown than one who has listened with fright and final callousness to endless bitter arguments and rows, who has bolted his food to escape them, who has at last come to think them a part of family existence and to expect, with a horrible resignation, that his wife will turn out to be the same noisy, bickering shrew his mother was at mealtime.

I think that it is a good thing, for many reasons, to have children eat at least half their meals at their own table, at the hours best suited to them, and removed from sight or sound of older people whose natural conversation would be as boring to the young ones as theirs would be to their elders.

But if, as was true when I was little, the children must have dinner with their parents, some such rule as the one my family followed should be law: business was never mentioned in any way, nor money problems, nor grown-up worries. And if any of us children had grouses to air, or peeves, we did it earlier or later, but never at the table. There we were expected to eat nicely and to converse with possible dullness but no rancor, and, being expected to, we did—or else were excused from the room.

My father, because of the endless evening meetings he had to go to as a small-town newspaper editor, had to dine early, and my mother, dependent on unskilled "help," could not arrange separate dinners at different hours for the children and for herself and him, but I have often thought it a pity that they had to refrain from any of the rich quiet talk that a husband and wife should indulge in over their evening meal, in order to teach us children one more rudiment of decent living. The only place where they could converse properly was in bed, and I can remember hearing their low voices going on and on, far after the house slept.

Even so long ago I used to think how dull it must be for my father to come home after the paper was off the presses and well onto the streets to find my mother deep in the unavoidable and noisy routine of getting four or five or six children washed and brushed and ready to be fed, with never a chance to sit down together and breathe.

Perhaps that is why, now in my own life, I feel that the quiet drink I have before dinner with my husband, after the children have been tucked away, is one of the pleasantest minutes in all the 1440. It makes the meal which follows seem more peaceful, more delicious. Physically it smoothes out wrinkles of fatigue and worry in both of us, which could, especially if we had been conditioned differently by wrangling parents, lead us inevitably into the Xanthippean tragedy of nagging, and bitterness, and anger. And that, I know because I have seen it happen, would be the world's surest way to send my husband from my table and my life—an ugly prospect indeed, and one rightly to be avoided, just as is the poison it would take to do it, brewed to the tune of a woman's shrewish voice and served, quick death to love, at the family table . . .

GARUM

100 A.D.—400 A.D. ROME

While Greece exchanged black broth and its accompanying simplicity for that more complex kitchen science nurtured by her new esthetes, Rome shadowed her some years behind, mimicking with fantastic exaggeration each of her calm inevitable developments.

For her Spartan pottage, Romans had a gruel of lentils. They too ate chestnuts and cheeses and fruits and green vegetables, with honey to sweeten and wine to gladden. Then when refinement, sure arbiter of a decadent civilization, crept into the Grecian cuisine, her tardy shadow Rome leaped feverishly in a grotesque and fascinating imitation.

As had happened in Greece, towns and villages vied for culinary honours. Certain cakes, cheeses of a special smell, and even fish from a named lake or river began to cause small feuds among the gourmets. Gradually shadow out-leaped self, and in their furious delicacy of palate and heavy-handed subtlety of selection the wealthy Romans left Greeks far behind.

Are *pâtés de foie gras* better made from cygnets than from milk-white geese? Of course! Not at all! Well, perhaps if the geese are nourished solely on green figs—But on the other hand, a diet of almonds——

Senators cut important electors in the streets; sons quarrelled with fathers, boys with their tutors. Even the philosophers considered such questions weightily, and uttered decisions which had but temporary effect.

When Cleopatra melted her pearl and six million sesterces into the world's most expensive recipe, she set a tantalizingly high mark. Until Rome fell, gourmets tried to outdo her. Undoubtedly the results were more palatable—but never more costly.

Rigid snobbism precluded all but the most extravagant citizens, and thus most plutocratic, from the inner circles of fine eating.

Juvenal drew the portrait of all Roman bon vivants when he wrote of one of the greatest, the general Lucullus:

> Stretched on the unsocial couch, he rolls his eyes
> O'er many an orb of matchless form and size,
> Selects the fairest to receive his plate,
> And at one meal devours a whole estate.

Lucullus, perhaps the truest epicure as we now think of one, was undoubtedly the most refined. He set the pace. Other Romans, like Trimalchio's vulgar prototype, might give banquets whose success depended upon the leaping of three naked virgins from a great crusted tart. It was Lucullus who gave his carefully chosen guests the exquisite compliment of letting them watch their next course die!

Mullets bred in the mountain lake he had transplanted to his estates, or trout brought living from one certain stream in all Italy, expired slowly in beautiful glass jars placed before the diners. Each throe was judged. Lucky the guest whose dying fish leaped highest and longest! The flavour would be unforgettable.

It was Lucullus who sorted his friends into different rooms, rather like the various restaurants in a large German railroad station. In some rooms, a meal cost only one or two hundred dollars for each person. Decoration there was relatively simple. More expensive surroundings showed that here Lucullus spent more on his food.

And finally, in the Apollo Room, where only his very intimate or important guests were invited, he spent one thousand dollars for each person.

Here he entertained most frequently, with the most precious foods laid upon tables now solid ivory, now silver or carved tortoise shell. For ordinary guests goblets of inlaid gold did well enough, but in the Apollo Room glasses hollowed from great gems were used with nonchalance.

Other men blinked at their own banquet bills, or complained bitterly, like Julius Cæsar when he found he had spent five millions sterling, one Roman summer, on suppers for his friends—and on barley water mixed with wine, for his favourite charger to drink from a golden trough!

Sometimes there was a suicide, nor was it from remorse for unpaid debts. Apicius, when he found he had squandered over a million pounds on banquets, and had but a tenth of that sum left, died as exquisitely as one of the mullets he had watched.

As Rome festered and decayed, the fever for fine eating mounted. What had been precious became vicious. Mark Antony's largesse of a town of thirty-five thousand souls for his chef's fine paste of flamingo brains changed to Heliogabalus' trick of fattening his prized conger eels on living slave-meat.

As much money was spent on perfumes as on food. It was the usual thing now to have rare aromatic essences blown into the air between the twenty-four courses of daily banquets, as in Nero's famous Domus Aurea, from whose revolving walls flowers and sweet distillations showered down upon the guests.

Indeed, such strange behaviour was necessary. Satiety, that monster behind pleasure, breathed into the stuffed bellies of the Romans. Excitants to their palates were prerequisite—those palates by now so ill-treated that some of the gourmets were forced to wear little tongue gloves to protect their delicate tasteglands from all but the most exotic flavours.

And where could they find new foods? They searched desperately. They had eaten every fish in the earth's waters, except Triton's sacred dolphin and perhaps a mermaid. They had sucked the bones of every bird and birdling in—But wait!

"Send hunters to Lydia," Heliogabalus ordered, "and pay two hundred gold pieces to the one who brings us back a Phœnix!"

But none came.

The fretful ruler tried colours. Perhaps they might whip up his dulled taste. For awhile Roman tables bloomed with shades as violent but not so harmless as those in a modern seed-catalogue. They soon faded.

Les Tables Volantes, which Louis XV of France proudly called his own invention, rose first for Heliogabalus. Laden with dishes resolutely emptied, these tables sank, to the strains of young boys' voices, into the marble floor. New perfumes from Araby spiced the air. Strange dances, increasingly erotic, occupied the dulled eyes of the diners. Then the beautiful boys raised their voices in mock amazement, and fell squealing back. From the floor lifted boards new-decked, like the Phœnix the king yearned for—each time with new plumes.

As the feasts grew longer and more extravagant, the guests lost gradually those stately good manners they had aped from the earlier Greek gourmands. Licence of the senses begot loose behaviour.

If the goblets seemed too small, or the wine-supply stingy or of poor vintage, banqueters howled until they were satisfied. If the dishes displeased them, they hurled food and vessel against a pillar or a serving-man. The host apologized.

Emetics were served with the beginning courses of any longer dinner—as they had been indeed in Greece, because of the difficulty of digestion in the reclining position assumed on the banqueting-couches. Now, however, the Romans found the capacity of their sated stomachs infinitely enlarged by the trick. By the time one dish appeared, its predecessor was well out of the way. Twice as much could be eaten!

This wholesale catharsis necessitated certain architectural changes. And suddenly these changes, luxurious privies to begin with, were metamorphosed once more. *Vomitoria* came into being.

They had a fine name, like a California real estate development. Little boys still hear it with fascination and disgust, in first-year Latin. Girls still invent other verbs, to avoid its nauseous root. Only one ever used it in public with the proper reverence: Colette, when she described an *éclair si vomiteusement chocolateux.*

Romans, however, their minds less on future derivatives of the word than on their next course, used their *vomitoria* with appreciation.

Their insides heaved too often. Quacks and honest physickers could not help. Rome grew dyspeptic, and heard clearly old Seneca's wry comment, "Are you astonished at the innumerable diseases?—Count the number of our cooks!"

We are inclined to agree with him. One course of a Roman meal would lay us very low, probably, and strip our palates for many days of even the crudest perceptions of flavour.

Look for a minute, hand over nose and a piece of ice on tongue, at the recipe for *garum:*

Place in a vessel all the insides of fish, both large fish and small. Salt them well. Expose them to the air until they are completely putrid. In a short time a liquid is produced. Drain this off.

And "this" is *garum*, most highly prized and used of all seasonings. In Cochin-China there is something like it, in these days, called *nuocman*—and of course we have our English meat sauces.

Romans, though, used *garum* not as a condiment in itself, but combined with a startling variety of spices. Dill, anise, hyssop, thyme; pennyroyal and rue; cummin, poppy seed, shallots and onions and garlic and leeks—almost every known savour except our parsley, which they wore in garlands on their heads, made the simplest banquet dish a mess of inextricable flavours.

Inextricable to us, that is. It is doubtful if even a professional taster, today, would be able to describe the sauce Apicius recommends for a boiled chicken:

Put the following ingredients into a mortar: anise-seed, dried mint, and lazar root which is a kind of asafoetida; cover them all with vinegar. Add dates and pour in garum and oil and a small quantity of mustard-seeds. Reduce all to a proper thickness with red wine warmed, and then pour this same over your chicken.

"The chicken," Apicius adds as an afterthought, "should of course be boiled previously in strong anise-seed water."

To cool your enraged palate after this strange dish you would most probably be served a goblet of red wine mixed with spices and sea water.

Then, while pretty slave children imitated worn-out lechers for your eyes' amusement, you would pretend to eat hungrily at a bowl of red mullet seasoned with pepper, rue, onion, dates, mustard, and the flesh of a sea-hedgehog pounded to a jelly.

With this, a fine cup of *vin rosé*, thickened to syrup with honey, myrrh, and spikenard. And after this, a piglet, soaked in——

A good old Roman custom—*vomitoria!*

FROM I IS FOR INNOCENCE

. . . and its strangely rewarding chaos, gastronomically.

There is a great difference in my mind between innocence in this gourmand interpretation, and ignorance. The one presupposes the other, and yet a truly innocent cook or host is never guilty of the great sin of pretension, while many an ignorant one errs hideously in this direction.

Almost any man who is potentially capable of thus cheating his guests is also incapable of telling the truth to himself and will sneak a quick look into a primer of wine names, for instance, and then pretend that he knew all along to serve red wine with red meat or some such truism. His lie will betray his basic insecurity.

An innocent, on the other hand, will not bother to pretend any knowledge at all. He will, with a child's bland happiness, do the most God-awful things with his meals, and manage by some alchemy of warmth and understanding to make any honest gourmet pleased and easy at his table.

The best example of this that I can think of happened to me a few months ago.

I know a large, greedy, and basically unthinking man who spent all the middle years of his life working hard in a small town and eating in waffle shops and now and then gorging himself at friends' houses on Christmas Day. Quite late he married a large, greedy, and unthinking woman who introduced him to the dubious joys of whatever she heard about on the radio: Miracle Sponge Delight, Aunt Martha's Whipped Cheese Surprise, and all the homogenized, pasteurized, vitalized, dehydratized products intrinsic to the preparation of the Delights and the Surprises. My friend was happy.

He worked hard in the shop and his wife worked hard at the stove, her sinkside portable going full blast in order not to miss a single culinary hint. Each night they wedged themselves into their breakfast-bar-dinette and ate and ate and ate. They always meant to take up Canfield, but somehow they felt too sleepy. About a year ago he brought home a little set of dominoes, thinking it would be fun to shove the pieces around in a couple of games of Fives before she cleared the table. But she looked hard at him, gave a great belch, and died.

He was desperately lonely. We all thought he would go back to living in the rooming-house near the shop, or take up straight rye whisky, or at least start raising tropical fish.

Instead he stayed home more and more, sitting across from the inadequate little chromiumed chair his wife had died in, eating an almost ceaseless meal. He cooked it himself, very carefully. He listened without pause to her radio, which had literally not been turned off since her death. He wrote down every cooking tip he heard, and "enclosed twenty-five cents in stamps" for countless packages of Whipperoo, Jellerino, and Vita-glugg. He wore her tentlike aprons as he bent over the stove and the sink and the solitary table, and friends told me never, never, *never* to let him invite me to a meal.

But I liked him. And one day when I met him in the Pep Brothers' Shopping Basket—occasionally I fought back my claustrophobia-among-the-cans long enough to go there for the best frozen fruit in town—he asked me so nicely and straightforwardly to come to supper with him that I said I'd love to. He lumbered off, a look of happy purpose wiping the misery from his big face; it was like sunlight breaking through smog. I felt a shudder of self-protective worry, which shamed me.

The night came, and I did something I very seldom do when I am to be a guest: I drank a sturdy shot of dry vermouth and gin, which I figured from long experience would give me an appetite immune to almost any gastronomical shocks. I was agreeably mellow and uncaring by the time I sat down in the chair across from my great, wallowing, bewildered friend and heard him subside with a fat man's alarming *puff!* into his own seat.

I noticed that he was larger than ever. You like your own cooking, I teased. He said gravely to me that gastronomy had saved his life and reason, and before I could recover from the shock of such fancy words on his strictly one-to-two syllable tongue, he had jumped up lightly, as only a fat man can, and started opening oven doors.

We had a tinned "fruit cup," predominantly gooseberries and obviously a sop to current health hints on station JWRB. Once having disposed of this bit of medical hugger-muggery, we surged on happily through one of the ghastliest meals I ever ate in my life. On second thought I can safely say, *the* ghastliest. There is no point in describing it, and to tell the truth a merciful mist has blurred its high points. There was too much spice where there should be none; there was sogginess where crispness was all-important; there was an artificially whipped and heavily sweetened canned-milk dessert where nothing at all was wanted.

And all through the dinner, in the small, hot, crowded room, we drank lukewarm Muscatel, a fortified dessert wine sold locally in gallon jugs, mixed in cheese-spread glasses with equal parts of a popular bottled lemon soda. It is incredible, but it happened.

I am glad it did. I know now what I may only have surmised theoretically before: there is indeed a gastronomic innocence, more admirable and more enviable than any cunning cognizance of menus and vintages and kitchen subtleties. My gross friend, untroubled by affectations of knowledge, served forth to me a meal that I was proud to partake of. If I felt myself at times a kind of sacrificial lamb, stretched on the altar of devotion, I was glad to be that lamb, for never was nectar poured for any goddess with more innocent and trusting enjoyment than was my hideous glass filled with a mixture of citric acid, carbon dioxide, and pure vinous hell for me. I looked into the little gray eyes of my friend and drank deep and felt the better for it.

He had not pretended with me nor tried to impress me. He knew I liked to eat, so he had cooked for me what he himself enjoyed the most. He remembered hearing somewhere that I liked wine with my meals, so he had bought "the mixings," as he knew them, because he wanted me to feel gay and relaxed and well thought of, there in his dear woman's chair, with her radio still blasting and her stove still hot. I felt truly grateful, and I too felt innocent. [. . .]

CATHERINE'S LONESOME COOKS
1533 A.D.—1810 A.D. FRANCE

Until well into the sixteenth century French cooking developed little. Lordly kitchens aped the British in the length, breadth, and depth of their enormous meals.

Restaurants there were none, unless you could so name that redoubtable hostelry *La Tour d'Argent,* old then, older today. Now it serves *crêpes Suzette* and *canards pur-sang,* but in 1533 it was still dishing forth such favourites of the Middle Ages as dormouse pasty and a mixed pie of snake, porpoise, swan, and plum-stuffed crane.

It was that year that Fate and Pope Clement VII changed the table manners of Europe. The Holy Father, probably conscious less of the gastronomic importance of his act than of its political results, married off his niece Catherine de Medici to France's young Henry.

And Catherine took her cooks to France with her. They were probably the first great *chefs de cuisine* in that land, and galling though the fact may be to those Frenchmen who mix patriotism with their love of fine food, they were Italians every one.

Paris seemed harsh and boorish to the lonesome Florentines. They moped for the gay lightness of their own banquet halls. There ladies and gentlemen were taught *The Fifty Courtesies of the Table* as soon as they were old enough to eat at all. Here in Paris many people still laughed jeeringly at "those Italian neatnesses called forks," and gulped down great chunks of strongly seasoned meats from their knife-ends or their greasy fingers.

Catherine's cooks shuddered, and conferred together in low voices.

It was not long before they acted. Their innovation burst like a bomb over all the noble tables of Paris. Sherbets appeared! In every shape and colour, with flavours as clear and subtle as summer flowers, sherbets were set before the startled Frenchmen by the Queen's wily chefs.

Roughened tongues were made smooth, and hot throats cooled; palates, long calloused by the indiscriminate spicings of the dark centuries, slowly grew keen and sensitive.

The chefs chuckled. These Frenchmen might be able, in good time, to appreciate their Italian sauces and their tarts and soups. In good time!

By the beginning of the next century the French palate had indeed grown much more sophisticated, and some knowledge of culinary tricks was a necessary part of any worldling's education. Louis XIII, it is true, became his own cook less for pleasure than because of his inherited fear of being poisoned. His court, however, led by Richelieu's careful genius, developed a passionate interest in cookery.

It became smart to cook the main dish of a supper oneself. Kitchens, suddenly invaded by guests in elaborate costumes and dainty shoes, were the centre of attention. They bloomed with new pots, crest-emblazoned: A hundred impractical inventions of the amateur chefs for turning spits and whipping cream were discreetly ignored by harassed cooks, who worked as expertly as ever in this new shade.

Kitchen gardens, as well, grew very amusingly under the ecstatic gushings of court ladies and the silent care of gardeners, and a bouquet of lettuces and shallots was as chic as lilies.

The greatest men in all France became authors of strange poems on food and stranger recipes, which were greeted with peals of respectful laughter. Some of them, like Cardinal Richelieu's invention of a sauce made with eggs and oil which he called *maionnaise,* are as familiar a part of our diet today as almond milk and brawn were in 1600.

The next Louis, the fourteenth, and the fifteenth who was his great-grandson, were less timid than the king who feared poison. They loved good food as they loved war and fine buildings and beautiful women, with a boundless and intelligent zest.

Kitchens and kitchen gardens were just as fashionable under their energetic reigns, but it now became even more stylish to own a famous chef. Great men stooped to the most childish tricks to win a rival's cook or steward, and recipes were guarded like coronation jewels.

Diplomats and nobles were proud to give their revered family names to a new sauce or a bonbon, or share kudos with the chef who so honoured them. Soubise sauce, so subtly oniony, and béchamel, that lifesaver of *la haute cuisine,* are only two of the innumerable recipes that have come to us from the snobbish palates of the French eighteenth century.

Great chefs were its oracles, and wrote serious treatises on the arts of carving and serving, or the complexities of gastronomic etiquette. The Prince de Condé's chef, Vatel, who committed suicide when fish he had ordered for a dinner arrived too late to be served, gave some indication of his own seriousness as well as his art's, in the essay *L'Escuyer Tranchant.*

"A carver," he dictates in one section, "should be scrupulous in his deportment; his carriage should be grave and dignified, his appearance cheerful; his eye serene, his head erect and well combed, abstaining as much as possible from sneezing, yawning, or twisting his mouth, speaking very little and directly, without being too near or too far from the table."

Oddly enough, Vatel's disciples earned their princely pay as much from those glamorous women kept by the diplomats as from the great men themselves. The pleasures of the table had become so important, by the time Madame du Barry and la Pompadour reigned over France, that no intelligent courtesan could afford to be without a fine chef. Dining eclipsed its old companion lovemaking, and many a beautiful *fille* was coveted more for her chef's skill with omelette than for her own artful thighs.

Waning passions, Louis the King's and Louis the fat silk merchant's, were fanned by the invention of a thousand new recipes. It was this, most probably, that started the extravagant fad for turkeys stuffed with truffles.

French interest in anything from the American Colonies ran high, and such dishes as Indian corn pudding and wild roasted turkey made any table smart. Prices for them ran into several figures—almost as expensive as truffles. It took a woman of unlimited income and capricious brain to combine the two whims of the moment, and serve a turkey stuffed with truffles to her admirers.

Immediately a rage for the crazy dish swept Paris. First the demimonde and then the court devoured it, with only slight qualms at its exorbitant cost.

Then, in an epidemic frenzy, the middle classes, the little shopkeepers, the laundresses and coachmen were seized with a mad appetite for *dinde truffée*. Truffles became so scarce that they were escorted through the city with armed guards, and men ruined themselves in order to prove their social stability by serving one stuffed turkey.

Only the courtesans and the great lords could afford the dish. They soon tired of it. In a few months Paris had forgotten it, except in the bankruptcy courts.

Under Louis XVI, gastronomy continued its somewhat debauched course. Louis himself was a plain man, more interested in locks and musical timepieces than in the intricacies of sauce-making. His simplicity, though, may have had its own subtle influence on the reigning vogue of the court, for under his poor giddy queen the pastoral life was lived most artificially.

Marie Antoinette and all her ladies became, for several hours of every sunny day, milkmaids more exquisite than ever spaded dung in any truthful farmyard. Gowned in picturesque and very flattering costumes, they sat on ivory stools to milk their perfumed animals, and churned at little silver churns until their arms grew tired.

A dainty pat of butter made by a noble lady's own hands, with the print of a strawberry leaf upon its smooth fresh bottom, was a love token almost more desired than kisses, and deserved at least a folk song in reply, or a country dance written for four partners.

Finally milk itself, so embarrassingly natural, was decided to be worthy of a true gourmet's attentions if it came from the hands of an aristocratic milkmaid. To add to the taste, so pure, so chastely sweet, the more promiscuous ladies gave special drinking cups to their courtiers. Made of the finest porcelain from impressions taken at the height of their owners' loveliness, each cup mirrored the curves of a woman's breast, wanton, fragile, evanescent.

Napoleon broke like a bull into this china shop. But then the Revolution had already scattered the aristocrats, demoralized the servants, and wiped out the depraved etiquette of court life. The Little Corporal brought with him another world of pretentious newly-rich, sharp-witted and vulgar. Paris blazed with jewels and affectations, all awkwardly displayed.

Napoleon himself was a bad eater. He gobbled. He had little patience with the long silences and deliberate smackings of his gourmand friends, although he tried at times to imitate them.

Once, in a sorry effort to pretend that he really cared a tinker's dam about such things as eggs, he insisted that he could flip an omelette better than his lady ever could. It landed on the floor.

For days he was morose, hearing in his head the muffled snickers of Josephine and his agile courtiers. He really preferred scrambling treaties, anyway, and men, and boundary lines.

THE SOCIAL STATUS
OF A VEGETABLE

Although we had walked into the little Swiss village restaurant without warning, an almost too elaborate meal appeared for us in the warm empty room, hardly giving us time to finish our small glasses of thick piny bitters.

We were hungry. The climb had been steep, through bare vineyards and meadows yellow with late primroses. We ate the plate of sliced sausages, and then the tureen of thick potato soup, without much speaking. We hardly blinked at the platter of fried eggs—ten of them for only three people!—with dark pink ham curling all around like little clouds.

We reached for more bread, sighed, and pulled off coats. The wine was light and appetizing.

Mrs. Davidson's old face looked fresher now. She straightened her shoulders, and settled her hat with a slightly coquettish movement of gnarled arms. For a wonder, she had eaten without mention of her self-styled "bird-like" appetite, with no apology for the natural hunger which she usually felt to be coarse and carnal. (Or so at least we had gathered from her many bored, sad smiles at any admission on our parts that we did like to eat.)

Now, when I realized that she was at last on the point of recognizing the existence of such low lust in herself, I rushed to forestall her with instinctive perversity.

"That was good," I said. "But I'm still hungry."

At once I was sorry, ashamed of myself. Mrs. Davidson looked cut into, and then settled her small handsome old face in its usual lines of refined disapproval. I had destroyed a rare human moment in her stiff life.

"So far, the meal, if you could really call such an impromptu thing a meal, has been quite passable," she admitted. "This inn, for such a small and unattractive village, seems respectable enough."

My nephew pulled the cork from another bottle, filled her glass, and quietly put more bread by her plate.

"I think it's awfully decent of you to come here while we eat," he told her, his face smooth and innocent.

She looked flattered, and finished the bread without noticing it.

The waitress, fat and silent, staggered in under a tray, her knees bending slightly outwards with its weight. She put down a great plate of steaks, with potatoes heaped like swollen hay at each end. We looked feebly at it, feeling appetite sag out of us suddenly.

Another platter thumped down at the other side of the table, a platter mounded high with purple-red ringed with dark green.

"What—*what* is that beautiful food?" Mrs. Davidson demanded, and then quickly mended her enthusiasm, with her eyes still sparkling hungrily. "I mean, beautiful as far as food could be."

My own appetite revived a little as I answered: "That's a ring of spinach around chopped red cabbage, probably cooked with ham juice."

At the word spinach her face clouded, but when I mentioned cabbage a look of complete and horrified disgust settled like a cloud. She pushed back her chair.

"Cabbage!" Her tone was incredulous.

"Why not?" James asked, mildly. "Cabbage is the staff of life in many countries. You ought to know, Mrs. Davidson. Weren't you raised on a farm?"

Her mouth settled grimly.

"As *you* know," she remarked in an icy voice, with her face gradually looking very old and discontented again, "there are many kinds of farms. My home was *not* a collection of peasants. Nor did we eat such—such peasant things as this."

"But haven't you ever tasted cabbage, then, Mrs. Davidson?" I asked.

"Never!" she answered proudly, emphatically.

"This is delicious steak." It was a diplomatic interruption. I looked gratefully at James. He grinned almost imperceptibly, and went on, "Just let me slide a little sliver on your plate, Mrs. Davidson, and you try to nibble at it while we eat. It will do you good."

He cut off the better portion of a generous slice of beef and put it on her well-emptied plate. She looked pleased, as she always did when reference was made to her delicacy, and only shuddered perfunctorily when we served ourselves with the vegetable.

As the steak disappeared, I watched her long old earlobes pinken. I remembered what an endocrinologist had told me once, that after rare beef and wine, when the lobes turned red, was the time to ask favours or tell bad news. I led the conversation back to the table, and then plunged brusquely.

"Why do you really dislike cabbage, Mrs. Davidson?"

She looked surprised, and put down the last bite from her bowl of brandied plums.

"Why does anyone dislike it? Surely you don't believe that I think your eating it is anything more than a pose?" She smiled knowingly at my nephew and me. He laughed.

"But we *do* like it, really. In our homes we cook it, and eat it, too, not for health, not for pretence. We like it."

"Yes, I remember my husband used to say that same sort of thing. But he never got it! No fear! It was the night I finally accepted him that I understood why my family had never had it in the house."

We waited silently. James filled her glass again.

"We missed the last train, and couldn't find a cab, and of course Mr. Davidson, who thought he knew everything, wandered down the wrong street. And there, in that dark wet town, lost, cold, miserable——"

"Oh, night of rapture, when I was yours!" James murmured.

"—cold, miserable, we were suddenly almost overcome by a ghastly odour!"

I repressed my instinctive desire to use the word "stink" and asked maliciously, "A perfume, or a smell?"

"A dreadful *odour*," she corrected me, with an acidulous smile at my coarseness. "It was so terrible that I was almost swooning. I pressed my muff against my face, and we stumbled on, gasping.

"When finally I could control myself enough to speak, I murmured, 'What was it? What was that gas?' My husband hurried me along, and I will say he did his best to apologize for what he had done—and well he should have!—by saying, 'It was cabbage, cooking.'

"'*Oh!*' I cried. 'Oh, we're in the *slums!*'"

"So you see what a terrible memory of it all I have kept. Is it any wonder that I shudder when I see it or have it near me? Those horrible slums! Its *odour!*"

We looked blankly at her. Then I asked, "But do you smell it now? Did it bother you on the table?"

Mrs. Davidson stared peevishly at me, and said to James, "Well, if you two have finished your food, I should like to go."

Then, as we walked down the stairs to the crooked narrow street, I thanked her for the pleasant meal. She almost smiled, and said, grudgingly, "It was, I admit, not bad—for the slums."

It is constantly surprising, this vegetable snobbism. It is almost universal.

My mother, who was raised in a country too crowded with Swedish immigrants, shudders at turnips, which they seem to have lived on. And yet there she ate, week in and week out, corn meal mush and molasses, a dish synonymous to many Americans with poor trash of the pariah-ridden South.

And my grandmother—I remember hearing her dismiss some unfortunate person as a vulgar climber by saying, quietly, "Oh, Mrs. Zubzub is the kind of woman who serves artichokes!"

Of course, to a child reared within smelling distance, almost, of the fog-green fields of those thistly flowers, such damnation was quite meaningless; but I suppose that to a Midwestern woman of the last century it meant much.

Just a few years ago, the same class consciousness was apparent in a small college in Illinois, where students whispered and drew away from me after I had innocently introduced a box of avocados from my father's ranch into a dormitory "feast." From that unfortunate night, I was labelled a stuck-up snob.

The first time, though, that I ever felt surprise at the social position of a vegetable was when I was a lower-classman in a boarding school. Like most Western private schools, it was filled largely with out-of-state children whose families wintered in California, and the daughters of local newly-rich.

Pretension and snobbishness flourished among these oddly segregated adolescents, and nowhere could such stiff cautious conventionality be found as in their classrooms, their teas, their sternly pro-British hockey matches.

One girl, from Englewood in New Jersey or maybe Tuxedo Park, was the recognized leader of the Easterners, the "bloods." She was more dashing than the rest; she used with impressive imitation her mother's high whinnying gush of poise and good breeding. She set the pace, and with a certain surety, too, for such an unsure age as sixteen. She was daring.

The reason I know she was daring, even so long ago, is that I can still hear her making a stupendous statement. That takes courage at any time, but when you are young, and bewildered behind your affectation of poise, and surrounded by other puzzled children who watch avidly for one wrong move, it is as impressive as a parade with trumpets.

We were waiting for the lunch bell. Probably we were grumbling about the food, which was unusually good for such an institution, but, like all food cooked *en masse*, dull. Our bodies clamoured for it, our tongues rebelled.

The girl from Englewood or Tuxedo Park spoke out, her hard voice clear, affectedly drawling to hide her own consciousness of daring. She must have known that what she said, even while aping her mother's social sureness, was very radical to the children round her, the children fed from kitchens of the *haute bourgeoisie* and in luxurious hotels. It was rather like announcing, at a small débutante ball in Georgia, "Of course, *I* prefer to dance with Negroes."

"I know it's terribly, terribly silly of me," she said, with all she could summon of maternally gracious veneer, "but of course I was brought up near Pennsylvania, and the customs there are so quaint, and I know you'll all be terribly, terribly shocked, but I *love*, I *adore* wieners and sauerkraut!"

Yes, it was surprising then and still is. All round are signs of it, everywhere, little trickles of snobbish judgment, always changing, ever present.

In France old Crainquebille sold leeks from a cart, leeks called "the asparagus of the poor." Now asparagus sells for the asking, almost, in California markets, and broccoli, that strong age-old green, leaps from its lowly pot to the *Ritz*'s copper saucepan.

Who determines, and for what strange reasons, the social status of a vegetable?

from Teasers and Titbits

In Plutarch's *Lives* he observed, "It is no great wonder if in long process of time, while fortune takes her course hither and thither, numerous coincidences should spontaneously occur." In other words, history repeats itself. Sometimes this can be eery, in even a tiny way. Occasionally it can be embarrassing, or funny. It can be good, too.

There is an unwritten law, as I assume it to be, that things go in threes, and in one week of my life three coincidences did "spontaneously occur," with such a subtle message that I felt instinctively I would prefer not to heed it. They sound innocent enough.

First, I was reading a collection of short stories written by authors of uneven quality in different decades of the past century, and near the front of the book was the term *félo de se*. It is seldom used in English, but this time it was perfectly in its place, and I enjoyed it, and thought about another one which rhymes with it and is only a little commoner: *auto da fé*. I wondered lazily why I had seen neither of these expressions for a long time. Would I ever write one of them? And then about three stories later in the book there was *auto da fé*. Full circle, I thought with the docility of anyone facing coincidence itself.

A couple of days later I was trying to remember the conclusion of a mistreated proverb beginning, "There is only one thing worse than a nagging woman, and that . . ." and I heard my father saying firmly, ". . . and that is one who *whangs* at you." I had not heard the word *whang*, even in my head, for at least twenty years. Dictionaries say that as a noun it means a blow, a whack, but the way Father said it, the tone of voice was what made it a verb: a loud, quarrelsome, stubborn punishment of sound, with hopelessness and ugly despair in it. I pondered the word, and the strangeness of its coming into my head . . . from a lost dream of the night before, perhaps? In Mencken's *American Language* I learned that in some prisons a whang is a dope addict, and that a whangdoodle is a mystical creature devoted to lamentations, but still I heard my father dismissing forever anyone, especially a woman, who might whang. And there it rested until the evening, when a friend came in for a glass of wine on the way home from work and said casually of an unfortunate neighbor we share, "I heard Bella Dobson out whanging away at her poor poodle." I felt a small peculiar shock, quasi-audible, like the click of a safe being closed in a TV thriller.

Half a glass later we talked about the other words, about the oddness, the mystery, of coincidences in life, no matter how puny. That was all.

The next day, this harmless and pleasurable chitchat almost forgotten, I started for the second or third time to write about what are correctly called titbits, the "dainty morsels," the "small delicious nibbles" which Puritanical dictionaries prefer to spell tidbits to protect the salacious. I myself think of titbits as little harmless appetite whetters served with drinks before meals: salted nuts, small flavored wafers. Increasingly I regret the custom of presenting elaborate canapés, mistakenly called hors d'oeuvres in our country, which more and more take the place of a first course at table and often serve adequately as a full meal, washed along on floods of strong drink instead of the once customary dry sherry or, for celebration, champagne. I feel almost violent about this, for personal and obviously prejudiced reasons, and when I start to talk or write about it, I am apt to grow malicious, or scoffing, or plain peevish.

This happened as I tried to compose a hopefully light and provocative article about titbits as such: I crossed out paragraphs, tore pages into scraps, made abortive new starts, with a special and mounting dislike for one word especially, the new American *dip.* Finally I found myself outlining an unpublishable credo of protest, based on the cold facts that I had never made a dip in my life, had never in my life tasted a dip (for I refuse to consider an honest *guacamole* as such, even though it is correctly eaten on the tip of a piece of crisp tortilla which, admittedly, must be scooped through the bowl of mashed avocado . . .), and was sure that never would I either make or taste a dip. I felt very firm and relieved about it, and turned my back smugly upon several new cookbooks with long chapters devoted to dips of varying extravagance. Men don't really like dips, I reminded myself. Dips are messy. The idea of all kinds of wafers and chips and vegetables and plastic skewers dabbling in a common bowl, and often breaking off in it, was repugnant. Down, down to hell itself, I said, with dips. Life tasted sweeter. . . .

Then the telephone rang, and my Third Time had rolled around: a kind neighbor, who found herself expected to serve thirty instead of ten people, to raise money for an eminently worthy purpose . . . and would I possibly make some kind of . . .

I interrupted her rudely and fast, for I had a wild feeling that if she said the word, I would go off into a helpless scream of laughter and shake her even deeper than she already had been. ". . . some kind of canapé, some little nibbles?" I asked almost sternly, self-protectively.

"Oh, no, nothing like that," she said. "Nothing that takes any time, really. You can buy several kinds already made, in the supermarkets, and I thought perhaps you could just mix a few together and add a little something, and . . . really, just any kind of easy *dip!*"

I kept in control, and promised to bring a "little something," and hung up before she tried to help me any further.

It sounds silly to admit that I was upset by this last coincidence. I pulled my diatribe about teasers and titbits out of the typewriter and threw it away, and sat down with an out-of-date newsweekly and a glass of dry vermouth to air my spirits. The trick worked its usually twenty-minute magic, and I felt only an occasional wave of hysteria as I read carefully some of the new cookbooks I had dismissed with prejudice and impatience not long before. I scanned recipes for Bean-Bacon Chip-Dip and Saucy Crab-Clam Dip and Blue Cheese Chili Fluff and Pink Devil Dip-n-Dunk. I also read conscientiously the formulas for many other somewhat less outlandish mixtures to be paddled in by drinkers armed with everything from raw green beans to reinforced potato chips. I agreed that not only guacamole but a true Swiss fondue and even a currently fashionable *bagna cauda* demand this communal enjoyment which seems to have become such a lifesaver, apparently, to American party givers. I closed the books and went to two large markets and stared for some time at the pretty plastic containers of dips in the cold-bins. I bought one, made of sour cream with a great deal of monosodium glutamate and not many minced clams in it, and ate some of it for lunch. I then faced the fact that I still refused, as a matter of integrity, to concoct even a reasonable facsimile of such a thing.

I would and did make something rather soft, easy to spread . . . but to *spread*. I compromised with a Tried-and-True from my mother's old files, and poured it while still warm into two wide-mouthed bean pots, and served them at my harried neighbor's Bash with several kinds of new crackers, tasty but not faked with imitation bacon and Cheddar and suchlike flavors. In each chilled jar I stuck two or three old-fashioned butter knives, comfortably broad in the beam. Everything went well. [. . .]

SET PIECE FOR A FISHING PARTY
1810 A.D. — 1900 A.D. FRANCE

The twentieth century may yet be remembered as one of monstrous mass-feeding. Certainly the nineteenth will never be forgotten for its great contribution to gastronomy—the restaurants.

After the Revolution, Paris found itself practically kitchenless. Scullions had fled, or fought for their new estate; great chefs had scuttled to safety with their masters; most important, the money that had bought rare wines and strange exotic dishes was gone now from the hands that had known so well how to spend it.

Paris recovered quickly enough. Her citizens, uncomfortably Republican and somewhat more affluent than before, cast about restlessly for a new, a significant diversion.

It was not hard to find. Word was noised abroad that in the cellar of Number So-and-so, Rue Such-and-such, the ex-chef, Jean Durand, was cooking again.

What! Durand, the inventor of *petits pois aux noisettes grillées,* the great Durand who for twenty years had made famous the table of the ex-Marquise Sainte-Nitouche, ex-mistress of the even more ex-Duke Volte-face? But certainly not that Durand who once corrected Citizeness Marie Antoinette for adding mustard to a salad dressing before she had put in the salt? Impossible!

But—but can anyone go to Number So-and-so, Rue Such-and-such? Hah! Then I, Jacques Maillot, and I, Pierre Doudet, shall order the ex-chef of the ex-marquise to prepare a good dinner. It is expensive? Pouf! It is certainly worth the pleasure of eating what the damned aristos used to!

Thus Parisian restaurants blossomed from a few dark corners. Their trembling chefs, not long out of hiding, grew confident—and rich. They gathered round them enough of the old guard of pastry cooks, roasters, and *sommeliers* to keep things moving, and soon had more apprentices than they needed. Their furtive restaurants moved into fine quarters, and quickly became those boulevard palaces of fat gourmets, twinkling mirrors, pink plush, and belles, that Zola and Maupassant knew so well for us.

Fine food, once the privilege of the moneyed aristocracy, was now at the summons of any man with enough silver and manners to go to a good restaurant.

As the century rolled forward, and Jacques and Pierre flourished, the palaces grew more glittering, and their patrons more extravagant and gouty. But new blood, vulgar as it could be at times, brought freshness and vigour to the somewhat depleted art of eating. Vim and zest chased out the satiety which had become almost synonymous with pleasure under the several Louis. People ate enormously, with a lusty bourgeois delight born of strong constitutions and palates untouched by preciosity.

The fine art of eating was not wholly a thing of the stomach, however. Great minds considered it. As early as the 1820's, the learned Doctor Villermet presented a short but important paper to the Academy of Science. In it he proved conclusively that gourmands live longest and in the best health!

Nor is only their physical state influenced by gastronomy. Even the modern critic, in discussing that bon vivant Dumas, observes that "his marked intellectual superiority over his son may be readily attributed to his greater knowledge of dining." *Le Grand Dictionnaire de Cuisine* helps prove it.

Indeed, the obsession for fine eating that swept over Europe, and especially France, during the nineteenth century, had a strange and wonderful influence on the literature of that world.

Grimod de la Reynière, who wrote *Le Manuel des Amphitryons* in 1808, and edited the great *Almanach des Gourmands;* Carême, who cooked for the princes of six countries and Baron Rothschild, and wrote books on everything from the maker of picturesque pastry to the history of ancient kitchens; Alexandre Dumas—all these skilled artists and many another lived then in the respect and admiration which were their due.

Strangely enough, the greatest of them was probably the least known, was in fact scoffed at by the Paris exquisites as a rough mannered provincial. Brillat-Savarin lived quietly and very pleasantly, ate with a refined and prejudiced palate, thought for many years, and a few months before his death in 1828 published *La Physiologie du Goût.*

This work, a masterpiece of clarity and charm in any subject, is still without peer among books on eating. It is difficult to write about physical pleasures without being either coarse or over-delicate, vaguely sentimental or dry and scientific. *The Physiology of Taste* is none of these. It is as near perfection as we yet know it, and a constant wonder. The temptation to quote from its clear, pungent prose is hard to resist. Infinitely better, however, is the companionship of the book itself, for there is no superfluous word in it, no dull page.

While Brillat-Savarin finished his unobtrusive days in Paris and Belley, speculating with deliberate wisdom on the problems of transcendental gastronomy, Europe went mad over the art of dining.

Never have Continental restaurants been so crowded, unless perhaps it was during the First World War. The atmosphere differed, however, almost as much as the costumes.

In 1914–1918 women wore tight sheaths of glittering cloth over their slender bodies, and helped all the sad young men to be gay and gather rosebuds. In the nineteenth century women were fuller, softer, smoother. They dined opulently at all the best tables of every good restaurant in Paris, and knew to perfection the whims and dislikes of their fastidious gentlemen.

Foyot's, the *Café de Paris*, the *Brasserie Universelle*—there were a hundred temples of fine food, some chic for a moment, some apparently eternal in their devotion to *la gourmandise*.

Their chefs, seldom as coveted by princes as the great Carême, rejoiced nevertheless in as respectfully adoring a public as any royal offspring.

Their smallest triumphs were town gossip before the last bite was swallowed, and their most insignificant utterances were lapped up by such hungry brains as Dumas' and Maupassant's, to appear later in solemn or witty conversation.

It was toward the end of the First Empire that Brillat-Savarin and Carême, by persuasive argument, substituted the "made dish" for masses of roast meat, piled high on a platter and held clumsily erect by skewers. That modern gourmet, Paul Reboux (whose witty essay on gastronomy in a reputable encyclopædia is, tactlessly enough, flanked by a large and greyly horrible photograph of a gastric ulcer!), remarks that "these enormous, barbaric accumulations of food were yet another Bastille which the French Revolution overthrew." And for a few years, at least, they gave the Parisians almost as much to think about.

Meats, fruits, vegetables, wines, were combined and cooked and served in a thousand new ways. Flavours and aromas never dreamed of ran and rose from the exciting dishes. Gradually their appearance grew more rigidly ornate, and their construction more difficult. Finally the most complicated of these "made dishes" were classed by themselves, and *pièces montées* came into being.

Pièces montées were to Frenchmen of the last century what modern-art exhibits and automobile shows and fan dances are to John Doe today. Public contests were held, schools were founded to teach worthy chefs how to construct the sacred tricks, great artists drew designs, and solemn tomes were written on the art.

The Romans had pies which spilled out dancing dwarfs, or let fly up a flock of blackbirds and white doves. Later, in England, ponderous subtleties set all the banqueters guessing on full stomachs. It was in France, though, the brilliant vital France of the last century, that these inventions reached their peak of artistry and popularity.

Every good restaurant had its special department from which a *pièce montée* could be commanded for any kind of festivity, christening party or wake. If the prices were too high, there was the neighbourhood bakeshop, where even the apprentice could turn out a passable sugar dove rising from a nest of mocha and pistachio cream.

Of all the real artists of the set piece, Carême was certainly the greatest. He had an uncanny ability to use pastry and sugar, and a mighty respect for them both. In one of his books he announces quite seriously:

The Fine Arts are five in number: Painting, Music, Sculpture, Poetry, and Architecture—whereof the principal branch is confectionery.

As the vogue for set pieces increased, he combined this reverential talent with all his others to produce amazing structures, dreamlike, fantastic. His disciples exaggerated his strange juxtapositions and his mixtures of irony and beauty. Finally, as with every school of art headed by one man, cheap imitators crept after him with their coarsening touch, and by the end of the century set pieces had become almost ridiculous, a synonym for the pretentious vulgarity of new-rich entertainment.

It is in Carême's own book on the subject, *Le Pâtissier Pittoresque,* or in the several other volumes of this period, that we must look to see *pièces montées* at their best. There countless engravings, as well as the restrained rhetoric of the prose, make very clear the incredible delicacy and variety of these strange dishes which cost thousands of francs and were seldom eaten.

One little engraving is very pleasant to remember. It shows a *pièce* which stands probably four or five feet high. A froth of green foliage forms its base—leaves of mashed potato as delicate as ever grew from pastry tube. From that a Doric column, garlanded with pale full-blown flowers of lobster meat, diminishes twice.

At the top, on a pedestal edged with little shells and shrimpy rosebuds, is a pool of the clearest blue-green sugar, crystallized. And from it, with only the ankles of his tail held in the crystal, curves a fresh plump fish, every scale gleaming, his eyes popping with satiric amusement, and a beautiful umbrella of spun sugar held over his head by one sturdy fin!

Above the engraving runs the legend, in that somewhat smudgy printing of the 1830's: *A Culinary Fantasy—the Cautious Carp.*

from THE PHYSIOLOGY OF TASTE

But, the impatient reader may exclaim, how can one possibly assemble, in this year of grace 1825, a meal which will meet all the conditions necessary to attain the ultimate in the pleasures of the table?

I am about to answer that question. Draw near, Reader, and pay heed: it is Gasterea, the loveliest of the muses, who inspires me; I shall speak more clearly than an oracle, and my precepts will live throughout the centuries.

"Let the number of guests be no more than twelve, so that conversation may always remain general;

"Let them be so chosen that their professions will be varied, their tastes analogous, and that there be such points of contact that the odious formality of introductions will not be needed;

"Let the dining room be more than amply lighted, the linen of dazzling cleanliness, and the temperature maintained at from sixty to sixty-eight degrees Fahrenheit;

"Let the gentlemen be witty without pretension, and the ladies charming without too much coquetry;

"Let the dishes be of exquisite quality, but limited in their number, and the wines of the first rank also, each according to its degree;

"Let the progression of the former be from the most substantial to the lightest, and of the latter from the simplest wines to the headiest;

"Let the tempo of eating be moderate, the dinner being the last affair of the day: the guests should behave like travellers who must arrive together at the same destination;

"Let the coffee be piping hot, and the liqueurs of the host's especial choice;

"Let the drawing room which awaits the diners be large enough to hold a card table for those who cannot do without it, with enough space left for after-dinner conversations;

"Let the guests be disciplined by the restraints of polite society and animated by the hope that the evening will not pass without its rewarding pleasures;

"Let the tea be not too strong, the toast artfully buttered, and the punch made with care;

"Let the leavetakings not begin before eleven o'clock, but by midnight let every guest be home and abed."

If anyone has attended a party combining all these virtues, he can boast that he has known perfection, and for each one of them which has been forgotten or ignored he will have experienced the less delight.

I have already said that the pleasures of the table, as I conceive of them, can go on for a rather long period of time; I am going to prove this now by giving a detailed and faithful account of the lengthiest meal I ever ate in my life; it is a little bonbon which I shall pop into my reader's mouth as a reward for having read me thus far with such agreeable politeness. Here it is:

I used to have, at the end of the Rue du Bac, a family of cousins composed of the following: Doctor Dubois, seventy-eight years old; the captain, seventy-six; their sister Jeannette, who was seventy-four. I went now and then to pay them a visit, and they always received me very graciously.

"By George!" the doctor said one day to me, standing on tiptoe to slap me on the shoulder. "For a long time now you've been boasting of your fondues *(eggs scrambled with cheese), and you always manage to keep our mouths watering. It's time to stop all this. The captain and I are coming soon to have breakfast with you, to see what it's all about." (It was, I believe, in 1801 that he thus teased me.)*

"Gladly," I replied. "You'll taste it in all its glory, for I myself will make it. Your idea is completely delightful to me. So . . . tomorrow at ten sharp, military style!"

At the appointed hour I saw my guests arrive, freshly shaved, their hair carefully arranged and well-powdered: two little old men who were still spry and healthy.

They smiled with pleasure when they saw the table ready, spread with white linen, three places laid, and at each of them two dozen oysters and a gleaming golden lemon.

At both ends of the table rose up bottles of Sauterne, carefully wiped clean except for the corks, which indicated in no uncertain way that it was a long time that the wine had rested there.

Alas, in my life-span I have almost seen the last of those oyster breakfasts, so frequent and so gay in the old days, where the molluscs were swallowed by the thousands! They have disappeared with the abbés, who never ate less than a gross apiece, and with the chevaliers, who went on eating them forever. I regret them, in a philosophical way: if time can change governments, how much more influence has it over our simple customs!

After the oysters, which were found to be deliciously fresh, grilled skewered kidneys were served, a deep pastry shell of truffled foie gras, *and finally the* fondue.

All its ingredients had been mixed in a casserole, which was brought to the table with an alcohol lamp. I performed on this battlefield, and my cousins did not miss a single one of my gestures.

They exclaimed with delight on the charms of the whole procedure, and asked for my recipe, which I promised to give them, the while I told the two anecdotes on the subject which my reader will perhaps find further on.

After the fondue *came seasonable fresh fruits and sweetmeats, a cup of real Mocha made* à la Dubelloy, *a method which was then beginning to be known, and finally two kinds of liqueurs, one sharp for refreshing the palate and the other oily for soothing it.*

The breakfast being well-ended, I suggested to my guests that we take a little exercise, and that it consist of inspecting my apartment, quarters which are far from elegant but which are spacious and comfortable, and which pleased my company especially since the ceilings and gildings date from the middle of the reign of Louis XV.

I showed them the clay original of the bust of my lovely cousin Mme. Récamier by Chinard, and her portrait in miniature by Augustin; they were so delighted by these that the doctor kissed the portrait with his full fleshy lips, and the captain permitted himself to take such liberty with the statue that I slapped him away; for if all the admirers of the original did likewise, that breast so voluptuously shaped would soon be in the same state as the big toe of Saint Peter in Rome, which pilgrims have worn to a nubbin with their kisses.

Then I showed them a few casts from the works of the best antique sculptors, some paintings

The Physiology of Taste

which were not without merit, my guns, my musical instruments, and a few fine first editions, as many of them French as foreign.

In this little excursion into such varied arts they did not forget my kitchen. I showed them my economical stockpot, my roastingshell, my clockwork spit, and my steamcooker. They inspected everything with the most finicky curiosity, and were all the more astonished since in their own kitchens everything was still done as it had been during the Regency.

At the very moment we re-entered my drawing room, the clock struck two. "Bother!" the doctor exclaimed. "Here it is dinner time, and sister Jeannette will be waiting for us! We must hurry back to her. I must confess I feel no real hunger, but still I must have my bowl of soup. It is an old habit with me, and when I go for a day without taking it I have to say with Titus, Diem perdidi."

"My dear doctor," I said to him, "why go so far for what is right here at hand? I'll send someone to the kitchen to give warning that you will stay awhile longer with me, and that you will give me the great pleasure of accepting a dinner toward which I know you will be charitable, since it will not have all the finish of such a meal prepared with more leisure."

A kind of oculary consultation took place at this point between the two brothers, followed by a formal acceptance. I then sent a messenger post-haste to the Faubourg Saint-Germain, and exchanged a word or two with my master cook; and after a remarkably short interval, and thanks partly to his own resources and partly to the help of neighboring restaurants, he served us a very neatly turned out little dinner, and a delectable one to boot.

It gave me deep satisfaction to observe the poise and aplomb with which my two friends seated themselves, pulled nearer to the table, spread out their napkins, and prepared for action.

They were subjected to two surprises which I myself had not intended for them; for first I served them Parmesan cheese with the soup, and then I offered them a glass of dry Madeira. These were novelties but lately imported by Prince Talleyrand, the leader of all our diplomats, to whom we owe so many witticisms, so many epigrams and profundities, and the man so long followed by the public's devout attention, whether in the days of his power or of his retirement.

Dinner went off very well in both its accessory and its main parts, and my cousins reflected as much pleasure as gaiety.

Afterwards I suggested a game of piquet, which they refused; they preferred the sweet siesta, the far niente, of the Italians, the captain told me; and therefore we made a little circle close to the hearth.

In spite of the delights of a postprandial doze, I have always felt that nothing lends more calm pleasure to the conversation than an occupation of whatever kind, so long as it does not absorb the attention. Therefore I proposed a cup of tea.

Tea in itself was an innovation to the old die-hard patriots. Nevertheless it was accepted. I made it before their eyes, and they drank down several cups of it with all the more pleasure since they had always before considered it a remedy.

Long practice has taught me that one pleasure leads to another, and that once headed along this path a man loses the power of refusal. Therefore it was that in an almost imperative voice I spoke of finishing the afternoon with a bowl of punch.

"But you will kill us!" the doctor said.

"Or at least make us tipsy!" the captain added.

To all this I replied only by calling vociferously for lemons, for sugar, for rum.

I concocted the punch then, and while I was busy with it, I had made for me some beautifully thin, delicately buttered, and perfectly salted slices of zwiebach (toast).

This time there was a little protest. My cousins assured me that they had already eaten very well indeed, and that they would not touch another thing; but since I am acquainted with the temptations of this completely simple dish, I replied with only one remark, that I hoped I had made enough of it. And sure enough, soon afterwards the captain took the last slice, and I caught him peeking to see if there were still a little more or if it was really the last. I ordered another plateful immediately.

During all this, time had passed, and my watch showed me it was past eight o'clock.

"We must get out of here!" my guests exclaimed. "We are absolutely obliged to go home and eat at least a bit of salad with our poor sister, who has not set eyes on us today!"

I had no real objection to this; faithful to the duties of hospitality when it is concerned with two such delightful old fellows, I accompanied them to their carriage, and watched them be driven away.

Someone may ask if boredom did not show itself now and then in such a long séance.

I shall reply in the negative: the attention of my guests was fixed by my making the fondue, by the little trip around the apartment, by a few things which were new to them in the dinner, by the tea, and above all by the punch, which they had never before tasted.

Moreover the doctor knew the genealogy and the bits of gossip of all Paris; the captain had passed part of his life in Italy, both as a soldier and as an envoy to the Parman court; I myself have traveled a great deal; we chatted without affectation, and listened to one another with delight. Not even that much is needed to make time pass with grace and rapidity.

The next morning I received a letter from the doctor; he wished to inform me that the little debauch of the night before had done them no harm at all; quite to the contrary, after the sweetest of sleeps, the two old men had arisen refreshed, feeling both able and eager to begin anew.

Anthelme Brillat-Savarin, 1755–1826

Translated from the French by M.F.K. Fisher

FROM V IS FOR VENALITY

. . . and for the mixture of gastronomical pleasure and corruption that helps senators and actresses pounce with such slyly hidden skill upon their prey.

Wherever politics are played, of no matter what color, sex, or reason, the table is an intrinsic part of them, so much so that Brillat-Savarin asserted, enthusiastically if not too correctly, that every great event in history has been consummated over a banquet board. Though I may question his statement, I still admit the loose rightness of it and bow to the companion thought that history is indeed largely venal, no matter what its ultimate nobility. Surely many a soldier has been saved from death because his general slept the night before the battle with Ottilia instead of Claudia, and more than one pretty creature in a Hollywood restaurant has missed stardom but kept her female balance because a producer did not like the way she ate asparagus.

Wherever politics are played, then, which means wherever in the world more than five men foregather, venality sits at table with them, corrupt, all-powerful. In every city from Oskaloosa to Madrid, there is one meeting place which above all others furthers and comforts the inevitable progress of the evilbent, and the ghost of a Paris senator who last lunched at Foyot's in 1897 would find itself perfectly at home in a certain air-conditioned restaurant in Washington, this year or next, or in some such place as Mike Romanoff's in Beverly Hills.

Some of the best food in America can be, and occasionally is, found at his eating place, although architecture rather than gastronomy seems at first glance to be what makes it a necessary part of the nourishment of Hollywood politicians.

The perfection of a rack of lamb served from Mike's over-poweringly beautiful silver meat cart is unimportant; it is where that lamb is consumed that matters. And the interior of this all-important chophouse is so cunningly arranged that its zigzag windowed partitions change it from a long dull store building into a series of rigidly protected social levels.

There are the few tables by the bar, known as Stockholders' Row, and with much of the well-padded comfortable aura of an exclusive club. Probably fifty people in the whole world are qualified to sit at them, and any slight deviation from the twice-daily pattern of familiar paunches causes as much local speculation as a mysterious drop in the market.

Then there is the Reinhardt Room, named for its professorial and omnipotent head-captain. It was rightly ignored at first because of its unbecoming pink sides and its dull isolation, until large peepholes were cut in the wall nearest the bar and a celebrated columnist was prevailed upon with true Romanoff tact to make it the center of her sharpest operations. Now anyone in Hollywood is glad to lunch or dine there, in order to catch her eye, and nod and smile, and guarantee himself one more kind printed word.

Off Reinhardt's stronghold and down a step or two, but still with low partitions so that no Keneth Hopkins hat, no famous toupee, need be missed by a quick-eyed loiterer at the bar, is a small quiet room where big deals are made. There fading stars form independent companies with other people's fortunes and themselves as writer-director-producers. Story editors buy unwritten masterpieces for a quarter of a million. Agents murder other agents with invisible bloodshed.

In spite of the fact that the silver meat cart is too luxuriously weighty to go down the steps, rack of lamb tastes better in the quiet little room, temporarily at least, than anywhere except Stockholders' Row. Certainly it would taste infinitely better there, basted with cyanide and laced with strychnine and garnished with Paris green, than it ever could if by some trick it were served plain and unpoisoned to the star or the story editor or the agent in the Back Room!

The Back Room, quite simply, is suicide. It used to be the whole restaurant, and a few old-timers smile fondly if discreetly at the remembrance of its early days, when Romanoff had not quite enough money to buy chairs and tables for it, and it was cut off from the half-deserted bar by long, gloomy curtains that flapped dismally in the draughts of debt and insecurity and emptiness. That was before Prince Mike and his loyal architect, in mutual desperation, had evolved their fantastically successful scheme of separating the local dukes, cabinet ministers, and lesser nobility into their proper groups, and their fair ladies into the correctly improper ones. Now the room, the dread Back Room, is reserved for a few miserable people whose options have just been dropped and a blissfully ignorant flow of Eastern visitors who do not realize that they are actually enjoying what to a local inhabitant would mean social death.

Well-groomed matrons from the hinterland chatter brightly over excellent cocktails and down great quantities of delicious pastries served with skill and tact, never suspecting that from the Row, and the Reinhardt room, and even from the far-west quiet corner where big deals are made, any glances that may come their way are heavy with scorn, boredom, or at best a faint pity.

Producers shudder at the thought of ever stepping over the sill of that airy pleasant limbo. Producers' girl friends in very new mink coats shudder at the chance that some crowded day they might have to sit two tables in. Ambitious and "promising young" writers of no matter what age recognize the ugly truth that in a pinch they might penetrate as far as the third small table to the left, but pray that it will never be necessary. And meanwhile the happy visitors from Iowa and New York sip and chatter under the same artful roof with countless movie-greats, oblivious of their wretched lot—and of one other room, which perhaps even the aristocracy up front might envy: a cool trellised garden off the kitchens, where one day I saw waiters and cooks and the lowliest busboys sitting at a long clean table in the dappled light, eating amicably together without benefit of silver meat cart but from bowls and platters that looked well laden.

Mike Romanoff and his architect had built exceedingly well, I thought with my own kind of snobbism. And I wondered if there, and at the Chambord still, and once at Foyot's, and once at the place in Amsterdam where there were, before the bombs fell, strawberries served two by enormous two upon white damask napkins, and at a hundred other great restaurants around the globe, venality and all its hugger-mugger of intricate play upon the senses did indeed work maggot-like through the kitchens as well as the bar and the Reinhardt Room. I looked at the men and boys eating with such seeming friendliness and pleasure under the vine leaves, and wondered if, for them, cuts of smuggled venison and truffles en papillote took the place of red-haired actresses, of senators of the Opposition, to be manipulated and wooed in the full sense of the word venal. It was harder to believe, there in the sunlight, than it could have been elsewhere. [. . .]

FROM SING OF DINNER IN A DISH

More than six per cent of the inmates of San Quentin give their previous occupation as cook (labourers form the largest group and cooks the second largest); but male cooks compose less than two-tenths of one per cent of the total U.S. population, according to the 1930 census.

I would like to know to what type of crime cooks are peculiarly given. I have heard it said by men who have been much up and down the world that cooks as a class are irascible men, with the instincts of dictators. It is an interesting speculation: does the profession attract men of a certain character, or are nerves and tempers shattered by the life they lead? Or does the emotional effect result from a physical deterioration of stomach and liver through too much tasting of their own cooking?

Just what, in brief, is the moral hazard involved in being a cook?

We Who Are About to Die, DAVID LAMSON

"Always have a Chinese cook," said the woman who had followed her sailor seven times round the globe, and settled at last inside the Golden Gate. "Yes, always have a Chinese cook—and never go into the kitchen!"

Is this foul slander, or the cool tongue of wisdom? When on the bottom of a casserole doth grimed grease hiss, is ignorance bliss? Probably.

Surely I have eaten many a tart that felt the floor before it felt my plate, and more than a hundred bowls of soup whose temperature was tested, consciously or not, by a fat thumb. I have even pushed dead flies to one side of an omelette or ragoût, and eaten to the last bite undaunted. I have not really minded, inside of me, because what I ate was good, and I do not think that good food can come from a bad kitchen.

It can come from a cluttered kitchen piled with used dishes, redolent with the escaped smells of garlic, vanilla, and wine-vinegar, a kitchen steamy and full of rattle and clash.

Madame Rigagnier's is like that—a dark cabinet not nine feet square, its walls banked with copper pots and pans, and a pump for water outside the door. And from that little hole, which would make an American shudder with disgust, she turns out daily two of the finest meals I've yet eaten.

Or good food can come from a gigantic factory of fine dishes, such as Arnold Bennett describes so well in a book he wrote about grand hotels.

But good food can never come from a bad kitchen. A bad kitchen is what it is for two reasons: either nobody cares whether it produces decent victuals, or it is filthy. And if it is filthy, it is, says Webster, defiled with filth; foul; impure; obscene; unclean; squalid; and above all nasty.

I know one like that. It is the back side of a kosher restaurant. In the window are pans of strudel and *auf-lauf* and rice *kugel*, which look good. Furthermore, the prices are low and the tables are crowded—favourable signs, surely. Perhaps this is one of those rare little places that lurk in big towns like pearls in the sea.

We go in. There is a great clatter. Nobody notices us. All the tables are occupied, and we push toward the end of the long room. The last table is freed by two silent men, and a large waitress slaps at it with a cloth. She looks at us dully with monkey eyes, and hurries away.

We slide our legs under the slimy tabletop. A pandemonium of cries and crashes swells in my ears whenever a waitress goes through the swinging doors beside me. I see Al, who faces it, peering with a strange expression, which he masks politely as I look at him.

My purse slips to the floor, and when I touch it again it is stuck all over one side with crumbs and nastiness.

I forget what we order. Whatever it is, we do not eat it. By now I too have peered through the swinging door, and I too have stiffened my face into politeness. We sit silently, watching with every pore, for this is a unique (Please God, unique!) experience, and we shall miss none of it by maiden squeamishness.

The kitchen is small and overcrowded and hot, as is Madame Rigagnier's—and our own. There the comparison ends.

The floor, slick and black, is uneven where dishtowels and utensils have been half-swallowed in its eternal ooze. Water from the grease-ridged sink runs over it in iridescent trickles, and crusts of bread and slippery wilted lettuce scraps lie everywhere, never too trodden for the rats of dawn.

Up from the floor and in and down from the foul walls and ceiling seeps a smell more evil and obscene than Mr. Webster dreamed of. It is acrid and heavy, a slippery, dark grey smell, like the piled-up excrement of a million ducks.

Waitresses go in and out with the look of women who have been so nauseated for so long that it can never matter any more. Fortunately, we do not see the faces of the two cooks.

They are men, evidently, wearing old tennis shoes, trousers, oily grey underwear, and bandannas knotted around their heads.

They yell at each other and at the waitresses, and the waitresses yell frantically back at them, and nobody ever yells at the strange brown man who walks among them.

He carries trays of soiled dishes, sometimes on his head, and sometimes not, from the front of the restaurant to the kitchen. He might be a Filipino, but more probably he is a last Hawaiian or Tahitian. He looks like the pictures we see of those fading races of the world.

His body is good, with no bones holding it up, but not soft, either, and his hair is fine and purple above his dark face.

He moves like a wave, steadily and impersonally. Other people are shoved and pushed, but as he walks through the restaurant, balancing his body easily under the tray, he is never touched.

There is no sign that he sees or hears. His face is expressionless and his eyes are contracted and dull. He seldom moves them, and when they light on my face he does not see me, as I do not see one telephone pole among all the other poles from a train window.

He is full of drugs, or hypnotized; he is mad; he is transcendental, taboo.

We begin to feel uneasy, and go away, turning as we pass the street window for one more puzzled look at the false *apfelstrudel* lying there.

The air tastes like mead in our throats. [. . .]

WHEN A MAN IS SMALL

When a man is small, he loves and hates food with a ferocity which soon dims. At six years old his very bowels will heave when such a dish as creamed carrots or cold tapioca appears before him. His throat will close, and spots of nausea and rage swim in his vision. It is hard, later, to remember why, but at the time there is no pose in his disgust. He cannot eat; he says, "To hell with it!"

In the same way, some foods are utterly delicious, and he thinks of them and tastes them with a sensuous passion which too often disappears completely with the years.

Perhaps there are little chocolate cookies as a special treat, two apiece. He eats his, all two, with an intense but delicate avidity. His small sister Judy puts one of hers in her pocket, the smug thing. But Aunt Gwen takes a bite from each of her cookies and gives what is left of one to Judy, what is left of the other to him. She is quite calm about it.

He looks at her with dreadful wonder. How can she bear to do it? He could not, *could* not have given more than a crumb of his cooky to anyone. Perhaps even a crumb would be too big. Aunt Gwen is wonderful; she is brave and superhuman. He feels a little dizzy as he looks at the bitten cooky in his hand. How could she do it?

By the time a man is ten or twelve he has forgotten most of his young passions. He is hungry and he wants to be full. It is very simple.

A few more years and he is at his life's peak of energy. His body is electric with young muscle, young blood, a newfound manhood, an awakening mind. Strangely enough, it is now that he whips himself up to greater speed. He drinks strong raw spirits and countless cups of coffee, hot and black. He devours such mild aphrodisiacs as chili, tamales, and rare beef drowned in bottled sauces. He pours salt and pepper over everything except desserts.

At this age, eighteen or nineteen, gastronomic perceptions are nonexistent, or at the most, naïve. I remember that when I was a college freshman my nearest approach to *la gourmandise* was a midnight visit to *Henry's*, the old *Henry's*, on Hollywood Boulevard which all the world said that Charlie Chaplin owned secretly.

There I would call for the head waiter, which probably awed my escort as much as I hoped it would. The waiter, a kindly soul except on Saturday nights, played up to me beautifully, and together we ordered a large pot of coffee and a German pancake with hot applesauce and sweet butter. ("Salted butter ruins the flavor," I would add in a nonchalant aside to my Tommy or Jimmy.)

When the pancake appeared, after an impressive wait, it was big as a tabletop, with curled edges. Two waitresses fussed over it, while people stared at us and I made sure that the applesauce was spread on *after* the melted butter, and that plenty of lemon juice and cinnamon were sprinkled about.

I always looked away while the monstrous thing was rolled: the waitresses were too nervous and stuck out their tongues. And I cannot remember ever finishing even my half of the pancake, when it was sliced and powdered and laid before me. Nor can I imagine ordering one now.

It is, however, these innocent experiments with food, mixed though they may be with snobbishness and "showing off," that indicate what kind of older person a young one may become. And he had two choices, the two oft-quoted oft-abused alternatives of eating to live and of living to eat.

Any normal man must nourish his body by means of food put into it through the mouth. This process takes time, quite apart from the lengthy preparations and digestions that accompany it.

Between the ages of twenty and fifty, John Doe spends some twenty thousand hours chewing and swallowing food, more than eight hundred days and nights of steady eating. The mere contemplation of this fact is upsetting enough!

To some men it is actively revolting. They devise means of accomplishing the required nourishments of their bodies by pills of condensed victuals and easily swallowed draughts which equal, they are told, the food value of a beefsteak or a vegetable stew.

To others, the stunning realization of how much time is needed to feed themselves is accepted more philosophically. They agree with La Rochefoucauld's aphorism: To eat is a necessity, but to eat intelligently is an art.

Critics of the resulting scheme of life are easily led to accuse its practicants of substituting a less pleasant word for "intelligent." So, indeed, do many of us. We sink too easily into stupid and overfed sensuality, our bodies thickening even more quickly than our minds. We sharpen one sense at the cost of losing many others, and call ourselves epicures, forgetting that Epicurus himself employed the same adjective as La Rochefoucauld when he advocated our finding an agreeable use for our faculties in "the intelligent enjoyment of the pleasures of the table."

Whichever school a man may adhere to, the protestant or the philosophical, he continues to eat through the middle years of life with increasing interest. He grows more conscious of his body as it becomes less tolerant.

No longer can he dine heavily at untoward hours, filling his stomach with the adolescent excitations of hot sauces and stodgy pastries—no longer, that is, with impunity. No more can he say with any truth: "Oh, I can eat anything. I can drink without showing it. I am made of iron."

He is confused by strange aches and rumblings, and shudders at the thought of being forced by old age to return to the pap and pabulum of his infancy.

Most of us, unhappily, shudder and ache and rumble as secretly as possible, seeming to feel disgrace in what is but one of the common phenomena of age: the general slowing of all physical processes. For years we hide or ignore our bodily protests and hasten our own dyspeptic doom by trying to eat and drink as we did when we were twenty.

When we are past fifty, especially if we have kept up this pathetic pose of youth-at-table, we begin to grow fat. It is then that even the blindest of us should beware. Unfortunately, however, we are too used to seeing other people turn heavy in their fifties: we accept paunches and double chins as a necessary part of growing old.

Instead, we should realize this final protest of an overstuffed system, and ease our body's last years by lightening its burden. We should eat sparingly.

It is here that gastronomy, or an equivalent, can play its most comforting rôle. Even in crude form the desire for a special taste or sensation has often helped an old man more than his critical family can know. They may call him heartless; he in his turn may as logically be acting with good sense, like the ancient sailor whose much-loved son was lost at sea. When at last some one mustered courage to tell the father this tragic news, the old man looked at him coldly for a minute, glanced out the window at the blown sea, and then snapped: "Dad blast it, where's my dish of tea? I want my tea!"

For many old people, eating is the only pleasure left, as were the "endless dishes" and "unceasing cups of wine" to the aged Ulysses. And between gobbling down an indistinguishable mess of heavy meat and bread, or savouring a delicate broiled trout or an aspic full of subtle vegetable flavours, how few of us would choose the distressful insomnia that follows the first for the light easy rest of the second?

But men are thoughtless and they are habit-followers. They have eaten meat and starches for years: they see no reason for stopping when they are old, even when they think enough to realize that every function of their bodies is carried on more slowly and with more effort than ever before.

They go on whipping up their blood with "well-done" roasts, which travel halt-ingly through the system to the final colonic decay that makes one of the great foes of senescence—constipation.

They are floated to their coffins on a river of "stimulating" infusions of beef extract and iron, usually fed to them surreptitiously by well-meaning daughters.

They plump out their poor sagging paunches for years with the puffed richness of such "nourishing" desserts as the typical English sweet which a friend described to me: "cake soaked with bad port, smothered in boiled custard stained a purple-brown with blackberry juice, which is in turn top-layered with warm ill-beaten white of egg tinted fuchsia pink, the whole garnished with small dirty-brown buttons of granite that are reported by us hardier Britons to be macaroons. This particular foul con-coction is called 'Queen o' Puddings'!"

No wonder old people are dubbed "quaintly crabbed and testy" by sentimental novelists, and "plain hell to live with" by their less idealistic offspring!

But we must grow old, and we must eat. It seems far from unreasonable, once these facts are accepted, for a man to set himself the pleasant task of educating his palate so that he can do the former not grudgingly and in spite of the latter, but easily and agreeably because of it.

Talleyrand said that two things are essential in life: to give good dinners and to keep on fair terms with women. As the years pass and fires cool, it can become unimportant to stay always on fair terms either with women or one's fellows, but a wide and sensitive appreciation of fine flavours can still abide with us, to warm our hearts.

E IS FOR EXQUISITE

. . . and its gastronomical connotations, at least for me.

When I hear of a gourmet with exquisite taste I assume, perhaps too hastily and perhaps very wrongly, that there is something exaggeratedly elaborate, and even languidly perverted, about his gourmandism. I do not think simply of an exquisitely laid table and an exquisite meal. Instead I see his silver carved in subtly erotic patterns, and his courses following one upon another in a cabalistic design, half pain, half pleasure. I take it for granted, in spite of my good sense, that rare volumes on witchcraft have equal place with Escoffier in his kitchen library, and I read into his basic recipe for meat stock a dozen deviously significant ingredients.

Such deliberate romanticism on my part can most easily be dismissed as the wishful thinking of an amateur cook who scrambles eggs very well but only reads, these days, about filets de sole Polignac and pâté de foie truffé en brioche. Or perhaps it is Freudian: subconsciously I might murder, or even seduce, by means of cookery, and therefore I ascribe such potentialities to someone whose culinary freedom I envy! Whatever the reason, in my private lexicon of gastronomy I continue to see the word exquisite ringed about with subtle vapors of perversion.

Most of the great historical and literary gourmets, in the sense of their being exquisites, have had the unlimited money, like Des Esseintes in Huysmans' *Against the Grain*. The very fact that they can command no matter what incredible delicacy adds to their satiety, and that in turn gives just the fillip of distortion to their appetites which satisfies my definition of their exquisiteness.

Huysmans' sad young man, for instance: his "farewell dinner to a temporarily dead virility," as the invitations shaped like bereavement notices called it, was a masterpiece of jaded extravagance. He needed to be a millionaire, as well as a determined exquisite, to serve—in a black-draped room lighted by green flames, attended by nude black virgins wearing silver slippers and stockings trimmed with dripping tears—a dinner beginning with blackest caviar and ending with black-heart cherries. He needed to be at least a demi-millionaire to fill his fountain with ink for that one dubious feast, and to line his ash-covered paths with funereal pine trees.

He needed, above all, to be sublimely indifferent to the taint of vulgarity, for his earnest efforts at eccentricity were indeed vulgar, and ridiculous too, in a basically shameful and extravagant way. All that saved him from oblivion was his dignified disregard of anything but his own kind of pleasure.

It is the same with some of the dishes we still read about with a strange fascination, those cooked for the most dissipated of the Romans two thousand years or so ago. Doubtless many of them tried to astound their sycophants by serving whole platters of the tongues of little birds that had been trained to talk before they went into the pot. We do not remember the names of these men, nor anything more than the vulgarly idiotic waste. But what if one of those epicures, greatly in love with a proud lady named Livia, had taught a thousand birds to sing her name, Livia, Livia, to the moment of most perfect diction, and then had served forth to the lady a fine pie of their tongues, split, honeyed, and impaled on twigs of myrrh? *Then*, I think, that fat lover would still be known to us for what he was, an exquisite—a silly one perhaps, extravagant certainly, but with his own dignity about him.

I remember deciding once, long ago and I believe after reading Elwanger's *Pleasures of the Table* for the first time, that the most exquisite dish I had ever heard of was a salad of satiny white endive with large heavily scented Parma violets scattered through it. It meant everything subtle and intense and aesthetically significant in my private gastronomy, just as, a few years earlier, a brown-skinned lover with a turquoise set in one ear lobe epitomized my adolescent dream of passion. It is a misfortune perhaps that not many months ago the salad was set before me in a bowl.

That it was not very good was relatively unimportant: the dressing was light to the point of being innocuous, and it was unable to stand up under the perfumed assault of the blossoms. What disappointed me, finally and forever, was that it was served neither exquisitely, nor by an exquisite, nor with an exquisite disregard of the vulgar.

Instead it was concocted and presented with both affectation and awkwardness and was at best an attempt at that insidious decadence which is a prerequisite of my definition. It suddenly became ridiculous.

I blushed for my long dream of it and felt a hollowness, for where again will I know so certainly that such and such a dish is *it?* What will it be? Expense is not enough, for sure, and no intricate silverware, no ritual of serving and compounding, can guarantee the magic. There must, for me at least, be a faint nebular madness, dignified no matter how deliberate, to a dinner that is exquisite. [. . .]

S IS FOR
SURVIVAL

from R is for Romantic

[M]ilk toast is part of the unwritten cookery book engraved, almost without conscious recognition of it, in the mind of anyone who ever tended the young, the weak, the old. It is a warm, mild, soothing thing, full of innocent strength.

There is no recipe for it in even my homeliest kitchen manuals, in their generally revolting lists under such titles as "Feeding the Sick" and "Invalid Receipts." It is, in other words, an instinctive palliative, something like boiled water. But since some human beings may by dire oversight have missed the ministrations of their grandmothers, or of such a great hulk of woman as cared once for me when I was low in body, I shall print an approximation of the rule, to be adapted naturally to the relative strength or weakness of the person to imbibe it.

Milk Toast
(for the Ill, Weak, Old, Very Young, or Weary)
    1 pint milk, part cream if the person is not forbidden that
    sweet butter, if butter is allowed
    4 slices good bread, preferably homemade
    salt, pepper, if not a child or very ill
Heat the milk gently to the simmering point. Meanwhile have ready 4 freshly toasted slices of bread. Butter them generously. Heat a pretty bowl, deeper than it is wide. Break the hot buttered toast into it, pour the steaming but not boiling milk over it, sprinkle a very little salt and pepper on the top, and serve at once.

It can be seen that compromise lies in every ingredient. The basis for the whole is toasted bread soaked in warm milk. The sweet butter, the seasoning, the cream and the milk—these are sops indeed to the sybarite in even the sickest of us.

I have used this bland prescription more than once upon myself, recognizing a flicker across my cheekbones, a humming near my elbows and my knees, that meant fatigue had crept too close to the fortress walls. I have found partaking of a warm full bowl of it, in an early bed after a long bath, a very wise medicine—and me but weary, not ill, weak, old, not very young!

And I remember going one night to a famous restaurant, the quiet, subtly lighted kind like the Chambord, for instance, with a man who was healthier than almost anyone I ever met, because he had just emerged from months of dreadful illness, the quiet, subtly mortal kind. He still moved cautiously and spoke in a somewhat awed voice, and with a courteous but matter-of-fact apology he ordered milk toast for himself, hinting meanwhile at untold gastronomical delights for me.

I upset him and our waiter, only temporarily however, by asking for milk toast too, not because of my deep dislike of a cluttered table, but because I suddenly wanted the clear, comforting feel of the brew upon my tongue.

While I drank a glass of sherry an increasing flurry surrounded us. It took me some minutes to realize that probably never before in the fifty or so years the restaurant had been there had anyone ordered milk toast—nothing but milk toast. I began to feel as if screens would be whisked up around us, like two unfortunate or indiscreet athletes on a football field. There was a mounting air of tension among the waiters, who increased gradually in our corner of the room from three to about twelve. By the time the silver chafing dishes had been wheeled before us, we had three captains, all plainly nervous, eying the maneuvers from nearby vantage points.

The thing began: butter sizzling here, toast smoking delicately there, rich milk trembling at the bubbling point but no further, a huge silver pepper mill held ready, salt, *rock*-salt, in a Rumanian grinder, paprika in a tin marked "Buda-Pesth." Helpless, a little hysterical under our super-genteel exteriors, my friend and I waited. The flames flamed. The three captains surged into action. And before we could really follow the intricate and apparently well-rehearsed ballet, two mammoth silver bowls, just like the nursery ones but bigger and more beautiful, steamed before us, and we sat spooning up the most luxurious, most ridiculously and spectacularly delicious milk toast either of us had eaten in our long, full, and at times invalidish lives.

It was a small modern miracle of gastronomy, certainly not worth having illness for, but worth pondering on, in case milk toast might help.

THE FLAW

There was a train, not a particularly good one, that stopped at Vevey about ten in the morning on the way to Italy. Chexbres and I used to take it to Milano.

It had a restaurant car, an old-fashioned one with the agreeable austerity of a third-class station café about it: brown wooden walls and seats, bare tables unless you ordered the highest-priced lunch, and a few faded advertisements for Aspirina Bayer and *"Visitez le Maroc"* permanently crooked above the windows.

There was one table, next to the galley, where the cooks and waiters sat. In the morning they would be talking and sorting greens for salad and cutting the tops off radishes for the hors d'oeuvres, and in the early afternoon they would eat enormously of some things that had been on the menu and some that certainly had not. There was always a big straw-wrapped flask of red wine with them.

Sometimes the head chef smoked while he drank, or read parts of a newspaper aloud, but usually he worked with his helpers. And if one of the two waiters sat there, he worked too.

We liked to go into the restaurant partly because of the cooks, who after a polite salute ignored us, and partly because of the waiters, who were always the same ones.

Of course, it is impossible that they were on every train that went to Milano through Vevey at ten in the morning. But they were on that train every time we took it, so that very soon they knew us and laughed and even patted Chexbres' shoulder delightedly when we appeared.

We always went into their car a few minutes after we started . . . after we had been seen by the conductor and what few travelers there were on the unfashionable train. The restaurant would be empty at that hour, of course, except for the table of amiably chattering cooks.

We would order a large bottle of Asti Spumanti. That delighted the waiters, whether it was the young smooth one or the old sour withered one. We would sit drinking it, slightly warm, from the thick train-goblets, talking and watching the flat floor of the Valais grow narrower and wilder, waiting as always with a kind of excited dread for the first plunge in to the Simplon.

The champagne would stay us, in that familiar ordeal. We'd drink gratefully, feeling the train sway, knowing a small taste of death and rebirth, as all men do in swift passage through a tunnel.

When we came out finally, into the light again and the high mountains, we'd lift our glasses silently to each other, and feel less foolish to see that the cooks too had known the same nameless stress as we.

Then people would begin to come in for lunch, and we'd go back to our compartment. The younger waiter would always call us when there were only a few more people to serve, in an hour or so.

Usually both waiters took care of us; they seemed to find us strange, and interesting enough to crack their cosmic ennui, and in some way fragile, so that they protected us. They would come swaying down the aisle as we ate, crying to us, "There will be a few bumps! Hold tight! Hold tight, M'sieu'-'dame! I will help you!"

Then they would grasp the wine, and usually my arm, and we would, it is true, make a few mild grating noises over some repair in the road. Then they would gasp with relief, and scuttle away . . . one more crisis safely past.

It made us feel a little silly, as if we were imbeciles of royal blood, or perhaps children who only *thought* they had gray hairs and knew how to survive train trips alone. It was fun, too; almost everyone likes to feel pampered by public servants.

The young waiter with the smooth almond face was more given to the protective gestures, equally lavished on Chexbres or me to avoid any sexual misunderstandings, but the older one, whose body was bent and whose face was truly the most cynical I have ever seen, was the one who watched our eating.

He hovered like an evil-visaged hawk while we ordered, and we soon found that instead of advising changes then, he would simply substitute in the kitchen what he preferred to have us enjoy that day. After the first surprise it was fun, but we always kept up the bluff of looking at the menu and then watching him pretend to memorize our order.

One thing he permitted us: simplicity. The people who traveled on that train were the kind who liked plain food and plenty of it. The menu might or might not list meat or fish, but it always had *pasti* of some kind, and lentils or beans cooked with herbs, and of course fine honest garden salad. Then there would be one or two *antipasti:* the radishes we had watched being fixed, and butter for them in rather limp and sooty curls, and hardboiled eggs and sliced salami. There would be cheese for dessert, with fruit . . . fat cherries or peaches or grapes or oranges, according to the season, and always green almonds in the spring.

The people ate well, and even if they were very poor, and brought their own bread and wine into the restaurant, they ordered a plate of beans or a one-egg omelet with dignity which was no rebuke to the comparative prodigality around them. The two waiters served them with nonchalant skill, and everyone seemed to agree that Chexbres and I should be watched and fed and smiled at with extra care.

"Why are they like that? Why are they so good to us, all the people?" we would ask each other. I knew reasons for him, and he knew some for me, but for the two of us it was probably because we had a sort of palpable trust in each other.

Simple people are especially conscious of that. Sometimes it is called love, or good will. Whatever it was in us, the result was mysterious and warming, and we felt it very strongly in places like the restaurant car to Milano, always until the last time.

That was in the summer of 1939.

We were two ghosts, then. Our lives as normal living humans had ended in the winter, in Delaware, with Chexbres' illness. And when we got word that we should go back to our old home in Switzerland and save what we could before war started, we went not so much for salvage, because possessions had no meaning any more to us, but because we were helpless to do anything else. We returned to the life that had been so real like fog, or smoke, caught in a current of air.

We were very live ghosts, and drank and ate and saw and felt and made love better than ever before, with an intensity that seemed to detach us utterly from life.

Everywhere there was a little of that feeling; the only difference was that we were safely dead, and all the other people, that summer, were laughing and singing and drinking wine in a kind of catalepsy, or like cancerous patients made happy with a magic combination of opiate before going into the operating theatre. We had finished with all that business, and they had it still to go through.

They looked at us with a kind of envious respect, knowing that war was coming to them, but that we were past it; and everywhere we went, except the one time on the Milano train, we moved beatifically incommunicado, archangels on leave. None could touch us, just as none could be harmed by our knowledge of pain yet to be felt.

The train was the same. By then we had grown almost used to miracles, and when the young almond-faced waiter stood in the door of the compartment and gaped helplessly at us, we laughed at him. He stammered and sputtered, all the time shaking our hands and laughing too, and it was plain that he had buried us long since.

When he saw what had happened to Chexbres, he turned very red, and then said quickly, trying not to stare, "But the Asti! At once! It will be very chic to drink it here!"

And before we could tell him how much we wanted to drink it in the old restaurant car, and look once more at the faded aspirin signs and listen to the cooks, he was gone. It was necessary for him to disappear; we were used by then to having people do impetuous things when they first saw us, ghosts come back so far. . . . We sighed, and laughed, because even that seemed funny.

The boy brought the champagne, wrapped elegantly in a red-checked napkin for the first time. He was suave and mischievous again, and it was plain that he felt like something in a paper-bound novel, serving fair wine that way at eleven in the morning in a first-class compartment. He swayed with exaggerated grace to the rocking of the car, and flicked soot from the little wall table like the headwaiter at the Café de la Paix, at least, with his flat black eyes dancing.

We saluted him with our first taste, hiding our regret at having to be "gentry" and drink where it was chic. The wine was the same, warm and almost sickish, and we looked quietly at each other, with delight . . . one more miracle.

But at Sion, before the tunnel, three Strength-through-Joyers got on, bulbous with knapsacks and a kind of sweaty health that had nothing to do with us. We huddled against the windows, not invisible enough, and I wondered how we could ever get past all those strong brown hairy legs to the corridor.

But there in the doorway, almost before the train started again, stood the little waiter. His face was impassive, but his eyes twinkled and yet were motherly.

"Pardon, pardon," he murmured. *"Entschuldigen Sie, bitte . . . bitte . . . "*

And before we knew it the German tourists were standing, trying to squeeze themselves small, and the boy was whisking us expertly, nonchalantly, out of the compartment, down the rocking aisle, and into our familiar hard brown seats in the restaurant.

It was all the same. We looked about us with a kind of wonder.

The old waiter saw us from the end of the car. His face did not change, but he put down his glass of wine and came to our table. The boy started to say something to him in an Italian dialect . . . it was like Niçois . . . but the old man motioned him bruskly aside.

His face was still the most cynical I had ever seen, but his eyes were over-full of tears. They ran slowly down his cheeks for a few minutes, into the evil old wrinkles, and he did not wipe them away. He stood by the table, flicking his napkin and asking crankily if we had made a good trip and if we planned to stay long in Milano. We answered the same way . . . things about traveling and the weather.

We were not embarrassed, any more than he was, by his tears; like all ghosts, I suppose, we had grown used to seeing them in other people's eyes, and along with them we saw almost always a kind of gratitude, as if people were thanking us for coming back and for being so trustful together. We seemed to reassure them, in a mysterious way . . . that summer more than ever.

While the old man was standing there, talking with his own gruff eagerness about crops and storms, flicking the table, he had to step in behind my chair for a minute while three men walked quickly through the car.

Two were big, not in uniform but with black shirts under their hot mussy coats, and stubble on their faces. The man between them was thinner and younger, and although they went single file and close together, we saw that he was handcuffed to each of them.

Before that summer such a thing would have shocked us, so that our faces would be paler and our eyes wider, but now we only looked up at the old waiter. He nodded, and his own eyes got very hot and dried all the tears.

"Political prisoner," he said, flicking the table, and his face was no more bitter than usual. "Escaped. They are bringing him back to Italy."

Then the chef with the highest bonnet saw us, and beamed and raised his glass, and the others turned around from their leafy table and saluted us too, and the door slammed behind the three dark men.

We got through the tunnel, that time, without feeling our palms grow sticky. It was the only difference: the train was the same, the people were the same. We were past the pain and travail, that was all. We were inviolate.

We drank the rest of the Asti, and as people began to come in to lunch, we made the signal to the suddenly active boy that we would be back later.

Just then there were shouts and thuds, and the sound of shattering glass. A kind of silence fell all about us, in spite of the steady rattle of the train. The old waiter ran down the car, not bumping a single table, and the door at the end closed sharply behind him. People looked strangely at one another.

Gradually the air settled, as if the motors inside all the travelers had started to hum again, and the young waiter took orders for lunch. When he got to us he said without looking at us, in his bad French, "I suggest that M'sieu'-'dame attend a moment . . . the restaurant is not crowded today."

As a suggestion it had the icy command of a policeman or a guardian angel about it, and we sat meekly. There was no more champagne. It did not really bother us.

Finally the old man came hurriedly back into the car. His face was furious, and he clutched his shoulder. The travelers stared at him, still chewing. He stopped for a minute by our table. He was panting, and his voice was very low.

"He tried to jump through the window," he said, and we knew he was talking about the refugee. "The bastards! They tore my coat! My only coat! The dirty bastards . . . look at that!"

He flapped the ripped shoulder of his greasy old black jacket at us, and then went madly down to the galley, muttering and trembling.

We stood up to go, and the smooth almond-faced waiter hurried toward us, swaying with the downhill rush of the train under a big tray of hot vegetables. "I am bringing M'sieu'-'dame's order at once," he called.

We sat down obediently. We were being bullied, but it was because he was trying to protect us, and it was kind of him. He brought two glasses of a dark vermouth, and as he put them in front of us he said confiding, "A special bottle we carry for the chef . . . very appetizing. There is a little muss on the platform. It will be swept up when M'sieu'-'dame have finished. *Santé!* "

As we lifted our glasses, willy-nilly, he cleared his throat, and then said in English, "Cheerio!" He smiled at us encouragingly, like an over-attentive nurse, and went back to serving the other people. The vermouth was bitterer than any we had ever tasted, almost like a Swiss gentian-drink, but it tasted good after the insipid wine.

When we went through to our compartment, there was indeed a neat pile of broken glass on the platform between the cars, and the window of the door that opened when the train stopped was only half filled: the top part of the pane was gone, and the edge of the rest curved like ice in a smooth fine line, almost invisible.

The Strength-through-Joyers leaped politely to attention when we got back to our compartment, and subsided in a series of small waves of questions in English . . . did smoke bother me, did we mind the door open, did we feel a draft. . . .

I forget the name of the town now where the train stops and the passport men come on. Is it Domodossola? How strange, not to know! It is as if I have deliberately wiped from my mind a great many names. Some of them I thought would stay there forever, whether I wanted them or not, like old telephone numbers that suddenly come between you and the sound of a new love's voice. I never thought to disremember this town, that man, such and such a river. Was it Domodossola?

That day we were there a long time. There seemed more policemen than usual, but it was always that way in Italy. We got the questions of visas and money straightened out; that used to upset me, and I'd feel like a blushing diamond-smuggler when the hardeyed customs man would look at me. This time it was easy, unimportant.

I kept thinking it would be a good idea to walk back to the restaurant car while the train was quiet, but Chexbres said no, we should wait for the boy to call us.

Finally we started, very slowly. We went past a lot of roadwork. Men were building beds for new tracks with great blocks of gray stone, and the Germans looked at them with a grudging fascination, leaning over us to see better and exclaiming softly.

We were glad when the young waiter came to the door. "Your table is ready, M'sieu'-'dame," he announced loftily, and the men stood up hastily to let us out.

When we got to the end of the car, the boy turned back. "Take care, please," he said to Chexbres. "There is a little humidity on the platform."

And the place was wet, right enough. The curved piece of glass was still in the window, but it and the walls and the floor were literally dripping with water. We went carefully through it, and into the almost empty restaurant.

The chef rested at the end, reading a paper, but got up and went back to the galley as we came in. Our table was nicely laid, with fresh linen, and there were two or three little square dishes of pickled onions and salami and butter. We felt very hungry, and quite gay.

The boy brought us some good wine, a fairly expensive red Chianti we always drank on that train, and we began to eat bread and salami with it. I remember there were some of those big white beans, the kind Italians peel and eat with salt when they are fresh and tender in the early summer. They tasted delicious, so fresh and cold. . . .

It was good to be eating and drinking there on that train, free forever from the trouble of life, surrounded with a kind of insulation of love. . . .

The old waiter came through the car. He was going to pass our table without looking at us. Chexbres spoke to him. "Stop a minute," he said. "Your coat . . . how is it?"

The man turned without answering, so that we could see the neat stitches that held his sleeve in place. I said something banal about the sewing . . . how good it was . . . and Chexbres asked quietly, "The man . . . the prisoner . . . did he get away?"

The old man suddenly looked at us, and his eyes were hateful, as if he loathed us. He said something foul, and then spat, "It's none of my business!" He hurried away, and we could not turn to watch him.

It was so shocking that we sat without any movement for quite a time. I could feel my heart beat heavily, and my throat was as if an iron collar hung around it, the way it used to be when Chexbres was first ill. Finally I looked at the few people still eating, and it seemed to me as if they met my eyes with a kind of hatred too, not as awful as the old man's but still crouching there. There was fear in it, and fear all around me.

Chexbres' face was full of pain. It was the first time it had come through for weeks, the first time since we started to drift like two happy ghosts along the old current of our lives together. The iron collar tightened to see it there. I tried to drink some wine, but I couldn't swallow more than once.

The young waiter hurried past us without looking, and Chexbres stopped him firmly. "Please," he said. "What is wrong? What has happened?"

The boy looked impassively at us, and for a minute I thought he was going to be rude. Then he whispered, still protecting us, "Eat, M'sieu'-'dame. I will tell you in a minute." And he hurried off to the galley, bending supplely under the last great tray of emptied plates.

"Yes, you'd better eat something," Chexbres said coldly to me. "You've drunk rather a lot, you know." He picked up his fork, and I did too. The spaghetti was like ashes, because I felt myself coming to life again, and knew he did.

When we were the only ones left in the car, the boy came back. He stood leaning against the table across the aisle, still swaying with the motion of the train but now as if he were terribly tired, and talked to us so softly that we could hardly hear him. There was no friendliness in his voice, but not any hatred.

He said that when the train stopped at Domodossola, or wherever the border was, the political prisoner was being taken off, and suddenly he laughed and pressed his throat down on the edge of broken windowpane. The old waiter saw it.

"That was probably the plan in the first place," the boy said. "The poor bastard was chained to the cops. There was no escaping. It was a good job," he said. "The border police helped clean up the platform. That was why the train stopped so long.

"We're making up time now all right," the boy said, looking admiringly at the rocky valley flash past us. "The old man keeps fussing about his coat. He's nuts anyway."

By the time we got to Milano everything was almost all right again, but for a few minutes the shell cracked. The world seeped in. We were not two ghosts, safe in our own immunity from the pain of living. Chexbres was a man with one leg gone, the other and the two arms soon to go . . . a small wracked man with snowy hair and eyes large with suffering. And I was a woman condemned, plucked at by demons, watching her true love die too slowly.

There in the train, hurrying across the ripe fields, feeling the tranced waiting of the people everywhere, we knew for a few minutes that we had not escaped. We knew no knife of glass, no distillate of hatred, could keep the pain of war outside.

I felt illimitably old, there in the train, knowing that escape was not peace, ever.

FROM BERN JOURNAL

1.viii.38

One thing about writing is that it takes time. This last month I have thought of perhaps a thousand things, to estimate conservatively, that for some perverse reason I should like to write about—sights or smells or sounds, or occasionally ideas. This last month—

It is 9:14 at night, a queerly noisy night, with at least two radios blaring from somewhere over the Kornhaus Bridge, and many people walking past the hospital, and trains racketing with extra fervor from the stop by the theater across the Aare to the Kursaal. I can look out and see the lights slide along the wet black bridge and the dull shapes of two floodlit towers push up into the sky.

I finish a glass of brandy, and want to write about this month, and know that I am too sleepy. And then I wonder why I do want to write about it, because I despise talk, and the people who talk, who tell others about themselves, and the dreadful necessity that pushes them to such confessions. They must talk. They must expose themselves. It helps them, and more horribly, it helps others.

That is what bothers me. I hate this need. I've never done much of it, and I despise it in others. But I know that I am more articulate than some, and I think, Well . . . my God in heaven! If what I've learned about pain or food or the excreta of the sea snail can help even one poor human, I am a rat not to write. Then I know I am wrong.

And now, at 9:23, I am writing, for the first time in more than a month. My eyes are sanded with sleep, and my back is numb against the two limp Swiss pillows.

I look up at the mirror above my washstand to see if there is light reflected from Timmy's room. We tried two pills tonight, which did no good, and then gave the old faithful shot of Analgeticum at 8:00. He is asleep, heavily, with his mouth dropped askew. I am fairly sure that by 12:00 he will call me. Then it will be Pantopon.

I can't understand so much noise from town, but, of course, people are still celebrating that there's no war. It would have been today. Yesterday Switzerland would have had general mobilization. Of course, we are all glad. I am, and so is Timmy. I don't like the idea of those bombs the Germans tried on Barcelona, which are made of aluminum filled with liquid air. I wouldn't mind being killed outright by one, but

I am sure that the people who were a quarter mile away and were stunned by them had dreadful headaches.

I hear the cathedral clock strike 9:30. It always rings first. I have tried to listen to one certain hour to see if all the clocks ever make the same pattern, but even at 3:00 in the morning they never strike the same way twice. Sometimes they make a beautiful sound. I heard that Shostakovich regretted using so many themes in his first symphony, because he had so few left. He should come here, to the Viktoria Hospital—the night bells across the dark Aare would tell him many new ones.

23.x.38

Today, after almost three weeks of fine blue autumn days, it is cold and darkly gray. I am listless, moonstruck. Timmy is in greater pain than usual, feverishly ill at ease. We go out, and after peering into several steamy cafés, whose floors, cluttered with dogs and cigar butts and spittle and a few children, spell disaster to crutches, we go to the Schweizerhof for beer and a gin-vermouth for me.

Home in a taxi, and while I watch Irma massage the smooth white curve of his hip, I am quietly horrified to see a purplish blotch above the bandage. It seems slightly smoother. Is it a bruise from trying on the temporary peg, day before yesterday? I am appalled and go away without speaking.

27.x.38

13:40

In a few minutes I go down through thick milky mist to the pharmacy, along the straight sleeping street lined with closed shops and pensions. It is cold. When I look out the window, here in the warm room filled with the staid strains of Handel's Concerto Grosso, I might be on a ship, fogbound to the sound of invisible cowbells from below, or in an airship, as well as in this snug Swiss hotel.

I cannot permit myself the doubtful luxury of thought. I am too close to frenzy, to a wild anxiety.

The first day was not bad. The second day, after only Timmy slept well, thanks to Analgeticum and Pantopon, was exciting. The Nigsts came. We had drinks on the terrace and then went down for lunch, with Nigst clucking like a hen over Timmy's agility on the stairs. Timmy overate, to please him. Later the local doctor, von Derschwanden, came for café on the terrace. At first he reminded me of a wretched sordid little snob I once knew from Manchester—not so much his manner, which was brisk behind his English pipe, but his mussed and pudgy English slacks and brown tweed coat. (Now I like him, even more than Nigst, I think. His hands are sensitive and investigatory, and he thinks of everything.)

That night was not bad. Yesterday was wretched, with fever for the first time above 37.5 degrees, and the right leg very painful. Last night was all right—injections, of course.

This morning the doctor came. I could see he was worried—congestion in the main artery of the right leg, general low condition.

Timmy lies for hours with an open book or journal before him. Occasionally he turns a page, but he has read nothing. Slow tears slip down his cheeks, and now and then he shakes violently and clutches me and sobs.

I must go down to the pharmacy.

I stay in the sitting room because I think I upset him a little when I sit in his room. I keep thinking, He may die—other people do—and then I will be sick at the thought of the times I spent here when I could be there. I'll try to begin a book today.

18:75 of the same day

Whenever I start to write, I seem to think of nothing but sadness. Perhaps it is because I never talk of it. Tonight I am almost intolerably depressed. I don't know quite why. I'm not one to be downed by weather that is usually thought to be mournful. But all seems wrong. Of course, the main thing is that Timmy is not so well. I try to tell myself—and him, when I have to—about the effects of altitude and so on. But I cannot convince myself that all those things could make such a difference in him—fever 37.8½ degrees now again, and surely higher at 8:00, and pain in the *other* leg, and this general withdrawal from me and life. He looks at me and seldom sees me. Everything he must save, all his various strengths, to fight the weariness, to hold at bay the bouts of pain, to keep himself on the right side of hysteria. I can see it all.

I stay near but away, where he can see me but not have to look at me. Often I keep the radio going. (It plays now, and it almost drives me frantic.) I tried to write, this afternoon, but I couldn't—Irma, a nap, talk, Tim calls me, so on.

I try to play the phonograph. That, at least, I have thought all along, will be wonderful, this wonderful. But it has something wrong, a grinding sound that creeps above everything but jazz. I tried to play "Es ist Vollbracht." It was terrible. And even with that grinding, it made things seem too sad. Then, when I said, "Do you like that, Timmy?" he answered, "What?"

I found that my favorite album is not here, the Sibelius concerto, and I paid for sending them all from Le Pâquis only today. Others are missing—and now it is too late to reclaim them.

And the man called about the car, to sell it at 2,700 francs. I said yes, probably unwisely. But it will be one less thing to worry about.

Of course, we have often been low before. Occasionally things seemed so bad, at the Viktoria, that I wondered if we could stand it. We never spoke about it. And then in the morning all would be well—a decent night, a blue sky, a good letter—

The strange faculty I developed, during my last years with Al, of shutting myself off has stood me in good faithful stead lately. It is only occasionally, as now, that it *almost* doesn't work. Usually I can shut parts of my realization, of my intelligence, off, rather as a ship's engineer shuts off various parts of a sinking ship. I can almost feel doors close—then—then. It is good, for the moment at least. I think it may have turned me into a duller person than I was—but at least I'm safer from myself.

There is much I can never write about. All this is superficial.

2.xi.38

I just posted, after much deliberation, an order for 115 Tanchnitz and Albatross and Penguin books. Aside from their costing about $80 and so becoming one of the most extravagant actions of my whole life, I felt from the first that they were an admittance of weakness in my nature. It is easy enough for me to justify wanting them, as Timmy said today that it was easy for any woman to defend her inability to eat less than she wanted. But the truth is that it is and will be much pleasanter for me to read book after book of silly "mysteries" than to make myself work. Of course, if I were a real writer, predestined, dedicated, I'd work in the face of everything. (And even without that fate, I write constantly in my head—stories, paragraphs, phrases, sometimes the skeletons of novels.) But as it is now, I feel almost hysterical at the thought of concentrating on one thing. I am never left without interruption (here are the self-justifications!) for more than fifteen or twenty minutes, and when I am in another room from Timmy's, his door is always open so that I can hear what he does or says and be ready to interpret Irma's talk or help her. I've never held one way or the other with some creative souls' demand for absolute privacy, although Woolf's theory of 100 pounds and a room of one's own seems attractive personally—but I truly don't feel keen enough at this time to be able to put aside all thought of the present while it is moving and moaning ten feet to the left of me.

I notice two things about this life, since the first night at the Bärem: my increased fastidiousness and my equally increased *gourmandise*. Since I can remember, I've been very clean, but now I spend long serious minutes, after my bath, drying each toenail; I wash my navel or my ears as if they were Belleek china teacups; a tiny hangnail sends me hurrying for scissors, oil, all the minutiae of a complete manicure. And I have become almost piggish . . . not in my manners, for I eat slowly and daintily . . . but I eat too much. The food here is good, especially after the tasteless monotony of the hospital. But there is too much of it. Today at noon there was a rich clear consommé with egg cooked in it, ravioli with tomato sauce and cheese, roast chicken with puree of potatoes, brussels sprouts, and a chocolate cream with wafers. So rich! I eat in the little sitting room. First I have a small glass of vermouth with T., while Marta is setting the table. Then I take him a cup of the soup and the crust of a slice of bread broken into bites. Then I sit down, with a book—today, *High Wind in Jamaica*. I ate all the raviolis, with a glass of wine. Then I took T. a little chicken cut into morsels and a little applesauce. I ate the brussels sprouts, and drank another glass of wine, and then some chocolate pudding and three wafers. Then I ordered a cup of coffee and drank a small glass of cognac with it. Usually I eat a lot of salad, on which I put a spoonful of meat juice with a strange voluptuous solemnity. I am interested in this slowness and this solemnity. I suppose it is a desire to escape, to forget time and the demands of suffering.

Another thing is the way I dress: I've always been rather finicky about colors and so on, but now I find myself looking at my reflection in any mirror with a smug satisfaction, noting complacently the way my sweater, my socks, the ribbon in my hair are the same blue as the shadow on my eyelids, and how the black of my slacks and my sandals makes all the blues more beautiful. It is queer, and slightly boring, but I suppose it won't get any worse.

After a day part cloudy and part sunlit, light from behind the western mountains beams suddenly across the valley and brings my mountains close enough to lean against. The snow of seven nights ago melts fast, and cliffs I never dreamed of stand out with abrupt starkness from the white slopes, their rock sides cozy in the unexpected light. Lower down, the pine trees are oily green-black, clustered like plant lice in diminishing dots up the mountain. At the bottom, the foamy, dirt-white ice water rushes, with a steady hissing, to the warm valleys.

7.xi.38

This afternoon, after a half-night of wakefulness, I began to write a book. It will be impossible to show it to anyone but Tim . . . if I ever get it that far along . . . because it is about this last summer. Of course, all of us, and above all myself, are changed, muted one moment and caricatured the next, by my own licentious mind. If a person could ever be seen truly, it would be by himself. But that seldom happens. Or perhaps, is that rare inward vision of oneself what explains the look of rapturous amusement on a dying person's face, which is always interpreted by good Christians as the first peer at heaven?

A letter to T. from his mother, fairly spitting and steaming from the envelope with rage that Anne, who had been two weeks home, had not yet come to Claymont, whereas *she* had defied nurses, doctors, and hospital to get home to welcome her errant darling . . . ten days too soon. I can understand her chagrin.

A quiet and prolonged scene with Schwester Irma today, solved finally by petting, cajoling, babying, playfully teasing her into a good humor. God, these complicated middle-aged nitwits who feed on attention! Am I headed for it, too?

After two years of having experts try to fix a gradual crescendo of whir and squeak in our extremely expensive and completely pleasing gramophone, the fumbling, puzzle-witted local radioman came in this afternoon and arranged it as it should be. Of course, I don't know how long it will last, but I enjoy it meanwhile. This afternoon I played a few things, and then the Brahms Second Concerto. The third (?) movement of it, I thought . . . my favorite piece of gentle music . . . it will soothe us, it will solace us. But I almost didn't hear it at all, so busy was I trying to keep T. from looking at the clock and crying wildly at the filthiness of a life that is only endurable with *piqûres*.

It is 10:00 at night. I'll try to stay awake until T. calls, about 12:30 to 1:30, to give him his shot. Irma has fussed so about how badly she feels that I'm bitch enough to want to fool her and do the night work myself for once. It's a shot-and-a-half, and I hate the idea of it, but I'm sick to death of her nobly stifled yawns in the mornings. I hope I can work it. *Piqûres* make me sick still, but not actively, as they used to.

It is satisfying, in a queer way, to have written the bones of a book today. I'm puzzled by it and feel quite doubtful that I can do it as well as I want to—but at least I'm working. As I told T. today, I've been proving with so much conversation that I'm through with the lost cause of literature that at least I can go to work now with the courage of my convictions. [. . .]

I Don't Like This

Tonight I looked at the cover of a current issue of a weekly magazine all about peace and war. The picture was of an angry mother in Texas or Israel or Beirut with her two hot-eyed sad children clinging to her proud heavy body, and I said firmly, I do not like this.

Then I was thinking about the word *like*, and I remembered one time when I was looking down at the poor anguished body of my love, while a group of young doctors and nurse nuns stood about the famous doctor who was using him as an object lesson of some kind. Tim lay in the cold Swiss light. There was a thick ring of faces above him, around the bed, trying to be dispassionate but still sad for him. His one leg lay firm and beautiful and naked, and the stump beside it twitched helplessly now and then and was open and angry, with yellow in the middle of the gaping open end. The doctor was speaking stolidly, elegantly, and the younger nurses hummed little sounds as he paused. He looked sternly at me, standing there, and asked, "And what does the lady think?"

I said in French against his German, "I do not like it."

There was a long pause, filled with shock and an almost physical disapproval. The ring of sympathetic cooing little nuns drew back, and behind them the young doctors stood like sentinels, alert and ready. The doctor looked straight at me, and then shrugged and smiled and said to the circle. "Madame does not like something, eh?"

He laughed shortly, and they all twittered in obedience and waited. I stood there and did not look down at Tim, who lay like a drugged beast—a small neat beast, like a fox perhaps, but still drugged and unknowing. The doctor laughed again, looking full into my open face. "Madame does not like this," he murmured as if to himself, and he bent over the open bone end of what had once been a fine leg and rubbed at it with a long swab. Every face drew closer, and I pulled away, forever outside of that or any other circle.

Tonight I do not like the faces of those three people who have no home. But what can I do for them? What could I do that time for Tim? We had no home, either. Still, I think these sad angry-eyed children may survive, just as their mother has, and perhaps as I have, too.

I am warm and I have, temporarily anyway, a place to call my home, and they do not. But the mother knows that there will be something more, I suppose, if she thinks about it at all. Perhaps she does not. I did not think any way at all when I said flatly to the great doctor, "I do not like this." The mother does not like what she sees now. But there is no arguing about it, except to make it clear that it is not right.

That is what I keep trying to do. I doubt that anyone listens, but I keep on saying it. I do not *like* this. It stinks. It is hideous. It is a filthy trick. It is a cruel trick. It will lead to intolerable suffering. It is ugly and twisting.

That day in Bern I stood while the doctor mocked me, and neither I nor the man drugged on the high white bed blinked an eye when all the little nurse nuns and the student doctors gave out a kind of exhalation of amused consent as the doctor bent over the stump and twisted expertly at some gauze, reverting into German as he continued, "And although she does not *like* it, she will have to see that the inflammation increases as the general state of vascular deterioration . . . "

Yes. Yes. Where can we sleep tonight? Will there be any food? Where will it come from? Will we live or die?

We do not ask. We say, if asked, that we do not like it—war or hopelessness or hate or love or or . . .

Glen Ellen, California, 1991

Introduction to the Revised Edition of
How to Cook a Wolf

How to Cook a Wolf was first published in 1942, when wartime shortages were at their worst. It was revised by the author in 1951, by the addition of copious marginal notes and footnotes and a special section of additional recipes. These have now been incorporated in their proper places in the text, and are enclosed in brackets, as is, for an example, the Introduction to the Revised Edition that follows.

THE EDITORS

[It is hard to know whether war or peace makes the greater changes in our vocabularies, both of the tongue and of the spirit.

Certain it is, however, that in less than ten years this book about living as decently as possible with the ration cards and blackouts and like miseries of World War II has assumed some of the characteristics of quaintness. It has become, in short, in so short a time, a kind of period piece. In its own way it is as curious, as odd, as any fat old gold-ribbed volume called, a hundred years ago instead of nine or ten, *Ladies' Indispensable Assistant and Companion, One of the Best Systems of Cookery Ever Published for Sister, Mother, and Wife.* . . .

Of course, it is difficult, in spite of the obvious changes in our physical problems since *How to Cook a Wolf* was first published in 1942, to say truthfully and exactly when we are at war.

Now we are free of ration cards (It was shocking, the other day, to hear that after almost twelve years gas rationing had come to an end in England. What a long time! Too long . . .): no more blue and red tokens, no more flimsy stamps to tear out or not tear out.

We can buy as much porterhouse and bourbon and powdered sugar as our purses will allow, given the rise of almost one hundred percent in the cost of such gastronomical amenities.

We need not worry, temporarily at least, about basic cupboards for blackouts . . . while at the same time we try not to think, even superficially, about what and when and how and where to nourish survivors of the next kind of bomb.

Thus stated, the case for Peace is feeble.

One less chilling aspect of the case for War II is that while it was still a shooting affair it taught us survivors a great deal about daily living that is valuable to us now that it is, ethically at least, a question of cold weapons and hot words. (In one week from the writing of this cautious statement, or one hour from the final printing of it, double ridicule can be its lot. Are weapons ever cold?)

There are very few men and women, I suspect, who cooked and marketed their way through the past war without losing forever some of the nonchalant extravagance of the twenties. They will feel, until their final days on earth, a kind of culinary caution: butter, no matter how unlimited, is a precious substance not lightly to be wasted; meats, too, and eggs, and all the far-brought spices of the world, take on a new significance, having once been so rare. And that is good, for there can be no more shameful carelessness than with the food we eat for life itself. When we exist without thought or thanksgiving we are not men, but beasts.

War is a beastly business, it is true, but one proof that we are human is our ability to learn, even from it, how better to exist. If this book, written in one wartime, still goes on helping to solve that unavoidable problem, it is worth reading again, I think, no matter what its quaint superficiality, its sometimes unintentionally grim humor.

That is why I have added to it, copiously. Not everything new in it is purely practical, of course. But even the wolf, temporarily appeased, cannot live on bread alone.

(And *that* is why I have added even more, I have sneaked other recipes into the book. Some are hopelessly extravagant—16 eggs!—and some are useful and some are funny, and one is actually for bread that even a wolf would live on.

These "extra" recipes are culinary rules to be followed with not a thought of the budget, not even half an ear cocked toward that sniffing at the door. I know, because I *know,* that one good whiff from any of these dishes will send the beast cringing away, in a kind of extrasensory and ultra-moral embarrassment.)]

M.F.K.F

How Not to Be
an Earthworm

Streamlined to the ultimate for functional performance the earthworm blindly eats his way, riddling
and honeycombing the ground to a depth of ten feet or more as he swallows.
Anatomy Underfoot, J.–J. CONDE

[This whole chapter has the faintly phosphorescent humor of decay about it. It is as outmoded as a treatise on how to treat javelin-wounds, now that we know even earth-worms are not inviolate.]

Other wars have made men live like rats, or wolves, or lice, but until this one, except perhaps for the rehearsal in Spain, we have never lived like earthworms.

Now we bend our minds, with the surprised intensity of any nonplused [In the face of continued disapproval I think this should have two esses, just as I think the word busses is proper in the plural for both a vehicle and a kiss. Buses, indeed! I am *not* nonplused.] creatures, to existing as gracefully as possible without many of the things we have always accepted as our due: light, free air, fresh foods, prepared according to our tastes. It can be done, of course, since we are humans as well as rats, wolves, lice, and earthworms.

You may have heard of one woman in England who withdrew to her tidy little bomb-shelter in the garden when the first siren sounded, and emerged, rather dreamily, some two weeks later. She'd been quite comfy, she told her worried neigh-bors, but she did hope the blinkin' raids would not always last quite so long.

There is more than a modicum of British deadpan humor in this wry story, as you will agree if you have ever stood, even for a few minutes, in one of the dreadful little strongboxes we are meant to hide in when bombs fall. No matter how much effort architects and decorators spend on making them habitable, they are shameful places, cramped and stuffy and ugly. They are a means to an end, which is to survive, but they have only that virtue.

Blacked-out rooms are another thing. Usually they are places we recognize, with familiar chairs and pictures. They are not cells or holes to hide in, but chambers with their lights blinded from the outside, where we can continue in an almost normal way our nightly life of supper, and reading, and playing the phonograph or rummy and always the game of Being Casual.

Blackouts happen at night, of course, and so, usually does dinner. For that reason it is wise, if possible, to have the kitchen one of the rooms most adequately equipped to operate normally under the various restrictions of your neighborhood and your own common sense, when the siren sounds.

In a small house you can make this one room into a very pleasant place for the whole family . . . unless you are unfortunate enough to have what used to be called a "kitchenette," which means that it is impossibly small, even for its original function. In that case, you should try to black out both it and the next room, never forgetting that there are a few other functions as necessary, if not as pleasant, as eating, and that an easily accessible toilet is more important than any stove.

Since this country went to war, a great deal has been done to prepare us for emergencies (a polite word for bombings, invasions, and many other ugly things). Much has been good, and intelligent, and it is too easy and perhaps very wrong to criticize some of the less good and intelligent moves. It is hard not to wonder, however, how some of the sensible women who are planning such things as emergency rations can be so blandly impractical, especially when most of them are graduate home economists and dieticians.

There are many lists being prepared by various organizations, mapping out twenty-four-hour emergency rations for school children, hospitals, and so forth. Here is a sample [I refer to this later as "nauseating," but no one word is strong enough to suggest my scorn of it, esthetically as well as biochemically. It is a shocking example of gastronomical panic, and if it were heeded would soon reduce us to malnourished as well as spiritually weakened creatures, past much harm from bursting atoms.] that is of course made up of foods that can be stored indefinitely, and which have been calculated down to the last soda cracker for five hundred people:

BREAKFAST
 Tomato juice
 Peanut butter
 Soda crackers or Melba toast
 Hot milk chocolate

DINNER
 Spaghetti with tomato puree
 Corned beef
 Peas and carrots
 Soda crackers
 Penny chocolate bars

SUPPER OR LUNCHEON
 Tomato soup with canned milk
 Soda crackers
 Fruit cup
 Graham crackers

These three meals, to be prepared for such a large number of people, most of whom are supposed to be children, would be heated on "a barbecue or make-shift inside camp cooking equipment," the folder says!

Aside from the obvious fact that few people eat three hot meals a day, even in peacetime ("Warm foods are not the only 'warming foods.' . . . Get out of the habit of cooking a hot meal every day," the British Ministry of Food urges in one of its regular newspaper bulletins.), it is foolish to think of the number of plates and cups and utensils that would have to be washed to provide for these impractical and nauseating feasts.

Have the earnest ladies of the Parent-Teachers Advisory Board forgotten that water may be as much of a problem as fuel, if things are so upset that five hundred people are hiding together in the basement of a schoolhouse? The old economy of paper cups and plates exists no longer, and the idea of washing at least twenty-five hundred different vessels into a passably sterile state is an uncomfortable one.

There are other problems than the main one of serving this pathetic attempt at a "balanced diet" to five hundred ill-assorted and bewildered people. The dieticians must begin, always with the hope that it will never be needed, to borrow knowledge from the women in England, who after the countless nights of this war have gradually evolved their own rules.

In the meantime, you feel, as almost all people do without even realizing it, that you would rather be at home than anywhere else, if enemy planes are scouting somewhere in the air. As long as it can be done without too much danger, that is just where you should be, and aside from the inescapable unpleasantness of your reasons for being there, it can be downright entertaining to spend your evenings in your blacked-out rooms.

There is something innately desirable about a room shut off completely from the eyes of other humans. [I continue to agree with something Colette once wrote about the primitive satisfaction of a low dark place to eat in. This is a fine conversational gambit . . . who can resist discoursing on *his* ideas of the perfect dining room, whether he be dyspeptic, ascetic, or simply hungry?] It makes you feel protected, probably the way a kitten feels when it hides in a coat-sleeve, or a child under the blankets. Unfortunately, like the coat-sleeve or the blankets, it can be very stuffy, as the English have discovered. Intelligent designers are thinking and writing about that, and such magazines as the January, 1942, *Architectural Forum* are very helpful.

Given a moderately well-ventilated kitchen, which is large enough in itself or is next to another blacked-out room, you can live there with people you like and find life decent indeed.

The people in England have found that electricity usually stays on longer than gas in an actual bombing, so most well-equipped private shelters have little electric grills in them, or at least toasters and hot plates. Now would be a good time to get out the old chafing dish, if you have not already done it. (The next thing is to hope that you can buy alcohol for it, but sufficient unto the day is the evil of that particular shortage.) [Ordinary rubbing compounds will do, in spite of their weird smells and the ugly incrustations they make upon the copper.]

In spite of your optimistic refusal to believe that anything could happen to *your* gas main or *your* power lines, it is a wise thing, if you know that you are to be blacked out that night, to cook as much food as you can during the day. Make things that can be reheated or served cold.

Another good reason for cooking while it is light is that few kitchens are as well ventilated as they should be at the best of times, so that at night with the windows closed and several people in the room, the air should not be overheated and filled with steams and fumes of food. This is especially true if you are reduced to cooking with an open flame or with coal oil: the air quickly becomes poor.

It is better, for the same reason, to cook things that do not have too strong a smell. Cabbage, for instance, is unwise. Kidneys, unless they are prepared beforehand, are too strong in the air. (They are easy, though, to fix in a chafing dish, smell or no smell.)

In the old days, before Stuka and blitz became a part of even childish chitchat, every practical guide to cookery urged you to keep a well-filled emergency shelf in your kitchen or pantry. Emergency is another word that has changed its inner shape; when Marion Harland and Fanny Farmer used it they meant unexpected guests. You may, too, in an ironical way, but you hope to God they are the kind who will never come.

It is often a delicate point, now, to decide when common sense ends and hoarding begins. Preparing a small stock of practical boxed and canned goods for a blackout shelf, in direct relation to the size of your family, is quite another thing from buying large quantities of bottled shrimps and canapé wafers and meat pastes, or even unjustified amounts of more sensible foods.

Probably the best way to stock your shelf is to buy two cans of vegetables and so forth when you need only one, if your local rationing allows it. Make a list of what you would like to have, and gradually accumulate it, if you can afford to.

Even if you cannot afford to, try to put aside at least an Iron ration of a few cans of tomato juice, a box of cube sugar (to eat for warmth and quick energy), a little tea, a sealed box of whole-wheat wafers, some tinned beef.

When you buy in cans, remember that many of the prepared "luncheon loaves" are extremely salty. It is impractical to give your family such food in blackouts, especially if the toilet is far away or nonexistent and the drinking water is limited.

A useful thing to have on your shelf is a supply of gingersnaps or vanilla wafers. [Much as I hate to admit it, weary English housewives have convinced me that packaged puddings are heaven-sent for such cookery: they have enough sugar in them to bolster energy, and even made with water they are palatable, at least to hungry and uneasy children and the gaffers.] These innocuous (or obnoxious, if you feel that way about them) cookies are useful at turning a can of fruit into a somewhat more nourishing and much more attractive dish, if you can put them all together and broil them for a few minutes, with the fruit on top. A little butter and brown sugar and even a dash of sherry will help.

Vanilla wafers may bring tears of anguish to the eyes of some self-respecting gourmets, but canned beef-gravy will make them sob aloud. And yet . . . may I be forgiven for admitting it . . . or may I? . . . canned beef-gravy is a "natural" for you if you have someone in your family who feels faint and weak unless he smells at least synthetic meat once a day. You can make many a good tricked dish, with a few mushrooms, some leftover rice, and a dash of wine, if you have one of those frightening, efficient cans of "rich brown *meat* gravy" on hand. It is spurious, maybe. It is chicanery. But it is economical and useful psychologically, especially if you are three miles from a market and the siren blows just as you are pumping up your bike-tire.

Another useful thing of doubtful origin for your blackout shelf is a moderate supply of cheeses in glass. The damnable things are fakes; they admit it on the labels . . . *simulated* Romano, Cheddar *type*, and so on. They are flatulently proud of being pasteurized. But they perform a special function, I think, in making people feel hungry. [I deplore the stupid overuse of monosodium glutamate, but in various "flavoring salts," called anything from Tang-oh to Mete-dee-lite, it does manage to lend a valuable if fleeting desirability to basically dull dishes.]

Cheese has always been a food that both sophisticated and simple humans love. And even if some doctors may not feel that it is wise to eat it, in a time of peril and unspoken fear it is an anesthetic and can make your guests, your own self, feel slightly stimulated by its unmistakable flavor and more than a little reassured to know that it still exists. Put a little bit on crackers, or on crisp toast if your oven is still working. Try it on a tired factory worker some day, or a nervous neighbor, with a glass of milk if possible or a cup of tea, and watch the unfolding of a lot of spiritual tendrils that were drawn up into a tight heedless tangle. [The lunch of draymen and farmers-at-market in French Switzerland is one of the best in the world: a slab of bread, a cut of slightly grainy mountain-cheese, a glass of thin white wine . . . I have seen it work miracles of restoration.]

If you are used to drinking, and can, it is pleasant to have whiskey or a good stable wine in your cupboard. A glass in your hand makes the ominous sky seem very high above you.

If by chance you want to be out in the streets, benefit by many a Londoner's experience and carry a little flask, since welcoming pubs are few and far between, and none too eager to open their doors even to old friends when unidentified planes are reported within sound of the listening posts.

(Do you remember that bar in Berne, during the Munich business, the night before what we all thought would be M-Day? There was a total blackout, and you went down a long hall through patent-leather curtains and then sat with a lot of other silent people in the dim room, while the tropical birds in the glass walls, which were really cages that imprisoned you caught in another and still another cage, flitted and screamed silently behind the glass. Everybody sat with a waiting look. It would have been better to stay away, probably.)

It is practical for blackouts, as well as for general "common sense in the kitchen," to cook more than you need for one meal. There are many simple recipes that can be made into a whole meal if you have some boiled rice handy, or some leftover green peas, or a bowl of cold cooked meat or spaghetti or almost anything you can think of (except maybe fried oysters!).

If you and your household are in a state of active emergency, you will survive, probably, without heat or light or anything but what you can scrape from the shelves. This picture is not one you care to dwell on, but it is a possibility. If it comes to that, no book on earth can help you, but only your inborn sense of caution and balance and protection: the same thing cats feel sometimes, or birds or elephants. Everything resolves itself into a feeling that you will survive if you are meant to survive, and every cell in your body believes that.

If you are not in a state of emergency, but merely living as so many people have lived for many months now, taking sirens in your stride and ration cards with a small cautious grin, you will be able to make very good meals indeed for the people who live with you. As long as the gas or the electric current supply you, your stove will function and your kitchen will be warm and savory. Use as many fresh things as you can, always, and then trust to luck and your blackout cupboard and what you have decided, inside yourself, about the dignity of man.

HOW TO BE
CHEERFUL THOUGH STARVING

*Obsession by economic issues is as local and transitory
as it is repulsive and disturbing.*
The Acquisitive Society, RICHARD HENRY TAWNEY

When you are really hungry, a meal eaten by yourself is not so much an event as the automatic carrying out of a physical function: you must do it to live. [I now disagree completely with this, and could and probably will write a whole book proving my present point, that solitary dining, no matter what the degree of hunger, can be good.] But when you share it with another human or two, or even a respected animal, it becomes dignified. Suddenly it takes on part of the ancient religious solemnity of the Breaking of Bread, the Sharing of Salt. No matter what your hunger nor how fiercely your fingers itch for the warmness of the food, the fact that you are not alone makes flavors clearer and a certain philosophic slowness possible.

And it is well to eat slowly: the food seems to be more plentiful, probably because it lasts longer.

There are many ways to make a little seem like more. They have been followed and changed and reinvented for ten thousand years, with small loss of dignity to mankind. Indeed, sometimes their very following is a thing of admiration, because of the people who are poor and who refuse to be obsessed by that fact until it becomes "repulsive and disturbing."

Of course, it takes a certain amount of native wit to cope gracefully with the problem of having the wolf camp with apparent permanency on your doorstep. That can be a wearing thing, and even the pretense of ignoring his presence has a kind of dangerous monotony about it.

For the average wolf-dodger, good health is probably one of the most important foils. Nothing seems particularly grim if your head is clear and your teeth are clean [Toothpaste now contains chlorophyl. Animals still chew grass.] and your bowels function properly.

Another thing that makes daily, hourly thought about wherewithals endurable is to be able to share it with someone else. That does not mean, and I say it emphatically, sharing the fuss and bother and fretting. It means being companionable with another human who understands, perhaps without any talking at all, what problems of basic nourishment confront you. [This still obtains, as my legal friends say. It is the condition most devoutly to be wished for. However, the years have taught me compromises, as they have all thinking creatures.] Once such a relationship is established, your black thoughts vanish, and how to make a pot of stew last three more meals seems less a nightmare than a form of sensual entertainment.

There was one person, though, who was a part of my education and who refuted all my tentative rules for fortunate wolf-dodging, and did it with such grace that I often think of her half-doubtingly, as if she were a dream.

Her name was Sue. She was delicate bodily . . . not ill, but never well the way most people are well. She flitted like a night moth through all her days, bemazed by the ardors of sunlight but conducting herself with wary sureness, so that she seldom banged against shut doors or hit her thin bones on sharp table corners.

She was, as far as anyone knew, completely alone. It was impossible to think of her in any more passionate contact with other humans than the occasional suppers she gave for them. The fact that once she must have been young did not change her present remoteness: you could not see her any warmer at seventeen that at seventy.

But her withdrawn impersonal attitude did not make her any less delicately robust. She loved to eat, and she apparently loved, now and then, to eat with other people. Her suppers were legendary. Of course, it depended on who was telling about them: sometimes they were merely strange, or even laughable, and sometimes they sounded like something from a Southern California Twelfth Night, with strange games and witchlike feastings.

Sue lived in a little weatherbeaten house on a big weatherbeaten cliff. At first when you entered it, the house seemed almost empty, but soon you realized that like all dwellings of old lonely people, it was stuffed with a thousand relics of the fuller years. There were incredibly dingy and lump-filled cushions that Whistler had sat on, and a Phyfe chair that had one stormy night been kicked into kindling wood by Oscar Wilde. It was held together with rubber bands, and naturally was not to be used as a chair, but rather as a casually treated but important altar.

When you went to her house, you ate by one candle, no matter whether you were two or eight at table. Of course this seemed intensely romantic to young Americans, but it was because she could afford neither more candles nor electricity.

The walls, covered with third-rate etchings by first-rate men, and a few first-rate ones by the almost unknown Sue, emerged gradually from the dingy darkness. There was an underlying smell, delicate as early death, of age and decay.

The main smell, though, was a good one. It never had the forthright energy of braised meat (although I remember one time, when I may have looked a little peaked, that Sue went against her custom and put a tiny morsel of cooked liver on my plate, and said, "Now, I want you to try to eat *all* of this!" It was no bigger than a dollar, and I made it into at least twelve bites, in a kind of awe).

There was always the exciting, mysterious perfume of bruised herbs, plucked fresh and cool from the tangle of weeds around the shack. Sue put them into a salad.

Then there was usually sage, which she used like a Turk or Armenian in practically everything that went into her pot. She gathered it in the hills, and dried it in bunches above her stove, and in spite of gastronomical scouts who wail now that California sage all has a taste of turpentine, hers never did. She knew only about a hundred kinds, she confessed quietly; someone had told her that the hills behind the village held at least fifty more.

Sue had only a few plates, and no knives. You ate everything from one large Spode soup-plate, when you went there, but it never seemed mussy. And knives were unnecessary, because there was nothing to cut.

As I remember now, her whole cuisine was Oriental. There were the little bowls of chopped fresh and cooked leaves. There were the fresh and dried herbs, which she had gathered from the fields. There was the common bowl of rice (or potatoes that Sue had probably stolen the night before from some patch up the canyon). There was tea, always. There was, occasionally, a fresh egg, which also was stolen, no doubt, and which Sue always put in the teapot to heat through and then broke over the biggest dish of food.

I have never eaten such strange things as there in her dark smelly room, with the waves roaring at the foot of the cliff and Whistler's maroon-taffeta pillow bruising its soft way into the small of my back. People said that Sue robbed garbage pails at night. She did not, of course. But she did flit about, picking leaves from other gardens than her own and wandering like the Lolly Willowes of Laguna along the cliff-tops and the beaches looking in the night light for sea-spinach and pink ice-plant. [For long now the cliffs have been covered with villas, and the wild herbs have vanished. I still taste and smell them in my memory, and feel the close-packed cold beads of the ice-plant's leaves and petals.]

The salads and stews she made from these little shy weeds were indeed peculiar, but she blended and cooked them so skillfully that they never lost their fresh salt crispness. She put them together with thought and gratitude, and never seemed to realize that her cuisine was one of intense romantic strangeness to everyone but herself. I doubt if she spent more than fifty dollars a year on what she and her entranced guests ate, but from the gracious abstracted way she gave you a soup dish full of sliced cactus leaves and lemon-berries and dried crumbled kelp, it might as well have been stuffed ortolans. Moreover, it was good.

I doubt very much if anybody but Sue could make it good. Few other humans know the secret of herbs as she did . . . or if they know them, can use them so nonchalantly.

But anyone in the world, with intelligence and spirit and the knowledge that it must be done, can live with her inspired oblivion to the ugliness of poverty. It is not that she wandered at night hunting for leaves and berries; it is that she cared enough to invite her friends to share them with her, and could serve them, to herself alone or to a dozen guests, with the sureness that she was right.

Sue had neither health nor companionship to comfort her and warm her, but she nourished herself and many other people for many years, with the quiet assumption

How to Cook a Wolf

[this is very important] that man's need for food is not a grim obsession, repulsive, disturbing, but a dignified and even enjoyable function. Her nourishment was of more than the flesh, not because of its strangeness, but because of her own calm. [And this, too, is very important.]

FROM HOW TO MAKE
A PIGEON CRY

Here's a pigeon so finely roasted, it cries, Come, eat me!
Polite Conversation, JONATHAN SWIFT

For centuries men have eaten the flesh of other creatures not only to nourish their own bodies but to give more strength to their weary spirits. A bull's heart, for example, might well bring bravery; oysters, it has been whispered, shed a new potency not only in the brain but in certain other less intellectual regions. And pigeons, those gentle flitting creatures, with the soft voices and their miraculous wings in flight, have always meant peace, and refreshment to sad humans.

Perhaps it is an old wives' tale; perhaps it is a part of our appetites more easily explained by *The Golden Bough* than by a cook or doctor: whatever the reason, a roasted pigeon is and long has been the most heartening dish to set before a man bowed down with grief or loneliness. In the same way, it can reassure a timid lover, or comfort a woman weak from childbirth.

It is not easy to find pigeons, these days. Most of the ones you know about in the city are working for the government. In the country there are few farmers, anymore, that have kept their dovecotes clean and populous . . . and fewer hired men who will kill the pretty birds properly by smothering them. By far the easiest way to make a pigeon cry, "Come, eat me!" is to buy it, all cleaned and trussed, from a merchant.

It is usually expensive, in a mild way. [How can extravagance be mild? And what is mild about a minimal $1.25 per bird? But I still say it is worth it, now and then.] But if you like the idea at all, it is worth saving your meat-money for a few days, and making a party of it; eating a roasted pigeon is one of the few things that can be done all by yourself and in sordid surroundings with complete impunity and a positive reaction of well-being. [And for two, four, or six people who know each other well enough to eat with their fingers, there is no pleasanter supper than hot or cold roasted pigeons, with kasha or wild rice and undressed watercress and good bread . . . and, of course, plenty of good red wine.]

[It seems impossible that there is, apparently, no recipe for kasha in this book so trustingly dedicated to my fellow philosophers in Operation Wolf. Kasha is a fine thing. In spite of unhappy political as well as gastronomical overtones just now, I must say that Russians are strong people because of it (. . . and cabbage and black bread and sour cream and floods of hoth*othot* tea). It can be bought most easily, at least in Western America, from "health food stores." Package directions should be followed carefully, for unfortunately some of the stuff is pre-cooked now, and turns into a horrid mush if you go on with the old routine of slow steaming. Properly prepared, kasha makes a wonderful aromatic nutty accompaniment to meat or fowl, and alone it is delicious, with an extra pat of butter, and combined with mushrooms it is heavenly, and and and. . . .

Kasha
> 2 cups kasha (whole or cracked groats)
> 1 or 2 fresh eggs
> 4 or more cups hot water or stock
> butter or fat, about 3/5 tablespoon
> salt, pepper

Put kasha into heavy skillet and mix egg into it until each grain is coated. Stir often over very low fire, until the grains are glazed and nut-like. Add liquid slowly, put fat in center, and cover closely, to cook until fluffy and tender (about 3/4 hour). Season and add more butter if wished. Serve.]

I have eaten a great many pigeons here and there, and I know that the best was one I cooked in a cheap Dutch oven on a one-burner gas-plate in a miserable lodging. The wolf was at the door, and no mistake; until I filled the room with the smell of hot butter and red wine, his pungent breath seeped through the keyhole in an almost visible cloud.

Supper took about half an hour to prepare (I could have done it more quickly, but there was no reason for it), and long before I was ready to put the little brown fuming bird on my one Quimper plate, and pour out my second glass of wine, I heard a sad sigh and then the diminishing click of his claws as he retreated down the hall and out into the foggy night. I had routed him, because of the impertinent recklessness of roasting a little pigeon and savoring it intelligently and voluptuously too.

This is the way I cooked that innocent brown bird, and the way, with small variations, I have often treated other ones since then:

Roast Pigeon
> 1 pigeon
> 1 lemon
> 2 slices fat bacon (or 2 tablespoons butter or oil)
> parsley
> red wine (or cider, beer, orange juice, tomato juice, stock . . .), about a cupful
> water
> salt, pepper

Melt the fat. [If bacon is used, cook it until crisp, and then remove it until time to serve it alongside, over, or even under the little bird.] See that the bird is well plucked, and rub her thoroughly with a cut lemon and the seasoning. Push the parsley into the belly. Braise well in the hot fat.

Add the liquid, put on the lid quickly, and cook slowly for about 20 minutes, basting two or three times. If you are going to eat the bird cold, put into a covered dish so that it will not dry out. [And if hot, make a pretty slice of toast for each bird, butter it well (or spread it with a bit of good *pâté de foies* for Party!), and place the bird upon it. Swirl about one cup of dry good wine and 2 tablespoonfuls butter in the pan, for 4 birds, and spoon this over each one immediately, and serve.] [. . .]

How to Practice
True Economy

Mere parsimony is not economy. . . . Expense, and great expense,
may be an essential part of true economy.
Letters to a Noble Lord, EDMUND BURKE, 1796

There is supposed to be something intrinsically satisfying about writing the last chapter of a book, even if it is written before the end. There should be something doubly so about writing of half-forgotten luxuries and half-remembered delicate impossible dishes at the end of a book of resolutely practical recipes for foxing the wolf and keeping him either at his proper distance, or well-jointed in a stewpan. It should be like waking from a dream of your loved one, and finding perfume on your lips.

Such impossible delights are necessary, now and then, to your soul, and your body, too. You can cope with economy for only so long. ("So long" is one of those ambiguous phrases. It means "so long as you do not feel sick at the sight of a pocketbook.")

When you think you can stand no more of the wolf's snuffing under the door and keening softly on cold nights, throw discretion into the laundry bag, put candles on the table, and for your own good if not the pleasure of an admiring audience make one or another of the recipes in this chapter. And buy yourself a bottle of wine, or make a few cocktails, or have a long open-hearted discussion of cheeses with the man on the corner who is an alien but still loyal if bewildered.

It is plain that a great many of the things in the following recipes are impossible to find, now. That immediately puts the whole chapter in the same class as Samarkand and Xanadu and the *terrasse* of the Café de la Paix. It is perhaps just as well; for a time there are other things than anchovies that must be far from actuality.

Sit back in your chair, then. Drop a few years from your troubled mind. Let the cupboard of your thoughts fill itself with a hundred ghosts that long ago, in 1939, used to be easy to buy and easy to forget. [This therapy, unconscious or deliberate, is known to any prisoner of war or woe, and some of the world's most delectable cookbooks have been written, at least conversationally and now and then actually, in concentration camps and cell-blocks.] Permit your disciplined inner self to relax, and think of caviar, and thick cream, and fat little pullets trotting through an oak grove rich with truffles, "musky, fiery, savory, mysterious." Close your eyes to the headlines and your ears to sirens and the threatenings of high explosives, and read instead the sweet nostalgic measures of these recipes, impossible yet fond.

Shrimp Pâté
>   4 pounds fresh shelled cooked shrimp or 6 cans dry-pack shrimp
>   1 onion, minced very fine
>   ½ cup melted butter
>   3 tablespoons lemon juice
>   ½ cup mayonnaise
>   salt, pepper, dry mustard, whatever other spice you want

[Now I use a full cup of melted butter, and more if the paste seems dry.] Mash the clean shrimp very fine in a big bowl with a potato masher, and add the onion as you do it. When you can mash no more, pour in the melted butter, mixing it thoroughly. Add the lemon juice and mayonnaise, and continue to pound it. It will be a stiff paste. Season it highly: if you plan to use it within two days use fresh herbs at your discretion, but if you will be keeping it in the icebox use powdered condiments.

Pack the mixture into a mold, and press it down well. Chill it for at least twelve hours in an icebox. When you are ready to serve, turn it out and slice it thin with a sharp hot knife. [I used to eat potted shrimps by the scoopful, in a small swank restaurant in London. They were shelled, whole and tiny, held firmly together in a little fat jar by an aromatic butter. I should think San Francisco's "bay shrimps" would be almost as good for such a forthright accessory to the pleasures of the table . . . but the shrimps must indeed be tiny, no longer than a bee, no thicker than a violet's stem.]

Or leave it in the presentable mold, preferably an oblong one, and serve it slice by slice as the *maîtres d'hôtel* used to do in little places like the Roy Gourmet and big little places like Lipp's and enormous little places like the Ritz, or the Casino at Evian in summer. There are still a few restaurants in the world that can think about *pâtés de maison,* and one of the best of their heady, almost phosphorescent, pastes is made essentially after this recipe—with perhaps a bristol mortar instead of a plain bowl and potato masher, and a good dash of smooth ancient brandy to lace it all together, just before it is packed into the mold.

Such a paste can be kept for weeks or months, or perhaps even for years, if it contains enough spices and alcohol, is correctly sealed into its mold with coagulated fat, and is kept reasonably cold. Given these three prime benefits, it can be produced when you will, like a mad maiden aunt, or a first edition (in Russian, naturally) of *Crime and Punishment.*

Eggs with anchovies. Ah me, to put it mildly! The recipe comes from an American woman who, for various reasons both sociological and esthetic, lived in Switzerland before this war. Although she was almost a stranger to me, I admired her house and many of the meals she served there, high above the lake with the vineyards pressing as close as their Swiss discretion dared against the terrace and the kitchen and the wide windows. She was I . . . and her recipe was good.

Eggs with Anchovies
    8 large fresh eggs
    2 tins or 1 cup filet of anchovies
    3 cups rich thick cream
    1 cup broiled mushrooms (can be tinned) in pieces
    2 tablespoons chopped parsley
    ½ cup grated Parmesan cheese
    fresh-ground pepper

Mash the filets of anchovies in the bottom of a shallow baking dish (save oil for a salad dressing). Mix the cream with them, and put the dish in a hot oven.

Stir two or three times after it has started to bubble, turning in the golden crust. Add the mushrooms and the parsley.

When reduced about one-third, turn off the oven. Remove the dish, and break the eggs carefully into it. Put the cheese over them, and the pepper. Then put back into the lowest part of the oven, and when the gentle heat has made the eggs firm but not hard, usually in about 15 minutes, remove and serve.

This recipe makes enough for three or four people, and is best with thin toast and a salad of little romaine hearts tossed lightly in seasoned walnut oil and lime juice. A recent Dazaley [This is spelled Dézaley. And, of course, the alcoholic pattern of another's feast would not be as Swiss as I made mine in 1942. Each to his own nostalgia! In the 1950s . . . would it start this way: an oily Dutch gin with the smoked salmon . . . ?] at cellar temperature should be served amply with it, and with the coffee, strong and plentiful and preferably in café-glasses, you would undoubtedly have a *marc du Valais,* rather yellow and well able to jar your guests slightly where they sit.

The first sip would be polite. The second would be dogged. The rest would be good robust happiness, especially after the bland delicacy of the supper. The summer fireworks would start across the lake at Evian, and the baker boy who worked at night in Vevey would come hurtling down the road on his bicycle, yelling like a hilarious banshee as he took the curves of the corniche. The marc would make a warmth in you that might well last for several colder years.

Bœuf Moreno, like Eggs with Anchovies, or any other good recipe, needs no nostalgic introduction except the one you will always give it in your mind, after the first time you eat it. It is, like so many of the classics [. . . as well as in the undying perfection of the Laws of Moses] a hideous combination dietetically, and well worth trying.

Bœuf Moreno

    2 tablespoons butter

    2 tablespoons flour

    3/4 cup stock

    4 tablespoons mixed parsley and chopped green onion or chives

    1/2 cup mushrooms or pitted olives

    2 tablespoons butter

    2 tablespoons chopped green pepper or pimiento

    1 pound leftover steak or roast beef, 2 inches thick, cut in thin strips

    1/2 cup sour cream [I have now increased this to one cup.]

    3 tablespoons brandy or whiskey

    hot rice or toast

Make a roux of the butter, flour, and stock. Add the onion and parsley, and simmer in a double boiler 20 minutes. Season.

Heat the peppers and mushrooms in 2 tablespoons butter in the bottom of a shallow casserole. Add the thin slices of beef and heat thoroughly.

Add the cream slowly to the roux, and stir in the brandy. Pour over the meat in the casserole. Serve at once, with hot fluffy rice or thin buttered toast.

A casserole that always makes me think of valentines, for no good reason, is made with young chicken and cream and is a fine way to ask, "Will you be my love?"

Poulet à la mode de Beaune

    1 tender chicken of about three pounds, cut in pieces

    1/2 lemon

    mixture of butter and olive oil [or chicken-fat from an earlier feast . . .

        and what is left makes a fine thing, once chilled, to eat upon good bread

        or toast.]

    salt and fresh pepper and a little nutmeg

    1 pint rich cream

    1 dozen large mushrooms

    3 tablespoons butter

    1/2 cup fine brandy or marc

Scrub the pieces of chicken thoroughly with the cut lemon. Dry, season, and fry thoroughly to a golden brown in the mixture of butter and oil.

Place the pieces in a casserole, and cover with the heated cream. Let cook in a moderate oven until tender.

Put butter in each mushroom cap, which has been washed quickly but not peeled, and cover the contents of the casserole with them. Broil quickly until done, about 5 minutes. Then quickly stir the mushrooms and the brandy into the casserole, and serve at once.

This is a rich and heady dish, as you can see. It needs a very cold and somewhat heavy white wine, like a Haut Sauternes. Or champagne will do nicely!

A refreshing delicate dessert that yet does not taste too sensible is indeed a rarity. Ices after heaviness are good, as the Italian cooks who first brought them to the French well knew, but they can seem overly thin. Fruit is the same, almost too natural and shocking after the high perverted flavors of some such masterpiece as Bœuf Moreno. But since a pudding or a soufflé would be unthinkable, why not serve thick slices of fresh pineapple soaked for several hours in an Alsatian *kirschwasser,* and then topped with a sherbet made with lime juice?

I ate this once in the richly muted dining room of a beautiful woman, and drank a dry champagne with it, and even if there had not been caviar in a big bowl long before, and little orchids like moths flying from a pink ruffled shell on the table, it would have been one of the perfect things of my gastronomic life.

The following recipe is very old, as age goes here. It was made often in Williamsburg, before there was any need of restoration, and undoubtedly pleased many a high-living Father of Our Country, both great and small.

Colonial Dessert
  2 cups thick cream
  4 egg yolks
  1 cup brown sugar
Boil the cream one minute. Pour over the well-beaten egg yolks. Heat in a double boiler 8 minutes, beating constantly. Pour into a shallow dish from which it will be served, and chill overnight.

  Two hours before serving cover with a half-inch layer of brown sugar, and brown very quickly under a hot broiler. Chill again, and serve with thin crisp cookies such as *langues de chat.*

A salad made of fruits, you could call the following eccentric dish. Paul Reboux, that antic gourmet, evolved it in his inimitable *cuisine au cerveau,* and called it, in the days when such things were slightly less impossible than now,

Fruits aux Sept Liqueurs
Put into an ample bowl the following: slices of orange, tangerines, and bananas; pitted cherries; wood strawberries and peeled grapes; sliced peeled peaches and plums and ripe pears. Sprinkle them with sugar and a little lime juice.

  Pour over them the following liquid, which has been made of a wine-glassful each of the following but no other liqueurs, all mixed thoroughly together: brandy, kirsch, Cointreau, Benedictine, maraschino, and a touch of kümmel.

  Stir the salad lightly, and put on ice for two hours. Just before serving, pour half a bottle of demi-sec champagne over it.

Yes, it is crazy, to sit savoring such impossibilities, while headlines yell at you and the wolf whuffs through the keyhole. Yet now and then it cannot harm you, thus to enjoy a short respite from reality. And if by chance you can indeed find some anchovies, or a thick slice of rare beef and some brandy, or a bowl of pink curled shrimps, you are doubly blessed, to possess in this troubled life both the capacity and the wherewithal to forget it for a time.

––––––––

[This book came to its own conclusion several years ago, and upon rereading it I myself have reached a few more. But both the book and I agree, on one point made much further back than 1942, that since we must eat to live, we might as well do it with both grace and gusto.

Those few of us who actually live to eat are less repulsive than boring, and at this date I honestly know of only two such lost souls, gross puffy creatures, both of them, who are exhibited like any other monstrous curiosity by their well-fed but still balanced acquaintances.

On the other hand, I cannot count the good people I know who, to my mind, would be even better if they bent their spirits to the study of their own hungers. There are too many of us, otherwise in proper focus, who feel an impatience for the demands of our bodies, and who try throughout our whole lives, none too successfully, to deafen ourselves to the voices of our various hungers. Some stuff the wax of religious solace in our ears. Others practice a Spartan if somewhat pretentious disinterest in the pleasures of the flesh, or pretend that if we do not *admit our* sensual delight in a ripe nectarine we are not guilty . . . of even that tiny lust!

I believe that one of the most dignified ways we are capable of, to assert and then reassert our dignity in the face of poverty and war's fears and pains, is to nourish ourselves with all possible skill, delicacy, and ever-increasing enjoyment. And with our gastronomical growth will come, inevitably, knowledge and perception of a hundred other things, but mainly of ourselves. Then Fate, even tangled as it is with cold wars as well as hot, cannot harm us.]

FROM A IS FOR DINING ALONE

. . . and so am I, if a choice must be made between most people I know and myself. This misanthropic attitude is one I am not proud of, but it is firmly there, based on my increasing conviction that sharing food with another human being is an intimate act that should not be indulged in lightly.

There are few people alive with whom I care to pray, sleep, dance, sing, or share my bread and wine. Of course there are times when this latter cannot be avoided if we are to exist socially, but it is endurable only because it need not be the only fashion of self-nourishment.

There is always the cheering prospect of a quiet or giddy or warmly somber or lightly notable meal with "One," as Elizabeth Robins Pennell refers to him or her in *The Feasts of Autolycus*. "*One* sits at your side feasting in silent sympathy," this lady wrote at the end of the last century in her mannered and delightful book. She was, at this point, thinking of eating an orange in southern Europe, but any kind of food will do, in any clime, so long as *One* is there.

I myself have been blessed among women in this respect—which is of course the main reason that, if *One* is not there, dining alone is generally preferable to any other way for me.

Naturally there have been times when my self-made solitude has irked me. I have often eaten an egg and drunk a glass of jugwine, surrounded deliberately with the trappings of busyness, in a hollow Hollywood flat near the studio where I was called a writer, and not been able to stifle my longing to be anywhere but there, in the company of any of a dozen predatory or ambitious or even kind people who had *not* invited me.

That was the trouble: nobody did.

I cannot pretend, even on an invisible black couch of daydreams, that I have ever been hounded by Sunset Boulevardiers who wanted to woo me with caviar and win me with Pol Roger; but in my few desolate periods of being without *One*, I have known two or three avuncular gentlemen with a latent gleam in their eyes who understood how to order a good mixed grill with watercress. But, for the most part, to the lasting shame of my female vanity, they have shied away from any suggestion that we might dally, gastronomically speaking. "Wouldn't dare ask *you*," they have murmured, shifting their gaze with no apparent difficulty or regret to some much younger and prettier woman who had never read a recipe in her life, much less written one, and who was for that very reason far better fed than I.

It has for too long been the same with the ambitious eaters, the amateur chefs and the self-styled gourmets, the leading lights of food-and-wine societies. When we meet, in other people's houses or in restaurants, they tell me a few sacrosanct and impressive details of how they baste grouse with truffle juice, then murmur, "Wouldn't dare serve it to *you*, of course," and forthwith invite some visiting potentate from Nebraska, who never saw a truffle in his life, to register the proper awe in return for a Lucullan and perhaps delicious meal.

And the kind people—they are the ones who have made me feel the loneliest. Wherever I have lived, they have indeed been kind—up to a certain point. They have poured cocktails for me, and praised me generously for things I have written to their liking, and showed me their children. And I have seen the discreetly drawn curtains to their family dining rooms, so different from the uncluttered, spinsterish emptiness of my own one room. Behind the far door to the kitchen I have sensed, with the mystic materialism of a hungry woman, the presence of honest-to-God fried chops, peas and carrots, a jello salad, and lemon meringue pie—none of which I like and all of which I admire in theory and would give my eyeteeth to be offered. But the kind people always murmur, "We'd love to have you stay to supper sometime. We wouldn't *dare*, of course, the simple way we eat and all."

As I leave, by myself, two nice plump kind neighbors come in. They say howdo, and then good-by with obvious relief, after a polite, respectful mention of culinary literature as represented, no matter how doubtfully, by me. They sniff the fine creeping straightforward smells in the hall and living room, with silent thanks that they are not condemned to my daily fare of quails financière, pâté de Strasbourg truffé en brioche, sole Marguéry, bombe vanille au Cointreau. They close the door on me.

I drive home by way of the corner Thriftimart to pick up another box of Ry Krisp, which with a can of tomato soup and a glass of California sherry will make a good nourishing meal for me as as I sit on my tuffet in a circle of proofs and pocket detective stories.

It took me several years of such periods of being alone to learn how to care for myself, at least at table. I came to believe that since nobody else dared feed me as I wished to be fed, I must do it myself, and with as much aplomb as I could muster. Enough of hit-or-miss suppers of tinned soup and boxed biscuits and an occasional egg just because I had failed once more to rate an invitation!

I resolved to establish myself as a well-behaved female at one or two good restaurants, where I could dine alone at a pleasant table with adequate attentions rather than be pushed into a corner and given a raw or overweary waiter. To my credit, I managed to carry out this resolution, at least to the point where two headwaiters accepted me: they knew I tipped well, they knew I wanted simple but excellent menus, and, above all, they knew that I could order and drink, all by myself, an apéritif and a small bottle of wine or a mug of ale, without turning into a maudlin, potential pick-up for the Gentlemen at the Bar.

Once or twice a week I would go to one of these restaurants and with carefully disguised self-consciousness would order my meal, taking heed to have things that would nourish me thoroughly as well as agreeably, to make up for the nights ahead when soup and crackers would be my fare. I met some interesting waiters: I continue to agree with a modern Mrs. Malaprop who said, "They are *so* much nicer than people!"

My expensive little dinners, however, became, in spite of my good intentions, no more than a routine prescription for existence. I had long believed that, once having bowed to the inevitability of the dictum that we must eat to live, we should ignore it and live to eat, in proportion of course. And there I was, spending more money than I should, on a grim plan which became increasingly complicated. In spite of the loyalty of my waiter friends, wolves in a dozen different kinds of sheep's clothing— from the normally lecherous to the Lesbian—sniffed at the high wall of my isolation. I changed seats, then tables. I read—I read everything from *Tropic of Cancer* to *Riders of the Purple Sage*. Finally I began to look around the room and hum.

That was when I decided that my own walk-up flat, my own script-cluttered room with the let-down bed, was the place for me. "Never be daunted in public" was an early Hemingway phrase that had more than once bolstered me in my timid twenties. I changed it resolutely to "Never be daunted in private."

I rearranged my schedule, so that I could market on my way to the studio each morning. The more perishable tidbits I hid in the watercooler just outside my office, instead of dashing to an all-night grocery for tins of this and that at the end of a long day. I bought things that would adapt themselves artfully to an electric chafing dish: cans of shad roe (a good solitary dish, since I always feel that nobody really likes it but me), consommé double, and such. I grew deliberately fastidious about eggs and butter; the biggest, brownest eggs were none too good, nor could any butter be too clover-fresh and sweet. I laid in a case or two of "unpretentious but delightful little wines." I was determined about the whole thing, which in itself is a great drawback emotionally. But I knew no alternative.

I ate very well indeed. I liked it too—at least more than I had liked my former can-openings or my elaborate preparations for dining out. I treated myself fairly dispassionately as a marketable thing, at least from ten to six daily, in a Hollywood studio story department, and I fed myself to maintain top efficiency. I recognized the dull facts that certain foods affected me this way, others that way. I tried to apply what I knew of proteins and so forth to my own chemical pattern, and I deliberately scrambled two eggs in a little sweet butter when quite often I would have liked a glass of sherry and a hot bath and to hell with food.

I almost never ate meat, mainly because I did not miss it and secondarily because it was inconvenient to cook on a little grill and to cut upon a plate balanced on my knee. Also, it made the one-room apartment smell. I invented a great many different salads, of fresh lettuces and herbs and vegetables, of marinated tinned vegetables, now and then of crabmeat and the like. I learned a few tricks to play on canned soups, and Escoffier as well as the Chinese would be astonished at what I did with beef bouillon and a handful of watercress or a teaspoonful of soy.

I always ate slowly, from a big tray set with a mixture of Woolworth and Spode;

and I soothed my spirits beforehand with a glass of sherry or vermouth, subscribing to the ancient truth that only a relaxed throat can make a swallow. More often than not I drank a glass or two of light wine with the hot food: a big bowl of soup, with a fine pear and some Teleme Jack cheese; or two very round eggs, from a misnamed "poacher," on sourdough toast with browned butter poured over and a celery heart alongside for something crisp; or a can of bean sprouts, tossed with sweet butter and some soy and lemon juice, and a big glass of milk.

Things tasted good, and it was a relief to be away from my job and from the curious disbelieving impertinence of the people in restaurants. I still wished, in what was almost a theoretical way, that I was not cut off from the world's trenchermen by what I had written for and about them. But, and there was no cavil here, I felt firmly then, as I do this very minute, that snug misanthropic solitude is better than hit-or-miss congeniality. If *One* could not be with me, "feasting in silent sympathy," then I was my best companion. [. . .]

WAR STORY

Almost all the books and stories now have touched war, vicariously or with true sweat and noise and fear. Of course, people, too, everywhere have touched it, even in the quiet dead-end valley where I live. I know that the iceman's daughter, soon to have a child, has lost her husband on some dry far island. I see the women in the unused store building bent over their piles of bandages, rolling and rolling, with their heads wrapped prettily in white and their hearts perhaps heavy with the pain they prepare for. And now and then a boy who graduated from high school a few months ago has his picture on the front page of the weekly paper. He is dead, or he wears a new medal maybe, or both.

Things like that go on, but when I read printed books, the war seems far from here. We have no stink of it, no frantic tortured eardrums, none of the strained gallantry of men and women who have touched it. I sit passively on my hill, reading about the stench, the roar, the high courage.

In letters from England, people I love say defensively each time they get a box of food from here, "We are really *quite* well off, you know . . . but the powdered lemon *did* avert a wretched chest cold."

And Emily Hahn in Hong Kong decides not to walk up to tea that day, because there is really too much going on, what with all the bloody bombs and then the ack-ack and the rioting. She has tea at home instead, with refugees and her baby and the cook saying Charles is wounded badly and she cannot get to him. . . . The tea is hot, what there is of it.

Or I get word from a man I've never heard of at an unknown Midwest college, saying that a friend of his has heard through the underground that Georges, dear gaunt fine-browed Georges, was safe a year ago somewhere outside of Dijon and sent word for none of us for God's sake to try to get in touch with him because of his kids who were still in Caen with their grandparents.

So I read all this—and even books by correspondents—and it seems sometimes as if I had already died, here on my quiet hill.

The other day, though, I knew I was still alive. J.B. came to see me.

J.B. is the son of Spittin. They all lived at the turn of the road where it went into the main part of the valley, and I had to shift gears there after the curves and the tricky ruts, and I got so I stopped to wave and then to talk. I would have had to stop anyway, because of all the children under my wheels.

One time I asked Spittin, who was called that because he spat so much, how many he had. He was slow in answering but finally figured out, "Abaht nine livin', and fahve dade."

But his wife told me that more than that had died, and she seemed sad about it. She was pregnant then, and soon after our talk I heard long cries, like a lost calf, and finally I drove down the mile of road and found her writhing on the bed, with only three or four of the smallest to watch. There was almost nothing I could do by then, and I was very ignorant, but by late afternoon when the children started coming home and Spittin rolled in from whatever pub he'd been at, things were fairly much all right again, and he could think a while and say, "*Six* dade."

J.B. was the oldest of this clutch of hostages to fortune. He was about seventeen when I first knew him, and probably the dullest of the lot, a tall thick boy with pasty skin and eyes emptier than a dead man's. He was still in school, but his grades were so bad that they weren't even marked on his card, and he and his teachers longed for his next birthday when he could legally stop going to classes. He used to shamble up the hill to see my husband, and I'd hear him talking, slowly, painfully, in the studio. Gradually he began to pose, and some good pictures came out of it, although he did not seem to see them but only the Coke bottle he held permanently in his hand. After perhaps ten Cokes, he would talk more, and we began to think that the reason he was so slow was that he was never spoken to as a grown boy but always as if he were the same age as the current baby in the brood. This was partly because Spittin and his wife were not much older either—about seven or eight, at most. They didn't realize what they were doing to J.B., of course. But he was *lonely*. We'd say something about how cool weather was easier to work in, something simple like that, and J.B. would think for a minute, and then his clay face would lighten and he'd answer, with a kind of piteous delight, "That's right." What he needed, we thought, was to get away from all the babies.

Finally he was eighteen, and right away he left school and drifted to the nearest beer parlor. He was too clumsy to play pool and too poor to drink much, but a couple of times I picked him up on my way home from the village and he was mumbling drunk, for the other men would give him liquor so they could tease him better, with his baby speech.

Spittin was worried, and whenever he saw J.B. come into a bar, he'd leave by the back way. He talked to my husband. We suggested that J.B. enlist—this was just before the first draft. J.B. did, but the night before he was to report he ran away. That was bad; we felt to blame. Then he came home, and as soon as he could, he enlisted again. He was in.

It seemed queer at first not to see him when I stopped by Spittin's house, sitting on the doorstep with his heavy puffed face between his hands and two or three little siblings climbing over his thick legs. His mother stopped doing the daily washing in an old tub over a fire of chopped-up auto tires, too, and when I went in one day to see why, thinking I might find her bedded again, she beamed and showed me the rattle-trap washing machine J.B. had made her buy with his first pay.

A few days later she walked up the hill to see us. She had on some kind of corset, and her hair was curled, and she looked almost my age, although I knew she was really younger. We sat formally in the living room. She thanked us for getting J.B. to go away. It seemed strange, because she never had mentioned anything personal, like the time I helped her when she made the long ugly noises. We drank Cokes in little polite sips, and then as she went away, she smiled shyly at me for the first time and said, "You see? I ain't got my bar' feet!" And I saw that she did indeed have shoes on, cheap high-heeled fancy shoes. She was really happy, and I never saw her again, although I have heard that she is working in the laundry of a training camp and has finally heeded the country nurse enough not to have any more babies. She left me a Christmas cactus, which still thrives.

I thought that was the last of them all, because they moved away, and new people came to the little house and picked up all the empty hominy cans and raked the yard clean of empty Coke bottles and dung.

Then last week J.B. came back to see me. When I went to the door, I didn't know him, of course; he seemed taller, thinner, with a fairly clear and almost intelligent face. His uniform was immaculate, with the shirt buttons, the buckle, the fly all in line, and the creases just so down his arms and thighs and over his deep chest. He looked fine, for Spittin's son or anyone's.

I was busy, but I was glad to see him, too. We sat in the garden in the gentle sunlight. He fidgeted, but not as he'd used to. His hands were still clammy to the touch, I noticed when we met, and there was nervous sweat on his face, but as we talked, he looked straight at me instead of sideways and almost didn't stammer. He was in the medical corps. He wanted to learn about surgery, he said. He shook his head about the fliers at his base.

"They're crazy," he said firmly, kneading his hands together. "They crash, and they see their friends spread all over, and they go right up again. They're crazy. They don't have to pick up the pieces the way we do."

He shook his head, and his hands looked moist and frantic, but he had improved. He spoke coherently, if very simply. He knew my husband had died, and when he said it was too bad and asked if he could have something, I went into the house and got a necktie. He folded it carefully and put it in his breast pocket and then went on talking about the hospital and an operation he'd watched there on his own stomach. I was glad to see how he'd grown up, but I was busy, too, and wished he'd go.

Then he seemed almost to pull his hands from their arms and told me, with his eyes on the ground, about how he had a three-week furlough because of the operation and had only been home two days and couldn't stand it.

"Nothin' to say," he said miserably. "My folks don't talk much. My dad was in France last time, but he don't know nothin' about this one. There's too many kids.

And I can't eat the food. It rises on me. We eat swell at the base. But I can't eat at home no more."

He was trembling. He was lost and terribly lonely for his prolonged childhood.

"I just can't stand it there no more," he said, so low I could hardly hear him.

"Let's have a Coke, J.B.," I said, and without waiting for an answer, I went into the kitchen from the garden, leaving him with his head low, as if he were wounded.

I felt awful. I felt that something was my fault: I had helped to pull up his roots, and now he was alone, nevermore to be a child with other children near him. Suddenly the hill seemed emptier than I could bear. I felt like running away. Alone, alone, my heart cried. *Seule, seule,* wept the dove imprisoned in the tapestry. I, and he, and all of us . . .

I left the Coke in the bottles, the way he used to like it, and when I got to the door into the garden, I stopped with a horror that seemed almost a natural part of my inchoate misery.

J.B. stood weaving and winding in the middle of the stone-flagged court, turning slowly round and round, with his hands hanging at his sides like an ape's. He has lost his mind, I thought at once. He has gone mad with all the blood and the pieces of fliers in baskets and not being able to talk to Spittin. I am here with him on the hill, and he is mad.

I stood for a minute with the two Coke bottles steady in my hands. Then I went out without banging the door and touched him on the shoulder.

He swung around until he faced me, and his dull little eyes were full of tears, and his face was lighter than I ever thought it could be, almost as if something had turned itself on inside his thick pasty head. He smiled at me, and a tear ran down into his wide mouth.

"Ain't nothin' changed," he said softly. He swung around once more, as if something had spun him from above, and his eyes touched the rocks, the hills, the far bending silvery eucalyptus trees, before he looked square at me again.

"Ain't nothin' changed, really."

He drained the bottle and handed it absently back and then very simply wiped his cheeks with the back of one clean pudgy hand. "I got to be gittin'. Gonna send myself a telegram to report for duty."

He looked seriously at me, with more intelligence in his face than I'd ever seen there. "We got ourselves to think of, you know."

We shook hands, and his was dry and firm, and then he swung off down the hill. He had escaped, and I, alone but no more lonely, felt that for a few minutes I had touched pain and death and strength very near me, instead of on the written page or even on the bed of childbirth or at the grave.

Bareacres, Hemet, California, 1940

17 RUE CARDINALE

*. . . the empty perspective of the old street, austere and patrician, where a delicate little Virgin, high
in a corner niche in the lacy leaves, bends her head to point out to her child the picturesque needle of the
fountain of the Four Dolphins, like a musical toy to lighten the lazy hours and charm the stillness of
this discreet and provincial neighborhood . . .*

Treasures of the Provincial Museums: Aix, LOUIS GILLET

i

In most college towns in America there are widows of professors, and even retired
female teachers, who hold on to their emptying family homes by renting suitably discreet lodgings to other people in their own social and intellectual strata. This is a
blessing, sometimes dubious but basically essential, to almost everyone concerned.
Well-run faculty clubs are few, and most people past thirty feel self-conscious in college "unions," even in the thin disguise of graduate standing.

As far as I know, though, France has a much better climate than the United States
for people who must find lodgings with another congenial family. On every social
level board and rooms are offered, usually with discrimination, to people who inevitably gravitate to their own chosen patterns, whether they be traveling salesmen or
nuclear physicists.

In Albion, Michigan, or Whittier, California, Dr. Doke's relict courageously
"takes in" one or two boarders to keep the taxes paid on her empty old house on
College Street. In France, almost any empty room in no matter what kind of dwelling, from hovel to mansion, is put to use: it helps pay the taxes, of course, and it salves
the instinctive guilt any good Gallic citizen feels about waste of food-space-energy,
and waste most of all of what can be called the sense of humanity, or more plainly
the basic and instinctive need of people for people.

I have lived with several families in France. More often than not while I was with
them I fretted and even raged at the strictures of sharing my meals and my emotions
and my most personal physical functions with people almost as strange to me as spi-
ders or nesting egrets. In retrospect I understand that they shaped such strength as
may be in me as surely as ever did my inherited genes and my environmental mores.
Of course they had these to build on, for I did not meet my first landlady until I was
in my early twenties.

She was a born Dijonnaise who lived down the street from the University because she liked to rent rooms to students, not because the house she rented was beautiful or otherwise desirable to them. She *liked* students. She liked to feed them and talk with them and play Chopin for them and occasionally sleep with ones who pleased her enough. She did all this with ferocious amusement. She was a kind of explosion in what had been until my first meeting with her a safe insular well-bred existence.

From then on I was aware.

She has been followed by decades of less robust but equally subtle relationships with French landladies. Now I know that I can live almost anywhere, with almost anyone, and be the better for it. This is a great comfort in contemplating the probabilities of the future . . .

First impressions are perhaps not as important as they are said to be, but they are good preparation for what may happen later, and I know that every landlady I ever met was part of preparing me for Madame Lanes, of Aix.

My mother would understand and accept my feeling that this old lady had almost as much to do with my development as did she, and would not ask for any explanation. It is at once an overt admission that I matured very slowly and a proof that people can grow at any stage in their lives. My mother would be pleased that I could still grow.

I was nearing fifty when I first met Madame Lanes, and well past it when last I saw her. It is improbable that I shall be with her again, for she is old and seven thousand miles away, but I feel serene and sure that if that happened I would be the better for it, and stronger to surmount the admiration, exasperation, impatience, ridicule, and frustration that she has always fermented in me.

The first landlady in my life happened as swiftly and irrevocably as a bullet's flight: I went to the students' office at the University of Dijon, the small elderly secretary gave me a list of boardinghouses, I walked two hundred feet down the first street on the right, rang a doorbell, and became part of a household for two shaking and making years of my life.

It was very different, the last time, in 1954.

I went to Aix for six weeks or at most three months. I stayed well over three years, in two or three periods, and partly it was because of Madame Lanes. I found her in a roundabout way, not at all bulletlike.

In my first interview with her she taught me the French meaning of the word "neurasthenic," which American friends in psychiatric circles frown upon, so that I am careful not to use it anywhere but in Aix.

I had not spoken French for several years when I sat in the autumn sunlight in her drawing room on the top floor of 17 rue Cardinale. I shaped my words carefully, listening to my rusty accent with dogged resignation.

"I have been told, Madame, that occasionally a room is available in your home," I said.

"Who told you, may I ask?" Her seeming question was politely direct as a police query: TALK, you!

I told her, and her firm rounded old face was as impassive as a Hindu postcard of Krishna.

"Why do you not stay in a hotel? There are many pleasant small hotels in Aix," she said, without any real interest but as if she were telling me to question myself, not asking me anything for her own information.

I took my first lesson, there in the thinning but still intense September sunlight, in speaking the kind of French that Madame Lanes expected of anyone who addressed her. It was a test I met intensely and even passionately whenever I saw her during the next seven or eight years, and even this long since, my accent in dreams is better when I am dreaming of her.

"Madame," I said, "I am very well installed in the Hôtel de France, where I was sent by Monsieur Bressan, the concierge of the Roi René . . . "

"I know him well," she interrupted. "A good man. A very reliable courageous man."

"He seems so. He saw that I did not like to keep my children in a hotel . . . "

"It is not the life for children. It is also expensive."

"Yes, Madame. So we went to the Hôtel de France until I got the children into Madame Wytenhove's . . . "

"Yes, I know her. Her sister-in-law's mother occasionally comes to my Afternoons. Your children will be subjected to a fairly good accent, vaguely Alsatian but better than Aixois in the correct sense of the word. Madame Wytenhove has had a sad experience; her husband died of cancer. Unfortunately her children speak like Spaniards after living in Spain while their father was an engineer there, but basically they are fairly well bred."

I felt desperate about my own way of shaping the half-forgotten sounds. "I do not like living alone in a hotel," I plowed on. "It is too impersonal. I miss my children. I hate the sound of the Vespas revving up in the garage on the Place des Augustins. I have no place to be except in bed. I hate to eat alone in restaurants. I feel unreal when I walk down the Cours at night from a movie where I have gone because otherwise I would have to go to bed."

All this suddenly sounded very voluble but logical and necessary to me, and my accent was forgotten in a relieving gush of words I had not used for too many years.

Madame looked dispassionately at me. We were sitting across from each other at a beautiful small chess table piled with her account books, bills, and correspondence, which I soon learned was cleared every night for cards or games. I do not know where she put all the papers, but they were out again in the morning.

"Madame," she said as coolly as any medical diagnostician but more frankly, "you are neurasthenic. Your surroundings are making you so."

I protested, for the English connotation of the word was not at all the way I thought I was. I thought I was bored and lonely but not at all neurasthenic in the dictionary sense: worried, disturbed in digestion and circulation, emotionally torn, tortured by feelings of inferiority.

"Oh no, Madame," I said. "I am very stable. I am very healthy."

"You are not mentally ill," she said. "You are simply moping. I have a small room, cold, ill heated, formerly for a maid, during the time when Madame de Sévigné's daughter used this as her town-house. I will show it to you. It is now occupied. But until it is free you may lunch and dine here."

I followed her across the tiles of the drawing room floor, and down the long dim corridor that split her apartment into halves, one sunny and spacious and elegant, the other small, with low ceilings and cramped dim space, made for servants and filled with people like me who lived there more happily, perhaps, than any varlets had.

ii

Ten years after the Liberation, French people were still steadying themselves. I became increasingly conscious of this the first time I lived in Aix. Anecdotes, some half-laughing and some apologetically tragic, came willy-nilly into almost every conversation, and little marble plaques saying things like *To the memory of six martyrs shot down by the invaders* still looked very new on the street walls. People were defeatist, and basically exhausted.

When I returned, some six years later, there was a feeling of comparative easiness of spirit, in spite of the mounting anxiety about the Algerian problem. Women who had seemed really harried to the point of masked hysteria in 1954, no matter what their social level, were relaxed and younger-looking.

This was true of Madame Lanes. She was on guard when I first knew her, wary but conscious of the fact that she had survived the Occupation (which was really three: German, then Italian, then American) and had escaped trouble in spite of being a staunch worker in the Underground for all its duration.

She was remote and hard. She fought jauntily a daily battle against poverty and rising prices and inefficient servants and inconscient boarders. She was like a tired aging professional dancer who would not dare stumble.

When I saw her next, in 1959, she was younger. A year later she was younger still.

Part of this, I think, was because her daughter Henriette had moved permanently to Paris. Most of it was because she had accepted the new stresses of postwar existence and recovered a little from the strains of war itself. She moved somewhat more slowly, for she may have been well into her seventies, and she used a graceful little silver-headed cane on the streets, but she still supervised the marketing and paid her calls on other ladies on their Afternoons, and went with composure and no apparent shortness of breath up the beautiful stone stairs with their wrought iron balustrades that rose from the street level of the Rue Cardinale to her top-floor apartment.

Generations of boarders had flowed in and out since first I met her, and instead of the cool acceptance, the remote calculation which I had first sensed in her, she seemed, the second time round, to feel a deep enjoyment in them. She was warm, and I could remember, with no regret and with real delight that she had changed, my early despair at ever having her like *me*, Mary Frances, the person who was me-Mary-Frances.

Often during that first stay there I would write home about this unaffrontable detachment. I would talk with my few friends in Aix about how I wanted Madame to accept me as another woman, and not as one more outlander who paid for her food and lodging and took as her due the dispassionate courtesy of the household which was forced to welcome her. Perhaps it is because I too was having to adapt my former ideas of the world to new necessities that I was oversensitive to this attitude of Madame Lanes and her like.

I knew that she approved of me as a person of some breeding, but there was always present an overt amazement that any American could really know how to hold a teacup, how to tell the difference between sixteenth- and seventeenth-century sideboards, how to say *Si* instead of *Oui* at the right places.

I would fight hard not to show my helpless hopeless rage when Madame would introduce me as the only American she had ever known who did not talk through her nose.

"Of course you must have taken many difficult lessons in voice placement," she would say blandly, and when I was fool enough to deny this and to say that both my parents were from Iowa but that I had never heard them speak with nasal voices, she would smile faintly and with heavy-handed tact change the subject. I would go to my room in a fury, and swear to leave the next morning.

This tumultuous resentment of my status lasted as long as I stayed with Madame. I never really accepted the plain truth that I myself could hold no interest, no appeal, for the cool gracious old lady. It was a kind of rebuff which perhaps Americans, very warm generous naïve people, are especially attuned to.

Spiritually we are fresh children, unable to realize that other peoples are infinitely older and wearier than we. We do not yet know much world-pain, except vicariously. Europeans who grow bored or exasperated with our enthusiasm are not feeling superior to us, any more than a group of "senior citizens" feel superior as they watch teen-agers rock-and-roll or do the twist. There may perhaps be a little muscular envy in the oldsters, but there is also tolerance and understanding which the young people are as yet incapable of recognizing.

Et cetera.

Et cetera.

This is the way I talked to myself, in an almost ceaseless monologue while I lived with Madame Lanes. It was good for me. Many things I should long since have known, about both outer and inner worlds, grew clearer to me as I learned that no matter how long I lived nor how many other lives I might be able to cram into my one span, I would never be as old as one of the children in the streets of Aix. I was the product of a young race of newcomers to a virgin land and must accept every aspect of my racial adolescence.

It was soon plain that I would stand a better chance of this with Madame Lanes than with any other of the people of her education and breeding who accepted boarders like me. They were more violently cynical and exhausted than she about the changes in their ways of living and the wounds of Occupation.

Some of them were openly resentful of my ambiguous state. I was too old to be a student, yet obviously not qualified to be a scholar or professor. I called myself a writer, but what did I write, and for whom, and even why? I was obviously middle-aged and yet the mother of two young girls whom I did not even live with. Neither fish nor fowl . . . and in spite of my appearance of respectability I was still an American, which basically meant that I must have been raised on De Mille spectacles, football and comic books.

iii

Madame Lanes, in spite of her deliberate detachment from her boarders as people and her overt acceptance of us as financial necessities, was unswervingly courteous and thoughtful. She remained unruffled through the maddest domestic upheavals, which occurred more frequently in her house than in any other place I have ever lived. She remained in full control of herself, a real lady, even at midnight with a maddened serving-girl whooping through the hall and down the corridor with her brain wild with nightmares of what the invaders had taught her. There was never any feeling of hidden frenzy in the old lady.

This was not true of other women I met, that first time in Aix.

Now and then, when I went back to Aix in 1959 to live again, I saw some of the people to whom I had been introduced just ten years after the Liberation, and I thanked God that I had made myself stay with Madame Lanes. She emerged from my memories as an unruffled monument of dignity and wisdom, whereas much that I had first felt about her fellow-landladies was plainer than ever on their ravaged proud old faces.

One, a Madame Perblantier, was their archetype. Her name was given to me by the head of the Girls' High School, a friend of an old friend from Dijon. Madame Perblantier would take two or three guests into her home. I should arrange an interview with her. I did.

Then I fled her, deep in sadness and depression about what had happened to a countless number of good French women.

She lived on the Avenue Ste. Victoire in a big house, nondescript from the outside, flush with the bleak street, very much like Spain. Inside, all the living rooms, the bedrooms, and the dining room faced toward the southwest onto a beautiful garden that descended gently to the edge of a little tributary of the Torse.

Inside, the house sparkled with that particular waxen clutter of the upper French bourgeoisie: varnished cabinets filled with Sèvres teacups; fans spread out in crystal cases; embroidered footstools from faraway military campaigns; a few minor etchings in recognizable styles from the eighteenth century, speckled in their heavy frames. There were flowers. The sunlight poured in through the beautiful windows, and stripped Madame's face like a scalpel, seeing viciously into the essence of her, the skin within the skin.

She was, like most of the other women of her class, used to a much easier life and was now accepting bitterly, bravely, with muted noisiness, the new ways. Probably she was raised as the child of a high official of landed if discreetly small gentry. She had inherited or been given as dowry this large elegant undistinguished house, with fireplaces and back-stairs and all the other necessities of well-run domestic slavery; and now the rooms were almost empty of family, thanks to death and taxes, and there were no more slaves.

In a kind of insane denial of reality the women like her (many of them saddled with senile husbands or horribly mutilated sons or unfortunate grandchildren kept as much as possible out of sight), these exhausted women, in background very much like my own aunts and their friends, tried to keep their homes running for "paying guests." They tried, and doggedly, to pretend that it was really intimates they were sharing their homes with, and kept them bathed in an utterly false atmosphere of well-being and charm and interesting meals.

Madame Perblantier invited me to come to dinner, for a kind of mutual and of course unmentioned inspection: perhaps I would *do?* I arrived (Madame Lanes had approved my invitation in a discreetly noncommittal way in which I could sense a tinge of professional curiosity) bolstered by an armful of flowers which were accepted almost absentmindedly, as if of course anyone would have known enough to bring them.

The evening was ghastly, because Madame, like all the other women of this level whom I had met in Aix, was incredibly stubborn and brave and wasteful.

The dinner was in its way as elaborately presented as was every meal at Madame Lanes': plates changed from four to six times, with the gold fruit knife laid this way and not that way over the steel cheese knife and the pearl-handled fruit fork, even if it took some three hours, twice a day, for the retarded or deformed little maid-of-the-moment to stumble around behind us and then finally serve the beautiful artfully mended bowl of grapes and pears . . .

After the endless ritual of coffee, Madame Perblantier sat like a death's-head, her eyes frantic and her speech witty and stimulating, and she and I knew, but nobody else seemed to, that she had been up since before daylight dusting the countless opulent gimcracks and waxing the beautiful tiled floors; and that she had gone halfway across town to the open-air markets and carried home heavy baskets of carefully chosen and delicious fruits and vegetables, and flowers for the sparkling rooms; and that she had supervised the laundry and had done part of the cooking and all the planning.

She was dying, literally dying of fatigue, I thought . . . and years later she would still be dying of it, although much less plainly as the strain of the war faded.

Her pettish elderly husband, sneering with thinly veiled ferocity at something she twittered about Montaigne or Voltaire to the young American engineer . . . the two English girls tittering over their cigarets behind the Directoire writing table . . . the old poodle going desperately into the corner and making a mess on the tiles because always before that there had been a *valet de chambre* to trot him out before bedtime and now Madame was simply too bone-weary to do it (and dared not ask it of her embittered feeble old husband, who had never been himself since his legs had been broken in several places during an "interrogation" in the War) . . . the sound of the slavey's feet shuffling heavily between dining room and kitchen with piles of dirty dishes, down the long corridor toward the last-century sink . . . the beautiful flowers: there we all sat in the luster of this insane bright shell, and I felt a child's fear and dismay.

I was caught with a blind woman, fighting with courage and stupidity to hold on to shadows.

I returned with eagerness to the imperturbable remoteness of Madame Lanes and her pattern, which suddenly seemed less mad to me, although still criminally wasteful.

Instinct perhaps guided me, for surely when I saw her, years later, she had survived it with enrichment and was younger in spirit than before. She permitted herself to smile with a real gaiety, and to make mischievous but gently amusing comments which before had been only malicious.

iv

Just as the waste of human energy in the upper-class landladies of Aix depressed me, so did their deliberate self-dramatization exasperate me. It made me feel like a bland phlegmatic "Northerner," I suppose, a cow caught in a flock of darting swallows. It seemed ineffectual, and actively stupid, to make such mountains and caverns out of trivia: screams, shrieks, vituperation, tears, passionate embraces of reconciliation were the daily music at Madame Lanes', over a broken cup, a few sous' cheating on the coal bill, a letter that did or did not arrive when expected.

Through all this hullabaloo Madame herself was the storm center, impassive and impregnable, and as I found myself growing fond of her in spite of her detachment toward me, I decided that she deliberately collected about her a group of near-maniacs which she used as tools: they would scream in substitution for her, and haggle in her place, and strike people she would like to punish with her own whip.

I also came to believe that one reason she kept me at a safe distance was that on the surface at least I too had been schooled to maintain something of her own calm and detachment.

All the time I lived there on the Rue Cardinale I floated on a hysterical flood of personal clashes which involved the boarders, the servants, the tradespeople, Madame's one child Henriette, and even the cats, who were perhaps the only creatures in the apartment with whom Madame permitted herself to be openly tender.

They slept with her on the couch in the salon, which she had made up at night into her bed after we had all decorously left her: that way she could rent one more room. Sometimes I would hear her singing and murmuring to them when she thought she was alone, as she attended to her accounts on the card table by the windows.

They were very handsome big cats, always lazy except when Minet would yowl for a night or two of freedom. This always excited Henriette and the maids, who obviously felt more desirable in an atavistic way at the direct approach to sex of the tom. He would pace in front of the wide windows that opened onto the garden far below, and then, practiced as he was, he would station himself by the carved wooden door to the apartment and at the right moment evade every effort to catch or chase him, and streak down the great stone staircase and into the staid street. In a few days he would return, thin and weary, and revert to his cushions and his voluptuous naps.

This blatant maleness, a never-ending titillation to the younger females of the house, interested neither Madame nor Louloute the other cat, and they seemed oddly free and happy when Minet was on the tiles.

Often Louloute would care for Minet after one of his escapades, and wash him gently and play with him as if he were a kitten. He accepted this as his due, plainly.

Once he returned with a bronchitic cough, and everything in the apartment, conversation, bickering, dishwashing, would stop while he wheezed and hacked. Another time was the most dramatic, for all of us: Minet came home drenched and shivering, and that same night developed pneumonia. A doctor was called: for three weeks the tomcat must be confined to quarters, not just the apartment but one small cupboard that led off the seventeenth-century boudoir of Henriette's room.

It was straight melodrama, played to the hilt of course.

It involved elaborate and increasingly smelly arrangements about his functions, all of which had to be attended to several times a day with infinite labor, since the cupboard was at the farthest end of the hall from the front door, and the front door was perhaps sixty broad steps up from the street, and the street was where all the rubbish was left for the city scavenger service.

The little maid-of-all-work stumped up and down the staircase with her face set and her arms loaded with carefully folded newspapers. I held my breath as I passed Henriette's toilette to my room. Conversation at meals hinged largely upon Minet's temperature, his chest rattle, and his appetite. The three weeks seemed longer than usual.

But everyone was relieved to find that the big tom's illness acted as a kind of release for Henriette's neurotic world-anger; she became for that time as serene as a young mother with a puling infant.

The head of the Lanes' household, after Madame herself, was Fernande, a tall, firmly stout woman of perhaps twenty-eight, who looked much older. She had a big stern face and a pasty skin that periodically turned bilious and yellow.

Her position was strange, as only that house could make it: she was the servant in charge of everything, and yet she was accomplice, personal maid, almost-governess to Henriette and almost-confidante of Madame. She was dictatorial about the continuous changing of charwomen, laundresses, and slaveys, and for the most part she was embarrassingly, mockingly servile with the boarders.

She and Henriette were violently jealous of their somewhat similar dependence on Madame's tranquillity, and had dreadful rows, screaming and cursing each other behind ineffectually closed doors. Madame would speak nonchalantly of nothings, with not a wrinkle on her round noble little face, while the wild yells pierced the clear air of Aix. At the next meal both ferocious unhappy women would be bland and released, for a time at least, from their helpless rage.

A good custom in the Lanes' house was that breakfasts were always served in our bedrooms. This made it simpler for Fernande, even though it meant ten or twelve trips for her down the long corridor with trays, and I always thought that it gave Madame a fairer chance to turn her narrow little bed back into an elegant couch again, in the salon.

Now and then Fernande would talk with me, as she knelt in front of my minuscule tile stove to start a morning fire with the five-inch kindling it would hold. Once she was open, and with no real bitterness, but only resignation.

That was when she told me how she never went to church any more, because of the day of Cease Fire, when everyone flowed helplessly into the chapels and cathedrals of France to thank God, and she cursed Him instead.

"It was all a lie," she said without obvious emotion, "and now I am damned with all the rest of us. But I am not damned for being a hypocrite."

And that morning she told me that she had once had a real gift for music, and that she had been considered very advanced in piano when her town was invaded, early in the war. Her family was killed, but she was kept on in what must have been her well-appointed home by the commander of the invaders, who chose it because of the fine concert piano in the salon. He heard that Fernande missed her music, so with what she called "relish" he permitted her to sit for hours to listen to him play. Orders were given that if she even touched her piano she would be shot, but as one music-lover to another the officer let her silently enjoy his own technique.

I came to know Fernande as a person so far beyond normal despair that she was magnificent. She did not even walk through the town like other people; she strode with a kind of cosmic disgust from marketplace to meatshop to wine merchant, a fierce frown on her dark-browed face, and her firm breasts high. She got a certain amount of money each day from her mistress for all provisions for the table, and if she could buy what was ordered for less than her allotment she was allowed to keep it. She marketed honestly, and we always ate well, although with an insidious monotony after the first interest wore off.

Fernande had a good taste for style and often made Henriette's clothes when she made her own. She also saw to it, in a tactful way, that Madame on her Afternoons or on her formal calls to other old ladies' Afternoons was neatly turned out, in a way unique to places like Aix and perhaps Paris where such rituals are still followed.

Madame's was every third Thursday, and on those days Fernande was the perfect domestic, plainly reveling in her characterization. She was deft, silent, attentive, almost invisible in her correct black and white uniform, which was somewhat like seeing the Cyrene Venus in livery but not at all ridiculous. The little cakes were delicious. The tea, one of Madame's self-indulgences, was of the finest in all Europe or even China.

And usually the supper that followed an Afternoon was pure hell, with sulks, screams, and general bad temper from Henriette, Fernande, Minet, Louloute, and a few of the boarders. Madame remained aloof, a pleased little smile on her lips to remember that the old Countess de Chabot had taken two sandwiches, and that little Lucie de Troubillers was finally engaged to an elderly diplomat from Istanbul . . .

Now and then Fernande would cry out that she could not stand her life any longer, and that she would kill herself unless Madame let her run away. These were tense moments, no matter how often they arrived. Madame would become pale and stern. Henriette would hide in her room and clutch at passersby in the corridor, to whisper about how evil and dangerous Fernande could be in one of her crises, which were decorously referred to as "liver spells," but obviously came at monthly intervals and involved violent headaches, nausea, and tantrums. They grew very dull, in a noisy way, but I always felt ashamed of my ennui in the face of such overt fury, and stolid and undemonstrative and therefore unfeeling.

One time Fernande got so far in one of her threatened escapes as to dress for the street, which was very correctly in hat, gloves, high-heeled shoes. (She always looked more like a young astute madam than a respectable whore.) She was leaving. The household held its breath.

We all heard her come down the narrow stairs from her tiny room in the attic-above-the-attic, which she once showed me and which she had painted to match a postcard of Vincent van Gogh's room in Arles. We heard her go firmly down the corridor to the toilet, and then come back and stop at the salon, where Madame was waiting for her, at her accounts.

Henriette sent the maid-of-the-moment slipping into my room. The trembling little halfwit held a big stylish handbag under her apron. She motioned me to be silent, and without a by-your-leave hid it under some papers on my desk.

I felt like a hypnotized hen, too dazed to protest, and when the door opened after a perfunctory knock which I did not even bother to answer, and Fernande stood stonily inside the room, I sat numbly watching the little maid pretend to dust the top of a table with her apron, and observing that Fernande was puffed out like a mad-dened turkey hen, with a face as yellow-white as frozen butter. She was handsome.

"Where have you hidden my purse, you filthy sneak?" she asked the maid in a menacingly quiet way.

I felt that she was very dangerous, and was glad my girls were at school, for I did not think their presence would have stopped this, even though she showed them more affection than anything else. She was always gentle with them.

The little slavey lied too volubly, and Fernande turned to me and said flatly, "Perhaps you will help me. I must flee this. I am desperate. I will stop at nothing. If these beasts keep me from taking what is mine, my own money, my wages, I shall kill myself. Here. Now."

It is perhaps as well that I have forgotten what I said, but I know it was ambiguous and basically weak: something about not knowing enough of the true situation to permit myself to be involved in it . . .

Fernande shrugged, looked once at the maid as if she were a slug under a board, and went out. I gave the purse to the maid, for Madame Lanes.

By suppertime that night she was back in her black serving-dress, and she had cooked an omelet with fresh chopped mushrooms which was superlative, along with the rest of the evening ritual of soup and salad and a delicate pudding. I noticed a kind of awed constraint in Henriette and her mother. The little servant trembled more than usual as she changed the plates endlessly.

The next day Madame said, almost in an aside to me when I paid my monthly bill, that the household was quite used to Fernande's crises. They were the result of the Occupation, she said. They were frightening but unimportant, she said. Fernande was a courageous soul if one came to know her . . . "And I cannot go on alone," she added almost absentmindedly.

vi

It is understandable that a woman fiercely enough disillusioned to curse God, as was Fernande, would find the human beings she must work with beneath her contempt. This complicated the extraordinary difficulties Madame Lanes faced in trying to find domestic help in Aix in 1954.

Many people had died. Many more were maimed in one way or another. The children born during the war years were not yet old enough to go into service. Worst of all from an employer's point of view, the few adolescents whose families were willing to have them go into service as they had done for decades were handicapped by malnutrition and worse, and were unfit for anything demanding normal wits and muscles. Many of them were Displaced Persons, who had been shipped here and there to labor camps all over Europe, and who perhaps mercifully hardly remembered who they were or what language they had first mumbled.

Map of Another Town

The procession of these human castoffs was steady, in the beautiful enormous apartment on the Rue Cardinale.

Sometimes a maid would last for two or three days. Then the orders of Madame about what plate to pick up and from which side, or the ill temper and loud mocking of Henriette, or the patent disgust of a boarder over a ruined dress or jacket would send her with hysterics to the kitchen, and she would vanish into her own swampland of country misery again.

Once there was a feeble old Polish woman. She spoke almost no French. She crawled slowly up and down the great staircase, carrying buckets of ashes to the trash cans on the street and loads of coke and kindling up from the cellars on the ground floor. I had to set my teeth to pass her, but if I had tried to help her she would have cowered against the wall in a hideous fear of my motives or my madness. She did not stay long. She was too feeble even to help dry the glasses without dropping them.

There were many Spanish refugees in Aix then, and one of them, Marie-Claude, lasted long enough for me to remember her as a person instead of a sick symbol.

She was sturdy and almost gay, and she and Fernande alternated laughter and passionate hatred in their relationship, for they must sleep together in the van Gogh attic, and eat together in the dark dank kitchen, and in general cope in the most primitive way with all the exigencies of living in an ancient house with several other people, archaic plumbing, and gigantesque rooms heated by drafty marble fireplaces or tiny porcelain stoves, which were set up like teapots every late autumn, after everyone was either in bed with severe colds or wrapped in all available shawls, sweaters, laprobes, and tippets. (For dinner, Madame often wore a finger-length cape of thick, long monkey fur which her husband had given her in Monaco in 1913.)

Marie-Claude was cursed with eyes so near blind that finally they were her undoing. She stumbled willingly about the apartment, knocking over little tables and leaving a thick film of dust and crumbs, which fortunately Madame herself was a little too nearsighted to notice. Fernande stormed after her, on the bad days, and yelled jokingly at her on the others, and between the two of them there seemed a general air of fellow-endurance, until on one of her days off the little Spanish maid ran her bicycle straight into a large truck, perhaps seeing it as an inviting continuation of the highway she felt fairly sure she was on, and a car in trying to avoid the zigzag truck hit it and then her, so that she was badly crushed. We felt sad. Her weak eyes were blamed on the hardships of her refugee childhood, and the motorists were dismissed as men whose driving undoubtedly had been influenced by the liberating Yanks and Tommies in '45.

There was one very strong coarse woman who for a time gave at least her physical makeup to the ménage, although Fernande shuddered often and volubly over her foul language. She was completely of the streets, not necessarily in her morals, which were undoubtedly as blunt and sturdy as she was herself, but in her skill at survival.

Every city evolves such people in its most evil districts. They are built in a special way, with bodies like brick walls, cruel eyes and mouths, stunted bowed arms and legs. They are as tenacious of life as it is possible to be in this world, and after plagues, famines, and wars they reappear from the holes in which they have managed to exist. They are not loyal or sincere, the way cats are not that. They are capable of unthinking devotion and tenderness, though. And unlike the more sensitive and highly organized people, they seem almost incapable of being hurt in their spirits. If they have not bred out their own spiritual nerves, they have at least developed through the centuries of travail a thick skin to protect them from weakness and above all from fear.

Louise was one of this breed.

I had never lived so closely with her kind, and I was glad to, for she was not at all unpleasing. Her manners were not uncouth with me, any more than a dog's would be, or a parrot's. Once she asked me if she might take my mending home, and I agreed gladly, but she would not let me pay her.

Like many charwomen in the world, she lived alone in a mean room in one of the ghettoes that every old town hides. Perhaps Aix could admit to more than its share of these sores, many of them sprawling behind some of the world's most elegant and beautiful façades, and I knew the quarter where Louise slept. It was miserable, with litter in the doorway and from far down its dank hall a sickening whiff that drifted out almost as tangible as sulphur gas into the street.

Louise admitted to being sixty-five, Fernande announced mockingly, the morning there was nobody to help her serve the trays. Where was she? On her way to Spain with a man . . .

Fernande read the note harshly: "Cheerio, old girl . . . I'm off on a *voyage d'amour* . . . he's young and handsome . . . see you in Barcelona? Yoicks."

Madame reached automatically for her list of domestic last resort, and said mildly, "Perhaps a proof that while there is life there is hope."

Fernande shrugged bitterly and closed the salon door without a sound behind her, but slammed the one into the kitchen with the report of a cannon.

The maid I remember most sadly in this procession of bedraggled broken women was the first I met there. Her name was Marie-Claire, and she walked with the shuffle of an old, weakened, exhausted person, although she could not yet have been twenty. Some of her teeth were gone.

Mostly she was unconscious of the world, so that she had to be told several times to pick up a dropped fork, or close a door. She used to exasperate Henriette to the explosion point, but Madame never allowed her daughter to scream at the little maid as she did at her own mother, and often Henriette would leap up from the table and run down to her room, sobbing frantically. The little maid never blinked at these outbursts, but they left the rest of us less interested in the amenities of the table, which were observed to their limits by anyone in Madame's presence.

One night, perhaps a few weeks after I had moved into my little *chambre de bonne* in the beautiful old house, I was propelled out of deep sleep and bed itself, and was into the dim hall before I knew that a most terrible scream had sent me there. It still seemed to writhe down toward me.

The two American girls who were staying for six weeks on their way to the Smith College course at the Sorbonne came stumbling to their door. One was weeping and chattering with shock.

There was another long dreadful scream. It came from up in the attic, where Fernande must share her bright décor with the current slavey, and already I was so imbued with the sinister spirit of the big woman that a logical sequence of unutterable crimes, crises, attacks flicked through my mind as I stood waiting.

The door to the salon opened, and Madame was there, calm in a gray woolen dressing gown and the kind of lacy headgear I had not seen since my grandmother died in 1922. I think it was called a boudoir cap.

There was a great crashing of heavy feet on the wooden stairs to the maids' room, and Marie-Claire ran out into the long tiled corridor. She was almost unrecognizable. Her eyes were alive and blazing, her hair stood out wildly instead of lying dull and flat, and she moved as fast as a hunted animal down to where Madame stood. She threw herself on the floor there, sobbing, "Save me, help me," and a long babble without words except for the way they sounded in the air.

Both American girls were crying helplessly.

Madame frowned a little. "Tell them to calm themselves," she said to me. "Get up, Marie-Claire. Stop that noise. Fernande, come down at once."

Fernande was halfway down the stairs, pulling her hair up with pins. She seemed as forbidding as ever, but not upset. She looked at Madame with a bored shrug.

"Here we go again. This is the last time, you understand?" she said, and gently picked up the half-conscious girl and carried her as firmly as any strong man could, up into her garish room.

Madame sighed. "We must retire. Thank you for being patient. That poor soul was cruelly tampered with when she was a child during the Occupation, and she stopped growing. Now and then she comes alive, and remembers, and it is terrible. Good night."

In spite of myself I reached out my hand to her arm. Perhaps it was because I was still hearing the first scream and then the second, and I too was shocked. Madame Lanes moved away from me with almost imperceptible reproof, and I turned from her with a polite good night and went along to my room, feeling chastened, reduced to clumsy childhood at my ripe age.

Marie-Claire was sent back to her farm: Madame respected her family as one sorely tried by the state of their daughter, but she knew that no patience from her could make the poor thing into even a slavey, and we started the long stream of nitwits, sick old whores, and dipsomaniacs again . . .

All this intimacy with the raw wounds of war was doubly intense with me, perhaps, because I was alone, and middle-aged, and scarred from my own battles since last I had lived in France. At times I felt myself almost disintegrating with the force of the incredible vitality of the people I was with. They were wasteful and mistaken and hysterically overt, and buffeted as I was by all the noise of their will to survive, I could not but admit, in my loneliest hours, that I was more alive with them than I was anyplace else in my known world. I was apart. I was accepted only as an inoffensive and boringly polite paying guest. But the people who blandly took what they needed from me, which was openly nothing but money, were teaching me extraordinary things about myself and my place in this new knowledge. I learned much from the warped malnourished drudges of Madame's household, that year.

vii

The physical climate of the Lanes' apartment was almost as erratic as the emotional, with dramatic fevers and chills from everyone and at unexpected times.

One night Minet the tom would let out a gurgle from his suppertime position on the dining room sideboard, and flip off onto the floor. Henriette would scream and rush to pick him up. Fernande would dash from the kitchen across the corridor and cry out, "No no, do not touch him, I implore you . . . He is plainly mad! He will bite you."

Madame would look in a mild way over her shoulder and say, "Leave him alone, both of you. He has perhaps a small stomachache. Fernande, you may serve the caramel custard."

Minet would lie on the floor, while Henriette gobbled viciously at her pudding, her eyes red with tears and anger. We all knew that after dinner she would slip out of the house to the Deux Garçons, the nearest public telephone, and call her vet. While she was thus secretly away, Madame would just as secretly carry Minet into her couch, give him half an aspirin . . .

Henriette herself was, inevitably, a mass of neurotic symptoms. They were of course unknown and inexplicable to any of the countless doctors she had consulted in her forty-odd years of world-sickness. They involved mysteries as yet unplumbed, at least by the medicos, and her fear of psychiatric help was almost frantic.

She had monumental hiccups now and then, which called for deep sedation. She had fits of dreadful weeping. She had dolorous shooting sensations in this or that part of her basically very strong body. All of these attacks were as close to the rest of us as this morning's coffee, and as inescapable, and her medical pattern added a kind of rhythm to our lives.

So did Fernande's periodic "liver crises." They usually meant that for at least one day we made short shrift in the dining room. This was basically agreeable: Henriette became helpful and almost pleasant, and Madame seemed to be less graciously remote.

The laborious and genteel clatter of changing plates and silverware diminished, and we lingered over two or three courses instead of five or six, which would be nor-

mal in the twentieth century, even in Aix, but which in the eighteenth-century manner still clung to on the Rue Cardinale was quaintly country-style.

Now and then Madame herself succumbed to human ills, and they always seemed
especially poignant to me, for except in dire trouble she insisted upon continuing the
serene pattern of her secretly frenzied efforts to keep the family head above water.
She would walk slowly to the table at noon, her face suddenly small and vulnerable
under her carefully combed white hair, and the conversation would lag a little in her
general apathy, but when she finally walked away we would know that she most
probably would be there again in the evening, ignoring boldly the fact that Dr. Vidal
had told her to keep to her bed.

Once she had to stay there, with a bad pleurisy. For the first and only time the
salon was openly admitted to be her bedroom, since there was no other place in the
big apartment to put her. I wanted to offer her my room, and finally did so, but I was
snubbed with exquisite tact for such presumption: it was a family problem, not to be
shared with an outsider.

Any such illness was complicated by Madame's insistence that the household try
to function as it would have done fifty or a hundred years before, with five servants or
even ten. It was insane. But it served to bring all of Fernande's ferocious courage into
full splendor, and we ate in muted satiety while in the beautiful room next to the long
airy dining room with the crests over the doors and mantelpiece Madame lay wheezing as quietly as possible.

Once she had a bad attack of sciatica. She hobbled gamely about, but gave up
her trips to market. My room was next to the bathroom, and one day I heard her sitting there in a steam tent made of old towels, trying to warm her poor aged muscles,
and she was groaning without restraint, although I had seen her a half-hour earlier
looking almost as always, if somewhat preoccupied.

It is very hard to listen to an old woman groan, especially when such is not her
custom. I had to fight my instinctive feeling that I was in some way her daughter and
that I must try to help her. I stood impotently in my little room. Finally I went down
the corridor and knocked at Henriette's door.

"Please excuse me," I said, "but Madame is in the bathroom and she seems to be
in considerable pain."

Henriette looked coldly at me. "Please do not worry yourself," she said. "She is
quite all right. She is simply making a little scene."

I went out for a dogged fast walk through the streets, and stood listening to several
fountains to get the sounds of the old woman, and even more so of the young one,
out of my head.

One time Henry Montgomery and I, two boarders for the time being, met a
decrepit old nanny trying to push an empty perambulator up to the first landing of
the house, where the Countess de Chabot was entertaining a niece with a recent
baby.

Henry insisted in the firm simple way of most Anglo-Saxon men that he and I help carry the pram on up. The old woman cringed and scuttled ahead, and for several weeks we were somewhat testily teased by Madame about this breach of etiquette: a man of a certain class, and Henry was unmistakably of the top level in his own country, does not assist in any way a man or woman of a lower class than his own.

This was a flat statement. Henry had betrayed his background. I on the other hand as a relatively uncouth American could not be blamed for my breach of breeding and manners, but I might perhaps have learned a lesson . . .

"But she was very old," Henry said flatly.

Madame's reply I can still hear. "I shall never forget one time I was about to cross the Cours Mirabeau. I felt very faint. I leaned against a tree. A kindly woman, very ordinary, came up to me and helped me across the street. It was most good of her, but it was rude."

We said, "But Madame . . . did you need her? Could you have crossed alone?"

"Yes, I did need help, and I could not possibly have crossed without collapsing, but she was not at all of my station, and it was basically forward and pushing of her to offer to help me. I would have preferred to fall where I was, unassisted by such a person."

Henry could appreciate this in his own inverted Scandinavian way, but I was, and I remain, somewhat baffled and very repelled by it. It was a conditioned reflex in the fine old lady, which was as natural to her as her need of a fish fork for fish and a game fork for game.

One more question we asked, before each in his own way pushed the matter into partial limbo: "Would you not have helped this woman if she had felt ill, just as we helped the old servant with her pram?"

"Never," Madame said simply, and we tackled the scallop of veal.

Letters from Madame between my two stays in Aix told of a series of ghastly operations, collapses, and maladies which afflicted Henriette in Paris, but never mentioned her own state of health, and when I saw her again in 1959 she did indeed look younger and less withdrawn.

She was perhaps encouraged by the fact that she of all her old friends was the one who had fought through the strange profession, come so late in life to her, of being a landlady. They, she told me mockingly, lived in their moldy shawls, playing bezique and bridge and tattling over their teacups. She alone supervised her household, her table, and her social life, and she did it with a late but appealing jauntiness.

Fernande was gone, in a cosmic huff. She finally ran away, convinced that Henriette had become the mistress of a man in Corsica for whom Fernande cooked during one of her summer vacations. If it was not that, it was something equally fantastic, Madame shrugged.

Life, she added, had been a dream of tranquillity since the big ferocious tyrant had disappeared, and now things progressed in seraphic perfection under the thumb of a sallow cricket of a woman, well-spoken and as sharp-eyed as a ferret, who "lived out."

It was she who hired the continuing but somewhat more palatable flow of maids-of-the-moment, and attended to the meals and the accounts. She coddled Madame. She put up with no nonsense from the boarders. One had the feeling that if it was her prescribed time of day to leave the apartment and return to her own home she would step neatly over any number of bleeding bodies and be deaf to no matter what cries for help, but that up until that moment she would do all she could to be a devoted and well-paid savior. I did not like her at all, and do not recall her name, but I felt thankful that at the end of Madame Lanes' troubled life she had fallen into the deft hands of this assistant.

I was glad for the look of relaxation in my friend's smooth old face, for by now I could freely call her friend. At last she had accepted me, perhaps for one of the rare times in her life, as a loyal and affectionate admirer in spite of my lack of ancestral permanency.

"Madame is originally from Ireland," she would say defensively, when I was the only American among her world-exhausted friends. "Her culture is obviously inherited."

At first this enraged me, but by the last time I saw Madame I was as unaffected by it as an ant by a fleeting shadow. I forgave her. She had accepted me for myself, in spite of any such linguistic protests.

We lunched together in a beautiful old converted château, the day before my last departure. She told me with laughing cynicism of how it had been declared a Historical Monument in order to reduce the taxes, and refurbished by a retired chef and his rich wife in order to profit by the armies of hungry tourists who wanted real French cooking in the proper Crane-fixtured setting. Meanwhile we ate slowly and delightedly, and drank with appreciative moderation, and savored the long reward of our relationship.

Never had there been any display of affection between us, beyond a cursory peck on each cheek, but no more did I feel pushed away, held at cautious distance because of my newness. At last with this adamant old woman I was me, Mary Frances . . .

She took my arm as we walked down the long stairway of the château-restaurant, and when she next wrote to me, in far California, she began, "Dear and faithful friend . . . "

Introduction to
A Cordiall Water

We have medicines to make women speak; we have none to make them keep silence.

ANATOLE FRANCK

This book is a collection of odd and old receipts to cure the ills of people and animals, mostly told to me by the believers.

There is no doubt that much of what we know of medicine comes from very ancient times, and from the birds and animals that we have watched. Myself, I do not know enough to say how or why one certain weed will calm a fever in a sick dog or antelope, nor can I guess what tells the beasts about that weed, any more than I can recite the new fine names for its magical components on a box of costly fever pills from a modern laboratory. All I can do is wonder, and everything that I have remembered and recorded here has made me do that.

It is easy to paraphrase a good saying, and the better the saying, the easier . . . as well as the harder to disguise. I could not presume to hide the fact that I am deliberately misquoting George Orwell's deathless motto about equality when I state that all books are written with a purpose but some with less purpose than others. This book of odd restoratives and remedies started with almost none, unless it was to put some order in my desk as well as my thoughts.

For a long time I have been noting strange things people have told me about illness and health. And recipes in old books would startle me by their foolishness and their faith; labels from old bottles and pillboxes, and clippings from newspapers, collected as if by themselves . . . and suddenly, in a move from one place to another, I saw that I had a disordered drawerful spilling from the table, fluttering in my thoughts. Innate tidiness stepped in, at least to help me make room for more.

At first I was interested as to why I had thought this or that hoarded note was worth its paper, and if there seemed no answer, it was thrown away.

Then I was astonished and dismayed to realize my growing confusion about how to classify all the cuttings and scribbled comments which I had collected for so many years with such careless compulsion. When does the ounce of prevention that is said to be worth a pound of cure stop being preventive and become restorative? What is the difference, then, between a cure and a remedy? Semantic dangers menaced me,

268   *A Cordiall Water*

and I groaned in the trap I had sprung on myself, as words like panacea and drug and nostrum took on sharper, meaner outlines. Who can say, still, whether Mother Periwinkle's Miracle Salve is a nostrum, a piece of arrant quackery, or a bit of instinctive folk medicine? Where, most of all, is the fine line that separates scientific from religious healing?

It has been exciting to knit into some kind of pattern all these "phisical receipts," as the old cookery books called them, and while I have found it impossible, for instance, to keep all the ones with liquor in them apart from the ones concerning alcoholic as well as actual snakebite, still I have managed with some license to separate the sheep from the men, and even the men from the mandrakes.

Best of all, I have made a few things clearer to myself, at least.

One is that we have long known and used much that the birds and beasts have taught us.

Another is that the great difference between our folk medicine and theirs is that we need, being men, to mix faith with our healing. We need to trust something unknown, and to count on more than the actuality of a potion in the cup, a pill on the tongue.

Animals go without any mystical query to the water or mud or herb that will help them, and as far as we can tell they do not question their going, nor pray to be led, nor offer thanks when they are better. Neither do they need our aid, except of course when we have caged and domesticated them past their own help. But we need them and learn ceaselessly from them.

All this is good to realize. It seems to bring natural order and even common sense into our acceptance of medical help, so that, being men, we can concoct trustingly from an Elizabethan herbal a drink which animals would create within themselves by eating various roots and flowers and leaves. *We believe* its claims, which although perhaps somewhat longer than others made in this little book of mine, are in reality not much different from them:

> To Make a Cordiall Water good against any Infections, as ye Plague, Poxe, Measles, burning feaver, & to remove any offensive or Venemouse Matter from ye Hart or Stomach, or to be used after surfetts or in Passion of ye Mother, or for Children in fitts of Convulsions, & is generally Good to Comfort or strengthen Nature.

III

———————

He went through the Wet Wild Woods, waving his wild tail and walking by his wild lone.
But he never told anybody.

RUDYARD KIPLING

[. . . Blackberry] was without doubt the rarest of many wonderful cats who have lived with me. I remember too many things about him, so that it is hard to talk of only one now: the way he healed himself after a mighty battle, really three times, for he waged four of them in as many years before he died after the last one.

This was when he was old for his race, because he was peculiar in that until he was almost nine he would have none of love and its warfare.

Females wooed him at least twice a year, and fought each other noisily to excite some interest in him, but he paid no attention except to yawn. I wondered about this, and with some regret, for he would have made a good father. He was beautiful, with fine but strong bones, small ears, a daintiness that was not effeminate, and great skill in hunting.

In the spring he loved to dance on the lawn with butterflies, who seemed to know that he did not intend to catch them and so would fly low and then up and past his deliberate frolickings.

Then when he was almost nine, and I was convinced that he had been born a feline eunuch, he went into such a passion for a little female kitten as I had never seen before. She was too young for him. I had to separate them, or he would have torn her to pieces a hundred times a day, blindly. It was sad and terrible. He was literally burning to death, and turned from a silky long-haired tranquil beauty to a wild-eyed snarler. He would not eat, and could not sleep.

Finally I gave away the bewildered and innocent kitten, thinking to calm him. Instead he ran away, no doubt to look for her, and I who had grown used to his tabbiness was forlorn for him.

In a week he came back, a shadow but quiet, and that year almost every kitten born in the Valley was Blackberry's, for when the moon was right he would leave again. Now and then one of his neglected wives would seek him out, and he would lead her away discreetly, being very gentlemanly in spite of his lost daintiness of manner.

A Cordiall Water

Finally, though, after about a year of this sustained libertinism, he returned to us in a most dreadful fashion.

I heard a small cheeping sound now and then, so like a bird's that I did not heed it at first. It came from the canyon, a narrow rocky place with a few straggly, ancient eucalyptus trees shading the muddy bottom, and for the knowing there were paintings on hidden and protected stones, done in the mysterious and ineradicable reddish stuff of ancient times, by Indians who came there to pray and be healed.

It was still said in the Valley that the water that trickled and in winter rushed down our canyon could be bottled and sold, for it would cure fevers and sores, and soothe pain, and in general was good for what ails one. Nobody, not even the modern Indians, did more than talk.

But down in that muddy slit in the hills lay the cat Blackberry, and his faint cheeping mews led me finally to him, after more than a day of searching through the rocks and reeds.

He lay so flat into the mud that I almost stepped on him, and he was stretched out so long and far that he looked more like the shape of a dead reptile than a living animal. The mud was so coated on his fur that it was cracked in the dry air. I could not tell which end was the head of the horrid dead-alive thing, until he made another faint cry and I saw the feeble opening of his caked lips.

I bent over him, really sick with shock. Such beauty once, now dying surely in this abject state . . . It was a shame, a shame, and I could hardly bear it.

I started to touch him, and then I felt what was like a bell ringing, or a flash blinding me, a warning as clear as any shout: I was not to put my hand on him.

I crouched above him for some time, and realized with a kind of awe that he was ripped from head to tail, and that in with the caked mud his flesh was mixed as it hung in strings from his skeleton. His mouth stayed open, with his tongue loosely hanging from it, and an occasional breath lifted his ribs almost invisibly. His eyes stayed closed. I withdrew, with farewell in my heart, for surely he was dying, and I seemed to have been told to let him do so alone.

The next day I went down to get his body. Of course it was not there, but a few feet further down the stream bed, and still living. When Blackberry heard me he mewed again, and again I bent over him, to see that he had dragged himself that far and that he lay with his other side in the black mud. Still I did not touch him, but I hurried back up the canyon for a pinch of ground meat and a flat saucer of water for him. Hours later they were still untouched, but his mew of recognition seemed stronger to me, and he had turned himself over again.

In the next week I watched a miraculous healing take place. When the caked mud fell off him and he rolled into wetter places I could see with horror that his flesh did indeed hang in strings, and many of his bones and tendons were laid bare. How he continued to exist I could not understand, for he ate nothing and never touched water for about eight days. Then he ate three or four times a day a bit of lean chopped meat which I left beside him, and his eyes opened and looked at me with what seemed thoughtfulness and amusement.

In about three more days he arose, licked himself stiffly, and walked up the canyon in easy stages to the house. He was a pitiful sight, but dignified.

A month of rest and genteel spoiling had him fine and sleek again . . . until the next year and the next, and finally the fourth such bout, which at first seemed to me the result of his tackling a wildcat or a lynx. Then I saw that three common Toms from the Valley must have attacked him together, to avenge his general seduction of áll their females . . . for sensing him to be old, they dared follow him this time up to the muddy bottom of the canyon, where he had dragged himself after God knows how long a battle down in the Valley. There they finished him off.

I have told a few people about this and they have not quite believed me, but I know it because I saw the end of it happen. I beat them away (it was their howls that drew me, for Blackberry made not a sound), but this time he was dead.

It was as well. Even the black mud of the Indian's healing stream could not have hung his legs back on his frame, his head on his neck. It did, though, keep him alive for the last wildly productive years of his long life, and now almost every cat for miles around has some of his strain in it.

One thing that has always interested me is that during the first three times Blackberry lay in the mud and let the hair and flesh grow back, no enemies ever came to bother him. But when he was old, and plainly not a match any more for them, they got him . . . and I think that not only the Toms, but probably almost any of the animals he had long hunted, would have come then, the fourth time he was downed, to get even with him.

XII

[. . .] *Dr. Meed's Certain Cure for the Bite of a Mad Dog*
Let the Patient be Blooded at the Arm, 8 or 10 Ounces. Take of the Herb
Call'd in Latin Lichen Cinercus Terrestris, in English Ash Colour Liverwort,
Clean dried & Powder'd, half an Ounce, of Black pepper two Drams. Mix
these well together, & Divide the powder into 4 Doses, one of which must be
taken every morning fasting, for 4 Mornings, Sussessively, in half a Pint of
Cow's milk warm.

After these 4 Doses are taken, the Patient must go into the Cold Bath or
Cold Spring or River every morning fasting for a month; he must be dipt all
over, but not stay in with his Head above Water longer than half a Minute if
the Water be very Cold; after this he must go in 3 times a week for a fortnight
Longer. N.B. the Lichen is a very Common Herb, and grows generally in
Sandy & Barren Soils all over England; the Right time to Gather it is in the
Months of October and November.

Most old herbals and receipt books have at least one or two such "certain cures"
for the bite of a mad dog in either man or beast, and it makes me wonder if perhaps
the word "mad" meant simply infuriated in those days, and not "rabid" as it does for
us. I have seen only two animals with rabies, but I have read that a man in the same
condition is even more appalling. Certainly none of these sufferers could last the six
and a half weeks of treatment prescribed by Dr. Meed, even with the magical simplicity of liverwort and cold river water!

Other illnesses, though, continue to respond to different waters, all over the world,
just as they have for thousands of years.

The nicest hydrotherapy I know about, I think, was told to me by one of my own
children, when she was little. She asked me with regret plain in her voice why she
had never had an earache, and when I said something like I-don't-know-thank-God-
but-why?, she told me that her dearest friend said it was the most fun in the world
because of what her mother did to make it well: she had the little girl lie with her aching ear pressed against a pillow, and then on the other ear, the well one, she put steamy
warm compresses for exactly one half-hour, while not a word was spoken and the
clock ticked. My daughter told me of this yearningly, and I pondered on the gentle

wisdom of it: the hypnotic half quiet, the warmth, the simplicity . . . above all, the trust in a wiser person's power.

Only lately I have heard of almost equally miraculous cures, of course bare of the mother-magic of this one, which are being worked in a suburb of Zurich by a self-styled doctor who submerges his patients in tubs of lukewarm water and then packs them with new-mown meadow grasses, mostly pink and white clover.

They emerge, I am told, feeling cleansed both inwardly and outwardly, and generally so refreshed that they are willing to sign statements swearing that they have been permanently cured of everything from "swell'd legs" and arthritis to a nagging wife.

This reminds me of another clover cure, which was solemnly recommended to me as a panacea for any form of cancer, but especially of the stomach or intestines: floods of tea made by steeping clover blossoms in hot water and adding a little honey.

The old carpenter who told me about this had cured himself, many years before, he said . . . and indeed when he died it was from a fall off a ladder, so perhaps he was right.

He is the man who showed me his bottle of Ozone once. He had bought it when a youngster from a traveling tent show, where the medicine man hung out charts of how active gangrene had been completely cured by a few applications of the Ozone. My friend said that with it he had saved the lives of several other carpenters with badly crushed fingers and blackening limbs.

I took a sniff of the grimy bottle, still half-full of a pale liquid in spite of its years of magic-making, and it did have a fresh stimulating smell, somewhat like good witch hazel.

"It has certainly lasted a long time, Mr. Addams," I said with no teasing visible.

He slipped it back into his hip pocket without a smile, slapped it protectively, and said, "Yep. Wouldn't be here without it."

I could not tell whether he was paying tit for my tat, and left the room . . .

I have never seen gangrene cured by anything from a bottle, even when it is marked Ozone, but I am sure that I have often dosed myself with that on the desert below sea level, especially in May and in the moonlight, when the air seems filled with a pungent revivifying sting, and the fleeting perfumes of the tiny sand-flowers are almost visible. I have breathed so deeply of this double air as to feel drunk on it, so that the stars wheeled.

And I have never seen a man recover from a mad dog's bite, even when dosed with powdered liverwort. But I have seen a wart push itself out and away from a boy's hand because of a wort called, plainly enough, wartwort.

This was interesting to watch. It happened a few summers ago, when a little boy called John came from California to stay on a farm in Provence with me. He arrived with several bottles which I could see had been very costly, and a habit of keeping one hand always in his pocket. He did indeed have the ugliest-looking wart I had ever seen, on the back of his right hand where it seemed to get hit with things, and to bang into them and rub against them. John said that he had used a dozen different medicines, and that if he had not had his ticket to Provence his mother would have arranged for an operation to remove this angry lump. Instead, he was supposed to dab on various things from the bottles, but they hurt and he kept forgetting. Meanwhile it grew worse, and I could see that he was humiliated as well as in some discomfort.

I told all this to a friend named Peter who lived in Aix and who knew so many strange things about other strange things—a kind of male Lolly Willowes really— that I thought he might well suggest something about John's burden.

"Of course," Peter said briskly. "Wartwort. Plain everyday old wartwort. We are walking right on it this minute."

And sure enough, the soft green carpet of June weeds, so soon to turn dry under the sun of the Provençal summer, was at least a third made up of this husky little plant. I do not know any other name for it, but I remember it from the hills of my childhood in the spring: of a tender green, fairly low to the ground but straggly, and with fragile juicy stems which when broken give out a drop or two of sticky white milk.

How I would have loved to know its impossibly silly name, when I was little! Now, even despairing John brightened at it, and when Peter told him the treatment he laughed with a mixture of doubt and delight and started it, right there on the path.

To Get Rid of a Wart in the Spring

Squeeze from the broken end of a wartwort stem the drop of milk, and dab it gently on the wart. Cover the whole wart, using as many stems of this limitless supply as you wish, but do not spread the milk past the edges of the wart. Do this three or four times a day for about two weeks. When the wart begins to push out of the healthy skin, take care not to joggle it and to push the wort milk gently under its loose edges. It will come off of itself, and then for a day or two put the wort milk on the place where it was, in case it left even a trace of its old tissue.

It was fine weather in Provence for the next two weeks, which meant that we ate outdoors and sat or walked or lay within arm's reach of John's remedy.

"Are you joking?" we had asked, and Peter had answered firmly, "You'll see," and we did, for the wart became almost a part of the family, not disgusting or humiliating at all, as we all picked the pretty weed and took turns touching its milk gently onto the intruder.

It changed every day, and once or twice at first it looked rather inflamed and rebellious and I got Peter to reassure me that I was doing no possible harm to indulge in this absorbing game. It began to grow out of the little crater it had made. In about ten days it was gone, one morning when John got up. He looked everywhere in his bed for it, because he wanted to keep it in a little matchbox he had found, to take back to California, but it never showed up.

I emptied the expensive bottles into the compost pit, feeling that plant decay would offset their noxious chemicals. It is possible that they contained exactly what hid in the pearly milk of the wartwort: I shall never know.

But when I look at John's smooth hand now, I remember what fun it was to rummage in the green weeds for the one we wanted, and then touch it so daintily to the ugly vanishing lump. Since that summer we have told a few people about it, but unless they are either from Provence or from very simple farm stock they do not really believe us.

XIII

Qu'a de saivi dins soun jardin
A pas besoun de médecin.
(Sage in the garden?
No need for Sawbones!)
Provençal Proverb

I know firsthand of a few other cures that use weeds, like the one for John's wart and the cure for burns from the leaves of the rabbit ear plant soaked in olive oil. Both these remedies came from Provence, where I think that everything that springs from its earth, here rust-red where the vanquished Saracens dyed it with their infidel blood, there gray with powdered marble and granite or bright white with salt, every single tough odorous leaf and stem is known intimately by the people of the country.

There is not a flower in the wild hills or the tamest gardens there without some quality of cure in it, whether dried, powdered, steeped, inhaled, pounded. Usually men and beasts eat the same plants, and for much the same reasons, but occasionally there is one like the autumn crocus, which cattle shun, but which is an active remedy in folk medicine against the gout.

Another cure I learned firsthand on the farm near Aix was for bad insect bites. It was a kind of rune in the dialect that Gaby the farmer's wife used, part Provençal and part Piedmontese, but I cannot rhyme it in my own language.

She sang it out in a rough shout when her husband came running into the courtyard from the olive orchard, rolling up his trouser-leg as he stumbled along. He yelled something at her, and "A scorpion bite . . . he's been bitten!" she cried out. She yelled, then, the rhyme at us, and when we did not understand she ran off herself and came straight back with a handful of leaves, which she scrubbed hard against the part of the farmer's foot where we could see a white blotch already formed from the bite, with pinkening skin around it. The crushed leaves made a greenish stain.

He grinned at us and his cursing died off, and we all drank a cool beer.

Once he had gone back to the orchard, Gaby taught me the remedy in her bad French, which still sang as she repeated it. Here is the only way I can write it, but it is good anyway, a perfect combination of superstition, instinct, and primitive knowledge which may well be part of our own pharmacopeia, for all I know:

Sure Cure for a Scorpion Bite

Run fast and find three kinds of leaves, one jagged (like the dandelion), one round, and one long. Crush them in your hand and rub them hard over the bitten place. Rub rub *rub*.

"Or if you can't find any leaves," Gaby said, "Rub rub *rub* with plenty of good wine vinegar. Same for wasp stings, bee stings. Or any plain brandy . . . But the three leaves work the best."

Another cure that needs leaves came to me from Tahiti, through [an] Italian who was raised in the Brazilian jungle and made delicious drinks for me in an air-conditioned Tahitian hut in California. It was used in Mexico too, he said, and the only difference was how to pronounce the plant: *wah*-bah south of the Border, and gou-*ah*-vah in the Islands.

"This is sure-fire for any bleeding at all," he said firmly over his refilled glass. "Deep cuts even. But you must have plenty of juice, that's it. Fill your mouth with tender guava leaves and chew them to a soft paste, and put them on the cut. Also for sores. The spit, if you will forgive my bad word, is what is the sure-fire. If you have guava leaves of course!"

And still another leaf cure, from Mexico, was told me by Nigel, who for a long time lived in Ajijic on the Lake of Chapala. It too uses a plant which animals will not touch, like the cows, even when the lake is dry and they are dying of thirst, a bush called the "gigante." Its cool green leaves when bound upon the forehead will cure any kind of headache, as well as soothe a fever.

This seems more logical to me than another receipt I copied a long time ago from one of the oldest collections of such medicaments that I have ever seen, called *A Booke of Phisical Recepts*. I would hate to have to drink this concoction, but I like the title:

Mrs. Sherlock's recept for a pain in ye head

2 ounses of Rubbarb leaves sliced, 1 ounse of Jensit's bark in powder, 2 ounses of sugar candy, 2 drams of Juniper Berris, Sinamon & nutmeg of each a dram: a Quart of strong wine infuse it in.

XIV

If you prick us, do we not bleed? if you tickle us, do we not laugh? if you poison us,
do we not die? and if you wrong us, shall we not revenge?

SHAKESPEARE

There are two more things I know at first or perhaps near-second hand, about how to stop bleeding. It is odd to me that both of them came from Negroes.

One of them was used by a Negro to save a white child, with human spit but no gou-*ah*-vah leaves. The other was used by white doctors to save a Negro woman who had learned the same remedy from her ancestors.

The first case happened the longest ago, perhaps seventy-five years, but the white man who told it to me still had bewilderment in his voice. A cousin came to visit him, he said, on the farm in Delaware. She was like a lovely fragile doll, with the palest skin he had ever seen, and silvery hair that fell in a soft cape over her little shoulders.

Everything about the farm was strange to her, and he led her by the hand from one marvel to another. Behind them always was black Tom. They watched lambs in the meadow by the great river, and Tom held the ewe while they straddled her for a short bumpy ride. They stood under the cherry trees and caught fruit in their hands when Tom shook the heavy branches.

Then once they went alone into the enormous dim barn. The man who told me this could not remember if his little cousin fell, but suddenly there she was, standing in wonder as red blood spurted out of her wrist from a long cut. The boy screamed *"Tom!"* and Tom was there from the shadows, and what happened next took perhaps seconds but not minutes, while Tom pinched the little girl's arm and the boy swept from the walls and rafters of the dim old barn great vague floating masses of cobwebs. They were gray with dust and age. They were without weight.

"More, more. Fast," the Negro commanded, as the little boy put the tenuous stuff into his free hand. He rolled it lightly into wads, and stuffed it against the deep cut on the little girl's arm. She watched without a sound. Tom packed the cobwebs as far as he could push them into her flesh. Then he took the last handful and spat into it and made a kind of plaster of it and put it over the wound. All the bleeding had stopped, but there was blood on the barn floor, plenty of it.

Tom took the little doll-like cousin into his arms and sat down with her against the hay, and sent the boy up to the Big House for a clean bandage and refreshments.

"You tell Maidie Miss Anne cut herself a little but all is well. Tell her Tom says so. You tell Maidie we could use some of her best eggnog, if she can spare the time. And you bring back a little clean bandage, boy, to cover us up."

The way it was told to me, Tom left the cobwebs in the wound, under the neat bandaging, and then removed them the next day. Nothing was ever said about how or why the cousin hurt herself, but there were two things about it that the little boy never told his mother: Tom's wife Maidie sent them an eggnog so well laced with good bourbon that all three of them drank it and slept in the hay, close together, for a good two hours; and Tom said, 'Don't you two ever tell that I spat in the cobwebs, hear me?'

They never did, but it puzzled the boy until he was very old that a Negro could save the life of a white child, and not want the whites to know that his own spittle had entered into her blood, along with the dust and spider tissue. In fact, he died still puzzled, still wondering why he had been weak enough, or even stubborn enough, to heed black Tom's request.

And in the second case of a good cure for bleeding, a fine Negro woman was in a way hoist on her own petard, for she swore that nobody but her Gramma knew the best way to cure a nosebleed, and she was proved wrong.

She lived in Pasadena, on Sugar Hill, and no life was more dramatic than hers. She was technically a "cleaning woman," with hours and even half-days promised here and there to white faculty wives, between her bouts with the medical profession. She was such a monumentally excellent servant as well as so exciting as a disaster-prone raconteuse that her employers paid her double, and put up with all her alcoholic and institutional absences, just to hear her recount them as she dusted and swept.

She was handsome to look at—a tall ferocious woman with the thin nose of a high-born Abyssinian. Her skin was coppery-black. She wore her hair in a regal pouf on top of her small head. Her gestures were as deft as those of a Chinese goldsmith while she mopped and talked of what had last happened to her at the hospital.

She was a historic figure there. It was said among the fashionable internes that they could recognize the tone of the ambulance siren when she was in it, and if she was in the throes of a miscarriage it was always with *three* little unborn creatures, not one; if she had just been stabbed, *all* her arteries were pierced; if she was dead-drunk, every facility of the great hospital would be needed, from oxygen to adrenalin, to save her, and every available doctor would stand by, fascinated, to watch her monumental renascence.

All these things made good conversation, and Pasadenans enlivened many a party with her latest medical tourneys. I think I came in last but best, though, because I actually saw her bow to Fate, and admit that she had exhausted the drama of Medical Emergencies.

She came into the kitchen where I sat with my cousin, who rose as if in the presence of a noble ghost and said, somewhat flatly, "I heard you were dead, Ruby."

The tall beautiful woman laughed impatiently.

"Almost, almost," she said. "Never was such a nosebleed. I swear I lost five quarts. Ask anybody. Ask those baby doctors, that's all they are. It was everywhere. All over. Everybody was crying I was really dead, this time.

"Never did go so fast in that ambulance in my life. There I was, bleeding to death, and no way to stop it, no way at all. I sure messed up that hospital. And you know what they did?"

My cousin and I were drinking vermouth and gin, because I had just got off a plane and we were arranging family problems, and we kept right on, thankfully. Ruby's voice was like a song.

"Hah," she said in a damning way, very cold and with her fine head up. "They slipping there at that big fancy high-tone place. You know what they did? They did exactly, precisely, in every way, what my Gramma taught me in Florida. It didn't cost them exactly *nothing!* You know what they did, those nothing-but-baby-doctors?"

She leaned over us, and I felt quite shriveled by her noble long copper body, and her scorn.

"They put bacon grease up my nose."

My cousin and I had nothing to reply to this. We sat stupidly in the prim Pasadena kitchen where we were really not supposed to be at that hour and sipped the gin we were not supposed to be drinking at that hour. Ruby pulled off her coat angrily and tossed it on the electric dishwasher.

"Anybody can do that," she said. "My Gramma always did it. With a very *serious* nosebleed. And now I nearly die and they do it at that big stylish place just like we would do in Florida. They saved my life, those baby doctors, for I was surely dying. And what they do is stuff my nose with bacon fat, is all! And here I am."

She stopped being so angry, and we all began to laugh.

XV

There is no cure for birth and death, save to enjoy the interval.
GEORGE SANTAYANA

Some receipts, like the raw potatoes that Jack London chewed in the Klondike to help his scurvy, are completely simple: one thing to cure one ill. Another as direct as this is gin for women's monthly misery.

"Gin is our best friend, girl," a fellow sufferer informed me soberly in a coal town in Southern Illinois. "It's not the liquor in it, it's the juniper juice that does the trick."

When I asked if a plain tea, made from the little berries or their oil, would not save us from the dubious bootleg gin we had to buy in 1927, she said a mysterious but firm No. The gin helped, she said, and whether she meant the berries or us I did not understand.

(Here is a somewhat more complicated remedy for this same complaint: white corn whiskey, or "mule," spiked with plenty of ginger and a modicum of hot water. It is called Ozark Stew, and has done much to keep mountain women happy, a happy mountain woman told me. She implied that Ozark females who manage to live past their years of childbearing owe it mostly to the stew, with snuff and the Bible rated as sure helps too.)

It is the cure-alls, though, that are the most interesting to reflect upon, as the simplest of the remedies that seem to have drifted into my life. They resemble in some ways my mother's "course of sprouts," although she never claimed that her panacea covered more than the myriad effects, many of them emotional, of a sluggish liver. Probably the simplest of them all, and the most all-embracing, is what in France is called "a little slice of ham."

Over some thirty years of fascinated observation, I have been assured that a little slice of ham, especially when taken in bed with a glass of good wine, will cure completely or at least help cure the following: exhaustion, migraine, grippe, gout, disappointment in love, business worries, childbed fever, dizziness, coughing, and indeed almost everything else except Death and Taxes.

The ham should be what we call "boiled," and what in France is named "diet-Paris-extra-fine" and whatever else sounds dainty to the person who wants it. In extreme cases it is served without the curls of sweet butter and delicately fluted little pickles that otherwise decorate and mask its stark, flabby pinkness. Usually it is a full meal in itself, complete with a discreet slice or two or three or four of fresh bread, or several crisp pieces of what we call zwieback at home. The wine that helps wash down this tidbit should not be ordinary, of course.

Perhaps the oddest thing about this prescription, besides the fact that people who follow it are as convinced as are the doctors who prescribe it that they are fasting, is that most of the hardy Frenchmen who believe so will recover.

They will not suffer from indigestion. Their livers will not shrivel in one last paroxysm of revulsion before the dainty fat slice of embalmed pork-flesh, and the salted pickles, and the mildly alcoholic flushing of the fermented grape juice. They will not, in other words, die.

(Then.)

Once more they will react to the balm of a quiet room, and of a simple meal, spiced with the extra sauce of loving care and consternation.

I have often thought with some regret of things I would like to inherit if I had been born French, but this panacea is not among them. It is too rugged for me. The few times I would have been deemed ready for it I was past wanting or needing anything but the prerequisite, the quiet room.

But I suspect that the sturdiness of the nation may stem from it, even if considered as somewhat the same test as the Spartan one, where a sick or spindly soldier was subjected to a drink made of warm ale, herbs, and iron filings: if he spewed it out or rolled up and died, he was still a boy, no man. If Frenchmen can survive the routine prescription given from Dover to Marseille, and can eat all the little slices of ham prescribed for them as they lie languishing, they will outlast many another Austerlitz.

Me, I think I prefer some such receipt as this following one, at least in contemplation. It promises to cure many things, and implies the easing of as many more.

It was first noted in a book by a pre-Elizabethan midwife named Dame Lethiculear, who most certainly soothed many more ills than the fleeting ones of childbirth. Its spelling is not ours, and it seems to go into a song which has in it all the magic, the atavistic knowledge, and the mixture of faith and good sense which are compounded in real medicine.

To make ye Green Ointment that cured Lady Probyn's Coachman's Back
Take of Sage and Rue of each one handfull, and of wormwood and
    leaves of bay
Each half a pound.
Gather these in the heat of Day, and leave them
All unwashed and Shreded small. Then take of
Sheep suet one pound and a half, and stamp it with the herbs
Until they be all of one couler.
Put into it one pint and a half
Of the best Sallet Oil from Spain.

Then stir all well together,
And put it in a pot,
And stop it close up,
And let it stop nine days.
Boil it then,
Till the strength of the herb be gone,
And take care in thus boiling that you doe not burn it.
Then of the oil of Spike add one ounse and a half
And keep it for your use.
It is good for all manner of wounds,
Of Bruises, of burns and sprains,
And the best time to make it is in the month of May.

FROM S IS FOR SAD

. . . and for the mysterious appetite that often surges in us when our hearts seem about to break and our lives seem too bleakly empty. Like every other physical phenomenon, there is always good reason for this hunger if we are blunt enough to recognize it.

The prettifiers of human passion choose to think that a man who has just watched his true love die is lifted above such ugly things as food, that he is exalted by his grief, that his mind dwells exclusively on thoughts of eternity and the hereafter. The mixture of wails and wassail at an Irish wake is frowned upon as merely an alcoholic excuse by the sticklers for burial etiquette, and the ancient symbolism of funeral baked meats is accepted, somewhat grudgingly, as a pagan custom which has been Christianized sufficiently by our church fathers to justify a good roast of beef and some ice cream and cake after the trip to the family burying ground with Gramp.

The truth is that most bereaved souls crave nourishment more tangible than prayers: they want a steak. What is more, they need a steak. Preferably they need it rare, grilled, heavily salted, for that way it is most easily digested, and most quickly turned into the glandular whip their tired adrenals cry for.

A prime story of this need is the chapter in Thomas Wolfe's *Look Homeward, Angel*, just after Ben has died, when his two racked brothers begin to laugh and joke like young colts, and then go in the dawn to Ben's favorite all-night beanery and eat an enormous, silly meal. Another good example is in D. H. Lawrence's *Sons and Lovers*, as I remember. There are many more, all of them shocking, and yet strangely reassuring too, like some kinds of music.

Perhaps that is because they are true, far past prettiness. They tell us what we then most need to be reminded of, that underneath the anguish of death and pain and ugliness are the facts of hunger and unquenchable life, shining, peaceful. It is as if our bodies, wiser than we who wear them, call out for encouragement and strength and, in spite of us and of the patterns of proper behavior we have learned, compel us to answer, and to eat.

More often than not, in such compulsory feastings, we eat enormously, and that too is good, for we are stupefying ourselves, anesthetizing our overwrought nerves with a heavy dose of proteins, and our bodies will grow sleepy with digestion and let us rest a little after the long vigil.

An Alphabet for Gourmets

I tried to say this once to a man who, being well raised and sensitive, was in a state of shock at his behavior.

It was late at night. He had been driving up and down the coastal highway, cautiously and in a numb way almost happily, ever since a little before noon that day when his love had died. She was one of the most beautiful women in the world, and one of the most famous, and he loved her for these reasons and even more so because she loved him too. But he had to watch her die, for two nights and a day.

When she was finally at peace he walked from her bedside like a deaf, blind man, got into his car and headed for the coast, and in the next hours he must have stopped at four or five big restaurants and eaten a thick steak at each one, with other things he usually ignored, like piles of French fried potatoes, slabs of pie, and whatever bread was in front of him. He had a flask of cognac in the car but did not touch it; instead he drank cup after cup of searing black coffee, with or without food, in a dozen little joints along the road, and then left them humming and whistling.

By the time I saw him he was literally bulging and had loosened his belt futilely to make room for the load in his middle. He put his head in his hands and shuddered. "How could I?" he said. "How could I—and she not yet in her coffin!"

It was a helpless protest, and I, more plainspoken than usual, tried to cut through his digestive fog, to tell him how right he had been to let his body lead him on this orgy, how it would tide him over the next hours, how his hunger had made him do what his upbringing had taught him was gross, indelicate, unfeeling.

He soon went to his bed, staggering, hardly conscious, certainly uncaring for a time at least of his own or the world's new woe. But years later, so strong was his training, he would think back on that day with a deep embarrassment, no matter how candidly he admitted the basic wisdom of his behavior. He would always feel, in spite of himself, that sadness should not be connected so directly with gastronomy.

PLACES ON A MAP

Introduction to
Map of Another Town

*. . . it is very probable that if I had to draw the portrait of Paris, I would,
one more time, draw it of myself.*

JEAN GIONO, 1961

Often in the sketch for a portrait, the invisible lines that bridge one stroke of the pencil or brush to another are what really make it live. This is probably true in a word picture too. The myriad undrawn unwritten lines are the ones that hold together what the painter and the writer have tried to set down, their own visions of a thing: a town, one town, this town.

Not everything can be told, nor need it be, just as the artist himself need not and indeed cannot reveal every outline of his vision.

There before us is what one human being has seen of something many others have viewed differently, and the lines held back are perhaps the ones most vital to the whole.

Here before me now is my picture, my map, of a place and therefore of myself, and much that can never be said adds to its reality for me, just as much of its reality is based on my own shadows, my inventions.

Over the years I have taught myself, and have been taught, to be a stranger. A stranger usually has the normal five senses, perhaps especially so, ready to protect and nourish him.

Then there are the extra senses that function only in subconsciousness. These are perhaps a stranger's best allies, the ones that stay on and grow stronger as time passes and immediacy dwindles.

It is with the invisible ink distilled from all these senses, then, that I have drawn this map of a town, a place real in stone and water, and in the spirit, which may also be realer.

from TWO BIRDS
WITHOUT A BRANCH

[. . .] We knew a woman who sold real estate in a small beach colony. She had a face like a brick wall, and a desire, some sixty years old and still undaunted, to play ingenue rôles on Broadway. Her past was cautiously shaded.

We said we were going to live in France.

She said, "Where?"

We said, "Here, there—maybe Dijon—"

Suddenly her face was blasted. "Oh, Dijon!"

She put her hands up to her eyes and wept, and then cried fiercely: "The smell of it! The smell of Dijon gingerbread! When you are there smell it for me!"

So we did.

We smelled Dijon mustard, especially at the corner where Grey-Poupon flaunts little pots of it. We smelled Dijon cassis in the autumn, and stained our mouths with its metallic purple. But all year and everywhere we smelled the Dijon gingerbread, that *pain d'épice* which came perhaps from Asia with a tired Crusader.

Its flat strange odour, honey, cow dung, clove, something unnamable but unmistakable, blew over all the town. Into the theatre sometimes would swim a little cloud of it, or quickly through a café grey with smoke. In churches it went for one triumphant minute far above the incense.

At art school, where tiny Yencesse tried to convince the hungriest students that medal-making was a great career, and fed them secretly whether they agreed or not, altar smoke crept through from the cathedral on one side, and from the other the smell of *pain d'épice* baking in a little factory. It was a smell as thick as a flannel curtain.

This is the Dijon recipe, without, of course, the mysterious quality that makes each little gingerbread shop bake loaves quite different from any others:

Take two pounds of old black honey, the older and blacker the better, and heat it gently. When it has become a thin liquid, stir it very slowly and thoroughly into two pounds of the finest bread flour, of which about one-third is rye.

Put this hot paste away in a cold place. It must stay there for at least eight days, but in Dijon, where *pain d'épice* is best, it ripens in the cold for several months or even years!

Wait as long as you can, anyway. Then put it in a bowl and add six egg yolks, one level teaspoon of carbonate of soda, and three teaspoons of bicarbonate of soda.

Next comes the seasoning—and it is there, I think, that lies the magic. Try these the first time, before you begin your own experimenting: some pinches of anise, a teaspoon of dry mustard, and the zest of a large lemon.

Now beat it for a painfully long time. Put it in a buttered mould or pan and bake in a moderate oven for one hour—or less if you have divided this measure into more than one pan.

In Dijon little gingerbread orange slices are stuffed with marmalade and glazed, or great square loaves are sliced several times and spread with apricot jam before they are put together again. Or currants and candied fruits are baked in the loaves. Or they are left plain, to be sliced very thin and be spread with sweet butter for tea.

Whatever you do with your *pain d'épice*, you should put it away in waxed paper and an airtight box. It will taste even better in two months or three. [. . .]

FROM THE MEASURE OF MY POWERS
1936—1939

I

Un pâquis, the French dictionary says, is a grazing ground or pasture. But when we bought our home in Switzerland, and found that it had been called Le Pâquis for several centuries by all the country people near it, we knew that it meant much more than "pasture" to them. The word had a tenderness to it, like the diminutive given to a child or a pretty girl, like the difference between *lambkin* and *lamb.*

One reason our Pâquis had this special meaning was that it was almost the only piece of land in all the abrupt terraced steeps of the wine coast between Lausanne and Vevey that did not have grapes on it.

Instead, it was a sloping green meadow, held high in the air above the Lac Léman by stone walls. A brook ran through it under pollarded willows, and old trees of pears and plums and apples bent away from the pushings of the lake winds. The ancient soil was covered with a dazzling coat always, low and filled with violets and primulas and crocuses in the spring, waist-high with such flowers in summer as I have only seen like shadows in real gardens.

They would be delicate in the beginning of the year . . . blue hepaticas along the icy brook, and all the tender yellow things. And then as the summer came and the time for harvesting, the colors grew more intense, more violent, until finally the wild asters bloomed, *les vendangeuses,* the flowers that meant all the village girls must go into the vineyards again to cut the grapes.

Three times every summer the man across the road reaped our hay, while we could not bear to look . . . and then in a week or so the flowers were back again, pushing and growing and covering all the short grass with a new loveliness, while the fruits ripened and the little brook ran busily.

There was a fountain, too, near the road by the stone house. It had been there for longer than even the Federal maps showed, and people walking up the long pull from lake level knew it as well as they knew their mothers, and stopped always to drink and rest their backs from the pointed woven baskets they wore. Even after we came, and planted more trees and added rooms to the house, they continued to stop at the fountain, and that made us feel better than almost anything else.

And all those things . . . the fresh spouting water, the little brook under the willows, the old rich bending trees, the grass so full of life there on the terraced wine-slopes laced by a thousand tiny vineyards . . . they were why when the peasants said Le Pâquis they meant The Dear Little Meadow, or The Sweet Cool Resting Place, or something like that but more so.

II

We started a garden before the ground thawed, while the Italian masons burned their fingers on the cold stones for the new part of the house. We had to make all the beds in small terraces; hard work in the beginning, but wonderful to work in later, when the paths were set and the little patches lay almost waist-high waiting to be cared for. As soon as we could we planted, while we kept on building walls and cultivating the rich loam, and by the time my father and mother came to see us, at our apartment down on the Market Square in Vevey because the house was not yet ready, the peas were ripe and the evenings softly warm.

We would go up the hills from town after the workingmen had left, and spread our supper cloth on a table under the terrace apple tree, among all the last rubble of the building. As fast as Father and Chexbres could pick the peas, Mother and I would shell them, and then on a little fire of shavings I'd cook them perhaps four or five minutes in a heavy casserole, swirling them in butter and their own steam. We'd eat them with little cold pullets cooked for us in Vevey, and good bread and the thin white wine of the coast that lay about us.

The evening breeze would freshen across the long sweep of the lake, and as the Savoy Alps blackened above the water, and it turned to flat pewter over the edge of the terrace, the first summer lights of Evian far down toward Geneva winked red at us. It was always hard to leave. We'd put our things silently into the baskets, and then drive with the top of the car lowered along the narrow walled roads of the Corniche, until we came to a village where we could sit again on a terrace and drink bitter coffee in the darkness.

Chexbres was a fine gardener; he read books and liked to experiment with new ways of doing things, but besides all that he had the feeling of growth and fertility and the seasons in his bones and his flesh. I learned all the time from him, and we worked together two summers in Le Pâquis.

The peasants of our village, and all the vineyardists, thought we were crazy not to leave such work for hired gardeners, gardeners who *knew*. They used to lean over the walls watching us, occasionally calling suggestions, and it embarrassed us when oftener than not we did things as they had never before been done there in that district, and got much better results for less effort in less space. That seemed almost like cheating, when we were newcomers and foreigners too . . . but why should we put in fifty tomato plants with elaborate stakes, as our neighbors told us to do, when we could get as much fruit from ten plants put in the way we thought best? Chexbres studied the winds, the soil, the way the rains came, and he knew more about how to grow things than the peasants could have learned in a thousand years, in spite of their cruel toiling. He felt truly apologetic about it.

Our garden grew and grew, and we went almost every day up the hill to the sana-torium for poor children with the back of our little green Fiat filled with fresh things to eat.

I canned often, too. We had three cellars, and I filled one of them with beautiful gleaming jars for the winter. It was simple enough to do it in little bits instead of in great harried rushes as my grandmother used to, and when I went down into the coolness and saw all the things sitting there so richly quiet on the shelves, I had a spe-cial feeling of contentment. It was a reassurance of safety against hunger, very prim-itive and satisfying.

I canned tomatoes and beans and vegetable juices, and many kinds of pickles and catsups more for the fun than because we wanted them, and plums and peaches and all the fruits. I made a few jams, for company, and several big jars of brandied things. I was lucky; nothing spoiled, everything was good.

When we left, before the war came, it was hard to give up all the bottles of liqueurs and *eaux-de-vie*, not yet ripe enough to taste, harder than anything except the bottles in the wine cellar, some still resting from their trips from Burgundy, and all our own wine made from the little yellow grapes of our vineyard for the two years past. . . .

In spite of the full shelves in the cellar, though, and our trips up the hill for the children and the baskets we took to friends in Vevey whenever we could stop gar-dening long enough to go down there, things grew too fast for us. It was the oldest soil either of us had ever touched, and it seemed almost bursting with life, just as it was alive with insects and little creatures and a hundred kinds of worms waiting to eat what grew in it. We ran a kind of race with it, exciting and exhausting.

One time Chexbres put down his hoe and said loudly, "By God, I'll not be dic-tated to! I'll show you who's boss!" He was talking to the earth, and like a dutiful wife I followed him up past the violently fertile terraces to the house, and listened while he telephoned to the Casino at Evian and reserved a table in the main dining room and ordered an astonishing meal and the wines for it.

I despaired somewhat in dressing: my nails were rough and stained, and I was too thin and much too brown for the dress I wanted to wear, and high heels felt strange on my feet.

But by the time we had driven over the Haute Corniche to Lausanne, right into the setting sun, and had sat at a little deck table on the way to Evian, wrapped in the kind of sleepy silence that those lake-boats always had for us, I felt more beautiful than possible, and knew that Chexbres in his white dinner coat and his white topknot was that way too. The maître d'hôtel and the barman and the sommelier agreed, when we got to the Casino, and it was a decadent delightful night.

But when we drove into Le Pâquis in the first shy sunlight, we shed our city clothes and bathed and put on dungarees again, and hurried down into the garden. We had been away too long. [. . .]

TEA WITH AGAMEMNON

One day in the spring in California, two women sit talking in a eucalyptus grove. There is a mountain behind them, snowy still, and under them sweet alyssum blooms with a wild heavy smell of honey in the sun. A dog lies watching, waiting for crumbs of love and cookies, as the humans drink tea with their own brands of easiness. Fredrika is the older, with long bare legs and a band of turquoise silk tied optimistically around her wisps of white hair; Mary Frances, the other, is remote and teasing. Both of them are shy, the way old friends can be without premeditation. Fredrika says, in her soft voice with the strange sweet crack in it, "They are all I remember about Greece, really. My mother got the recipe from her cook when we lived in Athens. I was about five, and Agamemnon and I . . ." Her voice fades vaguely, and she holds out a plate of little round flat cakes so dreamily that they almost slide off. The dog watches them, his tail wagging. Mary Frances takes the plate and puts it on her knees, and when she bites into one of the cakes, she sees the dog looking at her sadly, intently.

Mary Frances: They are good, delicious. Are they really honey cakes, the kind the gods ate?

Fredrika: Probably. Nothing changes in Greece—nothing basic, that is. Agamemnon lived next door to me and was about my age. His last name was Schliemann. His father unearthed Troy, you know, and his mother was Greek. I suppose she was beautiful—all Greek women are, in my mind at least, although I can't remember anything about them actually except that my nurse wore a black woolen dress that scratched my face when she carried me upstairs. My mother told me later how to make the honey cakes. Agamemnon and I would eat them in the afternoons on the long marble porch of his house, with goat's milk. That is, we did until my father discovered what the goats lived on in Athens.

Fredrika pauses and laughs in her shy way, bending over to put half a cookie between the dog's polite soft lips. Mary Frances drinks slowly at her cup of tea, watching her friend, smelling the honey in the air, and tasting it on her tongue.

Fredrika: Father couldn't understand why his children weren't thriving on goat's milk. It sounded so *Attic!* and therefore perfect. And then he saw that practically the only food the city goats had was the flour paste they licked off the huge paper funeral notices that were stuck up every day on the walls. He was horrified. He made himself taste a little of our milk, and sure enough it was pure paste, or so he swore later. So after that we didn't drink anything but lemonade, as far as I remember. (She adds firmly, as if reassuring herself:) I *don't* remember *much*, of course.

Mary Frances: Oh, yes you do. Tell more. Go on. Do these cakes really taste the same?

Fredrika: Not quite. Hymettos honey, from the hills around Athens, is sweeter, because of all the thyme blossoms the bees have there.

Mary Frances: It goes with the sweet alyssum, today. What else do you remember?

Fredrika frowns, a little impatient at her stubborn friend. She speaks slowly at first: Well . . . nothing about food, really. There were dry gullies, like the ones here in this country, but often they were like torrents, like floods of purple and rose and lavender, with anemones. The flowers were higher than my knees. And then . . . then at Easter there were big hens' eggs, blown out and painted with Christ Crucified, in beautiful colors. You exchanged them with people, and they were as light as feathers, but they didn't seem to break. My mother still had one or two, when I was growing up in Connecticut. And of course there were the paschal lambs, roasting everywhere.

Mary Frances: Well?

Fredrika: Well, there wasn't much meat in Greece, I suppose. I don't think people ate it often. But at Easter almost everybody had a lamb. You'd see the boys and men carrying them home, hung over their necks, bleating. My father said they were always killed very tenderly . . . part of a sacrifice. Then all the insides, *everything*—(She interrupts herself:) Once Father went up to the monastery on Mount Athos, pulled up in a basket. He was a man. Women couldn't get *near* the place. And as the guest of honor he was served the roasted eyes of the lamb. He ate them, too . . . but it never left his mind again . . . They don't throw away anything at all, you know, and when the lamb is dead, they put all the parts except the carcass on a long fresh skewer of pinewood, highly seasoned, laced together with strings of the cleaned guts. That's called . . . (Fredrika hesitates and then looks at once pleased and confused.) Now, how on earth do I remember that? I haven't even *thought* the word for years! It's *kokoretzi*. It smokes and cooks beside the carcass of the lamb. That's on another long fresh spit. I think there must be handfuls of thyme inside it, because I can smell that mixed with the heavy smoke of the fresh pine boughs. At Easter you smell that everywhere in Greece. Or did. (She closes her mouth bitterly, as if ashamed of speaking of food once eaten in a land so sorely tried.)

Mary Frances, quickly, teasingly, to divert her: I thought you'd forgotten everything!

Fredrika, weighing two halves of a honey cake in her thin, weed-stained fingers and then giving the larger piece to the dog Pinto: Nonsense. It's as clear as yesterday.

I stood looking from my window, and it was black-dark, so I was naughty to be awake. We lived near the great field where the soldiers had maneuvers. There was a circle three deep of evzones around the roasting pits, turning and basting. They laughed a lot, and they were the handsomest men in the world, with their stiff white skirts shining in the firelight, and their teeth flashing. There was music too, although I don't know know whether it was flutes or bagpipes or what. And the smell of the hot lamb meat and the burning pine boughs is something I'll never forget. Nonsense . . . it's as clear as yesterday. (Fredrika pushes back a lock of hair, and sits up very straight.)

Mary Frances: What went with it?

Fredrika: Oh, a pilaf, of course. My mother's recipe was for one cup of rice, washed well and dried, browned in four tablespoonfuls of butter or olive oil. Then one cup of tomato puree and three cups of good meat stock are brought to a boil and poured in, and the lid is put on tightly until the rice is tender and has absorbed all the juice. No stirring. Then the pilaf is shaken, and a dry cloth is put tightly over the top of the pan and the lid is put on again for about ten minutes.

Mary Frances: Like a risotto, practically. Simpler. Don't the Greeks use garlic or onions?

Fredrika: I don't remember . . . Yes, of course . . . but with the pilaf, I think, chopped fresh thyme or dittany, tossed in at the last.

Mary Frances: Dittany . . . it sounds like something from Ophelia's song.

Fredrika: It's a lovely herb. It grows wild on the hills, with tiny blue flowers. It used to be thought so powerful for healing that when stags were wounded they ate it and the arrows fell out of them. It was called *dictamnus* . . . or (and Fredrika coughs apologetically) so Father said. College professors' children keep strange things in their heads. But I do know a little dittany is wonderful in green salads. We should grow more of it in America.

Mary Frances: I read of a Greek pilaf of chicken in Escoffier, the other day. Mutton fat was used for browning the meat, which was cut up, and then . . . *here's* an onion! . . . an onion was browned, chicken consommé was added, and a chopped pimiento and a handful of currants. It was served in a ring of pilaf.

Fredrika: Yes. That would be Greek . . . and good.

Mary Frances: How about wine, though? I've heard people say they hated Greek wine.

Fredrika: I was a little young for it, even as a substitute for goat's milk. But of course it has a lot of resin taste to it. The Greeks like that. They still chew resin. It's a delicacy, and used to be reserved for the upper classes. It is supposed to sweeten the breath, cleanse the teeth, all that . . . And everywhere in Greece is that piney smell . . . even in the roasted meats. It's so clean . . .

Mary Frances: And did you and your Aristophanes—

Fredrika: Agamemnon . . . (She adds dreamily:) Agamemnon Schliemann . . .

Mary Frances: Did you have anything besides these wonderful, delicious, funny little honey cakes?

Fredrika: There were lots of cakes made of very thin layers of pastry called phyllo, with pounded dates and almonds and so on in between, but they were too rich for us children. Once in a while our nurses would give us a spoonful of rose-leaf jam. It was the sweetest, most perfumed thing I've ever eaten. I loved it then, but when I've tasted it since in Near East restaurants, I've almost hated it. Once I tried to make it, but I think maybe the roses weren't red enough, or my heart had grown up too much. (Fredrika coughs self-consciously, as always when she feels she has said something less restrained than she was brought up to feel was ladylike.) I took equal parts of clean dry rose leaves, the darkest red in the garden, and sugar. I moistened the sugar with equal parts of lemon juice and water until it was easy to stir the petals, and then let the whole thing lie in the sun until it was hot and well melted. Then I boiled it for about a half hour, stirring it all the time. And then I didn't really like it.

Mary Frances: Did you ever eat the jelly made from cactus apples that is served with grilled wild birds in northern Mexico? That is very sweet and perfumed, too.

Fredrika: No. But it couldn't be worse than the rose-leaf jam I used to think was so delicious. Of course I was young . . .

Mary Frances: And in love . . .

Fredrika, standing up abruptly and lifting the tea tray: Well, I *did* like having tea with Agamemnon!

Hemet, California, 1951

AIX-EN-PROVENCE

. . . 177 meters above sea level; 52,217 inhabitants; former capital of Provence; seat of an archbishopric since the fifth century, and of the departmental law courts and prison, and the schools of Law and Letters of the University of Aix-Marseille; one of the most beautiful art centers of Europe.

The town was founded in 123 B.C. by the Roman consul Sextius Calvinus, and was made into a prosperous colony by Julius Caesar. Between the fifth and twelfth centuries it lost much of its political importance to the town of Arles, although it was once more made the capital in the twelfth century under the Counts of Provence.

During the fifteenth century, before joining France, it became the hub of European culture under the benevolent administration of King René and his two queens.

Le Guide Bleu: France, 1960

So here is the town, founded more than two thousand years ago by the brash Roman invaders, on much older ruins which still stick up their stones and artifacts. I was as brash a newcomer to it, and yet when I first felt the rhythm of its streets and smelled its ancient smells, and listened at night to the music of its many fountains, I said, "Of course," for I was once more in my own place, an invader of what was already mine.

Depending upon one's vocabulary, it is facile enough to speak of *karma* or atavism or even extrasensory memory. For me, there was no need to draw on this well of casual semantics, to recognize Aix from my own invisible map of it. I already knew where I was.

I had been conditioned to this acceptance by a stay in another old town on the northward Roman road, when I was younger and perhaps more vulnerable. I lived for some time in Dijon in my twenties, and compulsively I return to it when I can, never with real gratification. And I dream occasionally of it, and while the dream-streets are not quite the same as in waking life (the Rue de la Liberté swings to the right toward the railroad yards instead of going fairly straight to the Place d'Armes and the Ducal Palace, for instance, but I always know exactly where *I* am going), still I am a remote but easy visitor, happier as such than as a visible one.

I do not, in my imagination, feel as easy there as in Aix. I have long since made my own map of Dijon, and it is intrinsic to my being, but the one of Aix is better, a refuge from any sounds but its own, a harbor from any streets but its own: great upheavals and riots and pillages and invasions and liberations and all the ageless tur-moil of an old place.

I feel somewhat like a cobweb there. I do not bother anyone. I do not even wisp myself across a face, or catch in the hair of a passerby, because I have been there before, and will be again, on my own map.

I can walk the same streets, and make my own history from them, as I once did in a lesser but still structural way in Dijon, my first return to the past, forever present to me.

The town was put on its feet by a Roman whose elegant bathing place still splutters out waters, tepid to hot and slightly stinking, for a ceaseless genteel flow of ancient countesses and their consorts and a quiet dogged procession of arthritic postal clerks and Swiss bankers and English spinsters suffering from indefinable malaises usually attributed to either their native climates or their equally native diets. This spa, more ancient than anyone who could possibly stay in it except perhaps I myself, is at the edge of the Old Town, at the head of the Cours Sextius, and more than one good writer has generated his own acid to etch its strange watery attraction.

Countless poems have been written too, in wine rather than acid, and countless pictures have been painted, about the healing waters and the ever-flowing fountains of the place. They will continue as long as does man, and the delicate iron balconies will cling to the rose-yellow walls, and if anyone else, from 200 B.C. to now, ever marked the same places on the map, in acid or wine or even tears, his reasons would not be mine. That is why Aix is what it is.

St. Sauveur

Almost thou persuadest me to be a Christian.
The Acts of the Apostles, xxvi, 28

i The Beginning

The structure of the baptistry of the Cathedral of St. Sauveur (end of the fourth, beginning of the fifth centuries) is strongly influenced by the liturgy of primitive baptism: immersion, conferred by a bishop upon adults once yearly during the night before Easter. To this sacramental rite of purification, performed behind curtains to protect the naked participants, two symbolisms are added: the passing from shadow to light (the water flows from east to west; two granite columns serve as entrance to the east, facing six of green marble; steps descend into the pool from the east . . .), and the resurrection and new life, symbolized by the figure 8, the primitive symbol for Sunday, the eighth day (the original baptistry was eight-sided, as was the marble-lined pool). In the sixteenth century the cupola was heightened . . .

Aix-en-Provence and Its Countryside, JEAN-PAUL COSTE

Many old towns like Aix in the Western world have grown the way a pearl does, in micromillimeters of skin against the world, around a germ, an alien seed, an itch, which in most of them has been a Christian church, at once fortress and prison and spiritual core.

Aix, however, grew around its baths, which still flow healingly behind the last of the old walls in the spa that is now run by the government. Even the Cathedral that later became the heart of the town was built over a temple bath, which in due time became its baptistry.

In St. Sauveur, the Cathedral of the Holy Savior, the pool is empty now in the octagonal room under the high vaulted ceiling, but beside it a cumbersome font still serves the parish, and from its walls local archeologists are still, discreetly between Masses, tumbling the bones of believers built into the niches.

Far above the stone ribs of the hushed room a small eye of open sky in the cupola looks down upon the empty basin that the first Christians found so conveniently ready for their baptismal rites, after decades of Roman ladies had bathed hopefully there to give themselves children. Perhaps, it is said, St. Maximin himself, one of Christ's disciples, stood beside that pool . . .

I remember it as about four feet deep, with crumbling steps down into it, and centuries dry. Once I was standing looking at it in the shadowy room, thinking of how long it and perhaps even I had been there, when I found myself a near-active party to a small christening that had suddenly shaped itself around the modern font.

There I was, and why would I be there for any other reason than to help make a new member of the parish? The parents and sponsors smiled at me with a polite preoccupied twitch, each probably thinking the other side of the family had asked me to come. I must not startle them, caught as they were in the hoarse whispers, the cold air, the irrevocability of the ritual.

I stood facing the fat careless priest, a man I saw often in the district of the Cathedral and never grew to accept as anything but obnoxious. His vestments were dirty, and he needed a shave and almost certainly a bath, whether Roman or Christian. He held the new child as if it were a distastefully cold omelet that might stick on his fingers.

The parents and sponsors were mute in their Sunday clothes, the convenient and almost essential uniform of black which will do for the next funeral, a vestment of respectability among poor people, who fortify themselves on what other poor people will think of them.

The new believer would most probably lead a long full life, although like many infants of its environment it looked moribund, a blue wax image faintly breathing, its eyes slits of world-weariness.

I prayed for myself that the lout of a priest would not ask me any direct questions about vouching for the little soul's well-being, and then, when the insultingly mechanical drone was plainly drawing toward a final benediction, I made myself disappear.

This is something that takes practice, and by the time I was standing there in St. Sauveur trying not to accept any responsibility for the sickly newborn baby I had become fairly good at it. It is mainly a question of withdrawing to the vanishing point from the consciousness of the people one is with, before one actually leaves. It is invaluable at parties, testimonial dinners, discussions of evacuation routes in California towns, and coffee-breaks held for electioneering congressmen . . .

As I flitted, almost invisible by now, across the baptistry, I nearly walked straight into the roughly paved pit where Roman ladies on vacation had splashed hopefully, where the first Christians had doused themselves, pressed down into the flowing water by the hands of disciples who had once heard the voice of Mary Magdalene praying in her cave.

I wondered as I righted my course around the dim room if anyone had ever fallen in. It would be only a bruise or two, perhaps a cracked bone . . . But why risk it? Why flee? Did I run from looking once more into the cynical eyes of the newest Christian, or did I escape from the more materialistic hazard of having to explain to the dismal young family that I was nobody at all, no cousin's cousin, an uninvited witness to the rites, not even real?

Map of Another Town

At the wide door into the comparative security of the nave I felt safe again, and the air had a different weight and coldness. I could hear footsteps up toward the choir stalls: chairs were being straightened between Masses on this Sunday morning. In the organ loft, Monsieur Gay flitted mockingly, tenderly, through two octaves of sound that came down to me as pure silver, like hollow clean beads on a string. I could not even hear the priest behind me. It was as if I had been bathed again . . .

ii Away, Away . . .

We hear the wail of the remorseful wind
In their strange penance.
Unrest and Childhood, ALEXANDER SMITH

The second time we returned to Aix for more than a few painfully nostalgic days, Anne and Mary and I made a point, with some trouble, of being there during Holy Week so that we could once again see the *reposoirs*.

They took place on Maundy Thursday, the day before Good Friday. It was like a fiesta. People walked gaily from one open church and chapel to another in a kind of jaunty quiet pilgrimage, part relief that Lent was almost over, part plain curiosity to see what the Order of This, the Guild of That would produce.

Chapels that were forever otherwise closed to the lay public were open that day, and in each one an offering of money could be left at the door. In the small convents and monasteries the whole main altar, with, as I remember it, no candle or flame burning, was turned into a wall, a solid wall, of the most beautiful flowers that could be found, which there near the Côte d'Azur meant beautiful indeed. In the larger churches the main altar was dim, and to the left of it, rising from floor to ceiling, sometimes perhaps thirty feet high, was the same solid mass of blossoms, now mixed all in a riotous jumble of spring, now austerely one kind of flower, one color.

It was a miracle that between the late night of Wednesday and the morning of the next day the old women and men could create such stormy pagan beauty, and then even more astounding that by dawn on Good Friday, or perhaps before, every sign of it would be gone, and the statues would be shrouded in black veils, and everything would be waiting for the recital of the Stations of the Cross.

When we saw the *reposoirs* in 1955 we decided that the most beautiful was in the Madeleine. It was, as I remember, mostly white tulips, with some scarlet.

Crowds filed into the great simple church with silent excitement, and gasped at its beauty, and as they left put money into the box to help pay for the flowers, and then went on to the next and the next churches, all over town, which echoed to the sound of thousands of leisurely feet.

One of the prettiest walls was in the small chapel of a convent of Sisters of Charity behind the facades of the Rue Gaston-de-Saporta, a little below and behind

Brondino's bookshop. It was never open to the public except on that Thursday of Holy Week. No nuns were in sight, of course, but a postulant stood by the coin box, pretending not to listen to the size of the sound of each bit of money hitting the rest. A little sign over another alms box said, *For the poor, the sick, and the ashamed.*

The most impressive *reposoir* was in the chapel of the Gray Penitents, or the Bourras, called that in Provençal because they wear sacks over their heads.

They are the last of the three active orders of Penitents in Aix, who devoted themselves, most strongly in the Middle Ages, to the burying of hanged criminals and abandoned victims of the plagues. The brotherhood today is a secret one, made up of businessmen and professionals who celebrate their rites and functions wearing over their regular clothes long tunics made of a gray sacking in much the shape of the Ku Klux Klan costumes, so that on the one time we saw them, silent and nightmarish in their chapel, their secular trousers and shoes showed absurdly beneath their grim disguises. They clanked with brutal-looking rosaries hanging from their waistbelts around their waists.

Their chapel is a plain room, without statues as I remember, but with the whole end an enormous carving, almost life-size, on tortured rocks, of the descent of Christ from the Cross, with the Act of Mercy of the Good Samaritan and perhaps a few others painted behind it. The carving is of gleaming gray-black wood. The altar, which of course was stripped the day we saw it, is in front of the carving and a part of it, so that the figures crouch and swoon and mourn above and behind it.

There were no flowers anywhere. A few of the Bourras stood clattering their rosaries and watching the silent frightened people, who filed in and then quickly went away. My children were scared.

And in a way I was too: it was a stern mercy that led those first hooded men to defy custom and disease, in the far days, and I wondered what bones and ashes they might rescue now, so silent behind their sackcloth maskings.

In the vestibule we bought some postcards of the altar, which I lost, and we left money in the coin box, beside which one last thin Penitent stood, perhaps listening to the size of the sound as if he had a real face with a real ear on either side.

We wanted to see all this with our older eyes when we were in Aix again in Holy Week. My sister and her three sons came too, earlier than they had meant, to see the pagan beauty of the flowers, perhaps the medieval fearsomeness of the Bourras. But the town looked the same on Maundy Thursday as it had on Wednesday or Tuesday, and in St. Sauveur there was not a sign of the blossomed wall, and plainly one could not enter the little convents that are still everywhere behind the facades of Aix.

We went into the Madeleine, and there was nothing to show that once at least a mighty wall of white and scarlet blossoms had stood at the end of the south transept for some short hours, long enough for us to see forever.

I was perhaps a little drunk with being in the place again, and while my family stood gaping at a safe distance, I went up to a tall rounded young priest standing near the door and asked him where the *reposoirs* were.

That was the only time a man of the cloth has ever been discourteous to me, and later I saw this same one be quite rude to elderly women and very irascible with children, in a strangely sneering way. He sniffed, and stared down at me even farther than he needed, and asked in a high petulant voice, "Why would anyone ask that?"

"Father," I said with polite boldness bred of my joy at being home again, "we came back for the *reposoirs*, and I wonder where they are."

He looked me up and down, as the old novels would say, and then remarked in a disdainful way, "Anyone who is a believer knows, and therefore it is plain that Madame is not a believer, that the *reposoirs* have been discontinued in Provence as unfavorable to true Christianity."

I knew at once what he meant about the pagan element in them, but was sorry to detect his puritanical triumph. I thanked him.

"Where, if Madame is a believer, has she been? This is not a new edict," the priest stated suspiciously.

"Away, away," I answered in a half-deliberately fey manner, and I disappeared from his immediate vision and returned to my family and told them that the *reposoirs* had been forbidden.

We went away, away . . . in this case to the Cours Mirabeau, where we consumed sherbets and vermouth-gins according to our natures, and as returned amateurs seemed to grow like water-flowers under the greening buds of the plane trees, in the flowing tides of that street.

When the violet-man came along, we bought from him, and held the flowers in lieu of that older vision, ineradicable, of the walls of flowers, and perhaps of the painful sternness of the altar of the Bourras.

iii The Ending

Of a good beginning cometh a good end.
Proverbes, JOHN HEYWOOD

The two best things for me, in St. Sauveur, were that I was able to know it full and know it empty, not of people but of the spirit.

Several times it was almost full when I went to concerts there, with an orchestra in the transept in front of the choir stalls, and then a full choir of men and of boys from the Maîtrise, and everything sacred delicately and firmly shut off. The organ was alive, with Monsieur Gay there at the console in his white cap and his wife beside him in a kind of choir robe to turn the pages, like two gallant old birds high above our heads, so knowing and so skilled in making near-celestial sounds.

Twice the Archbishop sat unobtrusively in one of the stalls to the right, in the big nave, and prelates and priests rustled beneath him and I sat close by, recognizing his spirit and looking, invisible and even more so than usual, at the hollows of his eye sockets.

The music sang out from in front of the dim altar, and I knew it was a good thing to play it thus in the house of God.

Once I went into the Cathedral and it was a shell, waiting. It was by accident.

We walked up from the Hôtel de Provence on Easter Eve, I think, for no reason that I can remember, along Gaston-de-Saporta and across the Place de l'Archevêché, and there at the entrance to the cloister some priests and acolytes were bending above a bonfire.

It was startling to see. The flames lighted their intense faces. Around them were a few old women, the kind who are always present at such rituals.

I am sorry and a little ashamed to say that I forget now what they were burning. It had something to do with the purification by fire and then water of the vessels perhaps, and probably it was old candles and such-like, or the robes of Judas himself, but at the end a large candle was lighted, I think, and then from it each of us lit a long thin taper given to us by an acolyte or perhaps a lay brother.

Then we walked silently through the passage and through the side of the cloister, where I had been used to watching my children playing handball against the Roman tombs, and into the St. Maximin aisle of the church. From there we went into the nave, and found seats.

It was in one of the most impressive darknesses of my life. There was no sound except for the muted shuffling of our feet and the mouselike whisperings of people telling their beads, and the darkness in that great place was as palpable as flesh. It was oppressive. It pressed in upon my skin like the cold body of someone unloved. There was no help for it, no escape, and so it was not frightening.

I looked toward the dead altar, and out and up, and there was nothing anywhere except from the few feeble tapers that seemed to unlight rather than to light the intense worn hands and faces that nursed them.

A long and to me very pagan ceremony unfolded before the altar and then down into the chancel. It had to do with fire and water and rebirth. I wish that I could remember more of it, but all that stays clear is that it was ageless and real. And then gradually light seemed to come.

Of course it was partly mechanical, electrical. But that did not matter. I watched the magnificent conglomeration, perhaps two thousand years old, come alive, softly, subtly, and then like a mighty blare of trumpets, and seldom have I been so startled in my soul. I had for once known true hollow blackness, and then light. And it seems to me now that there was music too, a great triumphant blast of it from the organ, but perhaps it was only the return of light that I heard.

And then the time that I knew the Cathedral full, not empty, was almost as enriching, for I went to a concert there during the Festival, and listened to even that great place hold as much sound as an egg its meat, or the sea its waters.

It was as full as it could ever be with people too, of course, who had come from many lands to listen.

There was a symphony orchestra. The choir and the middle transept were filled with one large chorus of men and women, and one of boys, with the four soloists for the oratorio. Monsieur Gay was at the organ. The walls hummed with the colors of the Canterbury tapestries; the triptych of the Burning Bush was open and glowing; artful lights made the stones vibrate with subtle colors, as I had often watched them do at sunset with a kind of absorption rather than reflection of the colors outside in the town.

But the thing that was real was the sound. It was awesome, whether from a little flute as single as a pearl, or mighty as Judgment Day from the whole orchestra. Everything was a part of it, and the breath that went into and out of the mortals there, and into and out of the great organ, was in a mystical way the breath of the place itself, very old and ageless. I have seldom felt myself more identified with anything. It was perhaps as if I were the right grain of sand for me to be, on the right beach.

Afterwards we were quiet and tired, and that too was in the right way.

FROM THE TIME HE SAT DOWN TWICE

[. . .] The Cours Mirabeau is probably the most beautiful Main Street in the world. A great many people have said so, in prose and verse and even poetry, for hundreds of years, and have seldom been contradicted, except perhaps on the dueling field.

Guidebooks, which always have a lot of other things to mention, usually do their best lightly by describing it as "wide and shaded, with many fountains, some dating to 36 B.C.," or something like that, which is true, of course, but inadequate.

It has several fountains of different periods of design, going down the middle. One, maybe the best, is called Old Mossback and is a great ugly lump of furry stone dribbling fairly smelly water, warm enough to send up steam on cold days, in which old aching people dip their wrists and dabble at their eyes. The others are more elegant, people and fountains both.

And the Cours is without a doubt one of the widest as well as shadiest streets that anyone has ever dreamed of: four majestic rows of giant plantain trees, with their roots down in a hidden river, rising up a hundred feet or more, straight and beautiful, and then meeting, artfully trimmed for it in the springtime, to form a thick green shade in summer, a delicate lacy cage in winter, a long three-arched tunnel from one end of the Cours at the *Place de la Grande Fontaine* for about a half-mile to the other, where a noble statue of King René stands, with him holding a bunch of grapes and smiling proudly enough at all this fine balance of the town he helped give it to.

He looks down the row of living fountains between him and The Big One. He seems to be listening to their ceaseless music. Now and then a little truck or even a Vespa bumps into one of their sides, and the police come and turn off the splashing for a few minutes, but in general the Old King sees to it that the whole Cours spouts and murmurs properly, and that it ripples with green shade when the time is right. . . .

In the summer the shade on that long street is so deep that people walking in it feel like fish in the bottom of a deep clean river. The great plantains are like immeasurably tall reeds. The air is pure and sweet and sifted, somewhat as river water should be to an unbothered fish. There is room to exist.

Even the sidewalks are as wide as most streets, with stone benches along them where old women knit and talk and jiggle their baby buggies now and then, and room for everybody in Aix to stroll and meet and stroll on again, room for perhaps hundreds of bright chairs around dozens of little round tables in the green dimness of summer shade or the thinner golden light of winter through the bare branches, or the tremulous green-gold of spring. [. . .]

FROM A COMMON DANGER

[. . .] All Frenchmen are reputed, at least by Anglo-Saxons and Italians, to be unpredictable, erratic, explosive behind the wheel, but they are the most expert backers I have ever watched. In a town like Aix, the street parking is a major problem, and it is as exciting to sit in a café and watch two drivers compete for a curb space not more than six inches longer than one of their cars as it is to look at West Germany beat France in football on television.

One man must and will win. The other laughs, waves, and drives on for another luckier try. All this involves not only perfect balance, but a basically philosophical approach to equally basic proposals like safety, insurance, even sanity. How can a harried young bank clerk, much less a rising barrister, stay cool and courteous in the face of such decibelic and logistical happenings, several times a day? France is a nation of daredevils, on the tightrope called *le parking*.

This, on a side street like Brueys, is even noisier and more dramatic than on the Cours Mirabeau, because there are no café-sitters to admire and gasp at the maneuverings, no cops to watch for and smile at. Here the action is compressed, and as if seen through the wrong end of an operaglass, but the sound of it has ten times the volume of a looser, wider place. The high walls, facing each other perhaps twenty feet apart; the lack of any trees or vines to absorb some of the noise; the implacable straightness to hold everything knife-sharp in a long, narrow box instead of letting it twist and fade and die as it would farther inside the Old Town: all this makes noise, and what best to do with it is a constant defiance to one's toleration point.

Brueys is marked as a one-way street, but cars can and often do enter from both ends at once, size each other up, and then agree without excitement or visible signals that one or the other will go up onto its nearest sidewalk while the other inches by. Seldom are there horn blasts or screeching brakes. The only sign of frustration is that both cars, purring along until they have passed, will suddenly spurt ahead with a roar worthy of the Grand Prix at Monaco. This unusual license (or tolerance) in Aix, where traffic problems are an increasing trouble for one hundred such reasons, makes for an especial lot of backing and filling on Brueys, already so narrow that it takes a good ten minutes to maneuver even a small car out of the deep garages.

The two wooden doors will be swung open, blocking the sidewalk as well as the view in either direction, or the heavy metal door will be shoved up with a violent crash, and the game will begin: little puffs of pressure on the accelerator, then short violent brakings, a ten-inch dart sideways, a four-inch dart forward, and then eighteen back at a new angle, on and on. Suddenly, the snappy fat new Citroën is *in* . . . or *out* . . . for a few hours, the garage doors slammed down or crashed shut, and the driver roars to the nearest end of the street, whichever way he is pointed.

The essential need to park three cars into every old wagon-room must perforce involve an intimate relationship between the tenants, for mutual agreement as to which one uses his car the most and the most urgently, or does not work on Wednesdays, or is a Sunday driver and can park in the farthest worst corner six days a week. Once, on my way over to the Cours Sextius for vegetables, I watched an old man in felt slippers and the kind of soft brown sweater some Frenchmen seem to grow into like a used skin as soon as they have been retired and start sitting around the house a lot. He looked frail, as if he had been ill during the past winter, but he was an excellent driver, and I felt almost invisible as I admired the way he got a big black sedan onto the street from his garage, in about eight minutes of precise backings and finaglings.

He parked it up on the sidewalk with deft ease, and I went on. When I came back, though, in about a half hour, with my two heavy baskets of vegetables, he was still at work. His elderly wife stood near the garage door, holding his sweater. He slowly wangled a third car up onto the sidewalk behind the black, and then a blue. She opened the trunk of the last car, threw in the sweater, and went into the house. He stretched himself carefully, and began to back the black car deep into the cave. She came down with a small suitcase and a wicker picnic basket. Neither of them seemed to see me, so I stayed to watch, as without a frown or a curse he maneuvered the blue car back into the long narrow room lit by one feeble dangling light bulb, and closed the wooden doors gently, locked his own car doors because of the stuff inside, and went into the house with his old lady. I suppose he had to change into shoes for the weekend . . . get a jacket . . . perhaps take a short snooze. I too felt tired. I wondered about their return. Would he soberly, as today, move out the two other cars and put his in the far corner and then move them back, as probably he promised their owners to do, if ever he and his wife went away for the weekend? Perhaps he would never come back. . . . But while I still stood leaning against the wall across the street, dreading to pick up my two heavy baskets, the people hurried out their door, with a little fat white dog on a leash, and hopped into their car like teenagers and roared off down the street. They were smiling contentedly, and I was still invisible.

Except on Sundays, big trucks turn ponderously into Brueys from about three o'clock in the morning until six at night, and if they obviously will meet head on, the one nearer his end-goal has the right-of-way and the other must back out. This of course makes for great growls from the frustrated engines, a lot of amiable shouting from the drivers and interested onlookers, and clouds of fouled air. And, from about 4:30 a.m., workers along the street are picked up by friends, and it seems part of the game to wait in one's flat until the car roars up and blasts three to six signals, and then lean out and shout down some pre-dawn badinage like: "Is that you, you old son-of-a-gun?" "Step on it, Marius!" the friend will yell back. "We're late already.

Give her a kiss for me, and get on down here," etc., etc. The motors drone in and out of the windows, and up past the rooftops, impatient, loud, soft, loud. Every Marius slams shut his door, slams shut the car door; his friend slams down the street. . . . They all try to sound belligerent and mean, *muy macho,* dragging off to work while their pampered Little Women snooze between the sheets. But really they are vigorous, enthusiastic men eager to get out, get away, and then get home again.

A little while after the last of the workmen has driven off with a friend, or has revved up his ancient *"deux chevaux"* and got it jerkily onto the street and banged shut the garage doors and shot off as loudly as possible toward one end or the other of Brueys, the Garbage Monster comes. It really comes twice, once halfway down the street and then backing out; next, about twenty minutes later, up the street from the other direction, after it has apparently gone to some spot and purged itself of the haul so far.

It is an enormous machine, as high as three men, a Juggernaut with a cab up in front and at the back a great revolving mouth. Two small people toss trash into it, everything that has been left out for it the night before, in cartons, plastic bags, old wooden crates. When there looks like a good mouthful, one of the men whistles, or occasionally yells a signal, which apparently can be heard in the cab over the noise of the machinery, and a dreadful crunching starts, with bottles and cans and even old bedsprings being ground and crushed and chewed into a stinking pulp of paper-plastic-metal-glass-rags-chips-of-plaster-and-stone, all held together by rotted food. There are a few more cabalistic whistles, and finally the gigantic Thing moves on toward the Place des Tanneurs and then toward wherever it will spew out what we have fed it.

Once or twice I have neatly and resolutely *not* heard all this pre-dawn rite, by hanging on to a perhaps hypnotic state of near-sleep, of awareness but not consciousness. The Monster has come partway, backed out, disappeared to disgorge itself into some municipal bowel where it will be treated, digested, turned in "fill" for a new subdivision. I have gone into a deep, deliberate trance, perhaps. . . . But then there it was, right under the window, its engine working doubletime to turn over the great glut, the two men chirping their signals before they all rumbled and crashed on down the street. I felt sleepily triumphant, in a very fleeting way. Mind over matter, I said, as the Juggernaut trundled along, rolling over past, over present. . . .

Once it almost got ahead of me. I heard it start along the street and then turn back. Something said very distinctly in my over-awakened consciousness, in a too-clear voice, "You are going to be afraid, this time." "Afraid of what?" "Afraid that on the top floor an old woman will toss her fat dog down into the great chewing mouth, or a young woman her baby, or herself, or you. . . . You might lean out, fall out, tumble, get sucked into it with such a crunch soft snapping. . . ." I said, "This is not a valid argument about anything at all." The voice yelled something about noise. We argued angrily, and my guts shook, and then the Monster had gone past 16 Rue Brueys without my really hearing it, and I took a peaceful post-dawn nap, with gentle dreams. It had been a bad moment, surely, but all was calm on the street for a few minutes after it, and there was a sweet air of survival inside me.

I have long held that everything, inside and out of one's self, is more intense in Provence than anyplace else I know or know about. Salt is almost dangerously saltier. Foods that grow from the earth taste stronger, or subtler, or stranger. If a person feels unwell, he is usually more miserable there than he would be in Sussex or Mendocino County, and if he is exhilarated and happy, it is immeasurably better than it could be anyplace else. In the same way, sound . . . *noise* . . . goes deeper into one's head-mind-innards. It is sharper, or rounder, or more cruel or beautiful. A very few times I felt a flash of panic and near-despair, on Brueys, because of a fear that I could not really tolerate its noise.

Almost everywhere in Aix and, I was told, in every population center in France, or perhaps the world, the constant scream and mutter of too many cars-motorbikes-people-sirens-TV-sets is something to cope with doggedly but not passively (i.e., "It *need not* be this dreadful, Mr. Mayor!"). Conversation is difficult and even impossible in a sidewalk café, and often was in my own flat. Thinking about a laundry list or perhaps a new pair of sandals, or why Pentecost is a national holiday, can for a few minutes or seconds become impossible, a smoke of sound, whirling and rising, a dizzy ride otherwise, before one is back at the desk again, noting and pondering. Sleep, if one permits even a slight tinge of exasperation to color the necessity of being acceptive, can be impossible. And a normal human being who cannot sleep, because he is protesting the constant harsh interruptions of his dark dream-world, can soon fall ill in any of a dozen ways.

So, early in my life on Brueys, I decided to do what I could to make myself a part of the occasionally mad sounds. Otherwise, I still believe, I might well grow wrathy and confused, and thus endanger the whole *élan vital* that I always feel in Aix. After much practice, I think that, except for a few flashes of irrational irritation at people's thoughtlessness or panic at my own craven subconscious, I stayed philosophical and on sane ground. I never ran a fever, and seldom felt dizzy. [. . .]

FROM TWO KITCHENS IN PROVENÇE

II

The second kitchen I had in Provence, when we lived in a part of an old farmhouse at L'Harmas, about three miles from Aix on the Route du Tholonet, was somewhat different from the one at the château a few years before. There was much more luxury. There was a small noisy electric refrigerator called, as everywhere in the world—except, perhaps, America—a "frigidaire." There was an imitation-modern white enamel stove with an oven and four burners. Two of the burners always blew out at once, so, except for the oven, which could not be adjusted to anything but a blasting roar and which I never used, I was just as before, in the older kitchen at the château, with the portable two–burner butane stove. There was the same slab of hollowed marble for a sink, with a round instead of oval basin scooped in it, but it had two taps, which usually had water in them, and quite often there was hot water without my having to light anything, unless someone had taken a bath in the past twelve hours, or there was a drought, or the farm pump was out of order. And there were several more shelves, for dishes and pots.

Two windows, not so high from the ground as in the kitchen over the stables, gave upon a terrace shaded by the tall trees of that country, which must bend to the mistral and shed their branches almost to their tops—a little like the wild pines in Monterey in California, but higher and thinner. The terrace was half wild, too, and could be deep in voluptuous sweet grasses and flowers in the spring, or dry and stinging with pointy weeds, or almost bare until the snow brought soft rains again. It heartened me to watch it and to smell its changing wildness as I stood in the kitchen, using it for its destined purpose—to feed people near me.

The food was the same in both kitchens; it dared me daily. But I must go to Aix for everything this time, for the jeeps and trucks that had come to the château did not seem to come this near the big town. I must get to the open markets and to a few little shops, and then on home, *fast*, before things spoiled. I went on foot. I did not want to have a car; it was too rare a thing to miss, that walking along the little Route du Tholonet—Cézanne's road—in all weathers, against all tides, between the farm and

Aix. I rose very early to head for town, carrying a nest of the light straw baskets that the Gypsies still wove, and then bringing them back full and heavy in a taxi. (There were few paper sacks in that country, and baskets and string bags were uniform.)

The Big Market is held three times a week—on Tuesday, Thursday, and Saturday—but every day, behind the post office, there is the Little Market. Both of them are beautiful and exciting and soothing, a tonic to the senses, but I think I loved the little one more.

The Place Richelme et aux Herbes is small, and shaded by very tall and noble plane trees, which in summer sift down such a green light as I have seldom seen. Perhaps some fortunate fish have known it, but for human beings it is rare to float at the bottom of the deeps and yet breathe with rapture the smells of all the living things spread out to sell in the pure, filtered moving air. There are snails in cages, ducklings bright-eyed in their crates, trembling rabbits. There are baskets of fresh herbs, and little piles of edibles gathered at dawn in a hundred gardens: peas and strawberries in the spring, small cabbages, apples, new potatoes, and onions and garlic, following inexorably the farmers' almanac, so that one soon accustoms the purchases and their uses to the crops that have been sowed and harvested thus for two thousand years at least.

Sometimes there was a man with a tiny donkey, selling baskets of fresh lavender, or crude mint drops from the Pyrenees, or cough lozenges made from Alpine herbs and saps. He always put a ringlet of what he was selling that day over the patient head of his little beast—in hot weather, on her hat. On one corner, behind the beautiful old grain market that now housed harried postal clerks, there was a quiet man with a folding table, making metal nameplates for people's doorways, in every kind of painstaking elaborate lettering. Once, he gave me a tiny ring, cut from a peach stone. It was for *me*, he said without irony, but it would not have fit a newborn babe.

At either end of the little square are small cafés and shops, and opposite the post office is a bleak, busy annex lined with fish markets and shops selling poultry, butter, and all kinds of smoked sausages and hams. Underneath this annex is a well-run and modern public toilet, new since our first stay in Aix and built by the city.

The other market, the big one, is comparatively gigantic, and always very crowded and amusing, but not dream-like, not deep golden green, even in its generous summer shade. I came to know it well, and soon. It is in a long square that is not square at all, with the Palais de Justice on one side, and many small shops and cafés and pharmacies and honorable bookstores and even the Girls' High School fringing it, dominated by the somber, vaguely sinister Church of the Madeleine and—at the time I was there—by two monuments. One of these, the statue of Mirabeau down by the Palais, is now gone. It is said to have been the most ridiculous public monument ever to be erected in France. This is a broad and daring statement, given the evidence against it, but certainly the small furious figure of Mirabeau, his wig askew and no pockmarks showing, with a knee-high lion cowering against him like a fat poodle, the two shooting up from a stony froth of great-breasted Muses, was very funny, even to the respectful. The monument that remains, the obelisk at the opposite end of the square, is fine indeed, and it rises pure and classical from the fountain at its base, where people dip water for their stalls and the flower women douse their posies.

At the low end of the unsquare square, on the regular Tuesdays, Thursdays, and—especially—Saturdays, is the Flea Market, a reputable debauch of canny snoopers for the great antique dealers of Paris and London and New York, and housewives looking for old wineglasses or copper pans, and happy drifters. Next come the merchants of nails and screws, junk jewelry, clothes, and kitchen stuff— and very few of them are fly-by-nights; most have their regular patrons among people like the farmers and the Algerians, who prefer to shop under open skies. Then there are always a few barkers under umbrellas, selling the kind of paring knife that for them alone will cut everything but the Greek alphabet with a flip of the wrist, or patterns for chic dresses that can be made from four dish towels. Even Bibles.

And then come the real market stalls, the ones where people buy to live. First of all, next to the café where we had long liked to eat couscous occasionally, there was (and probably still is) a woman who sold fresh peanuts in their shells. She was Algerian, I think, or half so, and she had such a delectable texture and color to her skin that I was glad she sold something I could buy from her, in order to talk a little and look at her. She was like a ripe, washed apricot, with the same glowing deep color coming through, as if from far underneath her smooth, tight skin. I have seen such tones in a few faces and in some stained glass in churches. Most of her customers were the thin and thick Algerian women who drifted by twos in their floating flowered dresses along the aisles of the market, and sometimes I listened to her speaking with them in their breathy language. She thought I was very funny, to be so plainly Anglo-Saxon and to be buying peanuts from her.

All the stands were alike and violently different, of course, and the prices were much the same, and the high quality was, too. It seemed to be a question of growing used to one vendor instead of another, and I soon confessed to myself that it was part of the pleasure to be recognized by some of the quick, tough people who carried on that never-ending business. They looked so fresh and strong, three times a week, and I felt flabby and exhausted to think that every day—not just three—they must buy, or grow, and load their wares, and drive to this town or that, and set up their stalls, and then at the end start home again. They were cheerful, and as watchful as cats and as impersonal, and yet they knew most of the people who traded with them, and smiled and joked as if I, or she, or that old woman with no teeth, or the smart young matron in white gloves, were a special pet. "Ah, how did they remember *me?*" one would ask delightedly, piling the brass weighing bowls higher with the new potatoes round and hard as plums, the stiff buds of artichokes purple and succulent.

Each time I went in to the markets from L'Harmas, I had quite firmly in my mind what we needed for at least two days ahead, what we might need in case of company, and what I would undoubtedly fall heir to or in love with at the last minute—that minute of decision between a good clean rabbit hanging with his own dignity, albeit naked, or some plucked, blackish pigeons I had just spied in the poultry woman's stand. I would start out with three or four empty baskets, and a coin purse full of the small change essential to such hectic purchasing. I would end with heavy baskets and the purse much lighter, of course; money goes fast for food, and even faster for good food, and although I knew better, I always thought in terms of pounds and ounces and I bought in kilos, so that often when I thought I had two pounds of new peas I was toting two kilograms, or more than double what my mind stupidly kept reckoning. Then I would add two kilos of soft, sweet Valencia oranges from Spain, and a half kilo of lemons; two kilos of beans as long as hairpins and not much thicker; two kilos of country tomatoes, smaller and more pungent than the big handsome ones from up near Avignon; a smoked sausage, the kind still packed into clean, uneven gut skin instead of smooth plastic; some cheese; a last generous basket of dead-ripe gooseberries; a kilo of fresh spaghetti from the fat woman by the fountain; and a clumsy bunch of pale-pink carnations: "Five dozen for two francs today—take advantage, my pretty ladies."

I would be hot, harried, and overladen. Down on the wide shady Cours Mirabeau, which, perhaps rightly, has been called the most beautiful Main Street in the world, there are taxis. I would push toward them. The peanut woman smiled always at me with gaiety and some mockery—she so solid and ripe and apricot brown, I so tottery and foreign—and I would feel stronger for her casual warmth. And under the trees of the Cours, Fernand or Michel would take all my baskets and then me into his taxi for the drive out along Cézanne's road, toward home.

Sometimes I would want him to go faster, for I could almost feel the food in the baskets swelling with juice, growing soft, splitting open in an explosive rush toward ripeness and disintegration. The fruits and vegetables of Provence are dying as they grow—literally leaping from the ancient soil, so filled with natural richnesses and bacilli and fungi that they seem a kind of summing up of whatever they *are*. A tomato there, for instance, is the essence of all tomatoes, of tomato-ness, the way a fragment from a Greek frieze is not a horse but *horse* itself.

As soon as I got back from the markets, I always reorganized everything I had gleaned, as fast as I could, against the onslaughts of time (especially summer time) and insects. First of all, there were the flies. The flies of Provence are said to be the most audacious in the world. People have remarked on this for at least twenty-five hundred years, and I have read that slaves being led in chains from the north to man the galleys anchored at Toulon marched fastest on this last lap of their death trip because of the flies that goaded them. Flourishing descendants of those foul, hungry insects still zigzag in a year-round dance there, especially in spring and summer, or perhaps autumn, and the grim acceptance of them is one of the requirements of life, especially on farms, where the soil itself is an age-old amalgam of droppings from beast and man. They were much worse at the château, of course, for there we lived close to the barns, where the shepherd kept all his sheep-goats-chickens-rabbits, and at least three or four pigs, in a timeless, fruity muck that must surely have glowed in the dark. At L'Harmas, there were only pigeons and two peacocks, but there was fine shade in the summer for the flies of that hillside, and warmth in the winter, and the general interest to be found in four families of two-legged creatures.

The ants are almost as powerful in Provence as the flies, surging relentlessly from the red earth, seeming to walk through wood and stone and metal and glass toward whatever they want. And there are other pests that like the cool tiled floors, or the dark of cupboards, or the moist dimness under old drains: scorpions, centipedes, bees, and wasps, earwigs, crickets, several kinds of gnats, now and then a snail or a tick. It was the flies and the ants I tilted with first and constantly, and I do not think I disliked them the most because they *were* the most but because I hated and still hate the sound and feel of flies, and the smell of ants. We are at odds always. Sometimes I can acknowledge their complacency—they will be here long after I have made my final stand against them.

In the part of the farmhouse where we lived at L'Harmas, there was a dim room that had once been a buttery, or even the farmer's office, I think. It had an uneven tiled floor, two windows with the shutters left bowed to form a kind of airy cooler, an old piano with no wires in it, and several hooks let into the plastered stone walls. From these hooks I hung whatever I need not cook the minute I got home from Aix: white onions in a crocheted bag, two kilos of long purple eggplants that not even a bee could sting, a basket of small, satin-skinned potatoes. On the old piano I would put a tray of red tomatoes, which I had placed gently, bottoms up, with some soft ones, already doomed for tomorrow, to be eaten tonight, even though they had all been firm and greenish a few hours before. I would do the same with a tray of peaches and apricots, and then cover them against the midges.

Baskets of green peas and one of beans I put upon the table in the dining room, with pans to catch them when they were shelled and de-strung by whoever passed by. It was a house rule, and since everybody talked and sat and drank and worked in that big white room, as well as eating there when we were not out under the pine trees on the terrace, it seemed a pleasant and nearly automatic thing to prepare for cooking whatever was set out for that.

In the little kitchen, I put things away as fast as I could. If I had bought meat, it must be prepared for cooking at once, or at best kept in the minute frigidaire overnight. (In winter, of course, things could be thoroughly wrapped and put on a window ledge or into a wire cooler, but winter is not long in that country, and the rats and half-wild farm cats are very clever about getting around such casual arrangements.)

Then I would pack the sweet fresh butter into a crock and put it on the old piano in a bowl of water. I washed the strawberries and cherries tenderly and put them, too, in heavy bowls in the buttery, to be eaten that day. Salads I stripped of their bad leaves and soaked for a few minutes in a dishpan, and then shook out and wrapped in a towel, to be eaten within twenty-four hours. Sometimes I could store clean curly endive or chicory and the coarser lettuces in cellophane bags for a little longer, but not in summer. It was fine, in winter, to have plenty of good Belgian endive—so easy to clean, to store, to serve in many ways.

It takes little time to learn the tricks of any new kitchen if it is a question of survival, and after only a few days at L'Harmas I knew which pans had bad handles, which skillets heated unevenly, which burners on the stove were not worth bothering to light. I knew where I was going to put bottle caps and broken corks and empty anchovy tins, all separate, and what I was going to do about garbage, and where I would hang the dish towels. I also knew where not to trip on a loose tile, and how to keep ants out of the honey jar forever. I remembered a lot of tricks from the last time in Provence, at Le Tholonet.

I remembered that in summer it is dangerous to make any kind of soup and hope to keep some of it for the next day; it will send off the sweet, sickly death smell in only a few hours, even from a jar in the frigidaire. And I remembered how to stew fruits lightly, to keep them overnight for a cool bowl for breakfast or lunch instead of having to eat them all and immediately. Once more I was washing everything fast in pure water from the well instead of the tap, to keep my people from the queasy gripes and grumbles that can plague countryfolk and that used to frighten pioneer American mothers with names like "summer complaint" and "fruit fever."

Soon I would go without thinking to the little icebox and that cool dark buttery, about twice a day, to sniff with my curious nose and to discard ruthlessly what it always hurt me to waste: a bowl of berries delicately veiled with a fine grey fuzz that was not there an hour ago, three more rotten tomatoes that were firm and fine last night. I would lift the lid from a pot of leftover ratatouille—was it really all right, or did I catch a whiff, a hint, of death and decay in it? A deep sniff might make me decide that it would be safe to bring it again to the boil, beat it well with some more olive oil, and chill it to be eaten cold with fresh bread for supper, before an omelet. There might be one lamb chop left. It would not be good by noon. I would eat it cold for a secret breakfast, with a glass of red wine, after the family had scattered. Tomorrow would be market again.

In winter, when alone, I ate by the fire on the hearth of the living-dining room. In spring, I carried my plate and glass into the new warmth of sunlight on the terrace, ankle-deep in wild flowers and a hundred tender grasses. In summer, I sat by the bowed shutters in the dining room, dim to baffle the flies, cool already against the blaze of white dusty heat, vibrating with the love call of the *cigales*. In the autumn, I walked a little away from roof and room to the meadows turning sere, to the pine woods past the wheat field, and I put my back against a tree and looked north toward the Mont Ste. Victoire, rising so arrogant and harsh above the curling foreground. I would think of what I must buy the next day, and load into the baskets, and then sort and store and serve forth in the order of Nature itself: first freshness, then flavor and ripeness, and then decay. And always there were the needs of the people who must live from Nature, and learn to do so to the best of all their powers and not die from the traps that she can lay for them, especially in this ancient teeming land.

It was a good way to live.

St. Helena, 1966

from THE PLACE
WHERE I LOOKED

One of the many tantalizing things about Marseille is that most people who describe it, whether or not they know much about either the place or the languages they are supposedly using, write the same things. For centuries this has been so, and a typically modern opinion could have been given in 1550 as well as 1977.

Not long ago I read one, mercifully unsigned, in a San Francisco paper. It was full of logistical errors, faulty syntax, misspelled French words, but it hewed true to the familiar line that Marseille is doing its best to live up to a legendary reputation as world capital for "dope, whores, and street violence." It then went on to discuss, often erroneously, the essential ingredients of a true bouillabaisse! The familiar pitch had been made, and idle readers dreaming of a great seaport dedicated to heroin, prostitution, and rioting could easily skip the clumsy details of marketing for fresh fish. . . .

"Feature articles" like this one make it seem probable that many big newspapers, especially in English-reading countries, keep a few such mild shockers on hand in a back drawer, in case a few columns need filling on a rainy Sunday. Apparently people like to glance one more time at the same old words: evil, filthy, dangerous.

Sometimes such journalese is almost worth reading for its precociously obsolete views of a society too easy to forget. In 1929, for instance, shortly before the Wall Street Crash, a popular travel writer named Basil Woon published *A Guide to the Gay World of France: From Deauville to Monte Carlo* (Horace Liveright, New York). (By now even his use of the word "gay" is quaintly naïve enough for a small chuckle. . . .)

Of course Mr. Woon was most interested in the Côte d'Azur, in those far days teeming and staggering with rich English and even richer Americans, but while he could not actively recommend staying in Marseille, he did remain true to his journalistic background with an expectedly titillating mention of it:

> If you are interested in how the other side of the world lives, a trip through old Marseilles—by daylight—cannot fail to thrill, but it is not wise to venture into this district at night unless dressed like a stevedore and well armed. Thieves, cutthroats, and other undesirables throng the narrow alleys, and sisters of scarlet sit in the doorways of their places of business, catching you by the

sleeve as you pass by. The dregs of the world are here, unsifted. It is Port Said, Shanghai, Barcelona, and Sidney combined. Now that San Francisco has reformed, Marseilles is the world's wickedest port.

(Mr. Woon's last sentence, written some fifty years ago, is more provocative today than it was then, to anyone interested in the shifting politics of the West Coast of America. . . .)

While I either accept or deplore what other people report about the French town, and even feel that I understand why they are obliged to use the words they do (Give the public what it wants, etc., etc. . . .), I myself have a different definition of the place, which is as indefinable as Marseille itself: *Insolite.*

There seems to be no proper twin for this word in English; one simply has to sense or feel what it means. Larousse says that it is somewhat like "contrary to what is usual and normal." Dictionaries such as the Shorter Oxford and Webster's Third International try words like *apart, unique, unusual.* This is not enough, though . . . not quite right. Inwardly I know that it means *mysterious, unknowable,* and in plain fact, *indefinable.*

And that is Marseille: indefinable, and therefore *insolite.* And the strange word is as good as any to explain why the place haunts me and draws me, with its phoenix-like vitality, its implacably realistic beauty and brutality. The formula is plain: Marseille = *insolite,* therefore *insolite* = Marseille.

This semantical conclusion on my part may sound quibbling, but it seems to help me try to explain what connection there could possibly, logically, be between the town and me . . . why I have returned there for so long: a night, ten nights, many weeks or months.

Of course it is necessary to recognize that there is a special karma about Marseille, a karmic force that is mostly translated as wicked, to be avoided by all clean and righteous people. Travellers have long been advised to shun it like the pesthole it has occasionally been, or at best to stay there as short a time as possible before their next ship sets sail.

A true karmic force is supposed to build up its strength through centuries of both evil and good, in order to prevent its transmigration into another and lesser form, and this may well explain why Marseille has always risen anew from the ashes of history. There seems to be no possible way to stamp it out. Julius Caesar tried to, and for a time felt almost sure that he had succeeded. Calamities caused by man's folly and the gods' wrath, from the plagues ending in 1720 to the invasions ending in the 1940s, have piled it with rotting bodies and blasted rubble, and the place has blanched and staggered, and then risen again. It has survived every kind of weapon known to European warfare, from the ax and arrow to sophisticated derivatives of old Chinese gunpowder, and it is hard not to surmise that if a nuclear blast finally leveled the place, some short dark-browed men and women might eventually emerge from a few deep places, to breed in the salt marshes that would gradually have revivified the dead waters around the Old Port. . . .

Meanwhile, Marseille lives, with a unique strength that plainly scares less virile breeds. Its people are proud of being "apart," and critics mock them for trying to sound even more Italianate than they are, trying to play roles for the tourists: fishermen ape Marcel Pagnol's *Marius* robustly; every fishwife is her own Honorine. The Pinball Boys are thinner and more viperous there than anywhere in Europe, they assume as true Marseillais, and the tarts are tarter and the old hags older and more haggish than anywhere in the world. . . .

Behind this almost infantile enjoyment of playing their parts on a superb stage with changing backdrops that are certainly *insolite,* and a full orchestration of every sound effect from the ringings of great bells to the whine of the tramontane and the vicious howl of the mistral, held together by sirens from ambulances and ships, and the pinpricks of complaining seagulls . . . behind this endlessly entertaining and absorbing melodrama, a secret life-source provides its inner nourishment to the citizens.

There is a strong religious blood flowing in that corporate body. Catholics and other Christians, Communists, Free-thinkers, Arabs, Gypsies, all admit to an acceptance of powers beyond their questionings, whether or not they admit to *being* "believers." The gigantic bell Marie-Joséphine, at the top of Notre Dame de la Garde, rings for every soul that has ever lived there, no matter how much a race-bound parishioner of St. Victor might deny the right of a Moslem in the Panier across the Old Port to understand its reassuring voice.

Naturally, in a place as old and *insolite* as Marseille, there is a strong dependence on forces that are loosely called occult, or mystical, or perhaps demonic. There are many fortunetellers, usually thriving in their chosen ways of neighborhood help or prestigious social acclaim. The best known of the Tarot cards were adapted to a special ritual that evolved there, and are called by the town's name. Cabalistic signs are often in or on graffiti, political or otherwise, and it is plain that the right people will see and understand them. Why not? After all, the churches build their altars over early Christian sepulchers laid in turn upon the stones of temples built to Artemis and Adonis, who in turn . . .

There is a good description of the withdrawn side of the noisy, rough-talking Marseillais in one of Simenon's books about Inspector Maigret. It was written about another French town, but it is Marseille to me:

> . . . a stone jungle, where you can disappear for months; where often you do not hear of a crime until weeks after it has been committed; where thousands of human beings . . . live on the fringes of the Law, in a world where they can find as many accomplices and hideouts as they need, and where the police put out their bait now and then and pull in a fish they were waiting for, all the while depending more for such luck on a telephone call from a jealous girl or an informer. . . .

This quasi-occult mutism is what has helped defeat the invaders of Marseille, I think. Certainly it baffled the last militant "occupants" in the 1940s. Many different stories are told about how and why a large part of the ancient Greco-Roman bank of the Old Port was destroyed by the Germans, but the basic reason for this move was probably that they simply could not keep track of what was going on in the deep warrens that went up from the Quai du Port past Les Accoules toward La Vieille Charité and the Place des Moulins. What was worse, they could not tell from the flat black eyes, the blank unmoved faces of occupants of this filthy old neighborhood, the pimps and bawds and small-time gangsters who went there as a natural refuge when their other ways of life were interrupted by war, which of them were working with what appointed or subterranean leaders, and even which of them might be town fathers in false beards rather than black marketeers dealing indirectly with the invaders.

The answer was to get rid of the whole infamous district, and it was easy to have the German-appointed city council approve a plan to blow up the mess from underground. It was done neatly, with complete evacuation of the helpless residents and full warning to the numberless unknown invisibles who were using the old tunnels for their special version of the Liberation. (Some other destruction during that dubious time was less circumspect, of course, and a few foul tricks were blamed on the invaders when an orphanage, or a clinic, say, was without notice shattered from above and not below ground. . . .)

Soon after the dirty tunnels and gutters above the Quai du Port were mined and hopefully wiped out, they were once more in full swing, of course: rats and moles know how to dig again. A lot of the diggers were summarily lined up and shot, but that did not seem to impress the strange breed called Marseillais for so many centuries. Some thirty-five years later, the whole quarter is threatened with a new demolition, to make way for high-rise housing projects, but the people who live there, as elsewhere in the big town, remain impassive and tough and sardonic . . . that is to say, *insolite.*

This cannot be a guidebook, the kind that tells how, with a chart to be got free from the driver of the tour, to follow a green line from A to G and then switch to either the red or the yellow lines to Z, depending on how weary or hungry one may feel. I am not meant to tell anyone where to go in Marseille, nor even why I myself went where I did there, and saw and smelled and felt as I did. All I can do in this explanation about my being there is to write something about the town itself, through my own senses.

I first spent a night there in late 1929, and since then I have returned even oftener than seems reasonable. Beginning in 1940, there were wars, both worldwide and intramural, and then I managed to regain my old rhythm. Each time I went back, I felt younger: a chronological miracle, certainly!

One reason I now try to explain all this is that when I cannot return, for physical or perhaps financial reasons, I will stay so enriched and heartened by what I have known there that I should be the envy of every crowned head of several worlds. I boast, and rightly. Nobody who has lived as deeply for as long as I have in Marseille-Insolite can be anything but blessed.

There is an almost impossible lot of things to see there, and for one reason or another I know many of them, and have been part of them with people I loved (another proud boast!). If I started to tell why I wished everybody in the world could do the same, it would make a whole book, a personal guide tour, and that is not what I am meant to write, according to my secret directives. I would say words like Longchamps, Borély, Cantini, Les Accoules, St. Victor, St. Nicolas, La Place des Moulins, La Vieille Charité, Notre Dame de la Garde, La Rue de Rome . . . and it would be for every unexpected reason known to human beings, from the smell of a sick lion in a zoo behind Longchamps to an obviously necrophilic guardian of the tombs in Borély to the cut of an exquisite tweed skirt in a Paris boutique on the Rome. Each reason I gave for wanting some people to know why I've been there would make the guide a long hymn, hopefully shot through with practical asides about how far Borély is from town, and how steep the walk is up through the Panier to the Vieille Charité, and how much to tip the elderly patient men at places like the Musée des Docks Romains . . . and yes, why did I not mention it before? Other places, other sounds: they tumble in my head like pebbles under a waterfall, and all I know is that I must try to understand why I myself go back to this strange beautiful town. [. . .]

from SOME OF THE WOMEN

[. . .] The native women of Marseille, the ones who are unmistakably of this place and no other that I have seen or read about, are short and trimly wide. As children they are thin wiry little monkeys, with large dark eyes. As girls they have a slim beauty that soon passes into what they will be for the rest of their lives, with breasts that stand up until marriage and then stay large after childbirth, without ever seeming to sag toward the ground in old age like those of taller softer females. They may develop paunches, the tidy kind that look made of steel, and among the lot of them there is never a snub nose, but instead the kind that grows stronger and beakier with time. Their arms and legs stay shapely enough, thanks surely to hard work, and their skins become like well-soaped leather, thanks perhaps to good olive oil and garlic and an occasional *pastis*, all taken by mouth in daily doses. (Tomatoes are also thanked for continuing their female vigor, according to many of their mates. . . .)

In all, the Marseillaises seem almost a part of their craggy land, like the thick trunks of the most ancient olive trees on the hills behind the city. And still they are from the sea, so that they smell of salt, and of what they eat and what they work with, but never of old sweat.

When they walk down a street, they cleave its air like small solid wooden ships driven by a mysterious inner combustion. Their men walk close alongside, often with an arm around the woman's waist or over her broad solid shoulders, pilot-fish escorting a trusted shark.

There is always the same kind of man with them, once they are mature: as short or shorter, often as stocky or else as thin as an eel. They seem to know each other as if they were born from the same egg, but there is obvious sexual enjoyment in their familiarity, and they look necessary to each other and are mutually respectful. The woman seems the more enduring of most pairs, and walks a half-step ahead, and makes decisions about things like where to sit down at what café for how long, and what to drink, and when to walk away alone so that the man can stay with other men for a time, and charge his batteries with a round of cards.

There is certainly nothing humble or timid or placating about the men. They are as male in their short strong bodies as their women are female. But they are as if pulled along in life by the dominant magnetism of their partners. They are necessary to each other, equal in their hard work, but it is plain that the woman can and often does survive several of the men whose arms lie trustingly over her shoulders as they walk together, and it is rare to see an old fisherman alone, while there are many ageless women, even shorter and broader than before, who stump strongly about, and sell fish with voices that are only a little more commanding than they were thirty years ago.

The voice of any female born and raised around the Vieux Port from countless parents of the same stock, the short dark strong breed that is a mixture of every Mediterranean race that ever touched foot there, that voice is unforgettable, once heard. It is harsh, but not hoarse, and rough and deep without being in any sense masculine. It is like the woman, built close to the earth and as strong as stone. Probably it can be soft and beautiful, in love or motherhood, but it seems bred to direct its own fate, over the sounds of storm and battle and even modern traffic. Without any doubt, a healthy fishwife could call easily from one side of the Vieux Port to the other on a busy day, and I know one Marseillaise, who sells flowers instead of fish because she lost a leg during the Occupation, whose voice (and with a fine lilt to it) carries more than a block during the worst noontime bustle. (People buy flowers in Marseille much as they buy fresh sardines or bread, and noon is the time to snatch up a posy along with the loaves and fishes. . . .) Voices like hers and all her sisters' are never a shriek or shout: they are simply a part of the whole amazing strength of their bodies, basically indestructible.

All this is not to say that the mature women of Marseille can be called beautiful, at least in our Western vocabulary, spoken if not felt. They have a toughness in all their attributes that is past beguilement and gentle allure. Still, they remain completely female, and therefore feminine, and while they often both outwork and outlive their partners, they seem always to be treated with a special kind of courtesy, no matter with what apparently rough bonhomie.

I have no firsthand knowledge of the private life of heterosexual couples in the lower social and economic levels in Marseille, any more than I do that of other more affluent or notorious citizens, but in public there exists a patent and perhaps strange equality among the native working class. I have watched it for a long time, in public, along the Canebière and all around the Vieux Port.

Of course on the Quai du Port most of the females are young. They are the chicks of the Pinball Boys, waiting impassively to grow out of their sleazy modish clothes, and the figures that demand them, for the uniform of the thickened strong bodies of the mothers, who six days a week sell fish on the Quai des Belges and on Sundays and holidays may double there, behind the fuming pots of sugared nuts or the little ice-cream wagons. [. . .]

from THE FOOD OF ARTEMIS

[. . .] I think that I have eaten once or even many times in every fishhouse on [the Rive Neuve,] over the last forty-odd years. They change, of course, and occasionally die, or linger pitifully past their prime, half-empty. For several years now, a small Chinese restaurant has survived where a good fish place used to be. It smells all right, but of soy sauce and mushrooms rather than, more properly, of seaweed and shimmering cold fishes and plump shells. One or two of the places are stylishly decorated: modern "rustic" furniture, copper pans and Camarquais cattle-prods on the walls, flowers towering over the whimsical displays of fish or strawberry tarts. There are a few plainer places with paper tablecloths and napkins, ample servings of fish soup, unlabeled rosé in liter bottles. Every class of restaurant is crowded, all year round, as long as its fish is of today's catch and is treated with respect.

The Two Sisters' place is in between, aesthetically at least. It has a small glassed terrace with five or six tables pinched into it, a little restaurant, an upstairs room for celebrations along with a window display of fish and a few proud lobsters languidly waving their feelers, and a steeply banked stand of shellfish with an elderly relative opening them with feverish skill as customers order trays of whatever they want and can afford. The trays are put on the tables on wire legs about ten inches high, and the diners pick what is nearest to them if they are polite . . . or reach for what looks plumpest on the far side. People in the money, though, trying to impress a girlfriend or the boss, or ignorant of the current value of the franc in dollars, pounds, lire, marks, will usually eat oysters: expensive, so fresh that the delicate dark flanges recoil a little at the touch. They are for special treats.

One good way to taste two or three of them, not the costliest Belons of course, but tangy lesser breeds, is to order a *panaché*, a mixed platter of every shellfish on hand. It is pretty, and fun. Like all other such platters, the open shells lie on a bed of cold seaweed, sometimes laid over cracked ice in warm weather, with halved lemons in the center. There will be one or two kinds of mussels: small darkish ones cultivated at Bouziques, very pungent; large fat ones with pale or orange-colored flesh, from the rocks along the coast. There will be a few urchins, and at the Two Sisters', the shell man snips out a bigger hole than their mouth, or whatever it is, and they are rather gritty. Then there will be a few clams, fat and crisp, and several of their little cousins, the *clovisses*. (When I am eating these sweet clams, I wonder why I think they are more delicious than any oyster . . . until I taste an oyster again!) There will be some *violets* in the *panaché,* unless ones asks otherwise, and if I am alone I ask exactly that, for they are the one real disaster in the whole orderly chaos of Mediterranean sea life, for me at least. They seem like a mistake, somewhere along the path of natural creation. They are misshapen lumps of dun-colored spongy stuff, not shell, not skin, and inside they have a yellowish flesh, not sticky, not solid, not runny. People like them, and break open a *violet* and spoon or suck out the insides and smile. Like egg yolk but subtler, they say, and reach for another. I give away my share, if we are eating a *panaché* together, and slyly accept a clam or mussel in exchange. . . .

At most of the fish restaurants, there are little dingy shakers of vinegar for people who like it on shellfish, but I have never once seen anyone use it. In fact, most of the cut lemons on the shellfish seem to go back unsqueezed. Perhaps this is because the fish themselves are so succulent and cool and generally revivifying that nothing can make them better. They seem to breathe pure sea smell into the air, and to melt something of this same purity into their shells, to be drunk slowly, one long sip, after the meat has slid down our hot hungry gullets. It would be a pity to rush through such a salubrious inner bath as a platter of just-opened shellfish can give two-legged people, and a *panaché* needs a good half-hour of spaced concentration. Fortunately there are dozens of places in Marseille where this somewhat ritualistic enjoyment can be found and I know a lot of them, and by choice I would return without question to the Two Sisters', forever, or as long as they were there.

Once the two women are gone, the restaurant cannot possibly be the same, no matter how hard and well they have trained their relatives. They are as forceful as any females I have ever seen in a town well known for its ferociously strong ones, and I can well imagine them as young fish peddlers along the Quai des Belges, braying their strident quips to draw idlers and customers to their trays of the morning's catch. Possibly they worked along the sidewalk of the Rive Neuve, before they acquired the restaurant itself; they seem basically tough enough, even in their later years, to have stood up to the *entraîneuses'* dubious art of dragging clients into no matter how shoddy a fishhouse.

By the time I met them, more than twenty years ago, they looked as they still do: the younger one with dark hair and mocking but kind eyes, the older with grey-white hair and the almost benign face of a reliable client of Central Casting, always ready to play a gentle old granny, a saintlike elderly nun. Of the two women, I feel certain she is the tougher. Both of them seemed fed on tiger milk, and rubbed with a potent salve made by Artemis herself, of equal parts of olive oil, garlic, tomato paste, and rosé wine, blended with enough flesh of new sea urchins to make a thick paste. (When I have eaten with them, I feel as if some of it had been rubbed off on me. . . .) I can see them in bed making love and birthing children as easily as I can see them zipping through the restaurant from back kitchen to front glass door, watching every table, talking constantly.

There are always some waitresses and waiters to watch and supervise, or a *loup* to grill and flame, or a steaming bouillabaisse to serve in a storm of ladles-spoons-plates. People need to be seated, need more wine, need an extra pastry or a feast-day glass of cognac. The oyster man disappears into the back room for fresh supplies, and one of the Sisters opens mussels and clams twice as fast as he, while the other pulls a big lobster from the pile on top of the stand and holds it up triumphantly beside a table. "Look at its fat load of roe," she commands in a modified shriek, so that all the surrounding tables will fall silent to stare in awe. "What a superb female," she cries, whacking its belly casually, as if its claw were not reaching for any part of her to pinch, and then she runs toward the kitchen with it. Another group of clients stands up, and there is a rush for their coats, with both Sisters helping tuck them on like nannies with sated children. "Come back soon, come back," they call out onto the sidewalk, without losing a step in their routine dance.

And this goes on twice a day, six days a week. What we see is the top of the iceberg, as in any good restaurant. Beneath it is the real organization: the staff, both seen and invisible; the provisions, constantly checked and renewed; the upkeep of the whole small tight place, with all its linens, glasses, table fittings, and its essential fresh cleanliness. Above all, there is the skilled synthesis of fast and slow *people*, that they will work together on bad days and hectic festivals, through heat waves and the worst mistrals. (There is one niece or perhaps friend who is somewhat simple-minded, and who has been there as long as I can remember. She is unfailingly sweet-faced and attentive, and is very slow. One or the other of the Two Sisters is always nearby, watching to see if she needs a deft hand with the serving, never telling her to hurry. . . .) Such an operation lives or dies with the control of its leaders, in this case two women, and every time I return to its welcome hum and buzz, I know before even seeing them that both of them are there. I doubt that one could carry on without the other . . . run the joint so joyously, except perhaps by plain momentum for a long time. When that wears off, weariness will settle like dust on the absorbed bright faces of all the relatives, and perhaps younger people will buy the restaurant, and perhaps it will stay a good one. Even in Marseille, though, the secret of Artemis' salve is not known to everyone, and the Two Sisters, changeless as they may seem, cannot live much longer than the rest of us. Selfishly, I hope it will be longer than I do. [. . .]

FROM THE OPEN EYES

I

There are many people like me who believe firmly if somewhat incoherently that pockets on this planet are filled with what humans have left behind them, both good and evil, and that any such spiritual accumulation can stay there forever, past definition of such a stern word.

For some of us, it exists strongly in Stonehenge, for instance, and can be a bad or good experience, depending upon one's ability to accept non-Christian logic. Almost as puzzling as Stonehenge, once in my life, were the front steps of a small doleful cathedral in central France, where I soon knew that it would be best for me to leave, rather than try to locate my uneasiness of spirit.

Then there are kindlier and even restorative places, which like the bad or merely disturbing ones influence people whether or not they are aware of their vulnerability before such old forces. The half-ruined garden in the Misión de San Juan Capistrano in Southern California, as I knew it more than fifty years ago, was such a spot, in spite of its comparative youth, and I suspect that it still gives even casual tourists an extra gift of serenity, no matter how unexpected or unrecognized . . . and that the Franciscans may well have planted it there on ground that had been loved by the Indians long before.

But to counteract such good, there is another pocket of ageless influences that can affect most human beings dangerously, if they let it and even if they do not: the wild white crag of bauxite in southern France called Les Baux. It is clearly a menace to us because of the accumulation of vicious brutality that has gone on there from the first greedy prehistoric Baussenques, who lived only for money, to Wise Man Balthazar's ruthless descendants, who lived only for power won through the graces of his holy star with its sixteen rays.

There have always been sorceresses and female prophets in Les Baux, whether from Rome or Romany. The treacherous grottoes carved by wind and human greed are peopled by millions of bats, called the mosquitoes of Hell, and there are remote black antechambers for nightmares and exorcism, and long dangerous tunnels leading to the Phantoms' Cave, and finally the Place of the Black Beast Himself. There is a buried Moorish treasure, deep somewhere, too horrible to dare search out. A

Golden Goat guards its keys, and often runs noisily through the narrow crooked paths of the fortress, kicking down obscene sexual symbols that crop up ceaselessly on the immense stones.

The Church has tried for several hundred years to dissipate this gathering of evil spirits in Les Baux, and in the end has got rid of all but one of its pagan ceremonies, so that the famous enactment on Christmas Eve of Christ's birth is a controlled gentle version fit for family viewing, complete with watered-down pre-Christian symbols, and pretty with traditional tunes from costumed piper and drummer.

And up on the wide meadow, so high above the Valley of the Rhône that often the sea is visible, near to the steep cliffs from which live captives used to be pitched by the descendants of St. Balthazar, there is a great cross, completely useless if it is meant to quell the incredible evil of the place, whose force has built up until now one wonders how it would be possible to live on that mighty rock, even as a guide or postcard seller . . . why the gentle little lamb (Lamb of God, in his cage blazing with lighted candles for the sacrifice), and the flower-hung powerful ran pulling him toward the altar to the tune of fife and drum . . . why they don't wither and die, each Christmas Eve. What would happen if the Church let them march straight out to the cross near the deadly cliffs, instead of only up the short nave of the chapel? Would the bats sing? Would the grottoes glow with their own answer to the holy candles?

Possibly not even an atomic bomb could unsettle, for very long, the collection of such an ancient mysterious mecca of damned souls. But of course not all the souls that have stayed in Les Baux have been damned, any more than all the people who built Stonehenge were filled with an awesome knowledge of celestial logic, or than the captive Indians who built San Juan Capistrano for their priestly invaders were filled with gratitude and joy. Both good and evil rimmed these receptacles perforce. Evil and good have been yeasts, bacilli, and one or the other has taken over, the way cancer or syphilis can either gain control of a human body or lurk in the shadows, held at bay by natural, spiritual, and even scientific forces.

The ancient port-city of Marseille, some fifty miles south of Les Baux, has a reputation for wickedness that is certainly wider spread than almost any other's in the world, partly because so many millions have passed through there and found what they were looking for, but unlike Les Baux, it seems to remain basically healthy. However, if one subscribes to the theory that some places collect curses or blessings as if they were pockets to be filled, buckets, vases, then it would be easy to blame the bad reputation of Marseille on some such thing as its three hundred years of building and servicing the galleys there and keeping them filled with slaves and criminals, most of them sending out great stinking auras of hatred.

The first galley made in France was toward the end of the fourteenth century in the Vieux Port, and it served as one of numberless fighting vessels built and docked in Marseille's shipyards. In 1385 the local fishermen outfitted one to protect their boats from pirates, and as the Church grew in strength, archbishops had their own escorts of slave-powered galleys, and carved saints rode every prow, from Michael to the Holy Sinner Magdalen. In 1533, for the marriage of Catherine de Médicis with the Duke of Orléans, there were eighteen royal galleys in port, and by 1696 Louis XIV kept forty-two galleys in Marseille waters, all outfitted and ready to fight.

The galleys designed and built in the great yards of the Vieux Port were called Marsilians, and were known wherever men rode the waves, for their two rudders and their catlike maneuverability. They could turn this way and that, and sneak up silently on any foe, for any prey.

These cats were manned by human beings who, if they were kept in good condition by their owners, could row six knots an hour through any tide or weather. And from an edict signed in 1564 by King Charles IX, they were either Frenchmen condemned to forced labor, or Mussulmen captured in war or bought as slaves, all called Turks but made up of real Levantines, or Senegalese Blacks, or North African barbarians. Their average price was high, around four hundred pounds, and they were bartered for, and traded, exactly as if they were precious silk or jute.

The Turks in Marseille were given their own mosque and cemetery. To keep things decent, captured French slaves in Constantinople also had a special chapel built for them. Everything was fair and square, and the bills of lading read like:

> Bought at Mallorca by order of Lord Beaufort:
> | For 9 Turks: | 6,453 | pounds |
> |---|---|---|
> | For Customs Duty: | 645 | " |
> | For Purchasing Agent: | 32 | " |
> | For Boarding-Vessel: | 16 | " |
> | | 7,146 | pounds |
>
> Signed: Séguin, Consul

There was hateful rivalry between the costly Turks and the cost-free French galley slaves, used cannily by their captains, of course, but little chance to express it. Mostly the men lived and died on their benches, chained by one leg, and wearing a gag around the neck that was ready to pop into the mouth on order, to prevent talk and make the ears more alert for commands. For a time all the slaves wore red caps like a brand, but later they had none at all against the sun and the sleet. Their officers were armed with a stick, a whip, and a lash. . . .

If a man became patently useless at his oar, he could be bought off: a Frenchman cost one high-placed purchase and replacement, but a Turk needed two backers and then two more Turks in his place. Madame de Sévigné more than once finagled galley spots for troublesome young countrymen in the seventeenth century . . . much as reputable Americans bought positions for their unwanted siblings or enemies in both sides of the Civil War. This exchange solved unwelcome political, domestic, and perhaps financial problems, and the risk of a resentful or even murderous revenge was slight.

The galleys of Marseille were from the first a tourist attraction, and perhaps it was there and then that pocket-picking became an art that still thrives, I am told, in broad daylight along the Canebière, on the Cours Belsunce, in murkier corners. It is said, for instance, that one bishop went on board a new galley to give it and the slaves his official blessing, and announced that he defied any man there to take his wallet, but when he left he found that he was without the heavy gold episcopal cross worn around his neck.

Once in port, often three or four thousand slaves at a time were housed in enormous barracks at the southeast end of the little harbor, used also for shipbuilding, sword sharpening, and the countless parties so dear to the city: the men would shout huzzahs like trained seals at a given signal, raise their oars in forty galleys at a time before the City Hall for some visiting admiral or prince, and sit helplessly under thousands of paper lanterns on the brightened water, while people danced and bands played.

Louis XIV loved to make war, or at least to have a good force behind him in case things came to that point, and by the end of the seventeenth century Marseille was the hub of his fighting navy, for building, arming, and maintaining an astonishing fleet of the subtle, sneaky, Marsilian galleys. A new Arsenal was built, an engineering marvel, from its prison barracks and ironworks and road factories to the elegant Commanders' House, hung with Gobelin tapestries, a fine place for celebrating everything from the King's recovery from a head cold to the overnight stay of one of his grandchildren. Three balls could go on there at once, complete with specially written operas and great suppers.

There was a real hospital for the condemned men, however, in those grand days: six big wards for the Turks to one for the French. This practical as well as merciful provision came from a gentleman of Provence named Gaspard de Simiane-la-Coste, apparently the only such benefactor without a statue in that country given to their erection in any and every little park or cranny. Above the hospital wards was the armory, rising up in four galleries around a covered hall, and known to house the most beautiful war implements in the world. It was a sight to behold, and countless travellers did so, and there were grand parties, at which living tableaux were given to martial music, with symbolic representations of Louis XIV's might, ringed by kneeling Turks hung with golden chains that were exchanged for their own irons as soon as the shows were over.

The Arsenal was, well before 1700, a city in itself, and employed free men along with its forced labor. Some of the slaves were allowed to go outside, and gradually they built shacks across the Vieux Port where under constant guard they could carry on their old trades as tailors, toymakers, and weavers. Many more men were used as domestics by the officers and rich citizens. They were returned to the Arsenal at night, and any Marseillais who let one escape was fined the price of a new Turk.

Once, during the dreadful Plague of 1720, Marseille ran out of gravediggers, and on August 8, twenty-six Turks were put into service, with the promise of their liberty. Two days later, however, they were all dead. Fifty-three more, then eighty, then a hundred and another hundred men were sent into the nightmare around the Port.

The job was to pick up the bodies, pile them onto carts, and dump them into the great ditches dug hastily for them. Twelve hundred people a day were dying, and on September 16, a brave gentleman named Roze commandeered enough galley slaves to clear a thousand cadavers off one of the quays, where they had lain for some three weeks, in less than half an hour. A commemorative plaque and a bust were erected to him. And back at the Arsenal, while only four men survived this forced service, the air was kept "perfumed" and most of the galleys were moved out of the Old Port, and of ten thousand slaves only about seven hundred died.

By the middle of the eighteenth century there were only eleven galleys left in Marseille, thanks largely to the fact that naval activities had been moved on down to Toulon and that slavery was beginning to seem "un-Christian." By 1784 the Arsenal had been sold by the King to outside speculators, since Marseille did not want to buy it, and only two galleys were left to be viewed by the tourists and then carted off. One of them, *La Patience*, served in the invasion of Egypt from Toulon in 1784, and was manned by free volunteers and then scrapped.

And by now nothing is left of the Arsenal . . . except that some people sense a pool of spiritual agony there where for hundreds of years men who had been ripped from their homelands by force, war, politics, must live and die chained to their oars or in their prison barracks. Up around the Opera, where the Hospital and Armory once stood, there are countless shady little hotels with their listless women waiting outside, and behind them rooms for shadier pleasures. Along the Rive Neuve, above the fish-bistros, there are "clubs" of varied repute, offering even more varied diversions to their members. Farther down toward the wholesale fish market, La Criée, and back of the waterfront, there are gathering places called names like the Galley Slave and the One-Eyed Pirate, where loops of tiny lightbulbs twinkle at odd hours, and sounds of bad dance-music seep up from the sidewalk, and some of the toughest girls I have ever seen lead young men toward the dark.

All of this is part of what was left by countless slaves who sweated blood and hatred and lust there. It will continue. A mysterious thing about Marseille, though, is that its collective evil is balanced by a wonderful healthiness. This too is what the galley slaves have left: the children they sowed in the sturdy stock of the Massilians, the children of Greek sailors from Phocea, and of wandering hardy tribes behind them, the prehistoric salt gatherers.

The reason, perhaps, for this balance of evil and good influences on the people of any such place is that it can be, as in Marseille, deeply religious.

It is "Christian" now, in the sense that this form of worship is the last manifestation of its ageless need for altars, altars behind altars, idols behind idols. It needs something to shout to and to dance around, to curse and to beseech, and because it is a natural gathering place on the globe for such human necessities, saints and sinners have collected there around the Vieux Port as irrevocably as water runs downhill.

When young Protis found himself married to the king's daughter and ruler of half the port-land, all in a few hours, he accepted the whole startling situation as a direct command of Artemis, the protector of sailors and therefore his own goddess. As soon as possible he built a temple to her, on the high northern hill above the city, and brought from Ephesus in Greece a handsome statue of her in her mummy-like wrappings covered with symbols and then her magnificent torso with its eighteen breasts in two vertical lines. She was accompanied by a famous priestess. A much simpler temple was built to Apollo, somewhat lower toward the sea with its face looking out for mariners, but Artemis must face inland, to watch ferociously the creatures of the hunt and to frighten off barbarians.

GARE DE LYON

Paris fairs and expositions, always attempted and sometimes realized on a grand scale, have been beset, at least in the twentieth century, by strikes, riots, floods, and other natural and man-made hindrances to such minor goals as opening on time. In the same way, they have left something strong and beautiful behind them, whether tangible or in men's minds and hearts.

In 1937, for instance, there was the Internationale. Strikes were an almost stylish necessity of life in those quaintly distant days before all hell broke loose, and the fair lagged in summer heat while opulent or simply eager tourists marked time in the cafés and museums; outlandish buildings were put up and torn down and picketed and sabotaged. I was there from Switzerland to meet my parents, who loved great fairs, as do most Midwesterners reared on St. Louis and Chicago and even San Francisco shivarees, and my father was excited by the violent scornful unrest in that year's Parisian air, as he had never been at home by giant mechanical toys like roller coasters.

We walked every day in the purlieus of the Exposition, to guess when a pavilion might possibly be opened or bombed. At night we looked at the lighted revolving statue of bright gold in the U.S.S.R. exhibit, but Father did not want to visit it, for vaguely political reasons. Once we went on the Seine in a *bateau-mouche,* and he was thrilled when every window in the Citroën plant was filled with striking beleaguered workers saluting us with raised fists. Nothing like that at home!

But from that fair, which never really came to life for us who waited, rose one bright star, the Guernica mural by Picasso. It was there. It was on view. It was well guarded. It was moving and terrible, and we went perhaps five times to look slowly at it, close up, far off, not talking. It was a difficult experience for my father, but one he faced with an almost voluptuous acceptance, so that we began to return compulsively to the long room where the painting unrolled itself. There were piles of rubble and discarded tools on the unfinished paths outside the building, but inside people walked silently up and down, finding parts of themselves in Guernica, even from Iowa and California.

Backwards to 1931, there was a fair called the Exposition Coloniale. As far as I know, some of it opened more or less on schedule, at least in time to assemble peculiar exotic hints of the imminent collapse of French attempts to keep their own sun shining around the clock on territorial land grabs. What else could it try to demonstrate? Why else would a reputedly thrifty nation spend hundreds of thousands of francs re-creating African villages and Indo-Chinese temples for visitors to gape at? From now in Time, it all seemed then to have some of the luminous gaiety of a terminal cancer patient's final defiant fling. I lurched about on camels, and watched silent backs squatting in front of their phony huts to carve cabalistic masks. Everywhere there was a heady perfume of leather, of raw silk and wool, of unknown spicy foods. As in the Internationale that came so few years afterwards, the Coloniale had a dappled green magic, under the summer leaves, and left behind it more than its rare polished woods and supple cloth.

But both those fairs seemed unreal. They were *there*, in spite of strikes and riots and general political uncertainty, but where are their physical traces? Where is the cardboard Angkor Wat by now? The painting of Guernica still exists, but where is the long shady building that harbored it? Where is the golden statue that revolved seductively, almost lewdly, above the Soviet pavilion? In the end, where are the dreams and wars that spawned all that pomp?

It was perhaps different in 1900. The hunger and shame of the Franco-Prussian War had been half forgotten by a new generation, and the Dreyfus Affair seemed temporarily under wraps. Paris needed and indeed deserved a circus. Architects were appointed, perhaps subconsciously, who could evoke all the rich weightiness of the Third Empire, before the late and current troubles, and they put together some pleasure domes for their fair that still enchant us: two palaces, the Grand and the Petit; the bridge across the Seine named for Alexander the Third; best of all, to some at least, the Gare de Lyon.

It happened before my time, and the French accounts are understandably vague about how and when that World's Fair finally ground into action. It seems natural, by now, that the enormous glassy station was formally inaugurated a year late, but it is still there to prove that in 1901, on April 17, the President of the Republic and countless international notables gathered in it to declare that the Gare de Lyon was indeed a reality.

No doubt other very solemn things have happened there in almost a century, like treaty signings and top-level hanky-panky connected with both railroads and people, and municipal banquets, but it is hard to imagine that they did not contain a certain element of enjoyment, in that magical place. Surely the ceremonial toasts tasted better there. . . .

As far as I can know or learn, no other railroad station in the world manages so mysteriously to cloak with compassion the anguish of departure and the dubious ecstasies of return and arrival. Any waiting room in the world is filled with all this, and I have sat in many of them and accepted it, and I know from deliberate acquaintance that the whole human experience is more bearable at the Gare de Lyon in Paris than anywhere else. By now the public rooms on the train level are more plastic-topped, chromium-benched, than in the first days of wood everywhere, with iron and brass fittings. But the porters seem to stay sturdy and aware, and there is a near-obsolete courtesy at the "snack bars," even five minutes before commute time.

For me, it began to come to life in 1937. I was there often, from 1929 on, always one more ant scuttling for a certain track, a cheap train south to Dijon, a luxury train to Lausanne. The station was something to run through. It was a grimy glass tunnel, and I felt glad when we pulled out and headed south.

But in 1937, when I could meet my parents in La Ville Lumière, I grew almost shockingly aware of the station. I went there early that twilight, to wait for their train. On the quai that looked far out under the glass roof and along all the gleaming tracks was a café, part of the big noisy bar-brasserie inside. There were little trees in long boxes, to sweeten the air and catch the soot, and the tables were of that grey-white marble that apparently was created by Nature solely for café tabletops. I sat waiting, drinking a brandy and water, realizing suddenly that I was not in a station, but in a place.

My family arrived, worn after a rough crossing, and it was not for perhaps ten days that I went back. My father was going down to Nice. For the first of countless times I cunningly arranged our getting around Paris so that we would have to *wait* for the train to slide in under the glass roof along the silver track, so that I could be there . . . in the place.

It was one of the pleasantest times I'd ever known with a man I'd always respected and loved. We were two people, suddenly. We sat behind the boxes filled with gritty treelings, and although it was only late morning we drank slowly at brandy again, with water and casual talk and mostly a quiet awareness of the loveliness of the great station.

It was not noisy. It was not stuffy. People did not look sad or even hurried. Trains whistled and chugged in and out, slid voluptuously toward us and then stopped. Big boards lit up here and there, high above the tracks, telling people where to go, when. A porter came to tell me that it was time for the gentleman to board.

"This is the way to do it! How can a railroad station be so beautiful?" my father asked happily, and I knew that I had marked off another mile in my life.

Then there was a war, and when I went back to Paris in the early fifties, I scuttled through without more than a shy shamed look at the glassed roof that the Occupiers had found too essential to destroy. I did not permit the station's magic to take hold again until about the mid-sixties, when I went alone to Paris, for the first time in my life: no husbands—lovers—parents—children . . . I was on a writing assignment, and I asked to be lodged in the attic of a hotel on the Seine in a room I liked most. My husband and I had planned, before the War and he died, to rent two little connecting rooms there and make a kind of pied-à-terre, a place where we could leave books and be warmer than in Switzerland. This all turned impossible, and when I went back so much later I felt scared, so that I asked to take one of those familiar rooms. And in the other, to my astonishment, lived a person I admired deeply named Janet Flanner. It was fine. My husband would have liked it.

And so it happened that I reported, that summer, to my friend about my love affair with the Gare de Lyon, and she in turn decided to take her own look, her view she admitted had always been sketchy in spite of some forty years in Paris, and with due reflection she reported the whole thing to André Malraux, who then controlled the governmental wires that could declare a French relic or monument legitimately "historical," and therefore supposedly immune to further human destruction.

Malraux had a rare and passionate belief in "the redemptive power of beauty," and seemed to know that a minor living art form is far more vital than a major dead one. From what I have been told, he started at once to safeguard the shabby old restaurant in the Gare de Lyon, so that by now it is a twinkling *Monument Historique*, worthy of all that was opulently cheerful, generously vulgar and delightful, about *la Belle Époque*.

Things were different from my lives before, in the mid-sixties. The job demanded that I go between Paris and the South quite often, and I was looked at as freakish because I insisted on taking the Mistral train from the station instead of flying. A waste of time, of energy, I was told by my bosses. But nobody could understand how totally renewing of many strengths it was for me to go there at least two hours before the beautiful train pulled out, to eat a slow breakfast, and then slide southward through the forests and farms and into Burgundian vineyards and then suddenly, like an explosion, into the Midi below Lyon . . . and on down, through poignantly familiar towns like Avignon to the spot past the Étang de Berre, just before the Quartier de St. Louis in Marseille, where there is a mysterious flash of gold from the tiny needle of Notre Dame de la Garde.

From then on it was less emotional sailing, with cliffs and twisted pines and strange villas, until I got to the familiar little station in Cannes and the resumption of my professional life, but always I felt brave enough for it, after the private meal in Paris.

The main room of the First-Class Restaurant-Buffet at the Gare de Lyon seems to run the whole length of what to us Americans is the second floor. Actually, if one enters by way of the noble staircase from the inside quai of the station, there are several rooms of varying importance to the left, closed and reserved for board meetings and other mysterious gatherings. Mostly, pundits and tycoons heading for them use a smaller staircase that goes up under the Clock Tower, and never set foot in the enormous Restaurant. (The Big Ben Bar and the cloakrooms are conveniently to their right as they enter.)

To the rest of us travelers, going up the staircase from the quai is much more exciting than the handy little "back stairs," and the huge room sweeps out, dream-like and yet inviting, and across from us the lace curtains move faintly in the drafts from the great square below.

Down at the far end, to our right, the Train Bleu is properly hushed and somewhat more elegant, if that is possible, than what any traveler can expect in the main room, only tacitly separated from its little offshoot. Service is swift or slow, according to one's logistical needs, and there is a comfortable feeling of *bourgeois* polish and sparkle everywhere: clean linen and brass, waxed floors, good plain food as well as a few fastuous dishes. Madame Maigret would approve of it. So, I feel sure, would Brillat-Savarin, if it were not some 150 years too late. . . .

It is one of the most amazing public dining rooms I have ever seen, or even imagined. The ceiling is very high and elaborate. The windows are tall, looking on one side upon a goodly part of Paris, and then to the right into and under the endless stretch of grey glass roof over all the tracks that come to a dead stop down below . . . Switzerland, Italy, Spain, the Near East, all France to the south. . . .

The walls, between and above the great lace-hung windows, are covered with more than forty huge murals of every possible scenic delight that the Paris-Lyon-Mediterranean trains could offer their travelers at the turn of the century, mostly peopled by plump Edwardian diplomats in top hats, and famous divas and courtesans in filmy garden frocks or even bathing dresses, all frolicking discreetly against breath-taking landscapes.

By now, the paintings have been cleaned, and their elaborate frames retouched. The lace curtains have been mended and starched and rehung, and the three monumental ceilings with their "crammed and gorgeous" paintings have been pulled back to life in our comparatively clean air, after years of collecting soot from the old steam trains below. And all the elegant *bancs* and chairs, comfortable in dark soft leather, have been refurbished, along with the sumptuous but functional brass racks for luggage and hats, and the tall lampstands along the middle aisle.

Perhaps best, at least for the waiters, is that the endless polished floors underfoot have been strengthened or repaired, so that there is no longer the steady creaking that I first noticed, when I listened there in the sixties.

I am not sure, by now, why I first decided to go to this station two hours before train time. Perhaps I wanted to sit where I had once been with my father. Perhaps I wanted to ready my spirit for the new job in the South. A porter (oh, a fine man, an angel in a blue soft blouse! I remember him clearly: tall, past middle age, oddly protective of me as was exactly right on that day . . .) told me when I asked to follow him to the café on the inside quai that he thought I would be better off upstairs, where he would come for me in ample time before the Mistral left. I felt docile, and followed him under the Clock Tower and past the end of the big noisy brasserie-café on the ground floor and up some back stairs, into the shrouded silent corridors of the First-Class Restaurant. I had never been there before.

He pounded on ahead of me with my luggage, and a waiter who knew him came from somewhere past the deserted old Big Ben Bar. My porter went straight down the middle aisle of what seemed like a silent gaudy cathedral to me, and stopped toward the far end, which as I remember was being remodeled for the new Train Bleu section.

"Madame is hungry," he said in a mild way to his friend. "She is taking the Mistral. I'll be back." I felt helpless but undismayed. This was part of important private history, I sensed.

The waiter was surprisingly young to be working in such an awesome monument. He gave me a menu, and I settled myself in the huge sunny temple while he went down to the newsstand where I had planned to sit in all the sooty racket behind a spindly box tree, drinking *café au lait*. When he came up again with two very solemn dailies, I told him that I would like bread and butter, Parma ham, and a half-bottle of a *brut* champagne that seemed quite expensive to me and that is no longer on the excellent wine list. He looked pleased, and scudded off, with the floor under him making a fine high racket in the emptiness.

In 1967 or whenever that was, I felt dismal about the state of bread in Paris, and had not yet found that it would be almost as bad everywhere, and I decided then that the fresh loaf served at the Gare de Lyon was the best I had tasted since before World War II. (It still is.) The butter was impeccable, not something from a tinfoil wrapping marked with either optimism or blasphemy *Beurre d'Isigny*. The ham was genuine, perhaps tasting of violets on the wishful tongue. The champagne seemed one of the best I had ever drunk.

The waiter saw that I was more interested in where I was than in where the grim newspaper editorials were telling me to be, and he stood tactfully beside the table while I asked him about some of the murals. He knew a lot, in a controlled but fervent way that I had long recognized in devotees. Now and then he flicked at one of my crumbs, to stay professional.

Then the handsome, thoughtful, strong, blue-bloused, honest, punctual porter beckoned to me from the gigantic doorway that opened onto cloakrooms and the Big Ben Bar and the far closed doors of a Belle Époque palace, and I left without sadness, knowing that I would return. I turned back at the end of the corridor, and the waiter lifted the bottle of champagne where I had left one glassful, and bowed and smiled. I felt fine about everything, even my job . . . generous, warm, floaty.

The next time that I cannily arranged to be in Paris so that I would have to take the Mistral again, I went somewhat earlier to the station. I forget whether there were only two waiters that morning, or whether it was later on, when I suddenly looked up from my habitual little meal and saw four or five of them drifting around the table. Mostly they were young, but there were some old ones, too, and they had decided they knew me, and what they had apparently decided to share with me was horrendous.

The Restaurant, they said, was doomed. *"One" ("they"* in our lingo) had decided that it was too old to live. The famous lace curtains were in tatters. The paintings were out of date, and filthy with some seventy years of soot and general neglect and pollution. The floors buckled under the weight of the men's trays. Yes, a promising young chef, probably a madman like them all, had opened the Train Bleu. But who but stunned starved travelers would come up to such a drab old wreck as this? "It is a crime of neglect," they said furiously, very quietly, as they stood around my table. "It must not happen. This beautiful thing must not be condemned to death . . . "

I looked at them, so proud, and at the gleaming glass and silver and linen and at my little meal, and then past all of it to the bedraggled lace, the dim dirty light, the flaking gold leaf above us. I would like to think that I said firmly, "Something will be done." The truth is that I probably whimpered a little as I let the men bustle me down the stairs to the train for the South.

I talked about all this, though, with my Paris neighbor, Janet. I told her about how passionately concerned the waiters were. And it went on from there. And by now the Gare de Lyon is in comparatively fine fettle, no way an aging beauty revived by hormones, but rather a mature female who has survived some unpredictable if foregone setbacks with good health and gracefulness.

Much is going on under the five storeys of the mansarded structure of 1900 (". . . a fairly discreet evocation of the Belle Époque," one government document describes it with equal discretion), and within a few years most of suburban Paris will commute from six deep layers of artful stations being burrowed out, for various environmental reasons. Currently, ridiculous bright-orange awnings in a garishly scooped shape have been placed over the seven majestic windows on the "Paris" side of the Restaurant floor, but doubtless they will fade, and fall off.

The interior style of this giant station is "pure 1900," whatever that may mean. On the ground floor thousands of people push in and out, buying tickets and meeting uncles and going somewhere, and the café-brasserie is always open and crowded. On the "train" side, the little trees in front of the marble-topped tables were sparse or gone when I last saw them in 1974, and the newsstand did not have its old inky glamour. This could be partly because I too was older and Colette and Simenon had stopped churning out their paperbacks, and partly because travelers do not feel as leisurely as they did when I once sat there with my father. By now there are snack-bar counters inside the busy buffet, and people drink and eat hastily. But a graceful stairway still leads upward, under the glass sky, and instead of one's being alone in the bright huge Restaurant, there seem always to be some *people*. They read newspapers or talk quietly at odd hours like my own; the place buzzes gently, like a rococo hive, all carvings and paintings and gilt.

Conceivably gentlemen throng at proper hours around the Big Ben Bar, where "all the cocktails of the Belle Époque" are said to be served . . . along with the British (and by now international) substitute of whiskey and water for the sweet pinkish drinks of 1900. (I have never seen a barman there, but then, neither have I seen more than a few travelers in the Restaurant at nine-thirty in the morning . . .)

Once in the seventies I ate an early lunch rather than a late breakfast in the Grande Salle. It was moderately filled with middle-class people who looked as if they were going somewhere soon, which of course they were. They ate quickly but seriously, in general the *plat du jour*, and read newspapers or peeked at their watches, or talked quietly with Aunt Matilda, who was going to see her first grandchild in Montélimar. The waiters glided miles and miles on the gleaming new floors. The incredibly long lace curtains pushed in and out over half-open windows onto the square, but there seemed little city noise. The ceiling with its three enormous murals looked somewhat lower since it had been cleaned, and the walls glowed richly. I walked about, looking at the paintings I liked best, sipping a "Kir au Chablis," and the waiters smiled at me as if they knew we shared a fine secret, which of course they did not know at all. Or did they?

I drank a Grand Cru Chablis, three years in bottle, feeling as extravagant as one of the well-kept women in the glamorous murals high above me, and ate a fine little soufflé of shellfish and mushrooms. Wood strawberries were listed, and their mysterious perfume would have suited the sudden sensuality of the meal, but the waiter shook his head. So I ate dark small raspberries with the rest of the wine, and leaned back to look at the ceiling crammed with color, in carved gilded curlicues, high above the incredible walls covered with their gaudily leering murals, all gold-scarlet-blue, a gigantic jumble of snowy Alps, fishing boats, trains, women, politicians, vineyards . . .

Even in its dingier days since 1901, the Gare de Lyon had stayed alive, I thought beautifully, and had made tired travelers stretch and smile. It had, one baffled but delighted writer said, "great harmony in spite of its decadent extravagance."

Yes, that was it: a strange massive *harmony!*

I thought of my friend Janet, who had grown angry with herself after she went there to lunch quietly alone, a double wonder for a person of her gregarious volatility. She felt baffled about not using, ever in her long years in Paris, more than the quick dashes through the station and onto the quais for trains going south to Lyon and then east and west and on further. She groaned, and scolded helplessly at human blindness.

Often people try to keep secret the charm of a tiny restaurant one thousand light-years from nowhere around the corner, in case there will not be a free table the next time they are hungry for its inimitable broth or brew. But who can hide the secret of a colossus like the Gare de Lyon, where thousands of people rush or amble through every day, according to the trains they must catch or leave or even think about?

Inside, under the misty glass, in the music of wheels and horns and whistled strange signals, there are signs guiding passengers to the toilets, the newsstand, the café, the Buffet, the upstairs Restaurant, the Train Bleu. There is no attempt to hide any of this vital and perhaps aesthetic information.

It comes down, I suppose, to a question of where one really chooses to be, and for how long. This is of course true of all such traffic hubs as railway stations, but nowhere is there one with a second floor like that of the Gare de Lyon, so peculiarly lacy and golden. It has, in an enormous way, something of the seduction of a full-blown but respectable lady, post-Renoir but pre-Picasso, waiting quietly in full sunlight for a pleasant chat with an old lover . . .

Glen Ellen, 1979

NOWHERE BUT HERE

It is very simple: I am here because I choose to be.

"Here" is a ranch on Route 12 in northern California, about two miles from Glen Ellen, where Jack London lived and drank and piled up the reddish volcanic stones of the region into strong clumsy walls, towers, cattle troughs, a dam. He devised a kind of sled drawn by oxen to come here for some of his best rocks, from up in the Ranch Canyon, where they have lain since Mount St. Helena blew its top about six million years ago, about twenty-five miles northeast of here as a tipsy crow would fly.

Some fifty feet south of my house there is a pile of the same rocks that flew through the air during the mighty blow. By now, native trees have grown up through their rich cracks and crannies: bay, madrona, live oak. One of the great rocks landed with its flat side up, to make a fine table. When the foundations of my little palace had been laid, more than ten years ago, some dear friends and I sat there on the other stones, and one of us ran along the top of the new walls, sprinkling a bottle of champagne on them in a ritual of goodwill that was actively religious.

And that was almost surely the first and last time that the flat rock has ever had a tablecloth on it, because I soon observed that the great pile was a perfect cool dark bastion for the rattlesnakes that still consider this their rightful territory. The day of the Blessing, they were courteous, recognizing our naïveté, but soon even my cat decided to stay away from their compound as long as they stayed off ours. We do not bother one another, even with more winy ceremonies.

It probably took a long time for those flying boulders to cool off, but by now they are beautiful and mossy to look at, and to leave alone.

Jack London was a born builder, no matter how untrained, and the man (David Pleydell-Bouverie) who owns this ranch is another, although highly shaped and skilled, and neither one could leave the rocks where they had fluttered down, as in my tumultuous little grove. Where London had his oxen drag their slow heavy loads for many miles, to build a gawky trough or a strangely perfect dam, David Bouverie simply hauled material down from his canyon to construct bell towers and gateways and suchlike. Where London was touchingly uncouth, Bouverie has been almost lightsome in his use of the seemingly limitless supply of solid ash that flew here.

To the east of my house, plumb with two tall stone gateposts that are in turn plumb with the bell tower, I look through and past them toward the mountains that separate Napa and Sonoma valleys. Between my house and the Tower are vineyards, and hidden from me as the Canyon curves back toward Napa there is the Waterfall. It is about 150 feet tall, and in winter I can hear it roar. At its base, behind the curtain of water that falls into a lovely pool, there is a long deep cave where Indians often hid, I'm told, from the white men.

The bell tower is mysteriously correct for this landscape. It is at once monolithic and graceful, unlike most of Jack London's piles of stone, and was built piece by piece by Bouverie and a local mason, of course Italian. It houses a fine bell, which Bouverie sometimes insists is the only reason he built the Tower.

He bought the big bell from Old Man Hearst, as one of the countless rejects from the European booty that now loads the castle at San Simeon. In a capricious joke, it was priced at thirty-six dollars, to be paid on the spot. Years later, one of the Old Man's sons offered Bouverie a hundred times that for it, but by then it was so firmly a part of this Valley, to see from the highway or to hear when the wind is right, that such a sale was unthinkable. It rings almost every day of the year, at sundown: twenty-one strong measured pulls. At midnight on New Year's Eve it is pealed longer, faster, louder. . . .

Ringing the bell, first made to summon monks here and there in a Spanish monastery, is no easy trick. Now and then a newcomer to the Ranch will ask to give it a few pulls, and its uneven stutter is painful. The appointed ringer, presently, is Jason King, going on fourteen, and after a few timid tryouts (ringing a big bell is like painting with watercolors: once it's started, there is no turning back . . .), this lanky redhead is in control, so that even the finality of the end of another day is acceptable in his weighty music. The bell rope is on the east side of the Tower, and hidden from me, but I often smile at the suspicion that my young friend is airborne at the end of it, no matter how seasoned and sure his peals sound.

When Jason, or his father the Foreman, or Bouverie the Builder swings up and down on the long rope, I go like a moth to the candle flame and stand on my East Balcony until the twenty-one rings have sounded. Then I stretch my arms and wave them, as the ringer steps around from the back of the Tower. There is no use to shout to him, for he is deafened in his cocoon of sound waves. He lifts his arms to me. It is a twilight ritual, sprung surely from some atavistic pattern.

On the north side of my house there was, for a few years anyway, a planted grove of several kinds of eucalypti, tall and healthy. Then in about 1974 there was a freakish period of day and night temperatures of under 20 degrees Fahrenheit, for eight days. It started early one morning, while I was staying overnight in San Francisco, and when I got home, everything was frozen tight. The pipes at this ranch never burst, as did most of them in our part of the Valley, but they were solid ice for much more than a week.

By then I'd lived here for several years, and was in close trusting relationship with the other people who lived all the time on the Ranch, whether the Boss was gone or not.

Joseph Herger, who had been Foreman here since the Ranch took shape in the forties, was a doughty Swiss peasant, a milker by trade, who had "pulled tits," as he put it, until he moved onto this 500 acres of wild country and started pulling poison ivy and pulling fence posts and pulling loads of cow pats into the gardens. And right then, in the Big Freeze, he was very ill with some kind of influenza. He lived in an isolated cabin, because he was a loner.

Phyllis Whitman, the Housekeeper, was really in charge of the Ranch when Bouverie was not here. She was and is a strong forceful person, at her best in emergencies, but also admirable at the kitchen stove. (Now she is far away, remarried after a sad widowhood.) And she looked after Joseph from her house in the Ranch compound, while I drove every day to nearby Boyes Springs to get water from a friend's outside hydrant, which by a fluke had not frozen.

I would load my station wagon with every big kettle from the Ranch kitchens and mine, and fill them with a hose and then ease back to the Ranch, trying not to slosh too much over the two cattle guards between the Ranch houses and the highway. (They are made of old rails salvaged when tracks were pulled out to prove that it was more patriotic to buy cars than to travel by train.)

Then Phyllis and I would flush all our toilets. Joe's and mine took only a few gallons of water, since we lived alone. Phyllis needed more, because some of her many children still lived here. That was when I decided firmly that every rural dwelling should have not only a battery-powered radio but a workable outhouse.

And then I would come down here, over the cattle guard and into the pastures and my grove, and try not to listen to the eucalyptus trees dying. They cried out and groaned and sometimes shrieked in the cold, for they were strangers here. The native trees growing up from volcanic rocks stayed strong and quiet, but the tall Australians perished noisily, and it was nightmarish to hear them, as they cracked down from tops to roots.

By the time Bouverie came back from Greece or perhaps Bavaria or New York, the trees had changed from their soft silvery greens to a strange black, and were plainly splitting into two long halves. They were a great hazard, since they could crash every which way in any wind from north or west, and burn like torches with their rich oils. People came finally and cut them down. It was almost as painful as their dying had been. Later lush sucklings came up from most of the roots, but the cattle trampled them. I saved a couple near the house, to catch up with the fourteen that were left, and now they look strong and promising as I smile at them through the north windows.

All this is no doubt part of why I live here.

Losing the grove of course changed the clear perfumed air, the climate in my house, the light on its walls, but it gave me a new view of the northern hills and mountains, past the flat green or golden meadows where aristocratically bred cows wait every spring and summer for their scheduled birthings. (The first bull here, when I came, was old and placid. He was called Maximilian. Since he retired from active duty, a succession of young ones of great race perform their jobs quickly and soon leave for other pastures.)

My house is between the two cattle guards, so that I am somewhat in limbo, literally on the wrong side of the tracks, while the Ranch life goes on under the bell tower and past the sprawling vineyards into its own courtyards and similar enclaves. Brave friends risk the railroad tracks to come down here, and even to go back. And since I need to cook simple meals the way some people need Bingo or Double-Crostics, a considerable number of hungry thirsty allies move in and out of this place where I have chosen to live.

The house is, as far as I can tell, a small gem. It is indescribably well conceived and constructed, so I must content myself by stating that it consists of two large rooms and a middle one for the privacies of life: toilet, shower, bath, washbowl, things that most of us Anglo-Saxons hide in small unventilated closets as if our bodily functions were perforce ugly and shameful.

My bathroom, thanks to Bouverie's forthright agreement with this theory, is large and low, with probably the biggest tub in this region, and a capacious shower and a long counter, all sane and practical but voluptuous. Everything is tiled a pattern made in Japan from a Moroccan design, and one long wall is painted the same Pompeian red as the ceiling, and has a changing pattern of pictures I feel like looking at for a time. I move them at will, and people who use the bathroom often stay there lengthily, in the nice old rocking chair or the shower or the tub, looking at what I've put on the red wall and thinking their own thoughts.

The bathroom is low-ceilinged, but the other two rooms of this *palazzino* are domed, in a fine conception of Bouverie's: random-width and random-laid redwood, never touched with oil or varnish, in a contrived curve (of course of straight lines!) that runs through the whole structure. Gradually the wood is turning darker, but I am almost unaware of this, since I live with it. In fifty more years it may be nearly black, from the strong indirect light of the days, and the subtle gases that cooking and laughing and sleeping people send out. Now and then, in a quick atmospheric shift, it will make snapping crackles, from west to east, in a mischievous but not frightening way.

There is a three-foot drop in the house, between the two rooms, but the ceiling goes straight through so that it seems higher in the western half. In "my" room, where I work and sleep, I look up at it when I am in bed, and its random symmetry cools my mind.

The western room is not only deeper but larger, and the big balcony outside it almost makes another room, and keeps the house cool in blazing summertime. From all this space, I look not only south into the native grove, and northward across meadows to the far mountains, but due west into a low range of wooded hills that are a county park, with easy trails, and then on to the high blue mountains of the Jack London Preserve. And now that most of the Bouverie Ranch has been added to the protectorate of the Audubon Society, the only houses anyone will ever see from my porch on the slope up from the meadows are already built down along Highway 12 . . . small, inoffensive, and tree masked.

And all this may be another reason why I live where I live.

For several years before I came here in 1970, common sense as well as various good friends had been telling me that it was foolish for me to plan to spend my last years in a three-storey Victorian house in Napa Valley, with no more nubile daughters to act as involuntary slave labor. At times it seemed that I was trying to run an unlicensed but popular motel-bar-restaurant there, instead of the welcoming warm home my girls and I had lived in for a long time, and most of my peers in St. Helena were either moving away or holding discreet garage sales before they settled into elegant mobile-home parks near supermarkets.

I did not want to leave the little town. Almost half of my heart was there, sharing honors with Aix-en-Provence, where I could no longer live as I would choose (in a second-floor apartment on the Place de l'Archevêché!). Time and taxes told me otherwise.

It would have been folly for me to rent or build a little house out in the hilly vineyards of the Napa Valley, because of the logistics of marketing and transportation and so on. The alternative was to find a nice old garage or tool shed in St. Helena, and install plumbing and wall-to-wall carpets, and accustom myself to air conditioning and viewless windows, and hope that if I didn't show up for a few days somebody might peek in to see what had happened to the queer old lady-authoress (found quietly dead between the stove and the icebox, with a glass of vermouth in one hand and an overripe pear in the other). The prospect was dismal . . . not so much the dying as the *living* that way.

Then my friend David Bouverie in Glen Ellen, westward in the next valley, proposed that I leave my beautiful old house and build a practical two-room *palazzino* on his ranch. I could use his land, and the little house would revert to his estate when I finally left it, and my heirs would be repaid what it had cost me. All this I did, especially since he proposed designing it for me.

And this *he* did, with all the bold skill of his earlier days as an English architect, and his knowledge of the winds and weather of this country as an American rancher. I said I wanted two rooms and a big bath, with an arch at each end to repeat the curved doors of his two big barns. I wanted tile floors. He did not blink . . . and I went back to Aix for several months to grow used to a new future.

It took a couple of years, once here, for me to feel that this was and would be, perforce and *Deo volente*, my "home." I had never before lived in a new house, and I felt like a guest in a delightful rented cottage, perhaps there to write a book, to hide, to escape. But there were familiar books and chairs and pictures, and Ranch people nearby to keep a kind eye on me in case of worry or trouble. Slowly but willingly I grew into the place, so that I was *here*.

The air is mostly dry and sweet, where I have chosen to stay. During the rains it is soft with seasonal perfumes of meadow grasses and new leaves. By mid-April the cows are back from their winter pasturage, usually heavy with imminent calvings, and they tread down myriad wild flowers into the volcanic ash that makes up much of this valley's earth, sometimes three inches deep and sometimes thirty feet.

Dear friends from St. Helena and even Aix and Osaka come here, or I go over the high hills on the beautiful Oakville Grade to be in St. Helena again, to walk down Main Street under its noble old electroliers and see dentist-doctor-CPA-librarians-winemen. In summer, here, I am a kind of female Elijah, fed by the kindly local ravens: fresh vegetables and fruits, all eminently meant for my table, which is seldom bare. For more than half the year, the air moves in four directions through the little house, and in winter I can be as warm as I want, with a Franklin stove in each room and an unending supply of madrona and oak from the Ranch, if and when electricity runs low. My cat and I like heat in the bathroom, but I am weaning him from this sybaritic attitude, if that is possible with felines, and plan to get him a little electric pad for the coming winter. I have not yet settled my own puzzlement about how to enjoy a chilly shower bath or toilet seat. . . .

It is plain that creature comforts are an acceptable part of my choice to live here in my later years. Aside from them as well as because of them, I find this house a never-ending excitement, and I think that this is as necessary when a person is in the seventies as in the teens and twenties. What is more, knowing *why* and *where* is much easier and more fun in one's later years, even if such enjoyment may have to be paid for with a few purely physical hindrances, like crickety fingers or capricious eyesight.

My eyes, for instance, are undependable by now, so that I do not drive. A young friend takes me marketing once a week. And my legs are not trustworthy, so that I have given up the walking that can be wonderful here on the Ranch: the sharp crumbled volcanic soil slides easily and is brutal to fall on. I move about fairly surely and safely in my *palazzino,* and water the plants on the two balconies. I devise little "inside picnics" and "nursery teas" for people who like to sit in the Big Room and drink some of the good wines that grow and flow in these northern valleys. I work hard and happily on good days, and on the comparatively creaky ones I pull my Japanese comforter over the old bones, on my big purple bedspread woven by witches in Haiti, and wait for the never-failing surcease.

How else would I live where I live? It all proves what I've said before, that I am among the most blessed of women, still permitted to *choose.*

Glen Ellen, 1980

JOURNEYS

Why is it that some people refuse, or are unwilling, to go back to a place where once they have been happy? If you ask them, they will say that they do not want to spoil a beautiful memory, or that nothing can ever be the same. (A wonderful thing can only happen once!)

Perhaps they believe that they are being kind and complimentary, thus to imply a perfection that must remain unflawed. Actually I think they may feel afraid that they will be disillusioned, if indeed they have had to convince themselves that a privately dull or ugly event was indeed a glamorous one. Or they may suspect that they are less attractive than they wanted to be, or that the other people are.

This has puzzled me since I was twenty-one years old and first married.

My husband and I went from Dijon in Burgundy, where we were students, down to the fishing village of Cassis for Christmas. I lived in a mist of clumsy passion and ignorant naive wonderment, and although I cannot remember a single word we spoke, almost everything else rings like crystal in my memory: midnight mass, with fishermen playing wild sad songs on oddly shaped *hautbois* and windy flutes, over the bleating of two sheep by the altar glittering with candles; a new human baby wailing in its modern cradle trimmed with blue satin bows, and filled with Christmas straw; all the short square women dressed in black, with shawls over their heads. We felt shy and bedazzled, later in the bright hall of the Hôtel Lieutard, when the villagers gave us thick glasses of a sweet brownish *vin cuit* and everyone talked a very fast dialect as if we understood it well, and finally kissed us and cheered as we went up to bed. And ten thousand other happenings that are yesterday and tomorrow for me.

Of course I never thought of anything but a long full life with my love, but a heavy foreboding hit me about two years into this planned bliss, when he said firmly that we must never go back to the fishing village where we had spent our first Christmas. And a cruel mixture of disbelief and sadness filled me as I came to understand how thoroughly and firmly he stood by his conviction, that if people know real happiness anywhere, they must never expect to find it there again.

I did not like to argue, then or ever, but I did want to find out why, and his basic answer was that it was foolish to try to recapture happiness. When I told him that I honestly did not have the faintest wish to be the ninny of two Christmases ago, to "recapture" anything, he was deeply hurt, feeling that I had considered him a fitting partner in our ingenuous love, a fellow fool. Plainly I was out of my depth; I fumbled along about how beautiful the wild hills were, back of Cassis, and how good the wine was, and how much I had learned since then. It would be wonderful to see it with older eyes, I said. Impossible, he said in a pitying way, as if I could never understand the pain of being a truly sensitive poet driven forever from his former paradises by crass realism.

So that year we went to Nuremberg, and the next year Strasbourg, but we never returned to any place we had been before, because once, according to his private calendar, we had been there. And in a few more years we parted. You might say that we ran out of places . . .

I remain astonished, and very puzzled. It was obviously impossible to find out why he felt as he did, or to understand it, because I did not, and I still don't. When I tried to tell him that I did not want to "go back," it hurt him that I had not recognized the bliss he had tried to give me. And when I said that of course we were not the same as we had been, he thought I was telling him that he was older, which indeed we both were, and that I was unhappy that we were, which I certainly was not. And so on. Yes, impossible!

Fear may be a reason for refusing to admit change. And why would anyone be afraid of that? It is as inevitable as death, or "the ever-returning roses of the dawn," or curdled milk. And what reasonable human being would want to see always with the eyes of a bewildered lovesick timid child, which I was in 1929?

Many years after I was told by my young lover that we must never go back, my sister Norah and her three young boys and my two little girls and I walked over the high white-stone hills above the little fishing port of Cassis, and I cried out, "There it is, exactly as it was! Nothing has changed!" And we ran down toward its quays feeling delighted and happy.

True enough, wisteria hung richly from the trellises above the fishermen's doorways, and newly washed jerseys hung bright against the blue and green and white walls. Tough bleached old boats moved up and down gently on the flat indigo water, and down the quay there was the sound of a pianola I remembered from some thirty years before. My heart pounded with delight, and I grabbed the hands of Johnnie and Anne. "It's all the same! It's exactly as I knew it would be," I babbled, and I gave a big happy whack to one of the old familiar rusted bollards that still stood like sturdy mushrooms along the quay.

And it was made of *papier mâché!* It tipped over like a match-box and rolled off into the dirty bay, and my sister and the children watched while (as I was told often and gleefully for several more decades) my jaw dropped like a startled puppy's and I seemed to *stop*—stop breathing, stop being. And then we all began to laugh, which we still do whenever we think of that wonderful return to the real-fake-phony-true place.

Maurice Chevalier was remaking one of Pagnol's movies there, maybe *Fanny,* and the whole village was a set, as much like Marseille of many years before as it could be made, and everyone was in a high giddy fever of participation, with the mayor and the priest talking together in the striped sunlight of the main café terrace, with some of the stars and grips and other people laughing as much as we were, if for different reasons.

My sister knew about my lasting puzzlement at my first love's firm refusal to go anywhere that had been happy for him, and we talked about it as we watched our five kids melt into the little gangs of actors' and fishermen's children. We sat under the paper wisteria in front of a fake café at the edge of the main set, and watched Maurice or Marius or somebody get out of a very ancient limousine countless times, for the cameras. Every take looked perfect to us, and every time the old actor creaked pompously from the backseat and stepped out, we smiled at his skill and then waited for him to do it again.

And I doubt that either of us had ever felt much more contented, serene, reassured. Quite aside from being well and with our children and filled with various kinds of love, we were in Cassis, exactly as we should be at that moment in history and time. And Cassis was there as it had been for more than two thousand years, and as it would be as long as there was a fjord-filled coastline between Marseille and Toulon on the north shore of the Mediterranean.

I think I was the first of our family to be there, between the two World Wars, when my love and I went there in 1929. A young fisherman rowed us far into some of the *calanques* to show us where the homesick German sailors from the submarines lurking there had climbed up the stony sides and painted their sweethearts' names on the highest rocks: "HANS + ANNA," "Ich liebe Huldi," "K. V. G." We ate the yolklike meat of sea urchins that he reached down for in the still dark waters. It was so still that we could hear a fish jump. We did not talk much, but the three of us liked each other, and for several more days we could call and wave and smile, along the three short quays of the village.

He might have been any of the older fishermen who stood about now for the cameras so long later. They wore their grandfathers' baggy pants and stocking caps instead of Levis and beat-up visored baseball gear, and the children of Cassis were blissfully arrogant as they strutted among the real movie kids and our envious five, in some designer's idea of how Marseille street brats dressed when Panisse ran his pub. One or two little boys had tried some makeup in their adventure as potential stars, and marked freckles over the bridges of their noses, like some blond blue-eyed urchin they had once seen in a Hollywood movie. They looked touchingly improbable: dark-eyed descendants of the Greeks and Saracens *never* freckle.

But they were part of our private return. They had been there forever. And so had I. And I realized that the dear man who had first gone there with me had never really been there at all.

Where had he been, then? We'd eaten and drunk and made love, listened to the wild sad rejoicings of the Christmas midnight mass together. Why did he fear to do it again with me?

Norah and I moved on down past the cameras and the serious village extras and the old actor getting in and out of his ancient car, and sat under the bamboo slats at the big café, and wondered. Lots of children came and went, and Mr. Chevalier came in alone and smiled tentatively at us, wondering why I looked almost like somebody from the Paramount lot in Hollywood a long time before. The white wine was cool and like delicate flint, as it had been even further years back. (Why had my love not wanted to taste it ever again, at least there and with me?)

Norah and I decided without words to stay by ourselves, and not smile back at the charming old actor, who looked suddenly lonely and wandered away. The children came along the quay with two American kids traveling with their movie parents, and several locals, still exhilarated by their professional debuts as extras. They were incredibly rich, at three dollars a day, even if their pay would go directly to their parents, but temporarily they were as broke as any proper thespians and consented graciously to drink a lemonade or two with us. The whole gaggle sat at the far end of the striped shade, like a scene from a child's version of *La Dolce Vita*. Norah and I looked remotely at them, and out into the afternoon shadows along the broad quays and the darkening water, and wondered how we could be anywhere but *there, then*.

I still think that first fine young man was mistaken. Perhaps his stubbornness was admirable, but his refusal to change his idée fixe was plain stupid, to my older wiser mind. Who wants always to look at a café or an altar or an oak tree with the first innocence and the limited understanding of a naive lovesick girl, or a homesick bornagain Byron?

Five minutes or five centuries from now, we will see changeless realities with new eyes, and the sounds of sheep bleating and a new child's wail will be the same but heard through new ears. How can we pretend to be changeless, then? Why be afraid to recognize the baby in the straw, just because it is not as it once was, innocent, but is now tied about with nylon ribbon? Is it wrong to see the phony painted mushroombollard on the quay and accept it, as part of the whole strong song that keeps on singing there, in spite of wars and movies and the turtling on of time?

Glen Ellen, California, 1984

THE ART OF AGING

REX I AND II

Rex I

There is a book I must write, and one I have long thought upon. Let me say that it will be about all good old people, of which I hope one day to be one; it is, perforce, about many I have known and lived with; it is about an oldster I would like one day to resemble. It is about Rex.

I shall draw upon my files I have kept for about twenty years, to put it safely, for long before then I was keenly conscious and even knowledgeable of the ways of old people. I thought, even so long back, that they must be even more important than I, and this, from a human being of fifteen or twenty years, is an almost monumental thought. Very soon after that I began to clip little sayings, quips, or bright quotations about the far from happy thoughts of people over sixty-five or seventy. (I do not rightly know when old age begins, but according to the welfare agencies and the insurance companies, two fairly respected authorities, it is at about such ages.)

I have kept my files going, to my intimates' amazement. I have countless clippings. I am glad. I can look, more or less at will, at what a baker's dozen of experts say about the physiological, emotional, glandular, gastronomical, gonadal-or-do-I-mean-glandular-again, psychological trends (if not traits) of those of us who are past fifty. It is a very reassuring picture.

I like old people.

I like to be old.

I'll write of Rex.

I have always known I would, but I've thought of it as past his coffin, over the hump of his disintegration, and in words tinged, imbued, weighted with the essences of my sorrow for a man lost to me.

Now I feel that I am strong enough, since he is, to write of him as an old man while he still is one.

Instead of waiting until he has died, and until my own harried emotions have settled into a kind of quiescent awe, I am, suddenly and unexpectedly, ready to write about him now, while he is alive, breathing, coughing, eating, defecating.

The best thing about this almost extrasensory decision is that I know it would meet with his approval if I cared to bother him about it. He acknowledges my small professional skills. He bows to my discretion. He would listen to my plan and smile with only slight apprehension, inevitable in a small-town editor, and then would read each chapter with a kind of patience impossible to anyone younger, fresher, less tolerant—anyone my age, for instance, forty-two instead of seventy-three.

That is why I think I should write the book about old age, about Rex, now, not later. It is the very fact that he does not much care, that he trusts me, that makes me want to put all these things into words—the things I have thought over a long time about old people and now *know* about such a fine, such an old, MAN.

I went in after he had turned his lights off and put the glasses beside his bed, and his face turned up to me like a child's when I leaned to kiss him. My heart turned over.

Whittier, California, 1950

Rex II

Hatred, hatred. What venom it distills. Tonight, filled with it, I give off poisonous exudations, I well know. Rubbing his feet, I could feel my hatred flow like bile through my fingertips into his strangely warm knobby venous toes ankles calves. Now, warm and alone in my bed, wrapped in a garnet shawl, sipping at an unwanted highball which I down almost as a punishment, I can smell the hated sourness on my hands, and can realize my puny foolishness to be so wretched, so voluptuously wretched.

My mind races volubly. Every word it says can lead in many a direction, and it is hard, as well as basically destructive, to force myself to follow one line of thought, or of suggestion.

God, but I have been angry tonight. By now I am coming into focus again. And even when I was most filled with the poison I knew my basic impotence, for I see no reason, really, for wounding Rex, no matter how slightly. He is old. He is tired. He is an astonishingly spoiled man: that is the crux of it, and I am too old and he is even too much older for me to try to show him how he could be easier to live with. Besides, I am not in love with him. Mother, and later Sis, tried hard to make him toe the lines they drew. They had rows. They wept. They stormed and sulked. As far as I can see he did not really ever hear them. But it was worth it, I suppose, because of the love. Me, I don't love him.

Now and then I loathe him, for the stupid waste, the basically timid arrogance in him. Mostly I accept him as a kind of foreshadow of myself, for we are much alike, glandularly and in the basic timidity and the arrogance. (But I think I am wiser, and therefore less impregnable.) There are times, like tonight, quite possibly dictated by the tides, when I am filled with a consummate revulsion. Most of the time I shed off things that other women squirm at openly or must turn away from: the dribbles of urine on the floor by the toilet, the long sensual belches at breakfast, the knowledge that he is restrained and charmingly gallant for any goddamned fluffy fool of a scheming small-town Bovary. But now and then I cannot, or do not, shed my deep and perhaps instinctive distaste for my intimacy with my father. All his odors repel me, and at his age and with his background of cautious midwestern plumbing, his odors are many. (I know about the difficulties of keeping clean in the aged. I know about earlier conditioning. I know . . . Still I hold my breath when I must step over the steamy underwear on the sitting room floor at night in order to reach the toilet; and I hold my breath again when after the fairly neutralizing oil I put on the alcohol and it pulls out from the blue-white feet a wave of bitter fumes; and I hold my breath now, an hour later, not to smell my hands, scrubbed, oiled, but still subtly stinking of those poor trusting rotten feet.)

Yes, the odors repel me, although I know they are largely involuntary. The sounds repel me, the long masturbatory belchings when he need not restrain himself—that is, when he is with the children and me. The equally long and voluptuous pickings at his nostrils, while he reads at night or even sits over his coffee: they repel me. And I am *agacée*, hurt, rebuffed, annoyed, everything like that, when he slams into his room, leaving all the doors open, and pees noisily. (Often when I rub his feet they are still damp with the urine he has dripped casually.)

Yes, many things about living with this old man exasperate me. Usually, given the situation and my increasing capacity for dispassion, I can sublimate my feelings fairly successfully. But now and then I cannot, and the thing I have the hardest time with *always*, no matter what the tides, is his spitting. I know he has to spit. I know what is wrong with him, I'm sure much better than he does himself. I know all that. But Jesus Christ in a handbasket, he need not be so thoughtless; so self-absorbed, so morbidly preoccupied. Or need he, given his seventy-four years of preoccupation and self-absorption? How can I ask, or blame?

All I know is that when I came home from getting the girls at school, and hurried into the kitchen to start organizing One More Meal, and saw a foamy blob of his spittle in the sink, I was as near physical revolt as I have been for several years. I thought I would vomit. And all the time I was thinking, This is a very *healthy* reaction, the best one yet—you are healthy now, much better. (I think I was right, too!) I had to go out, as soon as I had flushed the sink. I made myself a distastefully strong drink. I thought, This might even make you drunk. (But it did not.)

I was censorious and quietly horrid with the children, as my obviously easiest outlet. (They were patient with me, and now I think with a desperate resignation that I would to God I had the past hours back again, with those two budding beautiful little creatures.) I kept on sneering and blaspheming—no, that's not the right word—in my mind, and making chitchat and swallowing food and recognizing many of my familiar impulses toward escape. I kept telling myself how much more "normal" my present revolt was—no remorse, no guilt, just a damned good physical reaction followed by reasonable and reasoning resentment. Now and then as I sat amicably chatting, I contemplated A Good Scene. But I'm no good at them, and anyway I do *not* think they are right for children.

So—I went upstairs, and drew some creature comfort from an enema, which did indeed expurgate some of my rage. I lay down with Anne. She caressed me forgivingly with her slender dirty hands and made me feel both foolish and happy. Mary snored calmly in the other bed, but I did not feel that in her heart she was either calm or dormant. Then I went grudgingly downstairs, where a good fire burned. I felt mean and hateful. Rex picked at his nose in his own corner. I lay down, got up, moved about listlessly. It's either a scene or get out, I said. I'm no good at scenes. So . . . I got out. He felt my hatred, I know.

He went early to bed. He opened his sitting room door and tapped the jamb twice, our signal, and I turned off the tropical fish and the lights and fixed the fire screen and went in. I held my breath, and rightly. I flushed the yellow water down the toilet, and pushed the rug over the splashes of urine on the floor. I saw the teeth in the glass bowl, with flecks of food rising slowing in the water. The radio blasted, and as always, that annoyed me, for Rex knows it hurts my ears and that he can turn it up after I've rubbed his feet, but he never does. Often two or three stations blare together—two tonight. I thought that he'd bathed yesterday, but already he smelled like Wednesday instead of only Monday. I felt his toenails, like pieces of savage carving. He must go soon to the podiatrist—I must call for an appointment, and see that he puts it in his book, and then remind him and remind him.

All the time I was trying not to breathe, and increasingly I thought about hatred, and the different ways it can be what it is, and I grew more certain that this revulsion of mine tonight was a very healthy normal one. I did not hit anyone, except my children, with what I hope was a glancing spiritual blow (I do not say that lightly). I did not kick or yell or weep, although I was for a time near the last. *I* felt like hell. I took an enema. Then I drank a highball by myself with an electric pad turned to Low on my belly, and a chilly east air blowing over me, and the children breathing, perhaps disappointed but with confidence, in the other room.

I feel sorry, yes. Tonight I could not really *look* at Rex, because I was so angry at him for spitting in the sink: I knew he would see my anger. Perhaps that would have been a good thing. But I do not love him that way, and am not able to have good rousing battles with him. So I hide my bile. I don't think it really hurts me at all—except that I am still clumsy enough to vent some of it on the two people I love best, my innocent children. I sometimes feel that they know more than I, and therefore are as forgiving as they seem to be. But through my pores, through my lips pressed desperately upon their chaste temples, am I teaching them hatred?

Whittier, California, 1951

Notes on the Craft, Skill, Science, or Art of Missing

There is a commercial on, about a car called the Charger. A light-voiced man mimics an old-time vaudevillian. His timing is perfect, his mimicry impeccable. I prepare a salad or wash pantyhose or something on that level, the sound going on, and suddenly at a certain combination of rhythm-timing-voice play I am engulfed by a wrenching sense of missing June.

She and I never listened to this sort of music. There was always some going on, but she liked a schmaltzier beat than I did. When I stayed at her house I listened to it and enjoyed it. She liked big orchestras and a certain amount of uncluttered lilt.

When I lived for several years at my growing-up place, to help my widowed father a little and give my two small girls a good dignified man to know, June came as often as she could to stay for a couple of days with us. She and Father hit it off. We all did, and it was always fine.

He was deaf, though, and early in the mornings (he had breakfast and an hour of dictation before he got to his office at nine) we would be in the old kitchen. June would sit on a high stool, and I would be organizing his tray, coffee and all that, and a good meal for the kids and on weekdays their lunches, and we would listen to Fats Waller and Jelly Roll Morton.

I had the run Jelly Roll did with Lomax for the Library of Congress or wherever it was. (I still have it, but seldom listen to it now. I've heard it, thank God.) June would start out with a small cup of fresh coffee and then have a small glass of half water and half bourbon, while I moved around, my back mostly to her, and readied the other morning niceties, and changed records on the "box" I kept in the kitchen, as essential to me as the stove-freezer-refrigerator-toaster-ice crusher—all at the command of a person who hates gadgets.

Behind me I would know that June sat cross-legged on top of the stool, glass nearby, her eyes now and then filled with glad tears at a special word or sound from the old records. She was far from that kitchen, in a world nobody but she could ever fathom, and the trip there had some pain in it but she was willing to share it with her other selves and with me in those mornings when Rex, my father and our mutual friend, could snooze a bit later . . .

Now and then I would prance around a bit, at the stove or icebox, and she would chuckle, because we were both high on the music that pounded out. Long before in our separate lives we had heard it in different places, but those weekend mornings with light coming through the walnut tree by the kitchen windows at the Ranch, a good hour before my father and the little girls woke up, were a shared experience that is valuable enough to miss, in the highest sense of that word.

Tonight when I listen to that high affected voice, reminiscent of the old Orpheum circuit rather than what June and I listened to on early Sundays, the timing is part of other better jazzmen, and abruptly I am wracked by a sense of missing. I miss June. I miss being able to listen to the same music. Why did she dodge the trap before I did?

I feel puzzled about all of this. Why do I not miss my sister Anne at all? Now and then I have poignant regrets about how I failed her sometimes in her life, and how confused she was (to my mind), and how I tried with fairly complete nonsuccess to help her through financial-legal-emotional fiascoes. But I do not miss her. I am glad she has solved her own secret problems, although to do it she had to die a dog's death.

She introduced me to June, whom I miss more strongly.

I also miss one dog and one cat. The dog was registered as P'ing Cho Fung, but in the days when Butch did not necessarily mean a dyke haircut, I named him that defiantly, against his titles, and that he was. He was a highly dignified Pekingese dog. Now and then his spirit approaches my subconscious, and I feel that he is beside me, perhaps touching my hand subtly with his nose like a cool rose petal. And the cat, Blackberry, was ruler of the current roost, and by now is part of a hierarchy of the three great cats I have been privileged to harbor among countless lesser pensioners. He was a formidable friend.

There are other animals I miss almost physically, at times, as much as the two-legged ones like June. But here I must pull myself up, as I would a young pony, to ask what I mean by the word *miss*.

I can try to say that Missing is partly physical. There is a strong pull back to the warm kitchen with Jelly Roll and the friend cross-legged on the high stool, the friend gone now; to the princely little dog, also gone now. It is a wrench that is almost orgiastic, if one permits it to be, and it is always ready to pounce at unexpected moments, as when a canny-silly commercial comes over the radio.

Missing is also a more inward condition. It is something that must be accepted as part of any thinking existence, and made use of. It is a force. The special flavor of true Missing should be channeled. It is very strong. And I like to hope that the stronger the person is who misses something or someone, the stronger the force will be.

It continues to puzzle me that I miss June more than I miss my sister. It comes down to the fact, perhaps, that I am glad one died and sorry the other did. But I am not glad that Butch died. I am not glad that Blackberry did, either.

What is left is a vulnerable spot in my acceptance of vulnerability. These and many other people, like lovers and husbands and even friends, have slid off the scales. They seem, now and then for unknown reasons, to stand there stark and grabbing, in front of us. They want us. We say, No, not now. But the statement is a painful one.

That is why it hurts me when that silly commercial comes on, about some car named Charger that is selling for less than cost. The rhythm and timing—exquisite. The inexplicable anguish, fleeting but poignant to the point of true pain, of missing June, the little dog, perhaps a dozen other true beings, brought out by that shoddy takeoff: why should I submit to it? And why should it make me wonder why I loved them and not some other people?

Glen Ellen, California, mid–1980s

FOREWORD TO SISTER AGE

St. Francis sang gently of his family: his brother the Sun, his sister the Moon. He talked of Brother Pain, who was as welcome and well-loved as any other visitor in a life filled with birds and beasts and light and dark. It is not always easy for us lesser people to accept gracefully some such presence as that of Brother Pain or his cousins, or even the inevitable visits of a possibly nagging harpy like Sister Age. But with a saint to guide us, it can be possible.

This story about the portrait of Ursula von Ott, a forgotten German or Swiss lady, may seem odd as an introduction to a collection of stories about aging and ending and living and whatever else the process of human being is about. I know, though, that my devastated old piece of painted leather, half eaten by oil-hungry insects when it was already worn with years, has been a lodestar in my life.

Before I found the picture in a junk-shop in Zurich, in about 1936, I was writing of old people who had taught me things I knew I needed, in spite of my boredom and impatience. And years later, after I had sent away the boxes of notes made in the several decades since I first met Ursula, I realized that all this time when I had thought I was readying myself to write an important book about the art of aging, I had gone on writing stories about people who were learning and practicing it long before I was.

Sometimes we met for only a few seconds. Probably the old Bible salesman who stumbled to our door at the Ranch did not remember me five minutes later, but he was the one who first taught me that people can cry without a sound, and without knowing why. It was a valuable lesson, and as mysterious now as it was when I was about twelve, watching him walk slowly out to the dusty road again, and feeling the cool new tears run down my cheeks. And I forgot it, for about thirty years.

Sometimes the meetings with Sister Age's messengers are long, tedious, even unwitting. For instance, I knew my father's father for almost twenty years, but we never really met, and certainly did not recognize each other as appointed teacher or pupil. By now I sometimes regret this, because I see him as possessing great strength and dignity that were mine for the taking. I doubt, though, that he felt much more interest in me than I in him. We were as impersonal as two animals of different sex and age but sharing some of the same blood, unaware that we lifted our hooves in a strangely similar way as we headed for the same hay-mangers, the same high hills. Even now I cannot feel any strong reason for making notes about him. But I may, I may.

Certainly there were violent flash-like meetings, all my life, with people much older than I, of different colors and sexes and social positions, who left marks to be deciphered later. This was the case with the Bible salesman: I did not think consciously of him for a long time (Why should I?), when suddenly I knew that I must add some words about him to the boxes of notes. . . .

The art of aging is learned, subtly but firmly, this way. I wrote fast, to compress and catch a lesson while I could still hear it, and not because it had happened to *me*, so that *I* was recording it, but because it was important to the whole study. It was, for the time I made the notes anyway, as clear as ringing crystal that such hints are everywhere, to be heeded or forever unheard by the people who may one day be old too.

So all the notes I took were caught on the run, as it were, as I grew toward some kind of maturity. I never thought of them as anything but clinical, part of the whole study of aging that Ursula von Ott was trying to help me with. I kept on checking dates and places and events, not at all about my own self but simply as a student in a class, preparing a term paper and leaving scraps that might be useful to other workers in the same field.

By now some of my notes sound like fabrications, invented to prove a point in an argument. This is because it is my way of explaining, and it has always been a personal problem, even a handicap. When I tell of a stubbed toe or childbirth or how to serve peacocks' tongues on toast it sounds made-up, embroidered. But it is as it happened to *me*.

This may explain why I have spent my life in a painstaking effort to tell about things as they are to me, so that they will not sound like autobiography but simply like notes, like factual reports. They have been set down honestly, to help other students write their own theses.

And now my very long, devoted collecting is over. The reports are stored in some academic cellars for younger eyes to piece together, perhaps. The stories that stayed behind are mostly about other people than myself, and may at least prove that I have been listening for clues that Frau von Ott has tried to show me. Some of them may be useful, in moments of puzzlement as to what to do next in our inevitable growth.

So, with the usual human need for indirection, I introduce my Sister. St. Francis might call her, in a gentle loving way, Sister Age. I call her my Teacher, too.

The first time I met Ursula, and recognized her as a familiar, I was walking with Tim down a narrow street off the main bridge in Zurich.

Tim was to die a few years later, except in my heart, and Zurich was a cold secret city in Switzerland in 1936, and probably still is. We were there because we lived near Vevey and Tim was silently involved with some of the Spanish fighters living in Zurich during the "revolution" in their country.

We were innocent to look at, and Tim was useful in getting drawings and paintings out of war-wracked Spain, and I was strangely adept at drinking good coarse wine from a skin held far from my open mouth and then keeping it firmly shut, while all the men talked in the small dim cellar-cafés. We were treated with care. I was greeted politely and then put into a corner, with an occasional squirt of *roja* to remind me of true Spanish courtesy, while the schemings went on in more languages than Spanish and French and German.

At home again, we did not talk much about these smoky meetings, but usually they meant that Tim would be away from Vevey for a few days, always carrying a tightly rolled umbrella, like any proper Anglo-Saxon gentleman. Four or five years later, there was a big exhibition in Geneva, of treasures secreted from the Prado, and it was odd to walk past etchings and even small canvases that had come into Switzerland inside that bumbershoot, that prim old Gamp. . . .

So . . . one day Tim and I were walking down a narrow street in the old part of Zurich. There was a small shop ahead of us: junk, castoffs, rummage. There were a couple of bins of rags and a table of shabby books outside. Two or three empty picture frames leaned against the dirty glass of the dim window, and Tim stopped to look at them because he might be able to clean them to use for some of his own drawings. A man shuffled out of the shop, impatient to get rid of two tourists before he might have to turn on his lights for them.

And I saw the picture of Ursula, Sister Age. It was behind the old frames, and I pulled it out rudely, fiercely, so that Tim was surprised. In the twilight it seemed to blaze at me, to call strongly a forceful greeting.

I said, "We must get this."

Tim looked quickly at the dirty old picture and then at me. "All right if you say so. But we can't take it along to the meeting."

The junk-man said, "If you buy it you take it. I don't keep it."

I said, "Of course. I'll take it now, back to the hotel. I'll meet you at the café, Tim." I knew that he needed me, to add to the bland casual tourist-look the Spaniards seemed to want for whatever they were planning.

"No. We have time," he said, because he recognized the abrupt necessity in me, and we left the junk-man staring with surprise at the money in his hand, and hurried down to the bridge in silence. Under a streetlight Tim took the picture and looked at it and asked me what had happened, and I tried to tell him that it was the book I was going to write. What book? When? How did I know? I felt irked, as if we both had always known all about it, although it had just been born wordlessly in front of the drab little shop.

I was going to write about growing old, I told this dear man who would not. I was going to learn from the picture, I said impatiently. It was very clear to me, and I planned to think and study about the art of aging for several years, and then tell how to learn and practice it.

One fine thing about Tim was that although, a lot of the time, he thought I was funny, he never laughed when I was not. So that evening as we ran on over the bridge above the thick rushing water, he said seriously Yes and You are right and Get busy . . . things like that. We stopped again under a strong streetlight, and in it the remote, monkey-sad eyes of the old woman stared far past us from the picture as she thought perhaps about a letter in her dropped hand. Her face was quiet, but ugly veins stood out on her thin arm, as if her blood ran too fast for comfort.

"She will make a wonderful cover for the book . . . rich, dark, rewarding," I said.

"She's an ugly old lady," Tim said. "That moustache. She looks like a monkey, all right . . . that long lip, and melancholy eyes."

"Yes. She's removed from it, from all the nonsense and frustration. She's aloof and real. She's past vanity."

Tim said the book cover was already a *fait accompli*. Why not? "Go ahead," he said. "Get busy."

Neither of us questioned the strange unemotional decision that had been made, and after another wine-fed smoky night in Zurich Tim went away for a few days, and I waited in Vevey and looked long and deeply at the picture. It hung above my desk, as it was to do in many other climates, on its strong leather thong, and every time I looked at the old face, she reminded me of what I would do.

The picture is painted on leather, stretched clumsily on a heavy frame of unmitred fruitwood, about nineteen inches by twenty-five. It is awkwardly executed, in thick rich oils, by a fairly well-tutored young man full of romanticism and fashionable disdain. He was provincially worldly, probably the pampered son of affluent merchants, filled with the stylish yearnings of his peers in 1808. His work is cluttered with leaves and drooping boughs, an ornate marble pedestal carrying his stark white bust, small canvases of amorous conquests in his young life, always with the same beautiful hero lying like a half-clad exhausted child between ripe rosy thighs of uniformly blonde goddesses.

Of course his memorial bust is handsomer than any living youth could look; his neck is longer, his nostrils flare wider, his lips curl in a more fashionable sensuality than any mortal's could, even in 1808 in a provincial burg like Frankfurt or Zurich or Bonn. It is all a fine dream, down to the pinkest fattest Cupids born to hold up his nonchalant sketches of a would-be rake's progress from leg to leg or at least lap to lap of every available Venus, all exactly alike in his plainly limited field of pursuit. And the flowers that climb and twine are his own favorites; all in full bloom at once to symbolize his eternal loss. The flags in bold bas-relief on the pedestal are from the stylish regiment he may or may not have joined, and there are bold hints of more than a couple of noble family crests, in case he might marry well before taking off in search of Napoleon and glory.

Another dimmer pedestal to the far left in the picture is doubtless meant for his mother's urn, when her long empty life has finally wept itself to a close. It is crudely made, with plaster crumbling off, and a few bricks showing. There are no escutcheons or regimental flags to ennoble it. It is as plain and ugly, by stern design, as the old woman who waits to escape to a shabby urn atop it, in the shadows of the fine marble monument to her brave son.

And suddenly this angry and impatient adolescent becomes, for one moment, a painter. He learned the rudiments of perspective on a tour of the Greek Isles with his tutor in 1805, and his political caricatures titillated his classmates at the local Gymnasium in 1807, and then for a few seconds in Time, he seized the image of Sister Age herself. He was too blinded by ignorance of himself and his model and Life to see anything but the cruel cartoon of a once-beautiful bitch turned into a lorn crone abandoned to her grief. He did everything ugly he could, in his escape: her lined face is like pallid clay, with a full moustache and even the shadows of a shaven underlip. The one eye showing in half-profile is red-rimmed and shrunken, and her large ear is plebeian: pink, swollen, revolting, with its full lobe promising a hellishly long life. Her hair is grey and thin, topped with a tiny round black cap like a rabbi's but with two gold leaves on it to prove something like her Christian gentility. Her gaze is remote, behind her big masculine nose (*his* nose, but meant for a hero, not an old biddy . . .).

On the back of the painted leather, in strong black characters, is a legend in surprisingly schoolboyish German, that says it is a picture of Ursula von Ott, born in 1767, the mother of several sons, the last of whom has created, before leaving for the battlefield in 1808, this forecast of his death and the inevitable loneliness of his bereaved parent.

So here is the picture of Ursula that for so long hung above my desk or over my bed, speaking to me about life and death, more than I thought there was to learn. Tim never laughed at me, and nobody ever questioned the ugly dark old picture hanging by its crude thong on walls in Switzerland and then wherever else we were. It was a part of the whole, like wine or air.

I began to clip things I read about aging, because I felt that the picture was teaching me. I thought all the time, in a kind of subliminal fashion, about the anger and blind vision of youth, and the implacable secret strength of the old. I thought about human stupidity. It began to be a family joke, but not a foolish one, to transport my boxes of "information," as we moved here and there.

In perhaps 1970, long after too short a life with Tim, during which he subtly taught me how to live the rest of it without him, I found that for the first time since I was about two years old I was without commitments, responsibilities, dependents, emotional ties, and such-like traps. I decided to look at some familiar places, to see if they were new again. I closed a few boxes of clippings, to keep them from wind and dust, rubbed the painting of Ursula with good oil on both sides of the leather, and left. (Perhaps it is odd that I never thought of returning to Zurich.) I had gone away many times since Tim died, and had always put oil on the picture, so that its dream of weeping willow leaves and fat Venuses and Ursula's moustache would be alive and ready to welcome me back again.

This time, though, there was what I can only think of as an accident in Time. Silverfish, beautiful elusive predators, devoured most of the pigments on the ripe old leather, and then much of that too, so that held up to the light it is translucent, like dirty lace . . . except for one part. . . .

Ursula is still there. The omnivorous insects did not touch her. The striped respectable costume, the black cap on her thin grey hair, are all there. Her resigned stocky body still lays one hand with firm dignity on the pedestal under the bust, although the marble is shadowy. Her other skinny arm still hangs, swollen veins and all, against her skirts, and she holds listlessly the letter telling of her noble son's death. Her sad eyes, always tearless, look brighter than before.

There are still hints of drooping faded boughs and blossoms, but all the voluptuous rosy goddesses in their lush draperies, in their golden frames propped up by fluttering Cupids, and all the pictures of their young hero lying between their knees, and even all the crossed regimental flags and carved escutcheons are gone, digested by a million silent bugs. Nothing is left but Ursula von Ott, and the picture that was meant to be a cruel caricature painted in youthful frustration by a sentimental boy may well be final proof that even the least of us is granted one moment of greatness.

Nobody can know now whether Ursula's son came back from his dream of heroism and noble death and became a good Swiss burgher. All I can see is what he, and Time, and the silverfish have left for me: the enigmatic, simian gaze of a woman standing all alone. She is completely alive in a landscape of death, then and now. She does not need anything that is not already within her, and the letter of information hangs useless. Above her big strong nose, above the hairy shadows around her subtly sensuous mouth, her eyes look with a supreme and confident detachment past all the nonsense of wars, insects, birth and death, love. . . .

After too long a time to look at her, I finally knew that I had filled too many boxes with clippings about Old Age. I stopped thinking that I would write a book about the art of aging. (Ursula von Ott was teaching me humility.) I gave away all the boxes of notes and clippings. (She was teaching me how to be simpler.) Finally . . .

And here I would like to say *then* or *last night* or even *this morning*, I built a good fire, and broke up the brittle old leather, and burned it and the fruitwood frame and watched them consume and curl themselves into pale ash. But I cannot. (There is more to listen to, more to learn from the old lady. . . .)

The picture is beside me, leaning against a bookcase. Its leather thong is long since broken, and all that comes out to my eyes from the dark lacy background is the vivid figure of an aging woman with a little velvet cap on her sparse hair. She ignores the doomful letter with its once-red seal, and the once-fine marble bust, and the once-mockingly pretty pictures of venal pleasures and wishful trappings of a forgotten life. She waits, superbly aloof and untroubled.

She is my teacher and my sister, and will tell me more, in due time.

MOMENT OF WISDOM

Tears do come occasionally into one's eyes, and they are more often than not a good thing. At least they are salty and, no matter what invisible wound they seep from, they purge and seal the tissues. But when they roll out and down the cheeks it is a different thing, and more amazing to one unaccustomed to such an outward and visible sign of an inward cleansing. Quick tears can sting and tease the eyeballs and their lids into suffusion and then a new clarity. The brimming and, perhaps fortunately, rarer kind, however, leaves things pale and thinned out, so that even a gross face takes on a porcelain-like quality, and—in my own case—there is a sensation of great fragility or weariness of the bones and spirit.

I have had the experience of such tears very few times. Perhaps it is a good idea to mention one or two of them, if for no other reason than to remind myself that such a pure moment may never come again.

When I was twelve years old, my family was slowly installing itself about a mile down Painter Avenue outside Whittier, California, the thriving little Quaker town where I grew up, on an orange ranch with shaggy, neglected gardens and a long row of half-wild roses along the narrow county road. Our house sat far back in the tangle, with perhaps two hundred yards of gravel driveway leading in toward it.

There was a wide screened porch across the front of the house, looking into the tangle. It was the heart of the place. We sat there long into the cool evenings of summer, talking softly. Even in winter, we were there for lunch on bright days, and in the afternoon drinking tea or beer. In one corner, there was always a good pile of wood for the hearth fire in the living room, and four wide doors led into that room. They were open most of the time, although the fire burned day and night, brightly or merely a gentle token, all the decades we lived on the Ranch.

My grandmother had her own small apartment in the house, as seemed natural and part of the way to coexist, and wandering missionaries and other men of her own cut of cloth often came down the road to see her and discuss convocations and get money and other help. They left books of earnest import and dubious literary worth, like one printed in symbols for the young or illiterate, with Jehovah an eye surrounded by shooting beams of forked fire. Grandmother's friends, of whom I remember not a single one, usually stayed for a meal. Mother was often absent from such unannounced confrontations, prey to almost ritual attacks of what were referred to as "sick headaches," but my father always carved at his seat, head of the table. Grandmother, of course, was there. Father left early, and we children went up to bed, conditioned to complete lack of interest in the murmur of respectful manly voices and our grandmother's clear-cut Victorian guidance of the churchly talk below us. That was the pattern the first months at the Ranch, before the old lady died, and I am sure we ate amply and well, and with good manners, and we accepted sober men in dusty black suits as part of being alive.

When we moved down Painter Avenue into what was then real country, I was near intoxication from the flowers growing everywhere—the scraggly roses lining the road, all viciously thorned as they reverted to wildness, and poppies and lupine in the ditches and still between the rows of orange trees (soon to disappear as their seeds got plowed too deeply into the profitable soil), and exotic bulbs springing up hit or miss in our neglected gardens. I rooted around in all of it like a virgin piglet snuffling for truffles. My mother gave me free rein to keep the house filled with my own interpretations of the word "posy." It was a fine season in life.

One day, I came inside, very dusty and hot, with a basket of roses and weeds of beauty. The house seemed mine, airy and empty, full of shade. Perhaps everyone was in Whittier, marketing. I leaned my forehead against the screening of the front porch and breathed the wonderful dry air of temporary freedom, and off from the county road and onto our long narrow driveway came a small man, smaller than I, dressed in the crumpled hot black I recognized at once as the Cloth and carrying a small valise.

I wiped at my sweaty face and went to the screen door, to be polite to another of my grandmother's visitors. I wished I had stayed out, anywhere at all, being that age and so on, and aware of rebellion's new pricks.

He was indeed tiny, and frail in a way I had never noticed before in anyone. (I think this new awareness and what happened later came from the fact that I was alone in the family house and felt for the moment like a stranger made up of Grandmother and my parents and maybe God—that eye, Jehovah, but with no lightning.) He would not come in. I asked him if he would like some cool water, but he said no. His voice was thin. He asked to see Mother Holbrook, and when I told her she had died a few days before he did not seem at all bothered, and neither was I, except that he might be.

He asked if I would like to buy a Bible. I said no, we had many of them. His hands were too shaky and weak to open his satchel, but when I asked him again to come in, and started to open the door to go out to help him, he told me in such a firm way to leave him alone that I did. I did not reason about it, for it seemed to be an agreement between us.

He picked up his dusty satchel, said goodbye in a very gentle voice, and walked back down the long driveway to the county road and then south, thinking God knows what hopeless thoughts. A little past our gate, he stopped to pick one of the dusty roses. I leaned my head against the screening of our porch and was astounded and mystified to feel slow fat quiet tears roll from my unblinking eyes and down my cheeks.

I could not believe it was happening. Where did they spring from, so fully formed, so unexpectedly? Where had they been waiting, all my long life as a child? What had just happened to me, to make me cry without volition, without a sound or a sob?

In a kind of justification of what I thought was a weakness, for I had been schooled to consider all tears as such, I thought, If I could have given him something of mine . . . If I were rich, I would buy him a new black suit. . . . If I had next week's allowance and had not spent this week's on three Cherry Flips . . . If I could have given him some cool water or my love . . .

But the tiny old man, dry as a ditch weed, was past all that, as I came to learn long after my first passionate protest—past or beyond.

The first of such tears as mine that dusty day, which are perhaps rightly called the tears of new wisdom, are the most startling to one's supposed equanimity. Later, they have a different taste. Perhaps they seem more bitter because they are recognizable. But they are always as unpredictable. Once, I was lying with my head back, listening to a long program of radio music from New York, with Toscanini drawing fine blood from his gang. I was hardly conscious of the sound—with my mind, anyway—and when it ended, my two ears, which I had never thought of as cup-like, were so full of silent tears that as I sat up they drenched and darkened my whole front with little gouts of brine. I felt amazed, beyond my embarrassment in a group of near-friends, for the music I had heard was not the kind I thought I liked, and the salty water had rolled down from my half-closed eyes like October rain, with no sting to it but perhaps promising a good winter.

Such things are, I repeat to myself, fortunately rare, for they are too mysterious to accept with equanimity. I prefer not to dig too much into their comings, but it is sure that they cannot be evoked or foretold. If anger has a part in them, it is latent, indirect—not an incentive. The helpless weeping and sobbing and retching that sweeps over somebody who inadvertently hears Churchill's voice rallying Englishmen to protect their shores, or Roosevelt telling people not to be afraid of fear, or a civil-rights chieftain saying politely that there is such a thing as democracy—those violent physical reactions are proof of one's being alive and aware. But the slow, large tears that spill from the eye, flowing like unblown rain according to the laws of gravity and desolation—these are the real tears, I think. They are the ones that have been simmered, boiled, sieved, filtered past all anger and into the realm of acceptive serenity.

There is a story about a dog and an ape that came to love each other. The dog finally died, trying to keep the ape from returning to the jungle where he should have been all along and where none but another ape could follow. And one becomes the dog, the ape, no matter how clumsily the story is told. One is the hapless lover.

I am all of them. I feel again the hot dusty screening on my forehead as I watch the little man walk slowly out to the road and turn down past the ditches and stop for a moment by a scraggly rosebush. If I could only give him something, I think. If I could tell him something true.

It was a beginning for me, as the tears popped out so richly and ran down, without a sigh or cry. I could see clearly through them, with no blurring, and they did not sting. This last is perhaps the most astonishing and fearsome part, past denial of any such encounter with wisdom, or whatever it is.

THE WEATHER WITHIN

Several days after my two girls and I sailed from San Francisco on a passenger freighter bound for Antwerp, I permitted myself, feeling fresh and peaceful again, to look about me on the little ship and notice the actualities of pain and digestion and love in other people, and to face them as fellow-voyagers. By that time, it was plain that many people other than I felt clearer, less blurred by fatigue and the sound of telephones ringing now a thousand miles behind us, and the five o'clock traffic on the Bay Bridge. They were more in focus, thanks to the sea change. A man who wore an orthopedic boot upon his twisted foot limped heavily, freely, instead of trying to walk as if he had two straight feet, and a woman who at first had sipped sherry before dinner, her eyes desperate, now sat at ease in a beneficent flow of Dutch gin—quietly, openly, and with increasingly good nature alcoholic.

I saw all this with a familiar relief. I drifted through the corridors and up and down the gleaming stairs and in and out of my bed, my dining chair, as untroubled as a dot of plankton, and when in the corridors or on the stairs I met another dot of it we gradually exchanged a kind of acceptance, one of the other, which with the voyage warmed to as much love or hatred as such dots can know. Even in the small, gently tipping room where we ate together, in our most intimate act of public intercourse, we began as the ship plowed south and then northeastward to bandy the looks and smiles and other displays of recognition demanded, ultimately, by our enforced companionship, purified after so many days together upon the heaving foreign sea.

At first, I let myself exist mainly through my children, because I was trying to stay lazy a little longer. I saw that they were in a way in love with our monkey-like waiter, who one minute, with a sly scheming grin, served solid Dutch cookies as if they were almost too leaflike and light to stay properly on our plates, and the next minute, with a near wink at the girls, poured out my coffee the way a murderer might fill a cup with poison—attentively, hopefully. They found him as fascinating as a peacock-feather fan, and through them I did, too. In the same way, I loathed a man who before and after almost every meal would stop and lightly fondle them, murmuring of his own daughter in a subtly lascivious and self-righteous way. My girls drew away from him with admirable delicacy; their soft, rich hair fell over their faces, and with them I held my breath. Perhaps my revolt was deeper than theirs—or, at least, wearier—for I could see a thousand such impositions in the years ahead of them, whereas for them it was probably the first time they had ever had to sit politely through such behavior because they were in a public room and would not kick or spit.

Then there were the old ladies. One of my girls would say something about her old lady, who perhaps was feeling queasy or was having trouble with her dentures, and the other girl would say something even more protective and proprietary about *her* old lady, and a part of me would twist with a wry regret that I could not be as important as the indistinguishable white-haired females who had provisionally won my children's warm attention, and a part of me would withdraw with respect before the knowledge that there on the little ship, as everywhere, I could not even guess at the lives my children led.

There were almost more old ladies on board than there were junior officers or tons of canned pineapple, because it was a good time of year for an easy crossing and the food and service were as if designed for stiff joints and gastric crotchets. By the end of the voyage, I could recognize and, sometimes, name a handful of the small, gentle women, but it was mostly through my daughters that I came to have a general awareness of their quiet pains and problems, of how one had stumbled over the step between her bathroom and her cabin and had bruised her leg from here to here, and of how another had put her wedding band in her mouth and swallowed it three years ago and was afraid it was giving her bad pains now that kept her from sleeping. My younger girl's old lady wore, I was told, beautiful diamond earrings that she had not taken out of her lobes for forty-seven years, so that they had grown into her skin, but without causing any trouble at all. I never did manage to spot her, but after Mrs. Marshall died I noticed that she was not the one, although I forget what earrings it was she did wear. Perhaps they were small pearls; I remember pearls at her throat. I was glad neither of the children lost her own old lady, of course, for it was enough of a startling accident to have death turn up, without having it too immediate. As it was, it changed the complexion of our landing.

A few times after I stirred myself out of my post-sailing snooze, I met Mrs. Marshall walking step by step up to B Deck from where she evidently lived, on C. I judged from words the other passengers exchanged with her during her slow movings that she had been ill and that on coming aboard she had fainted from the excitement and had been in bed for several days—a bad heart. I identified an even older, smaller woman as her sister and attentive companion, and two or three times in the next couple of weeks I asked one or the other how things were going, and they always replied very gently and genteelly, and smiled and smiled. I said to myself that Mrs. Marshall did indeed move as if she was ill, and that she had the patient, sweet, sickening half-smirk so often found on the face of a person who is afraid and at the same time voluptuously involved with her fear. I remember being somewhat ashamed of my feeling of boredom on recognizing this grimace; I had spent a lot of time coping with other people's capricious outworn organs, and wanted to sit back—temporarily, at least—and contemplate my own.

One night, I was asked to be judge of a costume parade and party, and in all the noise and uninhibited prancing I was astonished to see Mrs. Marshall walk slowly past the official table, of course not prancing but still in step and with a restrained coquettish look about her. She was dressed with prim prettiness as a maid, and I wondered in whose luggage on the little ship she had found that uniform in these days of reduced domestic service. I also noticed, in all the brouhaha, that her sister was not to be seen. Usually she stayed quietly nearby, her eyes worried and her voice small and expressionless. Did she disapprove of this debauchery?

Both women were what can most easily be called nice. They dressed in good black or navy-blue clothes for dinner, even through the Canal Zone, and their hair was soft instead of in the tight waves of most elderly middle-class American women. They were dainty, their nails lacquered with an almost colorless pink and their stockings very fine. All in all, they were as nearly invisible as one can be after sixty-five and still breathe and defecate and chew.

Toward the end of the voyage, the mother of a small boy gave what was called a *thé dansant* to honor his seventh birthday, and all of us were invited. I did not want to go, because I hate to have to look at little cakes in the late afternoon, but the mother had toploftily stayed away from a cocktail party to which another woman and I had invited all the passengers, and I felt duty-bound to be polite and appear at her silly tea. I made myself look as proper as possible, and was pleased to find that the giddy if disapprovingly non-alcoholic mother was paying no attention at all to anyone but the captain and the third mate. This gave me a chance to feel self-possessed and superior, as well as to ignore the table loaded with sticky tidbits, and I made myself useful to the nearest social victim—in this case the smiling, quiet little Mrs. Marshall, whose name I still did not know. I only remembered that she had been ill and that she lived somewhat as if she thought of herself as a premature child in an incubator, on a gauze-and-cotton pillow, with a rarer air about her than she would have to breathe later when she became truly born.

She sat very straight, with her pretty ankles crossed, and I fetched cakes and tea for her, and sat beside her in another chair and listened to her talk softly and with a surprising degree of intensity about the year she and her sister planned to spend together, mostly in England. She had read a lot of books about English history and architecture and so on, and I was lucky to recall some of the things my mother had managed to pass along to me about people who were important to her, as disparate as Cardinal Wolsey and Victoria. I even managed to come up with Grinling Gibbons—names like that.

I got her more tea, feeling infinitely attentive beside our loutish hostess, who paid no attention to any of us. It was a tiny but enjoyable revenge, there in the confines of the ship world, and as I sat by the nice old lady who was without knowing it serving as my victim-tool, I noticed that she fumbled with a word, and then a few seconds later that her lips trembled slightly and that she looked once or twice around the big room. Her eyes did not seem frightened or even troubled, but, without knowing how or why, it was horribly clear to me that she had passed through one of those almost mortal waves of panic very sick people are prey to. Her voice did not change, nor did she turn paler than her plump withered face had always looked, but her fear was as plain and as dreadful to me as if she had screamed out or moaned. I told myself that she was tired, saw that she had a table where she could sit by her cup and plate, and left as fast as I could.

It was an incident that is, of course, much more meaningful to me now, but even then it left me questioning and scorning myself for using—no matter how unwittingly—someone weaker than I was simply in order to feel better mannered than a foolish fellow-passenger who did not know how to go to or give parties. I thought about the panic I had spied on, and I admired it; the woman was in terror, and she was handling it with grace. I reached this conclusion easily, and then went on to more immediate problems of survival for my own self and my children, since it was evident that Mrs. Marshall had things well enough in hand not to drop her teacup or even cry out.

The morning we debarked was one of generally repressed hysteria, after the slow crawl through the lines of sunken convoys in the North Sea and then the noisy night of docking and unloading all the canned pineapple. Breakfast was early and crowded, and my girls were pale with unheeded love for the table boys too busy to smile one last time with them. After the casual weeks, people looked strange in dark suits and stylish hats. There was an air of almost hostile caution everywhere, as if we regretted having been gay and friendly and unsuspicious for so long, and suddenly feared what the mysterious sea change might have let us in for.

For reasons at once too obvious and too intricate to unravel even within my mind, I wanted to be quiet and late in leaving the little ship. I stalled this way and that, and when almost everyone had gone I was glad to find that my girls could talk happily and quietly with their friends in the crew while I stood looking far down at the thinning crowd upon the quay and at the growing piles of cargo from the holds. The ship rose slowly, so that the end of the long gangplank was off the pavement by the time we headed grudgingly for it and the first touch of land.

A knot of the ship's men gathered at the top to say goodbye to the children, and I stood back for a few minutes more, tasting the warm kindness and the lonesome searching there, and noticing with only part of my outward civilized self that the two elderly sisters sat in the cabin nearest the last door to pass through. They were dressed in smart, quiet travelling clothes. Their ankles were nicely crossed and their backs were straight. Their faces were like powdered ivory. I smiled at them, but they probably did not see my perfunctory salute; it was as if they were concentrating on something that took them too far away for speech. I thought swiftly of all that the one who had been ill knew about English history, and then we were inching down the gangplank, which now bobbed and wagged foolishly, with at least a couple of feet to jump at the bottom.

The children stumbled along the quay, calling and waving up to the cabin boys and the barman and the bosun, who stood by the C Deck rails. I headed for the almost bare tables where the customs officers waited with my luggage lined up in front of them, and smiled and rallied my rusted French and kept a mazed account in my head of where we all were and what the agent was saying about trunks and what was in the suitcases the officers chose to open.

An enormous bus blasted its horn, and people shrieked goodbyes like sea gulls in a storm, and I felt eased to know that every passenger—and especially the man who had pretended he was not fondling my children—was probably forever gone from our lives and on that bus to catch the Channel boat for London, except the two sisters, who were heading first for Holland for a week and who probably knew more about England than any of them.

The customs man scrawled pink crayon over the last of my collection of some fifty years of family travelling bags. I felt a puff of relief rise from the ground through my body, as if an indiscreet ghost there at the quay to welcome me had blown up under my skirts. I was teased and excited and amused, and called out to the children, who stood, tiny as gnats against the ship's tall sides, mooning and bleating up at their white-coated friends, their backs to the new world that menaced them, their eyes glistening with tears of farewell.

They turned toward that new world at my call, toward me standing in it, and I saw them pull back, and at the same time I heard the older of the two old ladies, *my* old ladies, cry out in a small shocked voice, "Just like San Francisco! It happened there just like this. She'll be all right."

On the scarred boards of the inspection table, Mrs. Marshall half sat, half slumped against her older sister. She was as pale as always, with her eyes squinted and rolled upward in her plump face. Her smart black hat tipped crazily over one eye as she rolled back against the shoulder beside her, and I thought that she would hate to look that silly even as I hated myself for a feeling of irritation at the sweet, patient smile on her discreetly made-up lips.

Oh, God, these invalids! My mind was snarling as I put down my big heavy handbag and let her fall more against me than toward her sister. I don't know why I did this. It seemed natural; the sister was very small and old, and I know that a half-conscious body, which I felt Mrs. Marshall's to be and which it probably was at that moment, can be extraordinarily heavy. I eased her back against one of my softer suitcases, and behind me I could hear the sister saying in a quiet, desperate way, not especially to anybody but much as a nun murmurs toward a picture or a statue, "Oh, I did everything for her this morning, everything. She didn't even lift a finger. Not a finger. We didn't even talk. She was fine, too, just fine, not nervous at all. Get some whiskey. That's all she needed that time in San Francisco. Just some whiskey."

While she was murmuring this way, she came around the end of the table and stood near her sister's head, which I was watching while I took her pretty feet and tried to pivot her up lengthwise. Mrs. Marshall's face was changing rapidly, and there were no pupils in the narrowed eyes. Her skin became yellowish, and then darker and very subtly blue—lead blue—and I said to myself, "But this woman is dying and she is dying fast," and then I remembered how three times I had seen another woman turn this strange blue and how three times she had lived to question me piercingly about it all, so I said nothing aloud and pulled hard to lift up the dainty feet.

A dim old man with "Commissionnaire" printed in gold on his cap took the feet from me. He was drunk, with spit caked in the corners of his mouth, and he gave off a feeling of gentle strength. "All right," I said to the sister. "Yes yes, hold her head up more. . . ."

She went on in her small voice about San Francisco and whiskey and how whiskey was all that Mary Alice needed—really, really.

By now it was plainly too late to put anything into that blue open mouth, gaping subhumanly for air, sucking for it, then more and more slowly wheezing it out again. Somebody in the little crowd that had gathered said, "It's a fit. Don't let her tongue go back," but I knew it was not a fit at all, and I ran toward the ship for help.

The children were hurrying to me, their faces still pale from the intensity of their farewells, and twisted now with concern. They pushed almost past me toward the knot of people, and I turned them around toward the side of the ship again as I ran, and said, "It's all right. A passenger feels ill. She fainted, but it's all right."

"Is it my old lady?" one of them asked, and I said, "Of course not!" I was determined not to let them see Mrs. Marshall, for if she was dying she might have to fight it, and that was not for the children to know about yet, if I could help it. So I kept my voice calm for them, and my hands firm and gentle on their shoulders, but for the faces staring down curiously from the deck I let my own face show what I feared was happening. I called up to the young barman, spruce in mufti to meet his sweetheart, "Get the doctor! Hurry. Tell him to hurry!"

He stared for a second, freezing like me, and then he ran along the narrow deck and through the door, and another boy, the monkey boy the children loved the most, came down the bobbing gangplank, smiling warmly at them. "Keep them for me, Jantje," I said, and he took their hands and walked away with them toward the bow of the ship and the open river water.

I found I had their grey topcoats, and as I looked down again at the woman I put them over her carefully, perhaps to try to hide her from the flat stares of the little crowd, perhaps only to make it seem to her poor sister that it could possibly matter whether she were covered or bare as newborn. Her heart had almost stopped, and what air it could pull through her darkening mouth whistled slowly out, unused. She was suffocating as surely as if a cord had tied off her windpipe. I wished I could hide it from the sister, that I could put her little white-gloved hand, as I had done my children's, into the kind grasp of one of the seamen and send her along the quay toward the open water. But her look reassured me by its transparent blankness; she was shocked into safety for a time longer.

A cabin boy stared with horror at Mrs. Marshall's gaping dark face as he thrust a glass into my hand. I sniffed it—the ship's best brandy. Somebody must have relayed the sister's small prayer for whiskey as best he could. I would have liked to drink half of it in one gulp, for plainly Mrs. Marshall could not, and my stomach felt strange and I was breathing from the top of my lungs, carefully. I put the little brimming glass between two of my suitcases, and because I had nothing else to do I took one of Mrs. Marshall's ankles from the old porter. It was astonishingly heavy, like stone, and as I let it thump down upon the inspection table he picked it up again, without reproach, in his big, twisted, dirty hand.

The doctor was there, in civilian clothes, and without any preamble he and I started talking rapidly, easily, softly, in French, which neither of us had ever done before in our few chats on the ship. No, he said, almost no pulse . . . always complications . . . get her onto the ship . . . may have only a few minutes . . . injections . . . at least she did not die at sea, always very bad for the morale . . . this is very bothersome. . . . He muttered orders in a low, angry way at two of the crewmen, who ran up the wagging gangplank for the ship's stretcher.

The sister said, more loudly than I would have thought possible from her, "All she needs is some *whiskey*. That saved her in San Francisco."

The doctor glared briefly at her and then asked me in French, "Who is this person?"

"Her sister."

He asked her in English, in a curt, disapproving way, "Well, who gave her whiskey?"

The sister said firmly, looking up at him like a determined, unabashed child, while Mrs. Marshall's heart gave another great desperate jump and stopped again, "You weren't on the ship yet. A friend who is a nurse was saying goodbye to us and—"

He interrupted her haughtily. "And I am not a nurse. I am a doctor."

Oh you God-damned Prussian-trained Nazi-broken bastard, I thought. Protocol. Professional honor. My mind spat.

The crewmen were unfolding an ugly, stained khaki stretcher. The old porter and I lifted Mrs. Marshall clumsily onto it while they held it. She seemed made of cold lead, and her head arched back hungrily for some of the air we were breathing. Her sister tried to take her hand, but it fell into the pouch of stiff canvas.

"She'll be all right soon," I was saying without any shame. "He'll give her a shot to help her heart. He's a good doctor. A shot will be better than whiskey for your . . . for Mary Alice."

And then I closed a door on the past few minutes and turned toward my children and the things I had to do next. I waved to them where they stood with Jantje, watching the barges and the gulls, and with hardly a thought of the two old women in the ship I looked for the porter on the quay. When I saw him standing like a waiting horse beside the possible pasturage of my row of bags and boxes, I smiled at him.

His eyes filled with a kind of alcoholic urine. "Those poor, poor ladies," he said, and even though I had left them deliberately, my own eyes flooded with tears for them, which I ignored with an almost ferocious resentment.

All right, all *right*, I said angrily to the other parts of me. So I wanted to be last off the ship! But I'll be damned to hell if I'll let this hurt my girls and me, and all the fuss and bother of getting us this far. Life, death—they must know about it anyway. This will be life, not death. That is the way I talked to myself, while I reached for the glass of cognac I had put between two of my bags and thrust it, by now somewhat warm, at the old man.

He took it as if it were a natural thing to gulp a tot of four-star Fine Champagne on the quay, and then, with a swipe at his still brimming eyes, he yelled for a taxi—a prowler who had probably made two trips already into the city and was back for the last load of crew or officers. I counted the bags again as they thudded into the back of the car, and then I pushed the children onto the seat and gave the old man some money and once more we all said a warm, sad thank-you-and-until-we-meet to Jantje and I put my foot up into the car, thinking, Oh dear kind God here we are here we are at last quick driver into the city away from the salt smell and the sea gulls hurry hurry—and a voice called down my name with real desperation, twice.

We stood, the driver and Jantje and I, with our feet half here, half there.

The doctor was leaning against the rail, high above us, and his jaw was slack and he looked as if he were in panic or in a frantic state of disbelief. He must have run faster than he had been able to since the Gestapo broke all his leg bones after one of the first professional roundups in Amsterdam, for he panted and his thin grey hair was awry.

"But why is he calling *me*? Why *me*?" I asked angrily. I pulled my foot down onto the ground.

Jantje turned toward me, and even before the doctor spoke I was saying very fast and soft, "Can you stay here longer with the children? They'll be all right with you."

He looked at me wisely, and crawled past me into the back of the cab.

The doctor called down in a peevish way, "She is dead. She is dead," and I did not realize until later that he was speaking to me in Dutch or German, for I knew already what he was going to say.

I turned back to the children, with Jantje sitting now between them. They looked with unfathomable resignation into my troubled and perhaps angry eyes, which I tried to make nicer for them but could not. Then again one of them asked, "Was it either of *our* old ladies?" and again I said no and that I would be back soon and that Jantje would stay with them. The taxi was riding low, loaded with everything I possessed in the world, almost; I did not even bother to ask the driver to wait. He had a fat, although youngish, neck.

I walked back to the gangplank. The end of it was by now some three feet off the quay, and a crewman who a few days before had chased my ball of yarn across the deck and then tossed it to me with a saucy grin helped me haul myself up as if I were the Queen's first lady. His face was crumpled with a grievous surprise—the kind that had made the old porter cry, and then me.

From the top of the gangplank the doctor called again to me, as I crawled awkwardly toward him, "She is dead!" He was speaking in French, as he had done beside the customs table, and I cried up to him like a parrot, "Yes, yes, she is dead!" He took my elbow, and we ran in a dignified, cautious way down several corridors I had never known were in the ship, past the galley ovens and into dimmer regions, now awash with suds, where the filthy stevedores had walked for coffee or a glass of Genever. I had to talk sternly to myself for a few seconds, for my breath faltered and my tongue went dry, and my heart banged with primitive fear and civilized resentment.

Then I saw in a doorway the face of the barber, who also carried cases of beer up and down stairways between haircuts. He was a very stupid man, with enormous eyes and ears, and the crew called him Jackie the Clipper because he clipped their hair and also because he sailed in and out of every port with unexpected sexual prowess and a resulting state of alcoholic debilitude that only Rabelais could describe. There was Jackie then, peering at me with his great eyes, and in spite of the latent expectancy in them, the postponed amatory gleam and quiver of being in port again, they swam with tears that I knew were as real as my own helpless acceptance of the fact of Mrs. Marshall's death.

"Hello there, Jackie," I said in a mechanically cozy way as I pounded behind the rigid doctor down the corridor. Everybody talked to Jackie like that. I felt comforted by his great, drowned, simple look, and got my breath back. Whatever was next did not appall me anymore.

We were in a low white room half full of painted pipes twisting carefully along the walls and ceiling and even the floor. There seemed to be several people, but I remember only the doctor, stooping under the pipes, and, on the floor, the very small body of Mrs. Marshall with her jaw dropped and her hands looking as peaceful as a dead bird's claws, and the equally small sister standing with her back to us, holding their two heavy black handbags and my girls' topcoats. I did not know what to do, so I stepped over the high threshold and put both my arms around the living one, who seemed to shrink even smaller and cleave unto me as I know those words mean it. She sobbed in a way I had not heard before—with passion, but also rather like a rooster crowing. There was nothing ridiculous about it, and as I felt her feathery body pressed so completely, so unthinkingly against mine, I knew that I was blessed. I said softly a lot of things about how gay her sister had been at the silly tea, and how well she had looked that morning in the cabin next door, how untroubled—all half lies made without cavil.

The great eyes of Jackie the Clipper floated in the dark hot air of the corridor by the door, and I could feel a frightened hush through the depths of this unknown ship I had ridden so blandly for so many days and weeks. Having a dainty corpse upon it was something nobody wanted, but I was agreeing with the grey-faced impatient doctor that God had been good to all of us to postpone it this long.

"A sea burial is very bad," he said over his shoulder as we two hurried down the corridor. His French was impeccable, and by now I knew that his wife was waiting for him, after three months of voyage. "You cannot imagine a sea burial," he said, but he was mistaken and I could, so I agreed with him and said I could not. "And now here is the address of the hospital. Of course there are some complications: American Protestant corpse, Catholic Belgian port, Dutch ship. But the sister seems intelligent. The Red Cross will take care of everything. Give them half an hour and then call the hospital and have the sister speak with you."

And so on, very firmly, and I said yes and no and certainly, and tried to seem efficient, and all the time I was storming and roaring, but pretty much the way a child will when the light has been turned off and the door shut and he has heard his parents drive away in the family car. I could yell until I burst, but there was no real use. There I was, after so much trying to be, excited and somewhat scared in a strange land, with two little girls to watch over, and instead of our going at our own speed to a decent hotel and then wandering, as we had planned, toward the Zoo through the streets with all their new smells and sounds, I had already left the children with a Dutch steward and an unknown Belgian cabby and gone back down into the ship's depths to look at a dead woman, and was about to devote myself to getting her decently into some sort of coffin or urn or whatever in her god's name she would have wanted—and above all I must help the one still living, the birdlike sister whose name I did not even know. If the dead woman had not had a sister who still lived and must go on living, I would be free of the whole thing. I felt impotent and rebellious, and shook hands in a short way with the doctor, who already looked years younger at having rid himself so neatly of so many unexpected and unwanted responsibilities. He became almost debonair as we reached the top of the gangplank. By now it was a good four feet off the quay, and two sailors hoisted me down. I did not look back.

The children were pale and puzzled in the dim taxi. "Yes, the passenger died," I said to them and Jantje. He seemed upset and sad. He told me her name, Mrs. Mary Alice Marshall, and said that her sister was either Miss or Mrs. Pettigrew, and I looked at the piece of paper the doctor had given me and it was Miss. Jantje said they were very nice quiet ladies. Then he told me the cabdriver had kept the meter running but he had said that was a shameful thing to do in such a case, and later the children told me Jantje got out of the taxi and almost had a brawl with the driver before the little box was turned off. He left us, and the children looked after his springy back, his dark small simian head, with possibly as much plain love as they will ever feel for a man they trust.

Then we turned to each other, and I told them again that it had not been one of *their* old ladies. The children sighed and said good, and then we discussed the imminent problem of what to do with the remaining sister, Miss Pettigrew. They were both resigned and realistic about it, and filled with a real compassion, which to me seemed far past their expected capacity for such things, so that for the rest of that long day they did not protest in any way about having to eat lunch in a "nice tea-room" with the gentle little woman instead of in the glittering restaurant I had vaguely described to them, or about missing the Zoo entirely and staying alone in the hotel—a hateful thing—while I made numberless telephone calls to the Consulate and tried to get permission for cremation in the anti-cremation city, or about having late baths and supper in our rooms instead of going to see Charlie Chaplin, as we had thought of doing, because I had to make more telephone calls to Holland and California for Miss Pettigrew, whose voice had turned with repressed hysteria into an unmanageable but still genteel squeak. My girls were fine girls.

So was Miss Pettigrew a fine girl. She moved through the whole grim thing with hardly a falter, and accepted my presence unquestioningly. I, remembering my first resentful anger and the way I had heard my mind snarling, was abashed and suspicious at the same time. How could anyone stay as thoughtful and as self-possessed as this small aged lady, and how could she go on letting me parley intimate and even secret details of her life and her dead sister's for assistant consuls and functionaries and priests and doctors without hating not only my guts but my children's guts and my furtherest ancestors' guts? I saw that in a way I hated hers—or, at least, her dead sister's—and I bowed meekly before this knowledge, all the while snatching looks and words with my girls, and ordering tea and toast and a tot of rum sent to Miss Pettigrew's room, which I had naturally seen was next to ours. How she must hate *me*, I insisted to myself so that I would not feel myself hating her over all the larger and less ugly necessities, like What would the children really like for supper, and What valise did I put the toothpaste in, and Did I really say to the curé that I thought it was abominable to have to ship a body to Amsterdam to get it cremated or did I just mean to?

Miss Pettigrew and I discussed sleeping pills with brittle detachment. She had some; she seldom took them; she planned to take one or perhaps two that night; if I would be so good as to ask the night clerk to call her at seven, she would be ready for the morning train into Holland to stay with the friend of a dear friend. I knew she would do all this—or, at least, I felt that I knew it, and also I wanted her to. We said good night in a detached and carefully offhand way, and I went next door to eat a roasted chicken with my children. We talked softly, knowing who was next door and not wanting to sound as if we were too happy, but we had a very nice time. Just before I got into bed, an envelope slid under the door (she had been awake all the time), with a precisely written, lady-like note and two American dollars for a lunch or tea I had forgotten about. It asked for my address to be left with the clerk, so that Miss Pettigrew could write a letter I hoped I would never get.

We slept well that night, without any troubled dreams that we could remember in the fine grey daylight, and went on to Bruges. The only way I showed protest against what had happened was that when the children talked lengthily about dying and asked over and over again about turning black and decaying and how long it took, I felt inexpressibly annoyed and snapped at them and even said things like "For God's sake, stop talking about it! So she died! So let's *forget* it, shall we?" And they would look patiently at me and I would feel ashamed of myself and talk more gently and discuss at length the processes of disintegration and the effects of no oxygen on the bloodstream, as we slid along the silent canals of the dead town and the guide called out "All heads down" for the bridges.

And then I began to think that the small neat figure just ahead of us in the narrow street to the hotel, or the bowed head with the chic hat in the prow of the canal taxi that had just slipped by, was actually Miss Pettigrew's. Silent and shy, she was flitting behind me or ahead, filled with questions and sorrows that were really my own, hating me with my own hatred for having thus innocently thrust myself into her life, which, in turn, was becoming my own life. And I was in a kind of double focus, doubting my motives, wondering why I had been forced to be so generous of myself and of my helpless children—if I had done it because of a hidden hunger for the bird-like love and need of me, if I was indeed a ghoul! And then the questions were more mocking, and my brain went on shaping them this way and that, but always with Miss Pettigrew just ahead or behind, driven by something that had sent her after me, after us, to Bruges instead of northward to Amsterdam with the poor small body of her sister.

Perhaps I'll never know if the white-haired stronger sister reached Holland with her cargo, heavier than planned. I shall never know that she did *not* slip ahead of me in the dead streets of Bruges, or past me silently upon those silent, oily waters, as I shall never know if she hated me for being almost the last one off the ship.

THE UNSWEPT EMPTINESS

When the wax-man came around the corner of the house Matey was feeling sorry and alone, and that is why she cried out so warmly, "Why, it's my friend the wax-man!"

"Matey, Matey," her little daughter said, in a dance of excitement, "a visitor for us!" And the three dogs were barking pleasurably, their tails like banners and the bitch too heavy and near her pup-time now to jump, wallowing like a happy tugboat in the wake of all the noise. Matey looked up with a quick smile, and because she was full of sorrow about many things and lonely too, for her husband was far away and she could feel him missing her and the two little girls and the dogs, she cried out, "Why, it's my friend the wax-man!"

She put down the trowel, and rubbed her hands stained with weeds and earth on the sides of her overalls, and as she climbed up the embankment toward the man she thought of what always happened when she saw him. It was the same problem every time, and even though he had not paid his annual visit to her for five years, since gas rationing began, it still gave her a familiar hysterical feeling not to be able to remember his name, and to know that when she finally did she would want to laugh. He sold wax and took orders for wax, the way people sold brushes. If he had sold brushes his name would not be Fuller, which would be logical, but Kent, which was also logical but in a less obvious way: Fuller brushes, Kent brushes, one made in America and one in England. But he sold waxes. But his name was not Johnson, which in the same way would be logical. So what was it?

Matey tried not to feel gigglish and hysterical. She knew that before it was too late she would recall the wax-name that was the right one for him, and that then she must have a reserve supply of self-control, so that she would not laugh in his face with relief and amusement.

She saw as she climbed up toward him that he looked generally the same as five years ago, holding his heavy black hat in one hand and his little suitcase full of samples in the other, standing motionless in the swirl of dogs and noise while the small girl hopped around.

"Hello," Matey said, keeping her voice as it had been at first when he surprised her in her sorrow and loneliness, not wanting to hurt him by a quick change to normal politeness after that first warmth, for he had indeed come once more up the long rough dirt road to sell waxes to her. "I haven't seen you for a long time," she said, standing beside him.

"Who *is* this man, Matey?" her daughter asked in a gay excited voice, and the three dogs looked up at him gaily too, their tails still fluttering as they waited to know.

Matey felt the hysteria loom inside her. It is not Mr. Johnson, she said firmly, helpless to tell yet what the name would be, the logical name for her friend the wax-man. "This is my friend the wax-man, Sarah," she said, and then she felt shy and awkward, hoping once again as she always did that he would not find her rude to forget his right name, after his long ride up the hill.

"Oh," the little girl said, as if the answer were complete and deeply satisfying, and the dogs felt that too and sniffed courteously at his dusty black shoes, his creased pepper-and-salt trousers.

"No, I couldn't attend to my old customers during the war years," he said in his familiar gentle voice, and he was breathing in a guarded way, as if he tried not to puff.

"You're just in time," Matey said happily, as she always did to him whether it was true or not. It was ridiculous to infer that she was at this very moment almost out of the wax he had last sold her five years before, but it was so pleasant to see him unchanged and faithful, and to feel that she was one of his old customers, that she almost believed that the shelf in the broom-closet was indeed empty, and not well filled with bottles and jars of polish she had bought at the village hardware store. "I need *gallons* of stuff," she said.

She led the way through the patio to the side door, so as not to have the three of them tramping past the baby's room to waken her, and sank down in her familiar place upon the couch with Sarah tense with excitement beside her, while the wax-man dropped expertly upon one knee and flipped open the same suitcase, with the same wares fitted into it. It was as if five years had folded back upon themselves, like a portable silver drinking cup she once had that snapped back into a single ring, flat for her pocket, when she pressed it. Sarah was not her child born since last she bought wax from this same man, but perhaps just a neighbor visiting. There was no baby sleeping close by. She would give the order she always gave and watch him write it on a pad on his knee, and some time before he left she would remember his name, as she had always done.

"Now this is a new product," he was saying, "which I have supplied to many of my old customers, really very nice for kitchens and," he hesitated, "for bathrooms too they all tell me, and you can see," and he deftly held out an advertisement pasted to a sheet of cardboard, "here it is in the *Saturday Evening Post* of three weeks ago, very well displayed too I may say, one of our new products which I feel is a real addition to our list, as you will see if I may just give you a teeny-weeny hint of it," and before Matey could stop him he had sprayed from the fat atomizer in his hand a little cloud.

"Pee-*ugh*," Sarah said.

"Oh," Matey cried, "what is it?"

"We have Pineywoods, but this sample happens to be Arabian Nights," he murmured.

"Oh, it's simply awful," she said. "I'm sorry, but I simply can't stand it." She almost said, "It smells like a bad public toilet," and she almost called him Mr. Johnson. She began to feel impatient with her lagging memory, and a little hurt that he had shot this stink into the air, and beside her Sarah bounced nervously. Matey put one hand on her child's tiny knee, and said, "But I *do* need a lot of floor-oil and all that."

"Now here is something," he went on in his soft sleepy voice, "that I am recommending personally for a really high polish."

Matey laughed a little, because he always said that and then she always replied as she did now, "But these old floors! Rough pine! No use trying to polish them!" Then, as always, she looked at his remote thin face, knowing that he would glance very quickly, without any change of expression, at the floor at the end of the rug he was kneeling on, before he looked back at his sample.

Suddenly she was hot with discouragement, and almost overwhelmed by a rush of loneliness for her long-absent husband. If only he would unwind the red tape of discharge papers and such, and be home again, so that she would feel like a whole creature and be able to keep their house sparkling! If only he were home! Then there would be no dust, no murk of footprints on the oiled floors, no fluff of house-moss and dog hairs and untidiness under the piano. She leaned down in a welter of self-castigation and sniffed at the top of Sarah's head, and sure enough it smelled like the head of a hot dirty little girl. Ah, I should have washed her hair last Saturday, Matey thought morbidly. I am neglecting her. And she looked at the earth under her own fingernails, and then at her filthy old battered tennis-shoes sticking out from the faded overalls, and she felt unkempt and careless and desolate. When will he ever come home, she wondered, deep in a chasm of sadness.

"Absolutely no use," she said to the wax-man. "It's your good old floor-oil I need, gallons of it."

"This polish is really fine for furniture too," he went on softly. "I have always supplied it to my customers who value their antiques, you know." And he flicked his eyes imperturbably at the front of the walnut-secretary-from-Matey's-great-grandmother, all covered with smudges where the baby was learning to pull herself up.

Matey almost said, "Oh, Mr. Johnson, I've had *two* children since last you came! Yes, Mr. Johnson, I have *another* little girl, almost a year old! Such changes, Mr. Johnson!" But she did not. She said, "A pint of it, then. I think just a pint."

"Yes," he said gently. "Some of my best customers have always supplied themselves with it ... Mrs. Huntington Logan, you must know her, such beautiful antiques, and Mrs. James S. Reed but of course you may not know her so far away always used it, and Mrs. J. Howard Burnham, so very *very* particular about her antiques. . . ." He put the sample back tidily, and marked the order-blank on his knee.

Matey wondered, as she always had done at this point in their meetings, how he could kneel so long. She had read once that his company gave all its salesmen special training in such gymnastics. He folded down so neatly, and then at the end he stood up without making even a crackle or snap in his knee-joints, which she was sure she could never in the world have done. Perhaps Sarah could, but certainly not she. "And then of course a gallon of the regular floor-oil, for these horrible old pine floors," she said. "No, *two* gallons, I think."

"Two, yes," he murmured, flicking his eyes with no change of expression at the dust-blurred floors.

Matey once more sank down in herself with misery, and thought of the gleaming parquetry of all his other old customers, the shimmer under the piano of Mrs. Huntington Logan, the shine under Mrs. James S. Reed's maple dining table, the black glitter of antique oak beams under antique Mrs. J. Howard Burnham's antique armoire. They all have husbands, she thought bitterly, husbands out of Washington forever, husbands home and with jobs. That is why they have polished floors, all right. That's it, Mr. Johnson. "Two gallons at *least*," she said, laughing.

"I'll just mark down two," the wax-man said softly, licking the tip of his pencil. "I hope to be able to serve my regular old customers every six months now, since we no longer have rationing of gasoline. Two will suffice until my next visit."

In a daze, a glaze, of unhappiness Matey ordered two cans of wax for the icebox and the stove, and some liquid polish for the kitchen linoleum. They were goads to her, whips on her lazy slatternly back, sluttish hausfrau Matey. Never again will the wax-man oddly enough not called Johnson come here and see dustdustdust, smudges, smears, house-moss, she swore desolately. Never again, dear Mr. Johnson. She remembered as if it had been many years ago, five years ago perhaps, the light joy she had felt when he came this afternoon around the corner of the house, with all the barking and Sarah hopping excitedly among the dogs. How could she have felt so joyful, well knowing as she did that the house was filthy, *filthy?* How could she have been there in the sunlight, nonchalantly pulling weeds while the dust lay everywhere inside? Ah, if she could remember his name, then she would be more at peace with herself, she knew.

They stood up, the wax-man flipping shut his sample-case and Matey and Sarah as like as two peas, grimy and healthy, and while the two females waited on the terrace, so that perhaps the baby would not wake for a few more minutes, and the two dogs and the tub-like gravid bitch flounced and floundered about the man's legs, he went down to his old car for what had been ordered.

Matey held her checkbook and fountain pen. His name his name his name, she prayed, figuring ways to find out, in case the customary miracle did not happen and pop it into her mind. She would ask carelessly, "Shall I make it out to the company or to you?" . . . something like that. "Just what *are* your initials?" she would ask carelessly, laughingly.

Sarah said, "Matey, our old friend the wax-man is having troubles," and it was true: he stood halfway up the path with cans and cans of polish rolling out of his arms, and a look of dismay on his face at this inexpert unpracticed unaccustomed untidiness, so that they hurried down to him and Sarah went yelling and chasing after a round box of wax.

When everything was picked up and brought as far as the steps, Matey said, "Let's leave it all here, and my husband will help me," because even though she felt sure the wax-man knew that her husband would not be home for weeks-months-years she could not bear to have him come into the house again, for a nightmarish fear that he would fold down onto his knee and flick open his satchel and tell her once more about the clean sparkling gleaming homes of his other old customers.

"Now for the check," she said in a brisk voice that embarrassed her. What would happen? Would she have to ask his name? Would she remember, in a photo-finish? Was there still time for the familiar miracle, the name that was not as logical as it might at first seem, taken in conjunction with his profession as a wax-man, not as right as the name Johnson perhaps but still right, exotic, farfetched but right . . . ?

He slid a card onto the stone wall beside her checkbook, and then looked out across the valley, his back to her. He is discreet, she thought gratefully. He is a kind sensitive man. No wonder I welcomed him. The card, face down, said on its back "$12.56."

Matey filled in everything on her check but the name-line, and her stub and its name-line, and then asked in a voice that sounded a little too loud to her, "Shall I make it out to you? Would that be better?"

He did not turn, as she could tell without looking at him, but said very softly, "Please."

She turned over the card, still waiting to remember what it would say. And even as she read it she remembered too, so that there was surely not a half-second between the reading and the memory. Of course his name was Bee, Mr. J. M. Bee. It was unforgettable: Mr. Bee sells wax. What other man with what other name could ever sell wax but Mr. J. M. Bee? Real laughter, not helpless hysterical giggles, loomed in her, and all of a sudden she felt so full of relief that she wanted to cry out to him, "Oh, Mr. Bee! I am so happy that you came back, Mr. Bee! I missed you, these five years. I have always loved having you come up here on the hill. You have always been so nice, to come clear up here onto this dry rocky place, when most of your old customers have nice large shining houses on the flat of the valley, with lawns in front and no dogs and no children. I am really delighted to see you, especially today, Mr. Bee!"

She turned to him, waving the check like a flag. She felt young, triumphant, unconquerable. "Mr. Bee!" she cried.

He shrugged his shoulders in their neat pepper-and-salt suit, without turning toward her, and she stood looking with him at the far quiet valley, the two ridges of hills, one brown and one bluish behind it, and then the climbing jagged mountains and the final snow. Above the inaudible sound of the words her mind was still calling out so gaily she could hear a gobble of turkeys from a distant farm, and the droning hum of a tractor. She could hear, indeed she *did* hear, the little girl Sarah sigh once, close beside her, as if with a world-weariness, while the dogs sat in a silent row on the terrace wall, the bulging bitch in the middle, watching.

"Old Baldy," the wax-man said. There was still no immediate sound, and below in the valley the tractor and the turkeys made their small heartbeat into the thin clear air. "Old Baldy," he said again. "That old mountain always gets me, does something to me."

Matey still felt like telling him how much she liked him, because she was drunk with relief and amusement and well-being, at last to have his wonderful name safe in her mind. She thought in a flash that she would tell him about the name too, about her annual, semi-annual trauma or whatever it might be that made her suffer so, remembering Fuller-Kent-Johnson and then always the final miracle of *Mr. Bee*. But he whirled around and looked sternly at her, and said in a harsh shocking voice, "Funny what these old mountains do to you, all right!"

Matey saw in amazement, in a kind of horror, that his pale grey eyes were thick with tears, and that his mouth, which she had never really looked at, was trembling and bluish over his even white false teeth. She saw that his neat clothes were very loose upon his frame. He was old. He was much more than five years older than he had been five years ago, she saw. And then she remembered what she must have seen subconsciously in the living room, how he had stood up from his jaunty expert kneeling: he had unfolded in painful sections, in a kind of repressed agony of balancing and posing, of trying to maintain the good old wax-company stance, the tried-and-true ageless salesman's limberness. Oh Mr. Bee, she thought, weak with compassion. She knew that she could not tell him now about the name. It would not ever be funny again for her. And now she would never forget it: that she knew.

He blinked unashamedly, and a tear ran down one cheek and he licked it up with his tongue and surprisingly smacked his lips, the way the baby did sometimes when a whole bean got into the smooth puree of beans. It probably tasted awful, Matey thought . . . like alum.

She held out the check to him. He folded it neatly, thanked her with a jerky bow, and turned away without any confusion for the way his face was streaked. It was as if blaming tears on a far snow-white mountain absolved him of weakness.

Matey and Sarah and the three dogs watched him walk stiffly down the steep path to his car.

"Goodbye, friend the wax-man," the little girl called.

He turned, and said in his new scratchy loud voice, "Glad to have served you again. Things have certainly changed all right. Faces in the valley have all changed. I tell you, I hardly know a soul. All the old customers have gone."

Matey thought wildly, *Not* Mrs. Logan and Mrs. Reed, *not* Mrs. J. Howard Burnham too! Oh Mr. Bee!

"Well," she said, grinning fatuously at his blind face, "I'm still here. I hope I'm always here. I love it here."

He turned noncommittally and got into his car.

Sarah waved as it coasted down the hill. The bitch ran heavily along the road after it for a few feet and then turned and walked with caution toward her bowl of water on the patio, the other dogs after her. Matey stood waiting to hear the baby cry for light and air and *la vie joyeuse* after a long nap.

Everything was pretty much as it had always been: the wax-man had come; she had ordered with her usual lavish disregard of present supplies, oppressed by the thought of his long loyal drive up the hilly road; she had suffered and then been rewarded by the inimitable coincidence that the wax-man's name was, as it had always been, Mr. Bee, an unforgettable name forgotten annually.

But five years were not annually. . . . Matey thought of the two new children and the coming puppies, and of the emptiness and the smudged outlines of her present life, the undusted floors and the unpolished nails and the unwashed heads of sweet babygirlhair, and then for a minute she rose above all that the memory of blue-lipped Mr. Bee getting up so cautiously from the dirty rug of his last faithful old customer, and she was young and strong and happy and well-beloved. She knew that as fast as her husband could, he would come home to her. She knew that the floors would shine again, and the children's heads, and her own well-formed fingernails. But as she heard the cry she had been waiting for, the one full of hunger and sleep from the younger girl, she turned toward the far white mountain that had betrayed the wax-man into weeping and for a minute or two she could easily have wept, herself.

Notes on a Necessary Pact

I. There Is a Remedy

(. . . for everything but death
CERVANTES*)*

Once there was a woman who helped her father (Hodgkin's disease), her mother (grief and obesity), her child (premature birth), an unknown stranger in a war, two of her three husbands, and finally her dearest friend, die various ugly deaths. She resolved, at forty-some, that since she herself must die, she would do it as gracefully as possible, as free as possible from vomitings, moans, the ignominy of basins, bed-sores, and enemas, not to mention the intenser ignominious dependence of weak knees and various torments of the troubled mind.

For years she lived carefully. After much consultation and study she reached a state in which her bowels functioned almost perfectly, her bile manufactured itself in the correct amounts, and even her sweat glands responded more to the whip of her current diet than to the goad of temperature. She never sniffed or coughed, and so perfect was her superannuated but hyperdigestive digestive system that if she wanted to splurge occasionally she could eat a half pound of caviar and drink a quart of almost any commendable Champagne without belching.

Gradually, as her body, pickled in good health, ticked relentlessly and with no apparent slackening toward an infinity of common-sense living, she began to realize that she was all alone. At first she comforted herself by thinking of the weak self-indulgences of her poor friends: high blood pressure, of course, or cirrhosis of the liver. Why not, the way dear Amy loved her pastries, and Oscar his dry-Martinis-*cum*-Scotch?

Then, as this suddenly bereft woman roamed her various kinds of loneliness, she blamed her own firm limbs and well-preserved smooth sexless outlines on her basic chastity. She even invoked the rules of the Church, those equivocal utterances which laud celibacy and still encourage the lack of it. She thought of the years since she first resolved to die her own stainless death: of her occasional well-planned, exquis-itely fornicated affairs, which had left her feeling healthier than ever and without a care. Now that she was lonely and very old, she would remember a cheek, a sad, bewildered boyish eye like a fine colt's; her heart felt stirred in what had once been her bosom, and she felt a strange yawn in her well-preserved ageless thighs.

Then she thought of her cautious intellectualisms, of her daily hours for meditation, for thinking. How well she had done both, how thoroughly, during all those years when she had prepared herself to die an un-ugly death, when with one hand she had pushed away the crying-out orgasms of pain she had seen and with the other firm hand fondled the smooth comfort of Spinoza and Russell and Virginia Woolf!

But now, how lonely she was!

She thought for quite a few hours or weeks, and then she deliberately put away all her careful gourmandise and her life of planned asceticism and ecstasy, and her by now almost natural intellectualism. She ate chocolate candies, with some repressed faint nausea, and played Wagner's lushest music on the phonograph, since any more physical lovemaking was by now beyond her, and read the first serial novel she could lay her hands on in a "woman's magazine."

Nothing made her sick. Her guts, her private parts, her mind: all clicked on sturdily, as if she were a young unthinking virgin. She was, at last, ready to die, and nothing was able to kill her.

She lay down on her couch, in the vibrant hot summer twilight filled with little airplanes practicing power dives, and prayed with all the fibers of her stringlike nerves and her in-grown sad old soul to be able to vomit, to moan, to cough and whine. She wanted to die . . . but after all her early acquaintance with the lewdities of quitting this life, she did not know how to.

And exactly eighty-seven years, three months, and twenty-seven days after she had been born Susan Johnson, Mrs. Farstrey-Abbott-de Castranomi-Hodges died quietly in her bedroom in the Casa de Montana Hotel in Pasadena, California. It was plain to the servants that she had a look of deep disappointment on her face.

She lay in death like a ripe peach, and over her gathered myriad tiny flies, the like of which had never before been seen in that country. They gave off a soft light, so that for her wake no candles were required.

II. A Female About to Give Death

At first, the body lay crisscrossed. The arms were spread out and the legs stretched in welcome. Gradually the immediate impact of astonishment grew less. The legs came up, and crossed at ankles; arms folded softly across the racked chest cage, and the abandoned breast softened and came alive again. The body grew quiescent, receptive—a chrysalis, not dead, but reviving, curling into a further acceptance of the same process, the same physical position.

Within, there was still a mechanical protest.

"Why again?" asked the vigorous spirit.

This time is surely enough, to be stretched out and pinned, soused in the brine of dying.

"No," said the spirit.

But the legs straightened and then pulled up, the arms crossed with gentle resignation over the breasts, and the life began to slow to the waiting throb in the ever-hollowed still soft bosom.

Everything was ready for more.

III. A Communication

I went into the dark cool room again, and turned on the center light, and sure enough, she lay against the wall, her back twisted a bit and her eyes staring crossways at me, with her tail curled as beautifully as a fern frond or a twig. Yes, that is what she seemed, completely and suddenly: a twig, a dry frond.

It is a strange thing, to have been in at the death of anything, whether man or beast or lizard. This was a lizard.

I came into the basement room, a while ago, to see her walk clumsily past a bottle of gin and one of soda water I had put on a kind of buffet there in the side of the stone wall. She moved her fingers, such delicate ones, as if she were tired. The poor wee thing, I thought. She might even be a salamander away from any fire, looking for one.

She went halfway up her body length against the cold wall. I would have liked to move her down, but I knew she would not want me to touch her, even *in extremis,* just as I know some people in or out of it do not want me to approach them with words. I held myself away.

Her indescribably, unbelievably fragile fingers touched the wall. She turned to look at me. I felt alien. I had no right to see what I then saw, for she got down slowly from the stone and let her tail twist around in a frond-like loop, and that a lizard does not do unless she is dying. I looked, startled and disbelieving, into her eyes. I had never been allowed by a lizard to watch such intimacy. I felt shy.

But she did not. She died there graciously before me, before my eyes. Her own eyes fixed themselves, somewhat crossed, upon a goal I could not guess or comprehend. Her spine stiffened in a small sideways arch. Her little hands clung still to the rock and to the flat chill surface of the buffet with the bottles on it. Her tail remained like a frond, a Gothic artifact, a kind of earnest of the symmetry of death.

I stood looking at this, almost shocked that I had been permitted to see it. How could this tiny creature, breathing, alive, putting up and down its jewel-like head, have been subjected to the ordeal of dying in front of me, me of all people? Why had it not died alone? It could have gone under a log or a chair or even a warm pillow in this room. But instead it looked at me, curled its tail on the slab of concrete that made the buffet, and fixed its eyes upon me and then nothing.

It lies there, cold as the stone to begin with and now somewhat colder and dead.

I do not understand my feeling of amazement. It is as if I had been awarded a coin struck from a special metal, or allowed to peep through a special hole into

Heaven or Hell, to stand there and see this little lizard end. I lean back, my hands raised in astonishment and perhaps prayer.

The tiny scaled creature lies curled irrevocably upon the stone. I await, still warm and breathing, looking upon it as a miracle, wondering where what it was has gone, as I have wondered upon looking at my gone brother, father, even another. . . .

The thing that made this lizard what she was, made them and now makes me. The reason for my having to look at them and at her is still beyond my understanding.

When it comes to me, no matter where I am, I shall most probably fold myself into some sort of commendable shape and look far past the present, as did the little reptile. Someone will wrap me in a clean cloth and dispose of it all, as I have done before and shall do now. But I doubt that anyone in this world will ever know more clearly what I know tonight, from having the lizard look at me.

IV. The Question

For instance, it is like being with a very old person, one dying or near there. You are filled, bursting, with questions to be asked and things to be told about—things only that tired, caved-in stubborn one can even dare discuss.

He or she, by now past sex as well as most other hungers, could tell, might reply. But it is either too late for you to be presumptuous, this point of self-betrayal, or else you note the bone-weary patience, the kindness, and you dare not mar it.

Very soon it will be too late, to ask or to know. All that is left, other than your silent ageless cry ("Tell, tell me *now* . . . "), is the new strength, the fertile power left over to you, and then to your own questioners, not sooner but *later*.

V. A Rehearsal

I was told when young that my grandfather had often said that the climax of a sneeze was the nearest men could come to knowing what actual death felt like. I was also told that dreams are always in black and white, never in color, and that one cannot dream music or sounds. I am of course not sure about the sneezing, except that I enjoy the act, but I know for the truth that I often dream in full color and with anything from a shepherd's pipe to the New York Philharmonic as accompanists.

Another thing I was told is that no human creature can die in a dream without actually finishing it, doing it. That does not mean that death is a dream, but that it is a unique obligation that cannot be played with. I wish to refute that truism along with the others.

It may not be a common experience, but I think it is at least recognized by all but the Old Wives, that a person can indeed die in a dream, and then continue to live. And I did die once, and nearly twice. The second time I seemed reticent, or perhaps only cautious, about the final bliss (the sneeze) I had felt the first time.

I was almost asleep one night, lying on my left side, waiting without impatience for my dream life to begin. Suddenly I was recollecting, but without meaning to, a dream I had quite forgotten, one that happened a week or a few nights before. I knew that I was merely remembering, and that I was not redreaming. I did not question it, but I was conscious that this was a strange experience, never known to me before, a contradiction.

The second time, it was the actual dying that was important, much like the dénouement of a familiar novel. I felt the hole form around the bullet as it entered the base of my skull and proceeded firmly upward, toward the right eye socket.

Then, deliberately, but with no fear or repugnance, I stopped the thing, waking myself, and for a time was in full possession of the first dream, of which this was the near-end. (Already it fades, but a wonderment remains.)

In the beginning, the first dream, I was a fictional woman, having an affair with a strong, vicious, or at least ruthless man. We decided to kill his wife, and got a beautiful little gun. It was pale blue, I think . . . a pretty toy.

Then she was sitting at a table, her back to a low stone wall, and she became me and I her, as behind her/me the man spoke over the wall, framed in dappled sunlight and leaves and flowers, as from a gladsome pergola, and said that he had decided to kill me instead.

I turned slowly and saw the gun. I knew it was my turn to die, and at once. I felt a flash of fear, but only a flash, and a question about how long it would hurt, but there was no time for protest.

I leaned a little forward on the table, which was the stone one I once sat at in Provence. "Look," I had said jokingly that other day. "Here is my typewriter, and I am writing a book, a beautiful one, my best!"

Behind me now I knew the toy blue gun in the dappled light was aiming at me. I did not hear it fire, but as I dropped lazily onto the table the hole at the base of my skull formed itself to welcome the bullet, much as lips will form themselves for a good kiss. The kiss then went in an almost leisurely way toward my right eye socket. I was somewhat surprised at the obvious path it took, and at the general lack of confusion. I had guessed that there might be lightning, or ugly noises, but the only positive thing was its irrevocability. It was at once an accomplished fact.

About halfway through my head I began to fade . . . or rather there was a strong cloudiness that seemed to spread out from the bullet. I knew I was almost dead. There was no pain or fear. In another inch along the path I was nearly formless, a fog, a great mist. It was a merging of my identity with nonidentity, and never had I been so real, so vast, so meaningless. I disappeared, and the bullet no doubt emerged through the right eye socket, but it did not matter to anything.

THE JACKSTRAWS

Every thinking man is prone, particularly as he grows older, to feel waves large or small of a kind of cosmic regret for what he let go past him. He wonders helplessly—knowing how futile it would be to feel any active passion—how he could have behaved as he did or let something or other happen without acknowledging it.

The only salve to this occasional wound, basically open until death, no matter how small and hidden—is to admit that there is potential strength in it: not only in recognizing it as such but in accepting the long far ripples of understanding and love that most probably spread out from its beginning.

A good time for me to contemplate such personal solutions, or whatever they may be, is when day slides into night. In almost all weather I can sit for a few minutes or an hour or so on my veranda, looking west-southwest and letting a visceral realization flow quietly through me of what other people have given me that I can only now understand.

A clear one, tonight, was of the jackstraws my Grandfather Kennedy whittled for my siblings and me in perhaps 1922 or before. It was never pointed out to me, as I now think it should have been, that an old man had spent long hours making something to please us. I blame my mother for this: she was constitutionally opposed to in-laws, and her whole attitude was that they must perforce be equally antagonistic toward her as the bride who robbed their roost of a fine cock and as a person of higher social station. This was unfortunate for all of us, and my mother lost the most by it and realized it much too late.

Meanwhile, whatever Grandfather Kennedy did was put into limbo in a subtly mocking way, and as far as I can remember we laughed a little at the clumsy set of jackstraws and pushed them into the back of the game closet, tempted by glossier packaged things like a new set of Parcheesi and even the baby stuff Tiddly-winks.

I still have a couple of the jackstraws. They are made of fine dry hardwood, and I think that some at the first had been stained faintly with green and red—dyes Grandmother may have brewed for her dotty husband, grinning sardonically as she prophesied in silence about the obvious end to the caper. One of the straws (were there a hundred in each set, with one hook to be passed around among the players?) is shaped like a crude mace. There were others like arrows, daggers. . . . Each one, according to its shape and then its color, was worth a certain number of points.

I cannot find the rules anywhere in my otherwise somewhat gamey shelves, but I know that the person chosen to be "first" held all the jackstraws firmly in his one or two fists, depending on his age and the length of his fingers, with the hook or perhaps the king straw in the middle, and then twisted them while everybody held his breath around the table. Then the hand or little fists let go, and the pile fell into a contrived heap on the table. And then—yes, the hook was kept out, apart, in order to start the trembling battle, and it *was* the king straw we'd left in the middle!—then we took turns and delicately plucked out one straw, then another if we had not jiggled anything, no straw at all if we had, always aiming for the main glorious one so deftly buried under the little heap. The hook was passed around. Whoever got out the prize won the game, and unless it was time for bed we had another game, drunk with the taste of deliberate skill and *kill:* after all, if you have dug down to that king straw and tweaked it out smilingly, you are yourself king—no matter what your sex— for at least twenty-three seconds!

This sounds competitive, a boring word to me. It is: competitive and therefore boring and probably to be frowned upon by now. But it is a game that was played very quietly, over and over, by men like my midwestern grandfather no matter what his age, and he handed it on to us. It was a silent game, except for occasional shudderings and little groans from the younger ones, quickly snubbed as weak. Grandfather sat like a giant prophet behind his silvery beard, which we knew in a completely disinterested way (at that age!) had been grown to hide his beauty from a horde of young ladyloves, and with an enormous bony brown hand he plucked one jackstraw and then, when his turn came around again, another from the wicked pile. We watched him like hypnotized chickens and tried to do likewise. If one of us missed, there may have been a quiet moan from the others but never a chuckle: we were taught not to *gloat* in public.

Outside the quiet house there was, as far as I remember, no sound, except toward morning an occasional coyote. Of course, there were wild rabbits and moles and mice, but we paid them no heed. Inside, the game was as intense as in any elegant casino, although that connection would have outraged Grandfather: he did not believe in gambling, yet he practiced it every night of his life with jackstraws, Parcheesi, and later crossword puzzles that he transposed into Latin. He would never say "bet," but he would say "wager"; he never said, "My little mare is twice as good as yours," but rather "She is better, I believe." His differences were semantic as well as religious.

So we picked delicately and passionately at the pile of whittled sticks, with their faint colorings, when we played in Grandfather's house. It was *quiet* there on his ranch near La Puente, in southern California. At ours, the game fell flat. He was not there. I see now that such was the reason, although then I thought, if I thought at all, that it was a silly *kid* thing, to be played patiently and politely with an old man. And as I now remember it, I barely thanked my grandfather for the set he had so carefully whittled for us. I had grown past all that. I was in another environment, another age in my own rapid transit from here to there. He was, in a way, stopped at what I hope was the enjoyment of sitting at a table in soft light and watching young people fix their eyes and lick their upper lips and control their fingers to pluck one nicely carved stick from underneath another, in order to edge toward the king itself.

I wish that I had told my grandfather then, in all the hurly-burly of Christmas when he presented the little box of jackstraws to us after such lengthy whittlings and colorings, that I realized what he had done. But I did not. I had no actual physical conception, much less a spiritual one, of what his gift meant. He was an old person and I was a young one. I knew nothing of patience, pain, all that. He could not possibly have tried to tell me about it. So he made a set of jackstraws, and here and now I wish to state that I finally know how to accept them. (At least, I *think* I do.)

It is too bad that my mother waited so long to slough off her conditioned reactions to being related by marriage to people who, in spite of everything she did, were better educated than her own parents but not as affluent. She held us away, willy-nilly, from much warmth, and knowledge, and all that. I don't blame her now. I simply regret it, as I do the fact that I cannot tell Grandfather Kennedy how much I love the two faded pieces of the jackstraw set that he made, and that we casually pushed aside, and that I still have.

1987

LIGHT SLEEPER

Today is Sunday, and for a pleasant change in my schedule, there will be nobody here. At least no one is marked in the book. I could lie abed if I wanted to and for a long time I did. I think it was about ten o'clock when I got up. It did not matter, because the night had been long and easy and sweet: a few good dreams, and an unusually intense enjoyment about it, so that I lay mostly in a half-sleep or quietly awake, in order to enjoy it. And I wanted it to last, to keep my gentled sensations sliding me along toward what would be left of the horizontal day. Once on my feet again, I well knew, such passive sensuous pleasure would perforce change, no matter how positively.

The main thought, if such rambling snoozy contemplation can be called thinking, was that I am lucky to be a light sleeper, and not someone who through habit and other tricks of nature believes that anything but eight hours of complete unconsciousness means insomnia. One turn or toss, three minutes of alertness after a dog's bark, or the inward tweak of an outraged bowel muscle, and such a miserable creature honestly feels that wakefulness, the bane of honest healthy believers in Law and Order, has invaded him. Sleeplessness is an enemy. Anything except full dormancy is frightening. It means illness, or even guilt. A pill, a pill! Doctor, help me. I can't sleep—I turn and toss. I sweat.

All this is nonsense to me. I welcome dreams. I've never bowed to the word *insomnia*, and I often lie awake for many hours with real pleasure, knowing that some day or some night I will sleep again. I feel fortunate . . .

Glen Ellen, California, 1980

RECOVERY

The process of growing well after being unwell is an odd one and has always interested me. For instance, tonight is the twenty-second day after I was given a complete new hip on my right side, at my request.

All has gone almost phenomenally well, probably because I had faint and few qualms about the minor side effects of hospitalization, and chose after some deliberation to try for even partial mobility rather than a few more years of painful frustrated "coping" from bed or chair. The thought of being attended to, and dependent upon, other more active people was literally untenable. Yes, everything went with unusual smoothness. For instance, the actual surgery took about two and a half hours rather than the expected five. Only three one-pint transfusions were needed instead of the five or six that had been readied. And so on.

I feel strong and firm, and except for small times of annoyance when I drop things, or occasional twinges of peculiarly horrible pain when I am careless about doing something that I know I must not do, I am cheerful and courteous, and I keep myself well combed and washed.

But tonight I would like to be changed into another being. It is almost dark, and the air is cooling after unusual heat, and very still. I sit in the big ugly Victorian armchair that has been brought in from the living room, with a hard pillow to keep me from bending the hip at a right angle, so that I am leaning back awkwardly. I am not too hot. I am not unclean—that is, I don't want to make the effort to shower and dry and so on. I feel all right in my skin.

But I wish I could be transported somehow to my bed at the other end of the room. Perhaps a perfume would make me lean back on the cruel old cushion, and I would smile a sweet docile stupid smile, one that would say, Yes . . . Now. And then I would be lying naked, flat, on the bed. At least three very old witches, almost as gray and thin as smoke, would pull off my canvas shoes and hold up my two bony long thin feet and say, "Ah, yes, ah, yes," and they would blow softly on them, so that they would smell as if they were made of exquisite wax and not hot cotton and foot sweat.

So as I lie cool and naked on the sheet, my feet, fresh and sweet, seem to finish me off down there, thousands of fathoms or miles down there. Then the two other smoke people—witches, fairies, angels—smooth my skin, and through my skin my nerves and muscles and then the bones and then the marrow and gristle and whatever else it is that holds us into one position or another, and there is not a sound, except outside the summer song of the wee toads in the few hidden mud packs under the rocks. There is an invisible singing.

The smoke-thin smoke-clear fingers smooth me, and I lie on the cool sheet smiling a little, like an animal or perhaps like smoke. There are three of them, very see-through, like the angel Timmy painted who wept to see one green seed sprout from burnt-egg earth. It was Birth she wept at. I do not want to be born again, and the three smoke women do not wish it for me either, but there is nothing to do about it and they keep on silently rubbing my long tired body. By now it is thin, but I do not feel at all sorry, except for the deformed arthritic knobs on my inner knees, which I have always (seven years?) found an insult.

They came unexpectedly in Marseille, when Norah and I went up and down the old iron stairway at least once a day, on our way past the Vieux Port. (I forget now how many steps there were—perhaps 170. They clanged. During a bad mistral they swayed.) And one day I walked toward the mirror in my room and saw that on either side of my inner knees there was a soft meaningless bulge. I was astonished. I had always had straight legs. Later, in St. Helena again, I was told they were the natural result of my protective system giving my aging knees a bit of padding for taking that iron stair so often. I still have them, but since nobody sees my form now, I do not resent them. Tonight, as the three old smoke witches smooth me, one laughs or perhaps only smiles that it is all right. My good body has been kind to me, she says. I know.

And they keep on rubbing, in an almost intangible but completely knowing way, the way I sometimes press exactly the right nerves in the back of my cat when he has eaten a fresh kill and comes slowly to sit by my chair.

I hate him at first, and hold my breath, not wanting to breathe the fresh gut smells of the dead mole or gopher. Finally I lean a little, so that my arm touches the small of his back as he sits on the floor. Omnivore, carnivore, I curse him softly, and then I touch exactly the right nerves and muscles down toward the end of his spine, and know that I have communicated with him in a way neither of us had planned.

In the same way the smoky old old—well, are they witches? ghosts? nurses?—in the same way I am not here but I am on my cool bed, and they—they have touched or brushed or breathed upon or in some way made the tendons and even the flesh of my tattered body feel right again.

This is what recovery means, I suppose. I know that soon I'll be strong and firm. Tonight I like to know that even while the lights are still on and I talk and eat and awkwardly ready myself for a night that is not yet a good night, a rest that is not yet rest, there are the smoke ladies. I have not yet had to call upon them, and I hope I never do. But tonight might be a good time to try.

Glen Ellen, California, 1981

LES VENDANGEUSES

It is mid-September, 1983, and after ten at night, and I must stop everything to write about *les vendangeuses*, because I realize that they are very strong in my emotions right now, to my great surprise.

They are a small blue coarse kind of daisy that grows copiously in the ditches and neglected woods of Burgundy, the Savoy, the Vaud, every place I have lived where there are vineyards. And when the grapes are ready to pick, these wildflowers come suddenly into full bloom. They are the grape maidens, the blue-eyed faithful girls in even the brown-eyed countries like the Ticino.

And my house is full of them, and for the first time in my life I realize that to me they are Timmy. They have his strong blue strength.

When I met Patty De Joia, "La Ciuca," she brought me a bunch of them, and apologized for their being weeds but too beautiful not to pick. And I said, Oh, *les vendangeuses*, and I told her about them, and she said that she had brought them from a gully on the way home from her great-uncle's ranch where she and her husband Jim had been picking and then pressing the grapes since early morning.

Since then she plants them, I think only for me. When they are cultivated they make many more of the same blue flowers, with more small leaves and on stronger stalks. But they remain a kind of weed.

So now they are in jars and vases. And Patty and Jim are picking grapes, and everywhere the vineyards are bursting with promise, and I realize for the first time that *les vendangeuses* are Timmy.

Perhaps it is because I am quite old by now, into my seventy-sixth year, but I know that I am completely alive sexually for this man who died more than forty years ago. I have no need for anyone now, and probably physically I might prove to be narrow and withered in my sexual parts, although I have not cared or investigated for a long time. But I feel passionately aware of Timmy, more so than for a long time, and it is because of my new awareness of these strong little weeds, *les vendangeuses*, and the waning winy year.

I have had a few strong, not disturbing, fantasies lately about love with Timmy. There has been no orgasm, mostly because I do not want one. But I know that I love him with a continuing deep passion that has never been stronger than it is now. Occasionally I feel deep regret that I was not more knowing of the various arts of lovemaking, so that perhaps in his last dreadful frustrated years I could have solaced him, and probably myself too, with more physical pleasure than we dared permit ourselves. This will always be a sadness to me. But I did not know whom to ask, and Timmy was too proud. (Yes, I think that was it.)

So, now I am an old woman and I think passionately but with a partly cautious deliberate detachment of the man I love. I'll never lie again with him, and feel him within me, but I'm thankful that I still have the memory so strongly always, and that the little sturdy flowers have brought it again to me. Dreams and half-conscious stirrings of strong sexual awareness do not bother me at all, and all I can hope is that other people may know some of them too, as happily as I do. I have no desire to bring them to any culmination, perhaps because they have already been fulfilled to my full capacity. I do feel deeply sad that perhaps Timmy could have known some physical passion openly, in his last days of enforced impotency, but at least we were good lovers while we knew how to be, and he never doubted my undying love, as these flowers now tell me, so long after he first showed them to me.

Glen Ellen, California, 1983

TRAVEL

[. . .] My friend said that "at eighty, the last thing you feel like doing is planning a journey." This of course is a complete refutation of that heinous conclusion.

It is true that I am in my eightieth year, which means that I will indeed be eighty. (I find that many people prefer to add or subtract a year or two in this silly way.) And the truth is that what my friend states is the *last* thing I should feel like doing is increasingly the *first* thing, as I add a little chronologically every day to my fairly full span of life.

In fact, I plan several journeys a day, and even more than that at night. This morning I went to a Mexican village I first lived in some fifty years ago. This was easily accomplished, of course, since I was lying here in bed during the whole two years I spent there in Chapala!

Then, of course, I planned my second trip of the day, which took much more effort: I arose with extreme caution, reached for my cane, and with carefully measured steps went very slowly into the bathroom. There I performed my usual snaillike but always meticulous morning duties, and almost an hour later I was neat and tidy and feeling rather tired from this second long trip. And from then on it has been one journey after another.

A friend plans to buy a "perfect place" in Tuscany, of course on top of a hill and, of course, rather near Siena. So I went there with her, but not for much longer than to assure her that she must sign *nothing* without a local lawyer alongside. Then, I went quickly to Paris for about three days with another friend who has just come back from there. On the way home, we stopped in New York, since I would rather die than have to go through customs in Los Angeles ever again, as we would have had to do to get back to San Francisco. We went up to the Rainbow Room for a quick look at the new-old decor. It was fine, and the floor still revolved exactly as it had when I went there in 1937 to tea-dance to Paul Whiteman's orchestra. Then the phone rang, and while I was discussing going to a country club in Napa Valley in a few days, I was really in a small Swiss-Italian village with Romilda, who has just published a book in Napa about growing up in her native Ticinese (Swiss) village.

And I want to go over the hill from the Valley of the Moon to the Napa Country Club again, *not* to sign that silly book, much as I love it, but because I want to be once more in that little village.

Or perhaps on the way over the hill I may take another full-time journey and find myself in Athens. I have never been in Athens. Two of my friends are there this minute, though, and I don't see why I should not drop in on them. I might stay on, and learn enough modern Greek to read the newspaper every morning, and then go to a village on Crete and study the older tongue. I've always wanted to read Aristotle in the original language.

And all this is why I think it is incorrect that the last thing I want to do is plan another trip, simply because I'm not in my first foolish flush of youth.

Avanti!

Glen Ellen, California, 1988

ZAPPING

Unsent letter

Dear K.

Today is a wonderful day, really the first one of spring for me for some reason. I feel like dancing, whirling around any old way. It is astonishing and above all frightening, though, to realize that even before I am thinking this, I know that it is not possible. I couldn't dance if I had to. Actually I feel stiff and full of aches and pains, and why not? I am past eighty years old, and more than full of the usual woes—but I look out the window and it's so damned beautiful that really I am dancing. In other words, I feel quite silly today. What is even worse is that I would be willing to bet you ten cents or ten thousand cold ducats or whatever that you'd dance too. We'd go whirling off together.

Of course I got your letter, and you do indeed sound woeful. In fact, the letter is so damned miserable that it is very funny to me, and I don't mind telling you so right now along with all this dancing, which I am really doing. I am also laughing very hard. And all this goes on invisibly and inaudibly.

Of course, dear K., I've had a cataract operation. It was quite a while ago, and it went off very well indeed. I never felt as if I had two eyes in one socket, though. I am sorry you do, although really wouldn't two eyes be better than one, especially if they both work? As for the laser operation, I doubt that you will feel anything, except of course the boredom of having to go to the doctor's office and sit still for even a second or two.

Does your doctor say "zap"? The last time I saw mine, in Santa Rosa, he told me that of course he could zap me whenever I said to, but that he saw no point at all in zapping anybody who was as unzappable as I. Why bother? he asked. Quite possibly he would have to do it over and over. Why spend the money on it? I can make it with the help of other people, he said in a companionable, warm affectionate way. So I agreed, feeling properly warm and affectionate myself. But it's nice to know that I can be zapped whenever I feel like it *and* that he would do it. And I really do like him for talking to me that way. Maybe you have his twin zapping away at you.

I do agree with you that "something peculiar happens every minute" to make old age so "fascinating." Fascinating should be in quotes too because you said it when I would not. I do think, though, that aging is a very busy time. It can also be horribly expensive, "usually in a doctor's office," as you say. I am appalled to find or think of how much it costs to stay alive as one ages, and especially if kindly doctors are breathing down your neck every time some new symptom pops up. Symptom of what, though? I suppose deterioration implies that there is a constant process of disintegration or spoiling, but I don't see why these many aspects are called symptoms. The trouble with this steady fading away is that every aspect of it is viewed with alarm and is generally found unacceptable, when really it is the natural thing and is symptomatic of nothing at all. Doctors grow rich on it of course, and I often wonder why and how we are kept so ignorant of what is really a natural process. So one eye grows dimmer, and to protect its dimness a film forms over it. Help help help, and doctors are called in and operations are proposed and then performed as if each time it happened it was actually an unheard-of new development instead of something to be expected and prepared for.

So you had a cataract removed. It was the first time, plainly, and you wrote to me, "Ever had a cataract operation?" etc., etc., and I was amused and now I feel rather testy about it. "Of course," I said, and then I got even testier. The word *laser* made me angry too, after my first feeling of amusement and general danciness about it being spring today, with the new leaves looking very twinkly in the bright still pool of sunshine of midmorning. By now the words *cataract* and *laser* make me feel almost *angry*—not even testy but peevish, really peevish. Hell, I say, why does K. think he's the only man in the world who's ever had a bum eye? But is it really bum, or is it merely a signal that he is getting older, and does that mean that K., of all people, is caught in this silly syndrome of believing that he alone is fearing and hating aging? Hell and damnation, I say. This can't happen to K. Surely he more than most people has long since faced the fact that if he grows to be past fifty, chronologically anyway, he must perforce accept certain changes in his body. Yes, a little film will form over one eye, and then over the other perhaps, and he will feel astonished and finally he'll tell somebody about it. And then the doctors will move in, not because they are cruel or mean, but because they too must eat. And the jig's up. They will trot out little lasers that cost millions of dollars to operate, and they will make little tiny slits and marks on his most precious eyes, and he will shake and tremble and many people like me will laugh because they too shook and trembled. And we will all pay and pay, and the doctors finally will get little films over their eyes and they too will shake and tremble a little, and we all will be pouring out money and grumbling and fuming—and even dancing in the springtime.

In other words, K., I am as appalled as I always am at how completely unprepared we are for this inevitable game. What is most surprising probably is that I don't want anyone to be surprised (and by "anyone" here, I mean anyone that I love). I seem to think that if I love a person, he or she will perforce be above such common continuing universal things like fear and astonishment and anger and pain. I want people like you to know from the minute you are born that if you live long enough, you will of course find your eyes growing filmy, etc., etc. You will grow older. You will deteriorate. I do and you do, because we are both human beings and we are exactly like every other human being, except perhaps we are more fortunate because we admit it. And admitting that you are human makes it inevitable that you must admit to growing older, if indeed you are fortunate enough to grow old, and even to deteriorate, disintegrate, fall apart, and finally die. I am very fussy about words, as you know, and here I use the word *fortunate* with great care. I honestly do feel that anyone who can live decently, or even with some difficulty into and past middle age, and then attain old age is lucky. He is *fortunate*.

This does sound rather Pollyannaish, at least superficially. But it is a statement that I don't make lightly and I, am quite sure, not foolishly either. This is because I am old myself, and I know I have experienced many of the less pleasant aspects of deterioration. Actual years do not count, though. Often the symptoms that I am now feeling (and here I could say enduring or surviving or experiencing) have been felt by people much younger, men or women perhaps in their sixties or seventies. Of course I have heard of people almost 100 who swear they are not crickety and have all their own teeth, etc., etc. They are, to put it clinically or coldly, plain freaks. (Or liars!) You and I are absolutely normal just like countless millions of others in our same sorry, lamentable, miserable condition. So we sigh and moan, and call the doctor for some help, and everybody feels much better to have passed along his misery from himself to another human being.

And yet I am telling you how nice it is to feel dancy. Really, it is laughable, this part of the whole aging business, for me anyway. This constant contradiction in terms. I should be commiserating with you, which means with myself. Instead I am teasing you and therefore myself. Poor K.! You just had a cataract operation and on March 31 you are going to have a laser deal, and then you say, "Keep as well as may be" to me. And I can hear your sadness and your feeling of dismay and astonishment that this has happened to you. And all I can feel is real annoyance with you. *Of course* you are sad, miserable, and so on. And you know damned well that I am sad and miserable for you. But, and here I do mean a great big fat *BUT,* surely you must in some way have been prepared for this dreadful condition. You must have known somewhere along the line that you were bound to feel sadder and more miserable than you had in your whole life—you must have *known,* K., that if you lived past seventy you would ache and hurt and things would grow misty and so on and that you would endure them all.

I do think that women have it over men here. They are more accepting. And perhaps they are less hurt by actual pain and sorrow than are men. I do not mean that it is their lot to accept suffering and grief. I do think, though, that they make less fuss about some things, basic things, like hurting and dying and so on than men seem to do.

If this is the case, I am luckier than you. I am not sure, though. I know that I feel awful today, for instance, but that it would not occur to me to say so. I tell myself that I feel this way or that way, but I am very matter-of-fact about it. If I were a man, there would be more surprise and astonishment, as well as futile anger, in any such admission.

In your letter you betray, to me at least, your real fear and petulance and fury too. I am truly sorry about all this. I don't sound as if I am, but it is true, and the main trouble, I think, is that you were unprepared for what is happening to you. All your life you have seen other people spoil, deteriorate, fade away, and yet you have never really accepted the fact that it would happen to you too. I suppose this is the difference between empathy and sympathy. It would be very easy to remain pedantic and distant and keep it all a question of words, period, with or without any wisdom behind them. That, though, would be too easy. I think that faculty and experience should be put together, and that I have both of them and should be using them this minute to write an article for K., the famous compiler of philosophical mouthings and professorial snacks of wisdom and snippets of advice and so on, and here I sit trying to tell K. how miserable I really am because I am old and rapidly spoiling (i.e., rotting away in a puddle of blood and tears—"no sweat," as you might say), but instead my eyes keep going out the window to watch the sun on the dancing leaves. My poor old body is out there too. The grass looks beautiful, a sudden tender green after last night's little rain, and the red lava stones look redder than usual, and the vines have a new fuzz of green on them. In other words I feel like spring.

You say that in what I wrote about Henry Volkening there was no war between telling the truth and expressing affection. Of course there was not. Why should there be? I feel the same way about you. I think right now that you are peevish and grumpy about being old, and I don't want you to be because I love you. But the truth is that you *are* grumpy this minute. Of course you have a right to be, very simply because your age gives you that privilege. I honestly feel, though, that you are grumpy because you are frightened, and I am very impatient about that because by now you should know better. You've had a whole lifetime to face the fact that you too will be old and sad and aching, and now that you are old you are suddenly angry at being so.

Unfortunately, most people who have the rare experience of being your age and mine are exactly the same as you. They deliberately choose to close their eyes until it happens, and then they are peeved as hell that it has happened. It may be because they are just plain stupid, either deliberately or by nature. I would not call you stupid by nature certainly, but I think you are dumb (i.e., stupid) to feel so astonished that you, *too*, actually must go through the indignity of having a cataract removed from *your* eye. It's the first cataract removed ever from any eye, of course (empathy?), and you have the gall to ask me if I've ever had an eye or cataract operation. Hell, man, I've had two! And the only reason I'm not having it done at least once more is that I see no reason at all to risk bothering.

You say, "Old age is fascinating"—and I see your curled lip and the fake jauntiness and the hidden mockery cum bravery etc., etc., and I refuse to reply. You go on that something peculiar happens every minute, and I agree completely with you. It sure as hell does happen every minute, and I look out the window and the leaves are getting dancier than ever and suddenly I feel like shooting my wheelchair across the tiles, and then your letter floats onto the tile floor and I can't even pick it up and I start to titter and so does my helpless friend who is typing for me, and altogether I feel quite silly and giddy and happy, and I am not at all peeved at you, poor man.

Glen Ellen, California, 1989

THE DIFFERENCE BETWEEN DAWDLING AND WAITING

Right now I think, or I thought so until a few minutes ago, that I am dawdling. I think (or thought) that this was because I am trying to cope with the odd chill fact that I can no longer write clearly in what we were taught to call "longhand" (pen or pencil in one's trained or undisciplined *hand*). It is not only difficult but tiring to try to keep even my signature legible. And what may be even harder to accept in both present and future is that my typing is even worse than my script.

I reverse letters (*nda* for "and"), which I've often done in the past. But now I not only write *tifleau* for "beautiful," but I am at times *unable* to write all the letters. It is as if I were rushing, too fast and busy.

This is clearly an advance in what is amiably called PD—Parkinson's disease. I am finding it almost too difficult (boring?), now and then, to accept. So I *dawdle.* I put off looking at the mail. I get out a recipe, but I wait until later to make it. (I even get out all the ingredients and put the recipe near them, and then I lie on my bed, under my warm soft pouf.)

This morning I asked myself when in the rest of my unnatural life I had dawdled. Perhaps when I was about fourteen, when I was a miserable human brat. Or perhaps when I was drifting arrogantly from one college to another, I coasted. I slept, or I cleaned all night, or I played tennis. But perhaps I was *not* dawdling (wasteful human lazy behavior). Perhaps I was *waiting.*

I was waiting to escape from being *entre deux âges* when I was fourteen. Later I was waiting to escape from my young life, which then meant losing my virginity and marrying into another physical and even mental world.

So now I understand that I am *not* dawdling. I am waiting. I am waiting to move on, which at my age means dying. I wonder about how best to do it, most neatly. I must now wait, to learn more.

Glen Ellen, California, 1985